DOUBLE STANDARD

DOUBLE STANDARD

THE SECRET HISTORY OF CANADIAN IMMIGRATION

REG WHITAKER

LESTER
&ORPEN
DENNYS
PUBLISHERS

FIRST EDITION

Canadian Cataloguing in Publication Data

Whitaker, Reginald, 1943–
  Double standard

Bibliography: p.
Includes index.
ISBN 0-88619-172-6 (bound) ISBN 0-88619-174-2 (pbk.)

1. Canada - Emigration and immigration - Government policy. 2. Refugees - Government policy - Canada. 3. Discrimination - Canada. I. Title.

JV7225.W44 1987   325.71   C87-094327-8

Printed and bound in Canada by
Metropole Litho Inc. for

Lester & Orpen Dennys Limited
78 Sullivan Street
Toronto, Ontario
M5T 1C1

To my mother and to the memory of my father,
both immigrants to this country

Acknowledgements

Research for a book like this is always a collaborative effort among many people. The Access to Information Act is an extremely valuable tool for investigation of public policy; without it, this book would simply not have been possible. Yet the successful use of the act requires the assistance of many government officials. Some very grudgingly do their duty under the act: they shall remain nameless. It is only fair, however, to give due credit to those whose generous assistance to scholarship made the research not only fruitful but a pleasure as well.

Two agencies in particular stand out. The Federal Archives section of the Public Archives of Canada is a model of what a helpful public agency should be. In particular I would like to thank Robert Hayward (now with the Treasury Board), whose guidance and encouragement were invaluable from the very beginning. Others at the archives of particular assistance were Access Co-ordinator Lee McDonald, Dan Moore (whose infectious enthusiasm has been bestowed on many scholars), Gabrielle Blais, Bennett McCardle, Glenn Wright, Dave Smith, Paulette Dozois, John Smart, and Myron Momryk.

The Access section of the Privy Council Office was also especially helpful: in particular I would like to thank Lawrence Farrington and Thelma Nicholson.

Gary Marcuse, my partner in a related enterprise, read much of the original draft and offered many helpful suggestions. Others whose comments and suggested leads were of assistance include David Jay Bercuson, Howard Goldenthal, James Littleton, and Alti Rodal. None of the above, of course, bears any responsibility for the interpretations, which are entirely my own.

Special mention should be made of the Social Sciences and Humanities Research Council of Canada, whose financial assistance—providing research funds and giving me a year and a half away from teaching duties to devote myself to a larger project on Canada and the Cold War—helped facilitate work on this book. Thanks as well to the SSHRC for its Leave Fellowship. York University, besides providing a stimulating environment for scholarship, was generous enough to grant me a sabbatical a year after I moved there, which was crucial in allowing the completion of the project.

Particular thanks to Malcolm Lester, whose enthusiasm for seeing this project into print was immediate, warm, and un-flagging; no author could ask for a better relationship with a publisher. And particular thanks to my editor, Barbara Czarnecki, whose attention to detail, devotion to exactitude and clarity of language, and conscientiousness have made this a far better book than it would otherwise have been.

Finally, a word of thanks to Pam, Sarah, and Robin, who put up with this and much else besides.

Contents

Introduction:
"A Line Must Be Drawn Somewhere"

In the winter of 1985–86 two events took place within a few weeks of each other, on three different continents, that together introduce the subject of this book. One event, grisly and melancholy, took place in the Central American nation of Guatemala; the other, farcical and overblown, took place in the cities of Vienna and Toronto. Together they illuminate the effects of Cold War logic on Canadian immigration and on the human beings who are the object of immigration policies.

In Guatemala, a nation torn by civil strife and terrorized by a series of governments whose record for human rights abuses is among the worst in Latin America, Beatriz Eugenia Barrios Marroquin, a twenty-six–year–old mother and a student at the country's law school, had been receiving disturbing threats against her life. In Guatemala, where some 35,000 persons have "disappeared" over the past twenty years, where death squads wreak nightly vengeance upon those whom the right-wing forces accuse of "subversion" or "Communism", such threats are not to be taken lightly.[1] Beatriz Eugenia Barrios applied to the Canadian embassy for a visa to Canada. After the usual delays, the Canadians agreed—but stipulated that she would not be able to leave Guatemala for Canada for another two weeks. Beatriz Eugenia Barrios never made it to Canada. The night before her scheduled departure, she was kidnapped by "persons unknown".

1

When her body was found, it had been viciously mutilated: her hands cut off, her face disfigured.

Beatriz Eugenia Barrios was a victim of state terror in her own country. She qualified in every sense as a refugee under the United Nations Convention Relating to the Status of Refugees, to which Canada is a signatory. Yet the delay on which Canada insisted led to her brutalization and death. Beatriz Eugenia Barrios had the misfortune to have fallen (whether by choice or accident makes no difference) onto the "wrong" side in a local front of the Cold War that has been raging at varying levels of intensity for forty years. Canada, as a full-fledged member of the Western alliance, has certain duties to perform in this war. Among these duties are the security screening and control, using political and ideological criteria, of people moving across borders. Someone like Beatriz Eugenia Barrios—accused, rightly or wrongly, of being an agent of the Other Side against a government, however bloody and undemocratic, that is closely allied to the United States and to American economic interests in Latin America—starts out with certain disadvantages when contacting the Canadian immigration authorities or Canadian External Affairs officials abroad. Such a person may, after all, be a politically undesirable applicant, a potential threat to Canadian national security, and must be very closely screened.

In Beatriz Eugenia Barrios's case, permission to proceed to Canada was given, perhaps reflecting the somewhat more liberal attitude towards such cases taken in the 1980s than in preceding decades. Yet there was the fatal delay. Questions have to be asked. Was it caused simply by bureaucratic inefficiency, coupled perhaps with an aversion to cutting corners for a "left-wing" applicant, even for one whose life was in danger? Or was there a more sinister explanation? Canadian officials cited the necessity of clearing Beatriz Eugenia Barrios's brief transfer of airplanes at an American airport with US authorities before she could be allowed to depart. Was this just more bureaucratic red tape, or could it be something else?

The Americans have had a close relationship to the Guatemalan military and police ever since a CIA-sponsored coup, authorized by the president of the United States, overthrew a democratically elected and mildly reformist government in 1954, initiating the decades-long nightmare of military and police repression that continues to this day. The death squads are generally recognized to be made up of the police and right-wing military men, operating after hours. Could the Americans have routinely passed on their knowledge of Beatriz Eugenia Barrios's imminent departure to the Guatemalan police, who in turn tipped off the death squads, who then set their murderous plan afoot? This is speculation, of course, but speculation well grounded in the experience of American operations in Central America in aid of "anti-Communist" regimes. If there is any truth in it, it only serves to illustrate another shadowy aspect of Canada's Cold War role in immigration: the liaisons that have been established with the security and intelligence forces of other countries, either directly or through the Americans or the British, including some countries whose human rights records make some Communist countries look moderately liberal.

Canada is justifiably proud of its own record of freedom and liberal democracy. Unfortunately, Beatriz Eugenia Barrios did not have the opportunity to see for herself. Others are much luckier, especially if they happen to be on the right side of the ideological divide in the Cold War. One such person is Miroslav Ihnacak, a Czech hockey player. Ihnacak, allegedly in disfavour with the Czech national team because of his brother's earlier defection to Canada to join the Toronto Maple Leafs of the National Hockey League, travelled to Vienna with his girl-friend early in January 1986. Harold Ballard, the Maple Leafs' owner, whose anti-Soviet ideological zeal usually exceeds the prowess of his hockey team, dispatched an emissary to rendezvous secretly with the hopeful hockey player (through the good offices of certain shadowy "intermediaries" whose services reportedly left Ballard some $150,000 poorer).

The services of sports minister Otto Jelinek, former figure-skating star of Czech origin and a prominent anti-Soviet campaigner, were enlisted on behalf of the Maple Leafs. Within twenty-four hours a special ministerial permit was forthcoming from Flora MacDonald, the minister of immigration, who apparently found it "prudent to issue the permit because of Miroslav Ihnacak's concern for his safety." Within forty-eight hours, Ihnacak and his girl-friend were being proudly unveiled before a press conference in Toronto, where awed reporters were told thrilling tales of international skulduggery and imminent threats by the KGB to snatch Ihnacak back across the Iron Curtain to an unspecified fate.[2]

Ihnacak's future was apparently secure. The Canadian state had acted with speed and efficiency, not to speak of compassion for an athlete seeking the kind of compensation for his talents not available in his Communist homeland. At the press conference, his brother Peter reported that his first question for Miroslav when he met him at the Toronto airport was "How much money did you get?"

Speed, efficiency, and compassion had been rather less in evidence in the case of Beatriz Eugenia Barrios, whose gruesome death preceded Miroslav Ihnacak's well-publicized flight by only a few weeks. To be sure, there is no reason to begrudge Miroslav Ihnacak his good fortune, and no reason why the Canadian state should not have facilitated his removal to Canada to take up a job offer. But the double standard employed in these cases, a double standard that led directly to Beatriz Eugenia Barrios's death, should not be passed over in silence—especially as it is all too typical of a fundamental bias of very long standing in Canadian immigration policy and practice.

Czechoslovakia is no doubt a police state by comparison to Canada; it cannot be denied that in escaping Czechoslovakia for Canada, Ihnacak was escaping an oppressive state for a freer one. Yet however oppressive, Czechoslovakia is still not the kind of country where paramilitary death squads roam the streets snatching young mothers away to be dismembered and murdered in the name of ideology. Guatemala is that kind of country. But it also happens to be a country that the leader of the free world considers an ally against Communism. Canada may be marginally less enthusiastic about this kind of ally than its American senior partner, but the bias still shows. It was only coincidence that brought the cases of Beatriz Eugenia Barrios and Miroslav Ihnacak to our attention at the same time, but they belong together as symbols of that bias.

This book is an essay on the political bias that has underlain the process of immigration and the granting of citizenship in Canada in the postwar years. This history has never been written before, although bits and pieces have previously come to light. It is called a "secret history" for two reasons: first, the policies and practices of immigration security have been deliberately concealed from the Canadian public, the press, members of Parliament, and even bureaucrats with no "need to know"; second, most of the documentation upon which this book is based has until recently been classified "secret" or "confidential". Only the passage of time and the use by the author of the Access to Information Act, which came into force in 1983, have made this documentation available.

Some attention has been paid over the years to the effects of the immigration security system on immigration and on civil liberties, but only very sporadically. The Mackenzie Royal Commission on Security, which reported in 1969, briefly reviewed the system—mainly for the purpose of recommending that the security aspects of immigration policy be tightened up. Freda Hawkins cast a more critical eye in 1972 over the process, as did Gerald Dirks in a 1977 book that concluded that among barriers to "efficient refugee entry", the security screening process figured as a major barrier itself. Alvin Finkel has published a short but incisive article on the subject. The McDonald Royal Commission of Inquiry Concerning Certain Activities of the RCMP reviewed the entire security screening process in immigration in 1981 and recommended a number of changes; the commission sought a more flexible interpretation of the definition of security risks than had been the case in the past, as well as recognition of some right of appeal for persons adversely affected by screening. And since 1984 the Deschênes Commission of Inquiry on War Criminals in Canada has focused attention on the alleged shortcomings of the security process in weeding out Nazi war criminals and collaborators.[3]

Not enough detailed information about immigration has been made public, however, so our picture of policy in this area has been sketchy and incomplete. After detailed examination of the files of the Immigration Branch and of the departments where it was located over the years—sometimes through the instrument of the Access to Information Act—a much more complete picture can now be drawn. What is most striking about this picture is that the clandestine security operation in immigration turns out to have been far more important, more far-reaching and significant, than had previously been suspected.

Much of the detailed documentation presented here is from the 1940s and 1950s, when the apparatus of immigration security was put in place and the practices surrounding the policy took shape. The machinery and much of the mentality that it generated continued through the 1960s and 1970s into the 1980s, which are covered in later chapters. The 1940s and 1950s were the period when the Cold War was launched, by the two superpowers and by their allies and satellites. To fight a protracted international struggle that would fall short of all-out war (which would be mutual suicide in the nuclear age), the national security state was constructed.

The national security state is a set of institutional arrangements, along with a set of attitudes appropriate to the working of those arrangements, that re-creates in peacetime many of the conditions that made national mobilization possible in wartime. The prerequisite is an acceptance of a state of continuing emergency: the national security state is founded upon permanent national *in*security. The state is judged to be under threat of attack from an external enemy, and a much-expanded role for the state in national defence and economic and political warfare is enthusiastically accepted, especially by those who profess to oppose big government. But the external enemy is seen to have domestic extensions as well: those who sympathize with the external enemy constitute an enemy within. So a much-expanded role for the state in internal surveillance and in control over some political activities and associations is also legitimated and approved—often, again, by those otherwise opposed to such governmental intrusion.

This history details how the national security state in Canada, a junior version of the American model, built its system of political controls over the movement of people into and out of Canada. In the 1980s, as a renewed Cold War has intensified its grip over international relations, and the threat of international terrorism—which many argue is directed by Moscow—has superseded the old spectre of international Communist subversion, the question of political controls over the flow of people across borders in the name of national security has once again come to the fore. In this context it is timely to consider the past record of immigration and citizenship security, the apparatus of controls that has been constructed, and the lessons of past experience—a history that has been carefully concealed from the public over the years as a deliberate policy.

The secret history of immigration security is inextricably bound up in the history of the Cold War and its impact on Canada. Indeed, none of this history is comprehensible except in the historical context of the strange half-war, half-peace that emerged out of the ashes of the Second World War. What has become universally known as the Cold War—the division of the world into two hostile military, economic, political, and ideological blocs led by the American and Soviet nuclear superpowers— was the fundamental condition under which Canada adopted quasi-totalitarian police powers over immigration and citizenship. Because the Cold War was considered a crusade—a crusade against world Communism, against godless materialism, against totalitarianism—and because Canada lined up more or less willingly under American diplomatic, economic, military, and ideological leadership, the political leaders of the Canadian state also accepted a package of policies and ideas that came along with the Cold War.

Included in this package was a set of internal security measures—security screening of public servants and workers in defence industries to weed out "Communists" or "sympathizers" with Communism or the Soviet Union; peacetime controls over information in the name of national security; surveillance of domestic political activities; intensive integration of security and intelligence-gathering forces in the Allied countries; pooling and exchange of information between security and intelligence forces; and extensive reciprocal arrangements to control the movement of people from one country to another. All these features of the national security state were characteristic of Cold War Canada, but the question of control over the movement of people across national boundaries was one that had a particularly striking impact on this country.

Immigration was much more significant for Canada, its economy, its culture, and its people than for most other Western countries. By the end of the first quarter-century following the war, Canada had allowed entry to some 3.5 million immigrants. The postwar era has thus been one of continuous large-scale immigration and consequently of major changes to the composition of the Canadian population mosaic. This has often been remarked upon as one of the most significant features of postwar Canada.

The United States, by contrast, with ten times the population of Canada, did not take significantly more postwar immigrants than its much smaller neighbour. Only Australia rivalled Canada for the numbers of immigrants relative to population, and only West Germany, host to millions of displaced refugees—first when the countries to its east were under Nazi occupation, and later when East Germany and other countries came under Soviet domination—had to contend with the same administrative problem faced by Canada and Australia in screening and processing such numbers of persons. Canada wanted a much larger population for its economic future, and here its self-interest coincided with the desires of so many people to escape the Old World for the New (and later the Third World for the affluent Northern Hemisphere). Given the numbers of immigrants involved, relative to Canada as a whole, the Cold War apparatus of screening and control exercised over the inflow was of relatively greater size and significance than the same apparatus deployed in the United States. Ironically, it also received much less public notice and public criticism than the American controls received in the United States.

This book is an offshoot of a larger project on Cold War Canada. What began as a chapter in a book on the impact of the Cold War on Canada grew into something that took on a life of its own, as I realized the extent and scope of security policy in the immigration and citizenship area, and the serious impact it has had on immigration policy in general and on the lives of many individuals. It seemed to me that the national security state, as it emerged in Cold War Canada, found its fullest expression in its activities in immigration and citizenship, where entire groups of people could be walled off from the benefits of the normal restraints that liberal democracy exercises upon those wielding power, where natural justice and procedural fairness were mocked by arbitrary power, and where the state could pursue its discretionary course in dark and silent corridors unlit by publicity and unchecked by criticism.

This is a history that contains many surprises, one that presents a picture of Canada that is unfamiliar to those who see this country essentially in the rhetoric of its leaders and its publicists. The rhetoric of Canadian generosity to the less advantaged of the world, of Canada as a safe haven of peace and freedom in a world of war and oppression, is not altogether false, by any means: by comparison with most other countries, Canada has been generous to immigrants and refugees. The rhetoric is, however, inflated and ultimately misleading, as all self-congratulatory rhetoric by politicians and bureaucrats tends to be. Some of the tarnish on the rhetoric has already been pointed out by critics of immigration policies, particularly the racism and the rather narrow economic self-interest of much of Canadian practice. This book focuses on the political and ideological bias, the illiberality, and the duplicity that have all too often characterized the implementation of Cold War security policies. At the same time, some more familiar biases, such as racism, appear anew, cloaked under the magic rubric of "national security".

In 1987 refugees were seeking entry to Canada in numbers deemed to constitute a national crisis. An emergency session of Parliament was called to pass two new bills restricting the inflow of refugee claimants. This response by government—vigorously criticized by liberal and humanitarian critics—is no more than a reflection of the history of forty years of immigration policy and practice.

The Canadian state has erected a detailed framework of ideological and political criteria for selection and exclusion. It has insisted that it wishes to keep out certain ideas and certain beliefs, just as it wishes to keep out certain germs and contagious diseases. Canada has been at one and the same time the land of freedom, a peaceful refuge from the storms of oppression and persecution, and a country that, out of an extreme fear of totalitarianism, enacts what must be termed quasi-totalitarian controls over the entry of persons of differing political ideology and even, to the extent that this is possible, over the entry of the ideas themselves. These controls are quasi-totalitarian in that those exercising them are not responsible to the citizens of Canada or to their elected representatives, the controls have not been publicly debated, and the details are rigorously and zealously kept from public notice. Further, the people subjected to these controls are given no right to appeal, to examine hostile sources of information used against them, or to know why they are being denied entry to Canada, citizenship, or even continued residence in this country. And behind all this lies a secret police apparatus linked to other secret police forces in an international network.

This is not a pretty picture. But its ugliness is a legacy of the Cold War, which on a larger and more threatening scale continues to menace the earth itself with nuclear destruction. I believe it is important to expose the effects of this legacy to public attention, to write the history of the national security state and what it has done to us. This book is a contribution to that effort.

CHAPTER ONE

The Cold War and the Origins of Immigration Security

The atomic bombs that were detonated over the cities of Hiroshima and Nagasaki, instantly incinerating tens of thousands of Japanese, brought the Second World War to an abrupt and terrifying end in the late summer of 1945. To a fortunate nation like Canada, never occupied by a foreign invader, never bombed from the air, the war had been something experienced by its soldiers fighting on far-away continents. Yet in the aftermath of a war that had exacted a more fearful toll on civilians than any other single conflict in the history of the world, Canada could no longer stand aloof from the human consequences. The immediate postwar years would be ones in which a prosperous Canada, rich in natural resources and with a small population spread across one of the largest national land masses in the world, would be under continuous pressure to open its gates to the homeless, displaced, and discontented masses uprooted by the cataclysm of the war.

Europe at the end of the war was in ruins. The war itself had claimed the lives of perhaps 60 million people, the bulk of the slaughter being in Europe, especially central and eastern Europe. Savage bombardment from the air had reduced entire cities to rubble. As the infamous Nazi death camps were liberated and the skeletal survivors stumbled into the light, the world looked squarely into the face of an evil so monstrous it could scarcely be grasped. And of those who had not died from bombs or guns or gas chambers or starvation or disease, many millions had been uprooted by war from their homes, or what remained of them. By September 1945 there were perhaps 14 million such people. Michael Marrus describes this sea of desperate humanity in unforgettable terms:

> Among these was every possible kind of individual— Nazi collaborators and resistance sympathizers, hardened criminals and teenage innocents, entire family groups, clusters of political dissidents, shell-shocked wanderers, ex-Storm Troopers on the run, Communists, concentration camp guards, farm laborers, citizens of destroyed countries, and gangs of marauders. Every European nationality was present in both East and West. Some of the refugees remained shattered and bewildered by their experience, rooted to the soil where they were liberated. Others streamed in various directions, often without the slightest indication of what they would find at their destination. Endless processions of people trudged across the ruined Reich, sometimes with pathetic bundles of belongings, sometimes pushing handcarts, the ubiquitous refugees' conveyance, piled with household belongings. One refugee moving eastward through German territory cleared by the Soviets pictured the roads in 1944 and 1945 "like swollen mountain torrents in the spring, a Babel of languages, all former slaves of the Third Reich."[1]

Most of this storm-tossed human sea somehow found its way home, or to new homes taken as the spoils of war (often generating in turn yet more refugees as old owners were turned out). But by the end of 1946, a year and a half after the end of the surrender of the Reich, there remained over a million displaced persons in Germany, Austria, and Italy, of whom almost 800,000 were still in refugee camps. And taking Europe, the Middle East, and North Africa together, the United Nations and other international agencies claimed responsibility for 1,675,000 refugees.[2] This figure excluded Asia, where untold more had been uprooted, including thousands of Europeans, mainly refugees from Russia, stranded without hope in Shanghai. For countries like Canada, which had the capacity to receive refugees, the magnitude of the problem was manifest. And in the wake of the refugees there were all the others who would be ready to leave the homes they had retained to seek a new start in the New World as ordinary immigrants.

The Canadian government resettled more than 100,000 displaced persons; many of these in turn sponsored others among their relatives still in the camps. In all, during the first decade following the war, 1,222,319 people officially immigrated to Canada. In 1941 the population of Canada numbered only 11,506,655. By 1951 it had risen to just over 14,009,000. Over 20 per cent of the increase in that decade is accounted for by immigration. In the 1950s, in fact, the ratio of net migration to total population growth was the largest of any decade in Canadian history, with the exception of 1901–11, when the intense program to populate the western prairies was at its peak.[3]

Canada is of course a nation of immigrants, but the so-called charter groups of English and French Canadians have always been somewhat uneasy about later arrivals of differing ethnicity and foreign tongues. Often these reactions have taken the form of xenophobia, ranging from relatively mild forms of assumed cultural superiority to outright, even violent racism. In the prewar period, Canada's immigration laws reflected a fundamental racism: "Asians"—by which was generally meant non-Europeans and non-whites—had been overtly discriminated against for generations, sometimes excluded altogether, sometimes admitted only under the most demeaning and invidious conditions. British immigrants and other white, English-speaking applicants were favoured and offered the most generous of terms. Certain groups fell victim not only to law but to overtly discriminatory immigration practices as well: discrimination against Jews, themselves the victims of a systematic genocidal assault by Nazi Germany in the 1930s and the war years, has been well documented, although only recently.[4]

This background does not particularly distinguish Canada from other new nations built on immigration. America has a long history of nativist outbursts and of racial and national discrimination in its controls over immigration; discriminatory practices were further confirmed by the McCarran–Walter Act of 1952, the first major postwar revision of US immigration laws.

Australia until recently proclaimed a "white Australia" policy with regard to immigration. And there is no evidence that the Canadian state, in exercising this kind of discrimination, was acting against the wishes of the majority of its citizens; on the contrary, it was merely reflecting the prejudices of Canadian society, as well as confirming them.

Apart from the traditional forms of discrimination on ethnic or national lines, there was another class of immigrants that began to be identified in the early twentieth century as undesirable on political or ideological grounds. The Bolshevik Revolution in Russia in 1917 and the Winnipeg General Strike and sympathy strikes in other Canadian cities in 1919 together provided a new source of alarm to the Canadian state and to Canadians with property: the "dangerous foreigner", the alien as Red revolutionary, radical, anarchist, or labour agitator. This image was not entirely distinguishable from that of the racially or culturally undesirable immigrant. "Foreign" ideology was to many Canadians simply one more undesirable racial characteristic of non-British groups: alien ideologics and alien ethnicity, language, and customs seemed to reinforce one another in the eyes of white, Protestant, English-speaking Canadians, and in the eyes of white, Catholic, French-speaking Canadians as well.

Although immigrant labour was used extensively by Canadian capital to break strikes in the early twentieth century, the image of the alien radical as a threat to property and order became so intense that Canadian immigration law began to reflect this concern as early as 1910, when an amendment was added to the Immigration Act providing for the exclusion and deportation of those professing anarchist views. During the First World War, under the authority of the War Measures Act, thousands of "enemy aliens" were forcibly interned behind barbed wire. Under the same authority, various ethnic associations and foreign-language newspapers were outlawed. In the wake of the Red Scare generated by Petrograd and Winnipeg, the Immigration Act clause excluding anarchists was widened and strengthened. A 1919 amendment declared that any non-citizen who "advocates the overthrow by force of constituted law and authority" could be deported. This was used in conjunction with another clause that gave Cabinet the power to "prohibit or limit...for a stated period or permanently the landing...of immigrants belonging to any nationality or race deemed undesirable." Finns, Ukrainians, and Russians were discouraged from coming to Canada by immigration officials, because of their alleged association with Communism.

As for those "radical" aliens already in the country, the Immigration Branch of the Department of Immigration and Colonization began the practice of vetting applications for naturalization on political grounds, in close consultation with the RCMP. As one historian has written, "The Immigration Branch, which before 1914 had been mainly concerned to let people in, was now primarily concerned with the problem of keeping undesirables out. During the 1920s its liaison with the RCMP and provincial police forces became central to its operation." If naturalization was denied, there was a more alarming prospect yet, that of deportation. It was undertaken systematically on a massive scale during the Conservative administration of R. B. Bennett in the Depression years 1930 to 1935; almost 26,000 were shipped out of Canada in this period, some for being unemployed and indigent, others for political activities or union organizing. Again during the Second World War, certain ethnic organizations—especially German, Italian, and Japanese groups, but also left-wing Ukrainian and Finnish groups—were banned; their assets were seized and some of their members interned in camps; the threat of revocation of naturalization and deportation was again brandished by the state.[5]

In short, Canada already had a history of political control over immigration before 1946, although it appears to have been a somewhat crude and unrefined policy. There seems to have been little attempt at forestalling the arrival of undesirable immigrants, except by the rather clumsy expedient of impeding the entry of entire national groups, on the grounds of alleged association with radical politics. Most of the state's efforts were directed instead towards preventing the naturalization of politically undesirable aliens already resident in Canada and, in extreme cases, deporting them. In the postwar world the coincidence of two major interrelated factors was to force an unprecedented expansion and refinement of immigration security controls: first, the large number of persons seeking entry to Canada; second, the coming of the Cold War.

Just as the Second World War had a major impact on Canada as a nation, so postwar Canada was deeply affected by the Cold War between the two major victorious powers to emerge out of the war, the United States and the Soviet Union. In a sense, the entire history of the postwar world has been the history of the relations between the two military, political, economic, and ideological/cultural blocs under the hegemony of the American and Soviet superpowers, and of their attempts to fit the rest of the world into the mould of their bipolar conflict over a forty-year period. With hair-trigger mechanisms to launch the vast arsenals of nuclear overkill poised on either side, the Cold War is still the primordial political division of the postwar world.

In retrospect it is clear that the wartime alliance was already doomed long before the American and Soviet armies met on the shores of the Elbe River over the corpse of Nazi Germany. The ideologies were so antagonistic, the interests of the two great powers so contradictory, and their plans for the postwar world and their places in it so mutually exclusive that conflict was inevitable. The spirit of relative unanimity at the Yalta conference soon gave way to growing discord at Potsdam and the other postwar conferences. It soon became apparent that the Soviets intended to create around their borders a buffer zone of satellite regimes in Eastern Europe in which opposition would be liquidated. It was just as apparent that the United States intended to establish its economic and political hegemony over Western Europe and to maintain a leading presence in much of the remainder of the world as well. As early as March 5, 1946, Winston Churchill, occupying a platform with Pres. Harry Truman in Fulton, Missouri, declared that "from Stettin in the Baltic, to Trieste, in the Adriatic, an Iron Curtain has descended across the continent." A few weeks earlier in Moscow, Generalissimo Stalin had painted an equally dark picture of the imperialist powers gathered round the Soviet borders.

Soon a series of crises punctuated the Cold War. The civil war in Greece led to the Truman Doctrine and American intervention in 1947; the Czech coup of 1948 helped set the wheels in motion for the creation of NATO, which in turn inspired the Warsaw Pact; the Marshall Plan of 1948 helped regenerate the Western European economies, but further divided the two sides of Europe. The Berlin crisis of 1949 solidified the division of the two Germanys. The same year in China, Mao Tse-tung's Communist revolutionaries swept the American-backed Nationalists off the mainland. The division of Korea led to the Korean War, and the aggressive conduct of that war by the Americans led to the intervention of the Chinese Communists. The American monopoly of nuclear weapons led to a Soviet push to develop its own nuclear weapons. The defeat of the French in Indo-China at Dienbienphu in 1954 led to the division of Vietnam and sowed the seeds of future war. The Soviet tanks that rolled into Budapest in 1956, crushing the revolt of the Hungarian people against Soviet domination, were matched by the British and French armies that invaded Egypt to enforce Western domination over the former colonies. And all the time the arsenals of mass destruction— nuclear, chemical and biological, and conventional—grew on both sides.

Within the contending states, the coming of the Cold War also meant new domestic constraints, with new, intrusive methods of control and repression. Dissent was everywhere proscribed as being allied with the Other Side and thus treasonous. Everywhere there were demands for consensus and loyalty, everywhere the cultivation and enforcement of a peacetime equivalent of wartime discipline. On the Soviet side, there were bloody purges and show trials and gulags. On the Western side there was Mc-Carthyism and the ubiquitous apparatus of the national security state: screening of state employees, loyalty oaths, the purging of dissenters both in the state and in the private sectors, and systematic controls over immigration and travel.[6]

The Cold War had a profound effect on Canada. From junior partner to Britain within the Empire and Commonwealth, Canada graduated to junior partner to the United States within the American empire. From a position of peacetime isolationism, Canada moved to a permanent commitment to the military alliances of NATO and NORAD. From a country with a small, provincial, underdeveloped state apparatus, Canada moved to become a second-rank national security state, with an enhanced state machinery for surveillance and control over its citizens. Anti-Sovietism and anti-Communism became little short of official creeds, and commitment to the "free world" replaced the older loyalism to Britain. Canada, of course, also spoke of peace and the spirit of internationalism and the United Nations, but it did so from a position firmly within the military ranks of the Western alliance.

Canada was caught up in the Cold War from the very beginning. Canada had been a partner to the United States and Britain in the development of the atomic bomb, a partnership that deliberately excluded the Soviet ally. When Churchill was delivering his Iron Curtain speech in the United States, Canada was already agog with the sensational story that a Soviet espionage ring had been uncovered operating within the Canadian government. The defection of Igor Gouzenko from the Soviet embassy in Ottawa in September 1945 with documents incriminating a number of Canadians had been kept deep under wraps for many months, but the knowledge of Soviet espionage had been shared between the Canadian prime minister, the British prime minister, and the American president, as well as with the highest levels of British and American intelligence. When the story finally broke in February 1946, with the announcement that thirteen persons had been detained under the War Measures Act and were being held incommunicado for interrogation in RCMP barracks in Ottawa, it became an international sensation. Lurid stories, almost all grossly exaggerated, told of atomic secrets being passed to Russian hands.

A royal commission examined the documents, questioned the witnesses, and published a report that described a Soviet attempt to penetrate the Canadian civil service. A number of Canadians were named by the commission as willing accomplices in this betrayal of state secrets. That the government denied that atomic secrets were involved, that the "secrets" were mostly pretty paltry stuff, and that about half of the persons named were acquitted in the subsequent court proceedings did little to diminish the main effect of the Gouzenko affair. The Cold War was on, and it was being launched in Canada as well as in the wider world outside. Governmental and popular suspicion of the Soviet Union, which had always been relatively high—even in wartime, when the USSR was an ally—was strongly reinforced, and Canada was increasingly well disposed to the new anti-Soviet leadership being offered by Britain and the United States. Moreover, the Cold War was seen from the beginning as a war that was to be fought on two fronts, the one abroad, and the other on the home front. The "enemy within", Communism, was seen as a dangerous instrument of the Soviet menace from without, a fifth column that had to be struck down. Particularly in its early phases, the Cold War was very much a domestic struggle, as the cries were heard for purges of Communists and left-wingers in positions of influence in Canadian life, in government, the media, trade unions, and schools.

In the United States, public anxiety over the enemy within reached epidemic proportions as witch-hunting congressional committees and freelance patriotic vigilantes vied for public attention with wilder and wilder charges of vast conspiracies. Liberal democracy and civil liberties were the losers as McCarthyism ran rampant. In Canada uncontrolled public hysteria was much less in evidence. The Canadian way was to keep the fight against Communism more strictly within the confines of the state. Under the aegis of the federal government, purges were indeed carried out, and the apparatus for surveillance and intimidation of dissent was created, or refined where it had already existed. The defining characteristic of the Canadian Cold War on the home front was secrecy. The Americans played out their dramas in front of klieg lights and television cameras; Canadians were scarcely aware of what was happening here, for their government acted quietly, under the shelter of administrative discretion, even shielding its security operations from parliamentary scrutiny as much as possible. In America, the House Un-American Activities Committee held circus-like hearings in Hollywood to root out the "Commies" in the movie industry: the daily images of the Hollywood stars naming names or shouting defiance before the public inquisition became part of American folklore. Most Canadians were not even aware that a Red-hunting purge was being carried out in Canada's National Film Board around the same time; even today some of the details of this purge are still unclear, such was the secrecy in which it was shrouded.

In the wake of the Gouzenko affair, official Ottawa was certain that a security screening procedure had to be set up to ensure that civil servants were tested for political reliability. Communists or those associated with Communists would not be hired, and if they were already in the civil service they would be kept out of sensitive positions with access to confidential material, or fired. The RCMP's security service, which had been assiduously collecting information on left-wing Canadians ever since the Winnipeg General Strike of 1919, would be the investigative agency. To oversee the RCMP's operations and to advise the government on internal security policy, an interdepartmental body called the Security Panel was created in 1946.

This crucial body—the centre of the security establishment in Ottawa—was made up of senior civil servants and representatives of the RCMP and military intelligence, with a permanent secretariat housed in the Privy Council Office, the senior central agency in Canadian government. Through the Security Panel would flow all the important security questions to be decided and administered in Ottawa's internal Cold War. It was on this body that certain senior civil servants would have the opportunity to carefully shape Canada's national security policies, sometimes in conflict with the often bluff and acerbic representatives of the RCMP, sometimes in an alliance of convenience with the RCMP against their political masters in Cabinet.[7]

Among the legendary mandarins who were from time to time involved in Security Panel matters were Norman Robertson (a "man of influence", in his biographer's phrase), whose dark and brooding presence lay behind a surprising amount of government policy in the 1940s and 1950s; Arnold Heeney, whose precisely formal and conservative manner belied a certain liberal conscience exhibited in matters of national security and individual rights; Robert Bryce, the economist whose own marginal involvement in left-wing study groups at Cambridge in the 1930s marked him as a target for American witch-hunters in the 1950s, but who tended to take a hard line nevertheless against possible subversion within; and Gordon Robertson, a junior official in the 1950s who was later to become the mandarins' mandarin in the Trudeau years, who kept up an ongoing interest in security affairs throughout the 1950s and 1960s and into the 1970s.

Among prominent permanent officials of the Security Panel was Peter Dwyer, a former representative of British intelligence in Washington who was brought to Ottawa to carry out a kind of co-ordinating and policy role in security. Dwyer, who later left the security field for a second career in arts administration at the Canada Council, gained a reputation as something of a liberal, but as was true of most of the officials charged with responsibility for internal security, his liberalism was sharply circumscribed by an overriding concern about the Communist threat. These civil servants, who together with the RCMP and military intelligence formed the Ottawa security establishment, will make many appearances in this book.[8]

Employees of the state were at the front of the line for security screening and for possible designation as security risks. Moreover, because a government job was deemed a privilege, not a right, questions of civil rights and of liberal democracy were generally dismissed; if there were doubts about a person's reliability, they were to be resolved in favour of the state, never the individual. Security screening was extended beyond the state sector to private companies doing national defence work under contract; their workers were subjected to the same screening process. For a time it was even extended to shipping on the Great Lakes, where Canadian seamen were screened for traces of Communism in their past.

But loyalty checks and security screening were not limited to public servants and defence workers. There was another category of persons who, like civil servants, were considered potential threats and accorded limited rights. Immigrants were not Canadian citizens until they had been accepted for entry, had spent five years in Canada as landed immigrants, and had applied for and been granted citizenship. Even after citizenship was obtained, the process of naturalization could under certain circumstances be reversed. Throughout the process there was considerable scope for discretion on the part of the state, and this discretion was used to apply the political and ideological criteria of the Cold War to the selection and rejection of immigrants, to the processing of citizenship applications, to deportation on political grounds, to denaturalization, and to controls over travellers visiting Canada or leaving it. It was a massive operation, pursued largely in the secrecy guaranteed by the magic formula of "national security".

To put the Canadian experience in perspective, it is useful to look at what the Americans were doing at this time. During the McCarthy era the Americans became notorious throughout the Western world for the extreme application of anti-Communist criteria to immigration. Typically, the Americans enforced their Cold War controls over immigration, citizenship, and travel openly and with maximum publicity; their bad reputation for illiberality and narrow-mindedness was spread by their own penchant for openness.

Systematic political screening of applications for entry to the United States had begun in 1941, when a board composed of the FBI, military intelligence, the Department of State, and the Immigration Service was constituted to screen all visa applications.

Following the war, congressional opponents of large-scale immigration applied the security argument against the admission of displaced persons from Europe, citing the alleged implanting of Soviet agents—"numerous and important carriers of the kind of ideological germs with which it is the aim to infect the public opinion of the USA." The McCarran Internal Security Act of 1950 included provision for the exclusion of Communists from the United States. President Truman in vetoing the bill cited among other things the overly restrictive nature of this exclusion. Congress overrode Truman's veto.

The McCarran–Walter Immigration and Nationality Act of 1952 codified the exclusionary features yet further (while allowing for a form of renunciation of former Communist sympathies). The act was highly restrictive in intention, but it shifted the burden of restriction of immigration away from the older grounds of ethnicity towards ideology. McCarran–Walter pointed to the advocacy of ideas as the basis of exclusion: under its provisions many leading intellectuals, writers, and scientists were excluded, even as visitors. The thinking behind McCarran–Walter is perhaps best summed up in the words of Sen. Pat McCarran, father of the bill: immigration, he said, is "a stream of humanity [that] flows into the fabric of our society. If that stream is healthy, the impact on our society is salutary; but if that stream is polluted, our institutions and our way of life become infected.... This nation is the last hope of Western civilization; and if this oasis of the world should be overrun, perverted, contaminated, or destroyed, then the last flickering light of humanity will be extinguished."[9]

Canadians, as befitted mere attendant lords in America's holy alliance against Communism, were much less messianic than the Americans themselves. But in their quiet, understated, secretive way, Canadian officials shared many of the same assumptions and set out to implement aims similar to those of McCarran–Walter, but with a minimum of publicity. To some degree, Canada had to enact similar controls over immigration and travel simply because the Americans were doing so. There was the world's longest undefended border to consider, and the Americans would not allow persons to whom they had denied direct entry to slip across their northern border without visas. This was a factor in Canadian decision-making, but a minor one, and more of an excuse than a reason. More to the point, Canadian officials held the same world-view as the Americans and were just as determined to bar all bearers of the "germs" of Communism as they were to bar the carriers of communicable diseases from these shores. They did not express themselves publicly in the same colourful tones as Senator McCarran, but in the privacy of their political and bureaucratic policy-making conclaves, their assumptions were no less hair-raising for liberal democrats.

Canada had always exercised selective controls over who immigrated to this country and who was allowed to remain. What was different about the new era of the Cold War was the systematic application of specifically political criteria as a basis for mass exclusion from Canada of categories of persons. The application of political criteria had consequences beyond the mere administration of the immigration law. For one thing, they were part of a Cold War pattern of intervention by the state in the life of a society that claimed to be liberal and pluralist. Persons professing certain political beliefs or believed by the state to possess such beliefs, or even those believed to have *associated* with those who professed such beliefs, were declared unfit for citizenship and excluded from entry into the country. Others who did not even wish to immigrate to Canada but merely asked to visit were similarly excluded, apparently on the grounds that Canada had to be protected against their subversive ideas. Even Canadian citizenship and its privileges were called into question as the state considered such measures as revoking the citizenship of naturalized Canadians who fell afoul of the new criteria of legitimate political behaviour and restricting travel abroad for Canadians who displayed what the state judged to be subversive tendencies.

At the same time the ideological criteria for admission of immigrants happened to exclude certain national groups, while allowing others to enter, creating a new inequality of selection: not overtly discriminatory, but objectively so, when the consequences were felt. All this was effected by an administrative process carefully wrapped in an impenetrable fog of secrecy and assisted by procedures that were highly authoritarian and arbitrary. Administrators were not responsible to Parliament, and their decisions were usually not subject to judicial review or to appeal by injured parties.

In the postwar years the refugee problem was at the top of the public agenda. It was considerably complicated by the quick escalation of tensions between the USSR and its wartime allies in the wake of the Nazi defeat. A profound split developed between Western and Soviet perceptions of the nature of the problem.

The USSR and the Soviet-dominated countries of Eastern Europe were intent on the expulsion of millions of ethnic Germans from the East, as had been agreed at Potsdam. At the same time there were in Western Europe large numbers of displaced persons from the East, especially Poles and Ukrainians, who were violently opposed to being returned. Some had collaborated or fought on the German side; others deeply, and understandably, feared return to Stalin's Russia. The Soviets, however, demanded forcible repatriation, perhaps mainly seeking manpower for the heavy tasks of reconstruction, but partly no doubt for motives of revenge. Many, perhaps 2 million, were indeed forcibly repatriated—of these, many were executed or sent to labour camps—during 1945.[10]

By the following year, Western revulsion had grown as the Soviets stridently made their demands for further repatriation public at the United Nations during a protracted debate on world refugee policy and the creation of a successor to the United Nations Relief and Rehabilitation Administration (UNRRA). Western governments rejected Soviet demands; the constitution of the new organization—the International Refugee Organization (IRO)—reflected a Western rather than a Soviet model of refugee policy, favouring the principle of free choice over compulsory repatriation. The Soviet-bloc countries consequently refused to participate in the IRO. Liberal and humanitarian values may have prevailed, but it was none the less evident that the refugee question was already an issue in the developing Cold War.[11]

Late in 1945, the director of the Immigration Branch (now located in the Department of Mines and Resources) wrote a memorandum to his Minister in which he outlined the numbers of refugees from Nazi Germany and Stalin's Russia who would likely seek entry to Canada. "Read separately the facts in the individual cases present an almost unanswerable argument for admission," he conceded, "but collectively they constitute a problem extremely difficult to solve." An External Affairs report on the situation at the outset of 1946 warned that among the multitudes of refugees spawned by the war and postwar political upheavals were many who had collaborated with the Nazis, and it pointed to the "highly undesirable consequences" of the political activities of such persons, were Canada to grant them asylum.[12]

But the Cold War would soon shift the political ground away from the wartime emphasis on the evils of Nazism towards new criteria for what was politically unacceptable. The coincidence of the huge postwar flow of immigration with the height of the Cold War had very specific political consequences. In the past, Canada had been highly selective, sometimes brutally so and on a clearly racist basis, about the national and ethnic origins of would-be immigrants. The barring of Jews fleeing from Hitler's terror is now well documented.[13] Overtly racist discrimination against Asians and blacks had been a steady feature of immigration policy, and one that had indeed been publicly and proudly proclaimed in the past. Overt racism declined in the postwar period, and Canadian immigration laws and practices slowly began to reflect this change. But a new basis for discrimination was born with the Cold War.

CHAPTER TWO

A Secret Policy,
Secretly Administered

Even before the Second World War had come to an end, security screening of potential immigrants to Canada had begun. In early 1945, the Department of External Affairs and the Immigration Branch, assisted by the RCMP (which had earlier prepared contingency plans to round up and deport all refugees in Canada at war's end), began to regularize the status of those European refugees who had entered Canada during the war, including the civilian internees who had been dumped into Canadian custody by Britain early in the war. An order-in-council of October 1945 cleared the way for 3,500 wartime refugees to become landed immigrants. Well before the end of the war, Canada was already engaged in liaison with British and American intelligence agencies in planning for security screening of prospective immigrants from among the hordes of displaced persons and others in Europe who would be seeking admission to Canada in the aftermath of war. Early in 1945, Supt. Charles Rivett-Carnac, a security specialist in the RCMP who was to be the force's chief representative during the Gouzenko investigation, travelled to Britain to confer with M.I.5 (the counter-intelligence unit).[1]

In the summer of 1946, the newly created Security Panel noted that Parliament had recently amended the Immigration Act without prohibiting the entry of undesirable immigrants "other than by departmental administrative action". In other words, from the eginning the decision had been made to minimize public and parliamentary scrutiny and rely squarely on administrative discretion. The panel followed up on this by enlisting the services of the RCMP to join the teams of civilians sent to Europe to interview prospective immigrants from among the displaced persons; their job would be security screening and liaison with local security police, beginning with the UK passport control office. "The first two members of the Canadian immigration team to arrive in Germany in 1947 were RCMP officers, responsible for the political screening of refugees."[2]

The immigration teams faced a daunting challenge in the displaced persons' camps. Conditions were chaotic, all sorts of people from ex-Nazis to Jewish survivors of the Holocaust were jumbled together; the "truth" about what people had done over the war years was often as evanescent as the tattered "documentation" clutched in their hands; and over all there hung an air of desperation, a hunger to simply get out and start a new life elsewhere. Living out of suitcases, hitching rides, facing the daily sea of faces of the hopeful, the shattered, and the mendacious, the immigration officers either coped or failed. The turnover rate among officers was high. The administrative raw material was perhaps not promising.

The problems started at the top with a weak and ineffectual minister, J. A. Glen, whose "next to useless" performance in his portfolio drew the withering contempt of his boss, Prime Minister Mackenzie King, and the ire of the powerful minister of trade and commerce, C. D. Howe, who was concerned about securing a more aggressive immigration program to promote postwar economic growth. On the other hand, the new deputy minister was Hugh Keenleyside, a cultured man of liberal and progressive views with long experience in External Affairs, giving him some international perspective on the refugee question. Keenleyside had a mandate to clean house and make immigration a priority in his multipurpose department (which also included mines, resources, and Indian affairs). The task was not simple, however.[3]

As Keenleyside later recalled, the immigration service had been plagued by widespread corruption. In the process of selection of the displaced persons, there were "occasional reports of rough behaviour, mistreatment of women, and poor operational practices". Among the applicants, he also recalls, there was the widespread belief that "even the simplest and most proper requests had to be lubricated with monetary and other more personal favours." The temptations for misbehaviour were there, but the rewards for those who persevered in their duties were high, for here were new Canadians in the making out of the disasters of war—more than 120,000 of them by 1951 transported out of Europe and onto Canadian shores. This, said Keenleyside, was "as remarkable a performance as anything that is to be found in the history of immigration to Canada."[4]

No doubt it was a remarkable performance, yet the raw figures miss some of the darker shadings. Canada was highly selective in choosing from among the displaced persons. They were in effect skimming the cream of the camps in view of Canada's economic needs. As John Holmes, an old External Affairs hand and historian of Canada's postwar foreign policies, has put it, "In the light of the oratory accompanying the victory over Nazi bestiality and the revelations from Belsen, Canadian policy seems incredibly calculating." But the selectivity did not end with the potential value of the immigrant to the Canadian economy. Ethnic discrimination was central to the process. The exercise of prejudice against Jews, the worst victims of the Fascists, was matched by a favourable attitude towards certain more "Nordic" ethnic groups. And in the security screening process, with its notable right-wing bias, a record of discrimination on political or ideological grounds can be found.[5]

That the selection of displaced persons was itself a Cold War issue became apparent as early as 1946 when hearings before the Senate Committee on Immigration and Labour on the European refugees were the scene of bitter recriminations between ideologically opposed delegations from both the Ukrainian and the Polish communities, which were clearly divided between pro- and anti-Soviet elements. The pro-Soviet Ukrainians and Poles echoed the Soviet line expressed in international forums: it was the duty of all displaced persons from Eastern Europe to return home. A left-wing Ukrainian brief asserted that the "so-called 'displaced persons' " either were war criminals and Nazi collaborators or were "free to return to their homelands": in both cases, repatriation was the answer. Anti-Soviet spokesmen stressed that their homelands were now tyrannies, and those who refused to return were political refugees. This was certainly the view of the overwhelming majority of the displaced persons from the East themselves, who not only opposed repatriation in the most desperate manner, but most often cited opposition to Communism as the main reason for their stand.[6]

The pro-Soviet Poles (who quickly lost any influence within the Canadian Polish community once the reality of Soviet domination in Poland had become apparent) were reacting at the 1946 hearings to the government's willingness to admit some 4,000 Polish army veterans who had been placed under British military command after the fall of Poland in 1939. Admitting them seemed reasonable enough, given their service on the Allied side. Cabinet stipulated that the veterans be security-screened to prevent the entry of "subversives". It turned out that this screening was intended, however, to prevent Jewish veterans from entering along with their Christian comrades; so successful was this screening that of the first 1,700 admitted, there was only a single, token Jew. "Security screening" could be a coat of many colours.[7]

The RCMP established its overseas headquarters in London, which was the early collection point for applications from displaced persons and others who sought entry to Canada. By the time the London office began fully functioning in early 1947, it had become apparent to the civil servants in Ottawa that security screening was creating a problem of its own: an administrative bottleneck that threatened to seriously embarrass the government as it tried to carry out its stated policy with regard to immigration. With sponsored applications for relatives already numbering more than 10,000, and with departmental estimates reaching as high as 30,000 to 50,000 within a year or two, the RCMP had made it known that it could clear only twenty-five to thirty applications a day, or about 800 a month. Since the government was withholding approval pending security clearance, "it will be seen", wrote the director of the Immigration Branch, "that an ever increasing backlog would be created and that there would be very serious criticism both in Parliament and from the public."[8]

The Security Panel was put to work on the problem. When the suggestion was made that screening of sponsored relatives be discontinued, Rivett-Carnac of the RCMP bristled: "Any screening system", he asserted, "to be effective must be total. To undertake vetting in principle or under any partial system would mean that a great number of persons would be admitted to Canada without vetting and a very real danger exists of many undesirables entering this country." Since the problem was associated with the slowness of the RCMP in the first place, the insistence on a "total" screening system (whatever that might mean) must have caused some quiet irritation among the bureaucrats. Nor could the RCMP promise more manpower.

The problem bounced back and forth between Cabinet and the Security Panel. Finally the panel narrowed the options down to two. The major security problems, it was argued, were posed by emigrants from countries within the Soviet sphere of influence, on the assumption that these included planted agents; thus, one solution would be to restrict screening to applicants from those countries alone. For now, however, Cabinet chose the second option as a temporary solution: to reduce screening of sponsored applicants to spot-checking of about 20 per cent as chosen by the RCMP. Those who were not from Eastern Europe were placed under a "fourteen-day procedure"—if nothing adverse was received by Immigration from the RCMP within fourteen days after the police had passed the applications, visas were authorized. Screening in these cases continued, even though the applicants had gone on to Canada: they could, of course, always be deported later.[9]

A second problem arose during 1947 with regard to sponsored applicants. A number of cases arose in which the sponsored relatives of Canadian citizens were discovered by the RCMP to have left-wing or "Communistic" tendencies. It was out of the question that such persons be admitted, but the problem lay in what to tell their sponsors in Canada. In a memorandum to Cabinet, the minister suggested two options. The first was to reject the application and give no reason—an option described as "impracticable and not satisfactory". The second was to inform the sponsor that admission was not in the public interest and to refuse any further explanation, the "inevitable result" of which would be a "demand for additional information". In the event, Cabinet decided that the latter possibility was more alarming than following an "impracticable and not satisfactory" course; here began the policy, cited ever since as a precedent, of refusing to give notice that security was the ground for rejection. The Cabinet Committee on Immigration Policy also decided that "left-wing tendencies" as claimed by the RCMP should be accepted in all cases by the department as sufficient justification for a negative decision, and that the grounds for rejection were not to be reported to the civilians, merely the fact of rejection. It followed from this that an applicant rejected on security grounds by an RCMP officer could not appeal, although appeal procedures were available to those rejected by civilian visa officers. Moreover, the Immigration Branch and the RCMP agreed to an elaborate subterfuge whereby RCMP agents were never to be identified as such, but would pose as civilian immigration officers instead. The logic of administrative discretion was taking over.[10]

Although a new legislative authority was needed to support Canada's new approach to immigration in the postwar world, it was not until 1952 that a new Immigration Act would pass Parliament. In the spring of 1947, however, Prime Minister Mackenzie King made a major statement on immigration in the House of Commons that was to serve as the government's public articulation of its policies. The statement was drafted by Gordon Robertson and J. W. Pickersgill in the Prime Minister's Office and somewhat amended by King himself. Although no explicit reference was made to security, the statement strongly reiterated that immigration was a matter of domestic policy and that Canada was within its rights in selecting "with care" only those immigrants it wanted. This point may have been related more to the question of ethnicity—in particular, the government's stated intention to prevent any large-scale immigration from Asia— but it applied to the question of political suitability as well. Above all there was a strong statement of the principle that would-be immigrants have no fundamental human right to enter Canada, nor do immigrants have a right to Canadian citizenship once they are living in Canada. Immigration to Canada and Canadian naturalization were privileges, not rights. It was on this basis that a security system that emphasized virtually complete administrative discretion, with no judicial or independent review and no recognition of natural justice for the individuals affected, could operate quietly with little public notice.[11]

By the spring of 1948 the RCMP reported that some 22,000 out of 33,538 applications had been screened, leaving a backlog of some 11,000. Fewer than 400 had been rejected, a number that the RCMP commissioner admitted "seemed small". He promised to do better if only Treasury Board would give him more staff and a bigger budget. (By the last quarter of 1948 the rejections were running at over 100 per month, or a rate of about 4 per cent.) At the same time, the commissioner struck another, more controversial note when he drew the Security Panel's attention to the failure of the International Refugee Organization (responsible for the administration of the displaced persons' camps) to co-operate in the screening of displaced persons, a failure he attributed to the "infiltration of Communists and sympathizers" into that organization.[12]

This charge, which appears strange in light of the nature of the IRO ("From the beginning", wrote one careful contemporary observer, "the IRO was entirely an instrument of the West, and from first to last the opposition of the Soviet bloc to the IRO was bitter and uncompromising"), had an unanticipated result when it was picked up immediately by Col. Laval Fortier, associate commissioner of the Overseas Immigration Service and later the deputy minister of the Department of Citizenship and Immigration in the 1950s. Fortier, fresh from visiting the headquarters of the IRO, claimed that "there was a good deal of evidence to support the contention that communistic elements were trying to introduce undesirables into the immigration system" through infiltration of the IRO. On the basis of an eight-week trip to Europe, he painted an alarming picture of a continent ripe for Communist take-over and an IRO riddled with "Communist propagandists" not only in the field but in key positions in the organization. Their object was to infiltrate trained Communist agents into Canada. "It is impossible for me to bring concrete evidence on communist activities," he admitted, "but this was not the purpose of my trip overseas."[13]

The government was receiving many such alarming reports during 1948 from its officials abroad. The vice-consul in Shanghai, for instance, reported that 20,000 refugees from the USSR in that city were mostly criminals or "very active Communist agitators" and refused to accept any applications for immigration from them. The press in Canada and the US was whipping up hysteria about subversives and saboteurs among the displaced persons.[14] Fortier, however, went one step too far when he suggested that the RCMP security officers in Europe were not sufficiently trained in counter-espionage to offer effective resistance to this Communist offensive and demanded a "total reorganization of our security screening and a total change of the officers now employed on the security work". The deputy minister passed on Fortier's report to the RCMP commissioner for his comments, along with the suggestion that it "is admittedly based on opinion rather than ascertained fact" and "probably greatly exaggerates the problem." Commissioner S. T. Wood was more than happy to take the hint. His men had been ordered to conduct neither an intelligence nor a counter-intelligence operation in Europe, but to ascertain the political sympathies of applicants for immigration. The methods were scarcely infallible, but "in the chaotic condition which exists in Europe today...it would be impossible to raise a fine enough screen without the use of security forces, the cost of which would be prohibitive." With appropriately injured innocence, Wood—a venerable and seasoned anti-Communist of the purest stripe—wrote, "It would appear that Mr. Fortier is under the misapprehension that our men are not particularly interested in the detection of Communists. I may say that this is our primary interest...and all members of our security details are fully aware of this fact."[15]

Fortier clearly erred in attacking the RCMP on these grounds. Rare it was for the RCMP to be accused of softness towards Communism; the charge was so absurd that Fortier undermined himself. There appears to be no other example in the government records of a civil servant raising such a charge against the police. Indeed, the criticism was generally in the other direction.

To look into the charge of Communist infiltration of the IRO, which was echoed by the RCMP, a high-level mission was dispatched to Geneva in the person of Dana Wilgress, former Canadian ambassador to Moscow. Wilgress carefully selected a group of "trustworthy" English-speaking officials of the organization and raised the issue in private. In a lengthy report to the Department of External Affairs, he concluded that this Red Scare had "little justification"; significantly, American officials had dismissed the charges as exaggerated.[16]

Communists were not the only prohibited class, but they did hold pride of place. In a confidential memorandum sent to visa posts by immigration headquarters early in 1949, thirteen categories were listed, as follows:

> a) Communist, known or strongly suspected. Communist agitator or suspected Communist agent

b) Member of SS or German Wehrmacht. Found to bear mark of SS Blood Group (non-Germans) and non-German SS prior to Jan. 1, 1943, or who joined voluntarily later

c) Member of Nazi party

d) Criminal (known or suspected)

e) Professional gambler

f) Prostitute

g) Black Market Racketeer

h) Evasive and untruthful under interrogation

i) Failure to produce recognizable and acceptable documents as to time of entry and residence in Germany

j) False presentation; use of false or fictitious name

k) Collaborators presently residing in previously occupied territory

l) Member of the Italian Fascist Party or the Mafia

m) Trotskyite or member of other revolutionary organization

These categories were of course purely administrative, with no specific basis in legislation (other than the general category of "undesirable"). Later, under the Immigration Act of 1952, general instructions were issued to visa officers indicating that " 'security screening' means the examination of prospective immigrants and/or of their histories by the RCMP or other authorized agency of Government to determine whether, if admitted to Canada, such immigrants may be inimical to the democratic way of life and of government as such is generally understood in Canada." The specific interpretation of those "inimical to the democratic way of life" was indicated in this list of categories, which was strictly secret. The memorandum reiterated what was by now standard procedure: security grounds for rejection should never be disclosed to applicants, or to other than "senior officers". Even the memorandum itself, readers were advised, "should be kept under lock so that no one will have access to it."[17]

The strong emphasis on Communism as the main criterion for security rejection, especially in contrast to Nazism and wartime collaboration, is evidenced by a statistical review prepared by the Department of Citizenship and Immigration (where the Immigration Branch had been located since 1950) in the spring of 1951. In fact, the general criteria for security rejection did turn up a large number of rejections for non-Communist political categories, but these were treated very differently when subject to review. While only 20 per cent of all rejections were for the category of Communist, in only 2 per cent of these cases were reviews carried out, and a scant one in five of those reviewed was actually reversed. On the other hand, the prohibited category for enemy soldiers and former SS men accounted for 40 per cent of rejections, but of these 50 per cent were reviewed and over two-thirds were reversed. Similarly, former membership in the Nazi party accounted for 25 per cent of rejections, but of these over a third were reviewed, and 95 per cent of those reviewed were reversed. Former collaborators fared less well, although they accounted for only 10 per cent of rejections. Communism was not the only target of the screening process, but non-Communists fared much better upon review. Moreover, the efforts made in the early 1950s to streamline the system and relieve pressure on the RCMP were entirely directed to lifting the restrictions on former Nazis, Fascists, and wartime collaborators. No responsible public official ever appears to have suggested lifting restrictions on Communists.[18]

Yet there was also a fundamental contradiction inherent in the security screening process as an integral—while secret—part of Canadian public policy on immigration. The contradiction manifested itself in a continual tension between departmental officials, with their mandate to bring immigrants in large numbers to Canada, and the RCMP, with its mandate to filter applicants carefully and therefore slowly. As the director of the Immigration Branch indicated in a memorandum to the deputy minister early in 1951, it was government policy, as clearly enunciated in an order-in-council, to stimulate immigration. This had resulted in a marked increase of interest in Canada on the part of prospective immigrants, yet despite the department's "streamlined" procedures, this interest had yet to result in increased arrivals. "Unfortunately," he explained, "the present security procedure has hindered, and, as presently constituted, will continue to hinder the implementation programme."[19]

Since virtually all applicants (except British subjects, American citizens, and the wives, children, and elderly family relatives of naturalized Canadians) had to be screened, each had to be personally interrogated and enquiries made among local police and local sources of data. The London security section was "in essence the focal point of all security screening", taking referrals by officers in the field from all other points. Yet London, with limited access to facilities shared with the British, could process only thirty-five cases per day. "A backlog is building up which, as the immigration programme becomes intensified, will be even greater, with most serious effects." He pointedly went on to suggest that "consideration of the principles involved in security screening might be justified, when it is considered that since security screening was instituted, approximately 220,000 immigrants who required security screening have come forward and of the total number examined only 4,146 were rejected on security grounds." An opportunity existed: "To take advantage of the extremely great current interest in immigration, a review of the principles of security screening should be instituted as soon as possible."[20]

A new Immigration Act was already in the policy pipeline, enabling various interested parties to present their views on the security screening question. The RCMP lobbied for a sweeping extension of its discretionary powers of exclusion as well as deportation. The more liberal minds in the senior civil service, especially Norman Robertson and Gordon Robertson, were able to undermine these arguments effectively. But when the act was passed, broader legislative authority was given to prevent the entry into Canada of persons associated "at any time" with any group about which there were "reasonable grounds for believing" that they advocated or promoted "subversion by force or other means of democratic government, institutions or processes, as they are understood in Canada," or were "likely to engage in or advocate" subversion. Moreover, persons "likely to engage in espionage, sabotage or any other subversive activity" were also to be barred. This broad legislative writ offered little restraint on specific decisions made under its authority.[21]

Discretion to bar persons "likely to advocate...subversion of democratic government, institutions or processes, as they are understood in Canada," offers a defence lawyer's nightmare. But in the absence of any clear right to judicial appeals, in the absence of any right of rejected applicants to be given the reasons for their rejection, and in the absence of any right to counsel for applicants outside Canada or at ports of entry, there would rarely be defence lawyers to concern themselves with this problem. Further, in the case of landed immigrants facing deportation proceedings, the state's invocation of "national security" considerations could effectively override any appeal process. Finally, specific criteria for applying these very general terms—it was not even spelled out that Communists were the main embodiment of those forces of subversion to be barred—were not part of the legislation but secret administrative categories, never to be publicly divulged. And "subversion" is a notoriously difficult word to define in legal terms; when the legislation spoke of "subversion by force or other means" it appeared to imply broadly that certain kinds of lawful political activity directed towards change could bar someone from Canada, the criteria being left entirely to administrative discretion. Indeed, the entire act gave immense scope to administrative discretion, which was the real core of the security process.

Freda Hawkins, in her major study of immigration policy, cites "two fundamental defects" in the 1952 Immigration Act that have had "far-reaching consequences in Canadian immigration.... The first was the degree of uncontrolled discretionary power vested by the Act in the Minister of Citizenship and Immigration and his officials." Ministerial discretion was such as to give him "potentially the last word on every individual case", including the power to "confirm or quash...or substitute his decision" for the decision of any appeal board that might be set up under the act. Ministerial permits for entry for twelve months could be extended indefinitely. "He had, in fact, total authority over admissions, and total authority in relation to deportations over those immigrants who were not yet Canadian citizens and did not yet have Canadian domicile." In the latter case, there was no recourse in law. Section 39 read:

> No court and no judge or officer thereof has jurisdiction to review, quash, reverse, restrain or otherwise interfere with any proceeding, decision or order [that] the Minister, Deputy Minister, Director, Immigration Appeal Board, Special Inquiry Officer or immigration officer had made or given under the authority and in accordance with the provisions of this Act relating to the detention or deportation of any person, upon any

ground whatsoever, unless such person is a Canadian
citizen or has Canadian domicile.[22]

A perhaps unexpected result of this enormous discretionary
power vested in the minister was that mountains of files on
individual cases descended upon the hapless politician—along
with enormous pressures from private citizens seeking redress or
special considerations on behalf of their relatives, not to speak of
pressures from the major organizations representing the various
ethnic groups. In addition the act also devolved substantial
powers upon departmental officers, with an unfavourable public
image of an irresponsible and arbitrary bureaucracy as the result.
There was one significant court challenge to the 1952 Immigration Act. Criticizing the broadness and imprecision of the
grounds for deportation, the Supreme Court in 1956 ruled that
the government had exceeded its powers in delegating decisions
on admissibility and deportation of both immigrants and visitors.
The administrative basis of immigration selection was briefly
called into question, but within a few months the government
had drawn up new regulations that conformed to the court decision without significantly undermining the discretionary element
in the legislation.[23]
It was during the passage of the 1952 Immigration Act that
another element of Cold War repression was put in place:
discrimination against homosexuals on the grounds, among others, that sexual "deviants" constituted a security risk to the
state. Interestingly, there appears to have been no concern
among Canadian officials about denying homosexuals entry into
Canada; there is no record of the matter ever having been raised
at the Security Panel. According to Philip Girard, who has
addressed the introduction of the prohibition against homosexuals in the 1952 legislation, the pressure appears to have come
from the RCMP and, indirectly, from the American security
establishment, which had decisively linked Communism and ho-
mosexuality in its collective mind as part of a complex of Cold
War subversion. The clause prohibiting homosexuals was rushed
through Parliament with no discussion whatsoever and, it would
appear, to little or no effect in the administration of the immigration program. It was certainly unclear just what criteria security
officers were to employ in detecting homosexuals among the applicants for entry. Later in the 1950s the RCMP would launch

a veritable reign of terror against homosexuals in the public service, but the 1952 Immigration Act is the first example of legislative action in this area. Characteristically, however, both its passage and its implementation were shrouded in silence.[24]

The Immigration Act of 1952 was the sole legislative authority for immigration control for fourteen years. With its strong emphasis on administrative discretion, on the power of the state and the insignificance of the individual in the face of the state, it was an appropriate legislative vehicle for a security screening process that worked out of sight and, as much as was possible, out of mind. Hawkins' considered verdict on this legislation may serve as its fitting epitaph. It created, she writes, "a negative climate in immigration, a climate of suspicion.... The 1952 Immigration Act was a discouraging document."[25]

Administrative discretion was at the core of citizenship policy as well in this period. Parliament had passed the Canadian Citizenship Act in 1946. Until that time there had been no Canadian citizenship, at least technically; there had been only British subjects in Canada. The passage of citizenship legislation gave Parliament the opportunity to define the rights and obligations of citizenship and the necessary qualifications for admission to citizenship for those who had been born Canadian. The latter were not clearly spelled out. In fact, Canadian practice since at least the First World War had been to disqualify applicants for naturalization, as the acquisition of citizenship was then known, on political grounds. The RCMP had been an integral part of this screening process from the beginning, even though it never had any formal mandate for this activity. Nor did the act make any explicit provision for security screening, which was carried out instead under the provision for ministerial discretion to approve or disapprove applications, and under a section of the act that required that an applicant for citizenship be "of good character". By 1951 the procedures had become formalized, with the establishment of an interdepartmental committee to review cases of citizenship rejections on national security grounds.[26]

By enacting a Citizenship Act, the Parliament of Canada was defining the nature of Canadian citizenship.[27] Although Canada was ostensibly a liberal pluralist democracy, governmental practice had for some time defined certain political beliefs and associations as falling outside the acceptable bounds of the political community and thus as grounds for rejection of applications for citizenship—although these beliefs and associations were not, in fact, illegal. Moreover, the government did not spell out these criteria for rejection in the citizenship law. Once again, in matters of national security, administrative secrecy and discretion were the order of the day, at whatever cost to the formal principles upon which the country was supposed to operate.

Secrecy seems to be endemic to the process of security screening in immigration not only in Canada, but in other countries accepting immigrants in the postwar world. As Freda Hawkins comments:

> All the major receiving countries have practised a great deal of private administrative discretion. Security problems, exaggerated in the first place by Cold War difficulties and Cold War psychology, have involved considerable secrecy. Political pressures from all quarters have added to a sensitivity and desire for privacy on the part of governments.... Since immigration involves the direct action of one government upon the citizens of another, there is always something slightly surreptitious about it and departments of external affairs have avoided close association with it or have kept it well apart from considerations of foreign policy.[28]

Secrecy, like a good coat of paint, can cover a multitude of sins. Even the chronic overload of security work could be turned by the RCMP into an excuse for more secrecy. By the end of March 1949 the backlog of security clearances in Europe had reached 13,000, and the RCMP had concluded that the screening program had become "partially ineffective" through overloading and other problems. The whole procedure was sent to be reviewed by the Security Panel. Here the RCMP managed to refocus the entire discussion by complaining that the secrecy surrounding the screening process was not effective enough to allow the police to safeguard their sources of information. MPs or the minister, they complained, had been giving to the sponsors of rejected applicants "information from the highest levels which embarrasses the Police in respect to their relations with the U.K. and U.S. security services." Such leaks should be plugged, the panel agreed, and a Cabinet directive was later issued reiterating that "under no circumstances should the reason for withholding permission to enter Canada be attributed to security investigations." Security was in fact so tight around the screening process that very little publicity, good or bad, seems to have been generated in these early years: certainly there was little enough discussion either in the press or in Parliament. This did nothing to relieve the RCMP of the basic pressure of numbers. By 1950 there were between 2,000 and 3,000 applications requiring security clearance each month, of which about 3 per cent were eventually rejected.[29]

Secrecy was itself zealously guarded. When it was pointed out that "security" was sometimes stamped on forms, this was quickly rectified with the invention of the code phrase "Stage B", which in 1953 replaced "security" on all documentation. Similarly no mention was ever made officially of the fact that "Stage B" officers were actually RCMP personnel since, as one embassy pointed out, "anyone even slightly acquainted with Canada would be able to guess the nature of the connection between that Force and our immigration procedures." Visa officers were instructed that the term "Stage B" was "not to be used in unclassified messages in context with other comments or terms such as 'screening', 'screened', 'R.C.M.P.', 'clearance', 'security', etc., which might lead to a knowledge of its true meaning."[30]

The grotesque lengths to which security precautions could be taken can be glimpsed in one witless administrative excess in the early 1950s. When non-immigrants seeking visas to visit Canada were to be refused on security grounds, an elaborate system of ink dots placed under certain vowels in code on the applications was devised. ("The dots," intoned the instructions, "shall be carefully applied, not in a conspicuous manner, and not in the presence of the person under examination.") Within a few years the system had, inevitably, self-destructed. A British businessman was detained at the Montreal airport because a dot had appeared under the first "a" in his visa application. A security check on the enraged traveller revealed nothing: the dot was just an errant ink spot. The department privately admitted that there had been enough such cases to cause "considerable embarrassment" and dropped its schoolboy spy device.[31]

It was, of course, only a transparent subterfuge that security was not involved in particular cases. The deputy minister of immigration pointed out that "in public statements, we have always affirmed that immigrants to Canada are always security screened." In 1953 Peter Dwyer on the Security Panel recommended to Cabinet that where delays were caused by security screening of sponsored cases, the Canadian sponsors might be told that "arrangements for security screening are not as yet complete". Dwyer commented quite reasonably that "the fact of security screening for immigrants is well known and there seems no better way to explain the delays that are now and will in future be occurring." His advice seems not to have been taken.[32]

The theory appeared to be that security screening was acknowledged, and even pointed to with pride, in general, but that it was to be denied in particular cases. The instructions for security screening procedures issued to all visa officers (known as "Chapter 7") were quite explicit on this point. When applicants were rejected, "the only statement authorized in such cases is that the person concerned is unable to comply with Canadian immigration requirements." In 1955 one proviso was added: "When an order for deportation is issued for reasons of security, such information may be divulged only to the person ordered deported (or at the inquiry in the presence of his solicitor) and this only in cases where the RCMP have indicated their consent." The foreword to Chapter 7 contained this interesting, if somewhat tortuous, formulation:

> The security of Canada is the vital and legitimate concern of every resident of Canada; notwithstanding this, security procedures can remain in successful operation only when the responsible officers treat all security matters as strictly confidential. This places immigration officers in a position of trust which demands the utmost reserve and tact in dealing with the public. It is expected that every officer will realize the significance of the instructions herein, and carry them out with a full sense of the necessity for implicit compliance.[33]

The bureaucrats soldiered on with the pretence that what was acknowledged in general was not to be acknowledged in particular. In 1954 the *Winnipeg Free Press* questioned Laval Fortier, the deputy minister of immigration, as to why rejected applicants were given no reasons. "If rejected applicants were allowed to know why they were rejected that would be a very wrong thing for the protection of the country," he offered. Then he added: "I'm afraid I can't say why!" Yet the same deputy minister admitted to the minister that in "recent years" MPs, senators, and a "few persons considered trustworthy" were sometimes advised of security grounds for rejections in particular cases, but only by the minister and deputy minister, never by officials below that rank. An unexpected result of this practice was that "strong representations" were made by "various influential organizations and individuals" on behalf of rejected applicants, which "results in both the Minister and the Deputy Minister having to give much of their time to these cases."

Yet when the deputy minister suggested as an alternative that security grounds be given as a reason for rejection and that representations be referred to a special tribunal that would consider all the facts in the case, conduct an in-camera hearing, and render a final decision, the RCMP set up a classic bureaucratic smoke-screen. It would be necessary, the RCMP commissioner argued, for his men to "approach all their contacts in the various countries and advise them of the new procedure.... This was absolutely essential in order to determine whether their contacts would still be prepared to cooperate under the new system. He pointed out this would take some time to complete and while he would arrange to start enquiries immediately he could not guarantee" the outcome. The initiative, needless to say, fizzled out.[34]

The police stood fast, on the grounds of protecting their sources. This was the same justification they had invoked to protect the government's security screening of its own employees from any appeal procedure, but in the matter of immigration screening they had what in the climate of the time amounted to an unanswerable defence: the threat of non-cooperation from their counterparts in allied and friendly countries. At the same time an inevitable moral ambiguity is attached to this argument. To what extent was it really only self-serving, in that their own mistakes and their own sometimes dubious methods could be protected from scrutiny and criticism? Abraham Lincoln said of doctors that they were the only profession able to bury their mistakes. The RCMP was the only bureaucratic agency able to do the same with relative impunity, and it was zealous in maintaining that privilege.

In a situation in which the police held certain trump cards, the ability of the minister of immigration to assert civilian control was crucial. Two Liberal ministers headed the Department of Citizenship and Immigration before the St. Laurent government was defeated in 1957. The first was Walter Harris, who served for four and a half years. Harris was a successful businessman from Ontario, a war veteran, and a genuine power in the St. Laurent Cabinet who was very close to the prime minister. He had, in short, considerable clout as a minister, but there is little evidence that he used it to establish civilian control over the RCMP's growing sphere of autonomous activity within his department's operations. Harris was a very conservative Liberal (later, as finance minister, he would be anathematized by the Tories as "Six-Buck Harris" for his niggardly increase in the old age pension), and his conduct of the department was unimaginative, if competent. For the most part, Harris left the RCMP alone.

The same could not be said for his successor, the indefatigable Grit partisan and backroom boy Jack (J. W.) Pickersgill. Having come up through the Prime Minister's Office under Mackenzie King and into the supposedly non-partisan job of clerk of the Privy Council, the one-time Manitoban was parachuted in 1953 into the outports of Newfoundland, where he became an unlikely MP from Canada's newest province. Soon he succeeded Harris as minister of citizenship and immigration. His animated, mobile features and puckish sense of humour quickly made him one of the best known of St. Laurent's ministers. But the public image did not always give a clear picture of his abilities as administrator of the department, which were considerable. Pickersgill was an intelligent and able politician whose zest for machiavellian partisanship masked a liberal conscience, which found expression from time to time in initiatives in immigration policy—and sometimes brought him into direct conflict with the RCMP and with the Ottawa security establishment that ranged itself beside the police. When confrontations occurred, Pickersgill did not hesitate to stand fast. As we shall see, Pickersgill was one of the few politicians who had the courage to stand up to the RCMP and convince his Cabinet colleagues to back him.

The deputy minister for the decade of the 1950s was Col. Laval Fortier, one of the very small number of French Canadians who succeeded in reaching the deputy ministerial level in Ottawa before the days of bilingualism and biculturalism. Pickersgill recalled Fortier fondly: "Fortier was no yes-man and was direct and forthright in his advice. Whether I took his advice or not, and I sometimes did not, he carried out decisions promptly and effectively and was just as forthright the next time."[35] Fortier reflected, as did the prime minister, the very strong anti-Communist views that French-Canadian Catholics tended to hold in this era. The only real clash he seems to have had with the RCMP was his somewhat quixotic attack on them for being insufficiently alert to the Communist menace, as described earlier.

Pickersgill was no less anti-Communist, but he did take a broader, more enlightened view of how to pursue anti-Communism within an immigration program that had other, more important objectives. Fortier did not impede his minister's policy making in this area. Thus the degree of control exercised over the activities of the RCMP in the St. Laurent years derived from Pickersgill as minister, not from the permanent civil service in the department. This was as it should be; an active and assertive minister was no doubt the only force capable of keeping the RCMP within bounds.

Despite a degree of civilian control in Ottawa, tension persisted between the RCMP officers and the civilian officials in the field. It derived from what the chief of a special government immigration mission to Europe in the mid-1950s described as the "absolute responsibility" held by the security officers and their tendency in difficult cases to apply the benefit of the doubt against the applicant. The civilians were often less severe in their judgements and resented the lack of recourse when the RCMP ruled that an applicant had "not passed Stage B", especially when they suspected that the basis for rejection might be political judgement or even moral disapproval of character or behaviour based only loosely upon any statutory authority. Criminal records were one source of conflict; officials sometimes complained that much time was wasted by security officers zealously searching out evidence of minor offences committed twenty or more years earlier. An exasperated civilian declared in an internal memorandum in 1955: "We are a nation of immigrants and I am sure that our forefathers never had to submit to such controls when they decided to migrate." The tensions surfaced in other ways. One visa post reported that it routinely destroyed anonymous letters regarding applicants without passing them on to the

RCMP man, as a matter of principle—anonymous information was subject to abuse—but the RCMP felt that anonymous letters "helped to open up avenues of investigation which might ordinarily be neglected, and in this way have proved a very material aid." As usual, the RCMP won.[36]

As late as the mid-1960s, Freda Hawkins commented after interviews conducted on a tour of visa posts in Europe that she could find no particular evidence of strong political bias among the departmental employees, but the same was not true of the RCMP security officers attached to the posts:

> It is interesting to note, however, that immigration officers considered themselves to be a good deal more politically sophisticated than the RCMP (Stage B) officers who conducted the security screening at each post, and interviews with some of these officers, with rare exceptions, certainly confirmed this. Immigration officers were very critical at that point of the security screening process in relation to political unreliability. They felt that it was out of date and did not reflect a very intelligent approach to the problems of former membership in the Communist party in some countries.[37]

The RCMP also kept very close tabs upon any potential sources of publicity over immigration security within Canada. For instance, the RCMP gave forewarning to Immigration in 1954 that a Vancouver newspaper was planning to probe the screening of Chinese immigrants and was considering sending an investigative reporter to Hong Kong. Yet publicity did get out, and little of it was favourable. Organized labour was one source of hostile criticism. In 1956 a delegation from the Canadian Congress of Labour met with Walter Harris to raise complaints about immigration security screening. The labour representatives cited cases of mistaken identity and examples of persons barred who had no record of subversive behaviour. The minister was unimpressed, stating that agents of subversion had undertaken peaceful means and had attempted to destroy the faith of democratic peoples in the processes of democratic government. None the less, subversion by peaceful means, just like subversion by force, requires counter-action, even though he realized that such counter-action would have to be taken on more intangible, indefinite grounds than the definite grounds presented by forceful subversion.[38]

Two years later, the newly formed Canadian Labour Congress complained that while the government had been "highly successful in screening potential communists" it had shown "far less circumspection in admitting people with 'fascist' tendencies." "Many new Canadians", the CLC pointedly added, "showed no understanding of or respect for democratic trade union organizations." The CLC also criticized the lack of civil rights for applicants as contrary to natural justice and, in good Cold War fashion, declared that "disregard of those rights will certainly not help us in our struggle against world-Communism" and was "a very poor advertisement for Western democracy". Criticism of the arbitrary and authoritarian exercise of power under the security system was also echoed by the Canadian Bar Association, which argued that the right to be given reasons for rejection and the right to cross-examine sources of hostile information "seem to be self-evident but most people would be amazed to find that no such procedure is followed."[39]

The Canadian Labour Congress had expressed the vain hope that trade unionists might be represented at "some stage" of the screening process, but an earlier experience in the late 1940s with union consultation had already run aground over the presence of Communists among Canadian trade unionists. The government had sought the assistance of trade union representatives in selecting skilled workers from among displaced persons. An almost comic exchange of letters between the deputy minister of labour and the international representative for Canada of the International Fur and Leather Workers Union revealed a problem. The IFLWU had nominated Muni Taub, a Communist activist who, not surprisingly, was rejected by the government. A second representative was nominated and in turn rejected "by reason of doubt on the same grounds". The union then put forward a third name. The deputy minister wrote to the international representative asking for more information, explaining somewhat guilelessly, "You can take it as a fact that no one will be sent overseas to select displaced persons if he is a Communist. One of the duties is to ensure that displaced persons selected for admission to Canada are not Communists, and obviously it is my duty not to recommend a man who is himself a Communist."[40]

The irony is that he was addressing these words to Robert Haddow, a Communist activist in a Communist-led union. The RCMP informed the deputy minister that according to its files the third man nominated had in 1933 appeared in the role of Tim Buck in a play produced by the Progressive Arts Club of Toronto, "a Communist controlled organization" (the RCMP files were certainly complete). The deputy minister was warned that the IFLWU was "very badly infiltrated by the Communist element" and that any name put forward by this union "can be viewed with a great deal of suspicion". And so the charade ended.[41]

Despite the growing criticism from without, a growing perception within the government that the security component of immigration posed both administrative and morale problems (in 1955 both the Treasury Board and the Civil Service Commission turned their attention to the administrative difficulties), and the recurrent bottlenecks created in the flow of immigration, the RCMP successfully persuaded the Security Panel that "it did not appear possible to make any recommendations which would substantially improve the present system."[42]

Simply put, the RCMP had posed two stark alternatives: "It is either a question of continuing with our present arrangement or dropping security screening of immigrants altogether." Although this Hobson's choice had been posed within the context of an *obiter dictum* that immigration security was one of the "two duties the Force has which cause us more trouble than all our other work combined", the police showed little inclination to divest themselves of this trouble. Indeed, by the mid-1950s they were rejecting immigration applications on security grounds in greater numbers than ever before. Throughout 1954, for instance, the rejection rate was 4.6 per cent, almost double that of a few years earlier—and this despite the elimination of a number of formerly prohibited categories of Germans and former collaborators.

One of the undoubted benefits that the RCMP derived from its immigration role was the opportunity it offered for liaison with the police, and especially the security services, of friendly foreign governments. Immigration work enabled the Canadians to develop contacts and plug into a world-wide network of anti-Communist security forces. This was supposed to be a reciprocal relationship, but the Canadian security and intelligence corps had rather less to offer than its big brothers in Washington and London. "In principle", according to confidential External Affairs instructions to its posts abroad in 1949, "our understanding with both United Kingdom and United States services is that the exchange of information will be reciprocal, although in practice it is recognized that our contribution will be very small."[43]

For a security service that had been limited to a domestic role, this was a positive asset, offering a kind of window on the world. But there were serious questions about some of the company it was keeping. British and American security and intelligence agencies were, of course, heavily relied upon, with few qualms— although American co-operation presented special complexities at times, which will be discussed shortly. Local security police in friendly democratic European countries such as France, Italy, West Germany, and the Scandinavian countries presented only rare problems along with a degree of assistance and liaison that was much appreciated by the RCMP.

But if there was no question of any co-operation with the police in the Communist countries, there was little reluctance to engage some dubious elements in repressive dictatorships that happened to proclaim their strong anti-Communism. Spain, Portugal, and Turkey—three of the most brutally undemocratic regimes in the West at that time—were judged to have "more or less efficient police services", liaison with whom was left to the RCMP's discretion. Israel, on the other hand, for reasons that will be discussed later, was judged with much less indulgence. Latin American countries presented some problems, although the Security Panel believed that in the case of "the more stable countries" the police forces were "not inefficient". The FBI and the CIA, of course, kept close tabs on left-wingers in Latin America, although the RCMP worried a little about reliance on American agencies leading to "an interpretation that immigration to Canada is dependent upon U.S. approval". Contact in Latin America was made with the FBI, with British intelligence, and with local police forces, again at the RCMP's discretion.[44]

In Germany the Allied intelligence agencies had access to the Berlin Documentation Center, a veritable cornucopia of Nazi intelligence on German citizens, including more than 20 million individual files dating back to the 1930s. The centre was, and continues to be, an excellent source for discovering war criminals, because of the Nazi regime's meticulous documentation of its bureaucrats; it was of signal assistance in uncovering the murderous past of Albert Helmut Rauca, the postwar immigrant to Canada deported to West Germany in 1983 as a war criminal. Thirty-seven Germans were employed full-time by British intelligence perusing these voluminous files, and Canada drew indirectly upon their services for screening immigration applicants.

In 1952 the Canadian government was forced to begin paying $24,000 a year for the use of these facilities, as well as $5,000 for access to the Hamburg central registry of police records. But the government believed, according to the Security Panel, that continued access to these centres was "essential to the success of the immigrant screening programme". The essential thrust of the screening program was to be against Communists rather than against former Nazis, making it unclear just what purpose the Berlin facility was being used for. Was Nazi intelligence being relied upon to detect "Communists"? The question had occurred to West German authorities, as evidenced by a report by the Canadian ambassador to Bonn of a conversation with an official of the German foreign ministry: the latter "wanted to know whether our Immigration people used the Berlin (Nazi) Document Center as a basis for information regarding Communist sympathies of a prospective immigrant. (He did not think Nazi documents were reliable on this point.)" It seems that the German official received no answer.[45]

The RCMP did rely to a considerable degree on the American Counter-Intelligence Corps (CIC) in West Germany. The CIC in turn co-operated with some ex-Nazis, who were, in exchange, protected for their anti-Communist intelligence. Among the more notorious of these was Reinhard Gehlen, a former Wehrmacht general in charge of military intelligence on the eastern front who assembled, under American auspices, an organization that carried out offensive operations within the Soviet bloc. At hearings in 1984 of the Deschênes commission investigating the possible presence in Canada of war criminals, former RCMP commissioner William Kelly averred that Gehlen was a "very hardened anti-Communist" with whom the RCMP did not work since it wished to avoid any association with offensive operations behind the Iron Curtain. At the same time he admitted that the RCMP relied upon the CIC, which in turn was

"very interested in ascertaining if there were Communists within
Germany and they actually favoured the Galland [*sic*] Organization as a source of their information." In short, the RCMP
appeared quite happy to accept information from ultra-rightist
ex-Nazi sources, so long as it was first laundered through the
Americans.[46]

Close liaison with the Americans may have offered many
advantages to the RCMP—which was thereby connected, in
however junior a capacity, with the leading edge of the Western
security and intelligence front in the Cold War—but the relationship brought its discomforts as well. Willing enough to accept
the necessity of a subordinate role abroad, the Mounties still bristled when the Americans moved onto their turf. In the late 1940s
the US Immigration and Naturalization Service began gathering information in Canada concerning the political background
of Canadians visiting the United States. In 1949 the RCMP se-
cured what it thought was an understanding with US officials
that such enquiries would be directed through it alone. Instead
the Americans conducted their own investigations on Canadian
soil and in the process often bypassed the RCMP to consult municipal police sources. According to an angry commissioner, "a
situation occasionally arose where Canadian citizens seeking to
enter the U.S.A. were dealt with unfairly on the basis of unreliable information provided by a municipal police force. This was
sometimes attributed wrongly to the R.C.M. Police and caused
embarrassment. In addition, the municipal police forces would
sometimes pass on sensitive information which in the opinion
of the R.C.M. Police should not be given." External Affairs
was similarly outraged, and in 1953 the Security Panel asked
External to inform the Americans that henceforth the RCMP
was to be considered the "sole source of security information in
Canada"; the Panel added the rather elastic proviso that "information would be provided only on those Canadian citizens who
either desired permanent or extended residence in the U.S.A., or
about whom doubts existed on the part of the U.S. authorities."[47]

Two years later the RCMP complained to the minister of justice of the "trouble" this arrangement caused the force, mainly
in the form of bad publicity when Canadians were barred at
the US border or, on occasion, summarily deported as undesirables. If the RCMP took full responsibility for liaison with the
Americans, it could scarcely escape the odium of providing the

information upon which McCarthy-era America made decisions that appeared to many Canadians as arbitrary and illiberal. As the commissioner explained, passing on criminal information (as the RCMP had been doing since the 1930s) was one thing, but passing on information from the subversion files was quite another: "Information from our subversive files does lead to misunderstanding as from its very nature it is frequently indefinite and, furthermore, it cannot be made known or displayed to the Canadian applicant for entry into the United States in the same manner as can a criminal record." In other words, the RCMP was hoisted on its own petard of secrecy, and the commissioner was reduced to admitting: "I do not know how we can improve our present policy to any significant extent." Thirty years later the problem of Americans barring Canadians on security grounds remains— author Farley Mowat's 1984 experience was a well-publicized example—as does Canadian complicity in the process.[48]

On balance, however, the RCMP found that the international connections opened up by immigration security screening were an asset (as did its counterparts in Australia in the same era), and this gave the RCMP a vested interest in perpetuating the screening process, as well as an excuse for continuing to shroud its business in the utmost secrecy.[49] But if the RCMP constituted a powerful pressure group from within, it should not be thought that the policy lacked strong support from other quarters. First, it was plain to all that the United States government would not have tolerated a Canadian immigration security policy that was significantly less rigid in its Cold War logic than that of the United States itself—after all, there was the world's longest undefended border to consider. Secondly, there were influential domestic pressures as well. The bulk of the early postwar European immigration effort was directed to admitting unskilled and, later, skilled labourers. Canadian employers wanted no radical foreign agitators to organize discontent among an immigrant work-force that they expected to accept relatively low wage levels. While there is little evidence of direct pressure by employers on the state, it is clear from reading the business press of the era that Canadian capital expected its government to screen out potentially dangerous elements and indeed was reasonably grateful that this had been done.[50]

Above all there was the pervasive Red Scare atmosphere of the time, kept alive by the press and by opposition politicians who could be expected to pounce upon any examples of government laxity at the immigration controls. This was a point nicely made by Gordon Robertson in the Privy Council Office when Peter Dwyer, formerly of British intelligence and now freshly installed as the senior permanent official on the Security Panel, with a mandate to review policy, looked at the screening process in 1952 and suggested what seemed to him to be a more logical course. Why not, Dwyer mused, concentrate on screening only those applicants whose skills would destine them for industries engaged in the kind of defence-related activity that would require security screening on the shop floor? Why bother with the rest, most of whom could not conceivably brush up against the national interest in their humble day-to-day activities? "I feel", he wrote to Clerk of the Privy, Council Norman Robertson, "that an immigrant's profession (and hence the probability or improbability of his access to Canadian secrets) should condition that degree of examination which he is to be given." The logic was impeccable, but Dwyer had failed to grasp the political aspect. Gordon Robertson—an accomplished mandarin who served successfully under six prime ministers, with an ongoing interest over the years in security matters— shrewdly noted in a marginal comment on Dwyer's memo: "Govt. immigration would be attacked if Communists were let in, whether they would do harm or not. Must be a certain amount of general precaution for political reasons."[51]

The government thus believed that public opinion demanded stiff controls. Is there evidence of this? Given the secrecy surrounding the security process, it is not surprising that little evidence was gathered of public opinion in the matter. However, one Gallup poll in 1955 asked if respondents would approve or disapprove of European families moving to their neighbourhoods. Thirty-seven per cent disapproved of the idea. Of this category, 3.1 per cent gave as their reason (in an open-ended question) "better screening needed". A year and a half later, of respondents indicating disapproval of "Canada's immigration policy" (36 per cent of the sample), 7.7 per cent gave "not enough screening" as their reason. One can speculate that those who formed the larger percentages, who approved of immigration policy, were satisfied with the results of the screening process or had no views about it.[52]

The security mania of the Cold War years sometimes affected Canada's international obligations in regard to immigration. The abortive attempt in the late 1940s to question the bona fides of the IRO on the grounds of alleged Communism has been discussed. There were two other examples of more serious difficulty with international obligations.

The first episode had to do with refugees. In 1951 the Office of the United Nations High Commissioner for Refugees was established in Geneva, and the UN Convention Relating to the Status of Refugees provided an agreed-upon international definition of refugee status and of the obligations of signatory nations to refugees. Despite the widespread expectations that Canada would sign this convention, it did not do so. For seventeen years, the Department of External Affairs attempted to gain Canadian approval but was blocked by the immigration bureaucracy. Behind Immigration stood the RCMP, because the real reason for Canada's refusal to sign was the belief that the convention would restrict Canada's right to deport refugees on security grounds. It was not until 1969 that Canada finally signed the convention. Gerald Dirks comments:

> Canada at last had become formally associated with the vast majority of countries beyond the developing world by acceding to the Convention Relating to the Status of Refugees. Close to a generation had passed, however, since the Canadian representative at Geneva had first argued strongly for this country's ratification of the international agreement.[53]

The second example had to do with the successor body to the IRO, the Intergovernmental Committee for European Migration (ICEM), established in 1952. Canada joined the ICEM at the outset for reasons that, according to an interdepartmental committee on immigration, were strongly anti-Communist: "The political stability of such countries as the German Federal Republic, Italy and Greece are menaced by a continuation of social conditions which facilitate the spread of communist ideology. If those countries are helped to become more economically viable, by being relieved of some of their excess population, they should be in a better position to resist the appeal of international communism."[54]

It was ironic, then, that Cold War attitudes made Canada increasingly negative towards ICEM. By 1953, the Department of Citizenship and Immigration was demanding that Canada get out of ICEM altogether. The core of opposition was concern with ICEM's desire to process and screen refugees itself; Canada tended to see this as an infringement of its sovereignty and a potential security threat. In 1955 Cabinet considered the question of withdrawal. Some ministers were worried about pressures being brought through ICEM to admit refugees from the Soviet bloc who had not been screened according to Canadian standards. On the other hand, there was also concern that withdrawal might cause "a bad reaction amongst Slavic groups in Canada whose kin were assisted by the organization." Notice was given that Canada intended to withdraw by 1957. By that time, however, External Affairs persuaded Cabinet that the ill will generated among the NATO allies by such a move would not be worth the benefits of withdrawal, and so Canada remained for a few more years, until 1962, when a Conservative government ended formal membership in the international body.[55]

CHAPTER THREE

Canadian Roulette: The Unequal Incidence of Security Screening

The complex apparatus for security screening in immigration did not operate with equal force in all the various nations from which immigrants to Canada were being drawn. In fact the effects of the screening process were highly discriminatory. The number of applicants rejected as security risks was not the only measure by which immigration screening was judged; more important to many prospective immigrants, and their relatives and supporters in Canada, was the treatment of those of certain national origins. This was evident in long backlogs in processing applicants in certain countries, in conditions that sometimes made it impossible or extremely difficult for certain would-be immigrants to get their applications processed, and even in outright ethnic discrimination masquerading as considerations of national security.

France: Deliberately Undermining Public Policy

If the security apparatus formed a sort of "secret state" within the state, there can be no more telling example of how the secret considerations of security could undermine the stated principles of public policy, as formulated by an elected government and justified to the people, than the case of immigration from France. Here a clearly stated public policy, purporting to bring to a close a long-simmering controversy in immigration practice that had pitted English Canada against French Canada, was secretly subverted from the very moment of its inception by the same officials who had proclaimed it.

Immigration had always been a bone of contention between English and French Canada, with the latter often viewing large-scale immigration as an attempt, conscious or otherwise, to swamp francophones with anglophone newcomers or with ethnic groups who overwhelmingly opted—even within Quebec—to assimilate into the anglophone majority of North America. French-Canadian sensitivities were not eased by the well-known reluctance of the European French to emigrate, and by suspicions that Canadian immigration officials were biased against francophones and towards British immigrants. These suspicions of bias were given some foundation by rules and procedures that discriminated in favour of British and American immigrants and thereby placed French applicants in an inferior position. For instance, neither British nor American emigrants needed visas, but French emigrants did.[1]

Resentment was further fuelled by a widely publicized airlift of some 10,000 English immigrants to Ontario in 1947, sponsored by the blustering Tory premier of Ontario, George Drew, with the promise of more to come. The federal Liberal government, with its strong Quebec caucus, responded to this resentment with a series of orders-in-council in 1948 that placed immigration from France on exactly the same basis as immigration from Britain, the Commonwealth, and the United States. In Quebec and in francophone areas outside Quebec, this action was proudly pointed to by Liberal spokesmen as evidence that henceforth English and French Canada were on an equal footing with regard to immigration. In fact, the ink was scarcely dry on the orders-in-council before public officials were scurrying to develop subterfuges to carry on discriminatory treatment of French immigrants—in the name of national security.[2]

The problem was that France was seen by Cold Warriors as a Trojan Horse for Communist penetration of the West. The French Communist party, with more than 5 million loyal voters, was by far the largest party in the country and had been a participant in coalition governments until Communist ministers were expelled in 1947. The Communist-led Confédération générale du travail, with more than 5 million members, was the largest trade union federation in France. To the Canadian security establishment,

France already represented a gigantic security risk to the Western alliance, and now French immigrants were to be allowed to show up unscreened at Canadian ports of entry as Britons and Americans had always done.

To the RCMP, to security-conscious civil servants, and to the Cold Warriors in Cabinet, the new policy was intolerable. To Lester Pearson, it was a "known fact that the Soviet Union is using France extensively as a point of despatch for its agents". To a leading official in the Immigration Branch, it was evident that once France was put upon the same basis as Britain, "many undesirable types of individuals" would seek entry. And to the RCMP security officer stationed in Paris, the changes were sufficient to draw three pages of complaints to the RCMP security service in Ottawa with the warning, "This matter is of grave importance to Canadian security."[3]

Under the new policy, there was no way that Canada could insist that French travellers secure a visa before setting sail for Canada—which effectively precluded the normal security screening practised in other non-English-speaking countries. And justice minister Louis St. Laurent, shortly to assume the highest office in the land, was torn between his public posture as the leading French-Canadian representative in Ottawa and his zealous anti-Communism. To the various complainants, he attempted to draw a fine distinction: the French must, he reiterated, be treated just the same as Britons, but only "if not Communists". This distinction was put into practice by a series of secret devices designed to make the French last among equals. Prospective emigrants were to be encouraged (although only informally and not in any official way) to get a medical check in France, from an approved list of French doctors, prior to passage. Their names would then be passed on to the French Sûreté for a security check. Warnings could be sent ahead, and the unfortunates who fell afoul of this surreptitious screening would then be turned back at the Canadian port of entry.[4]

Other devices to allow prior screening were also put in place. Even non-immigrants from France arriving for visits were to be put through security checks to which English-speaking arrivals were not subjected. All this was, however, to be kept very quiet. When one official indicated to his superior that "extreme care is to be taken in answering any inquiry" regarding French visitors barred from Canada and that "no hint of the security aspect" be given, the latter replied: "Sorry—too open. Say it without say-ing it!" Indeed, so sensitive was the matter that no reference was made to the special treatment of French immigrants and visitors even in the "Chapter 7" instructions on security screening sent out to visa officers abroad. As one internal memorandum in 1956 explained, this was because "technically" French nationals were not subject to screening, although "in practice" they were (a pe-culiar bow in the direction of bureaucratic legitimacy). French admission cases referred to the RCMP were given special blue "urgent" tags: "Speed was considered of the essence to avoid embarrassing questions." When changes in procedure were in-voked, instructions were not entered in the manuals; instead, supervisors were advised to instruct their officials verbally.[5]

Although officials had originally expected that 3 to 5 per cent of French applicants for immigration would be rejected as "Communists" or "Communist agents", in fact the level of rejec-tions was somewhat lower through the early 1950s. Moreover, the general flow of immigrants from France was not high, so the numbers involved were relatively small (seventy-two native-born French applicants for admission to Canada were rejected on security grounds from 1952 to 1955). The numbers involved did not, however, change the growing feeling among French Canadians and French immigrants that French applicants were being treated differently from British applicants, despite the pub-lic protestations to the contrary. The demand that they be treated equitably—that screening be extended to British immigrants or not applied to the French—rose in intensity during the 1950s. Jack Pickersgill, as minister of immigration in the mid-1950s, re-sponded favourably, expressing dissatisfaction with the inequity and advising that "we should relax", but by 1957, when a full-scale review of immigration security was launched, no change had been made. The duplicity continued unabated, casting an ironic shadow over the 1948 public decision to put French and British immigrants on the same footing.[6]

Britain: The Most-Favoured Nation

It is not possible to evaluate the case of France without at the same time considering the privileged status of British immi-grants with regard to security. Certainly French Canadians in government and the civil service constantly raised the comparison and demanded a response to a fundamental anomaly—a response that never came.

The unequal treatment of applicants from the two countries had been raised by Laval Fortier at the time of his unfortunate charges of Communist infiltration of the IRO in 1948. Fortier, soon to become the deputy minister of citizenship and immigration, was one of the highest-ranking French-Canadian civil servants. In fact, his appointment had been made quite consciously by the government in the hope, as the former deputy minister, Hugh Keenleyside, put it, that it "would make things easier with Quebec". Freda Hawkins comments, however, "Unfortunately this had no effect whatever, and Quebec remained a negative presence, a ghost at the banquet, if only seen by some."[7]

Fortier's ghostly representation of Quebec was nowhere so obvious as in the case of the treatment of French immigrants. He never was able to get across his point regarding the discrimination against French applicants. In 1948 his suggestion that Britons should be screened was dismissed by the RCMP commissioner with the argument that "the security organization which would have to be set up would not be worth the heavy cost to locate the few Communists who might be expected to come to this country from England." Keenleyside, still the deputy minister, agreed that the proposal to screen British immigrants was "disproportionate to the problem". The insouciance of the commissioner regarding the "few" Communists who might slip in was very uncharacteristic of the RCMP's usual hard line on security; could it be that pro-British sentiment might have clouded the otherwise undiluted anti-Communism of the force?[8]

George Drew, who took a back seat to none either in anti-Communism or in pro-British sentiment, did not go so far as to dismiss the possibility (or danger) of British Communists. Apparently his Ontario government had badgered Ottawa to institute screening of the participants in the massive airlift of Britons to Ontario. Even the RCMP began to waver: as its representative on the Security Panel admitted, there was a case to be made that either French or British Communists would be potentially more dangerous than those coming from countries that spoke neither of Canada's two official languages.[9]

The problem grew more acute during the Korean War in the early 1950s, with the imposition of security screening of employees in defence industries. Many of Canada's skilled workers came from Britain. External Affairs reported in 1951 that "a number of persons who had come from the United Kingdom to seek employment in Canada and had subsequently been dismissed from positions in Canadian industry as a result of adverse security reports, had made representations to the High Commissioner for the United Kingdom in an effort to obtain financial assistance to enable them to return to the United Kingdom." In the early 1950s about one-third of all immigrants deported from Canada were British; official statistics are unhelpful on the point, but it does seem that a substantial proportion of these deportations were for security reasons. To the degree that this is so, deportation constituted a kind of retroactive screening of Britons, but one that was particularly nasty for the individuals involved.[10]

The Immigration Branch suggested that upon their arrival in Canada, the names of British immigrants be relayed by the RCMP back to British security police, who could then check the names against their files. Upon receipt of adverse information, the immigrants could be deported immediately. The RCMP replied that the British would not accept the level of paperwork involved. The Security Panel finally compromised by instituting a thirty-day delay between application for citizenship by British landed immigrants and the granting of citizenship. This would enable the RCMP to run a simple file check to determine if any adverse information had been accumulated on applicants during their required five years of residence in Canada. This was a small compromise indeed.[11]

Three years later Fortier once more tried to establish equity, this time by reducing the screening of French immigrants. The RCMP commissioner fired back that there were difficulties "in securing liaison with the French security service to a point equal to that enjoyed with the British", and added as a clincher "the fact that there are approximately 5,000,000 Communists in France as compared to only 35,000 in the British Communist Party." When a full-scale intramural review of immigration security was launched in 1957, the discrepancy with regard to screening of French and British applicants remained, and the same arguments were once again rehearsed to demonstrate that the situation ought not to be changed. Not until the 1970s would

British immigrants be placed on the same footing as all others, when security screening was made universal for all independent (non-sponsored) applicants.[12]

Britain's status as the most-favoured nation was evident again in 1956, when the twin crises of the Hungarian revolt and the British-French-Israeli invasion of Egypt in the Suez Crisis spawned two quite separate movements of refugees to Canada. The much-heralded arrival of 38,000 Hungarian "freedom fighters" and refugees from Soviet Communism took place amid a veritable press orgy of self-congratulation about the generosity of the free world and the horrors of totalitarian Communism. Rather less heralded, but much more significant in size, was the tidal wave of 109,000 British immigrants, disillusioned by the sad spectacle of Britain's collapse and the ineptitude of the Eden government. This was three and a half times the number of British immigrants who had come the previous year. Cabinet authorized the chartering of 350 air flights to transport these immigrants. The Cabinet minutes included mention of French as well as British immigrants (Suez had been a joint British-French disaster) but the number of French immigrants was negligible. There were no security barriers to impede the arrival of the British refugees.[13]

"A Long and Arduous Struggle with the Italian Masses"

In the history of postwar immigration to Canada, the two largest groups of new Canadians have been the British and the Italians. In the first two postwar decades, as Hawkins comments, "these two movements were closely related in an interesting way, namely in the anxiety of Canadian policy-makers...to keep one ahead of the other." She goes on to say that "beneath the outward appearance of civility, the Canadian government was engaged for some years in a long and arduous struggle with the Italian masses, eager to join their Canadian relatives in large numbers."[14] In this struggle, the security screening apparatus formed part of the government's armoury.

Italy was a focal point of the Cold War in Europe. The national elections of 1948, following the dismissal of the Communists from the postwar coalition ministry, were widely believed in the West to be a crucial test of strength between alleged Soviet expansionism through the instrument of the Italian Communists and Western resolve embodied in the Christian Democrats. In that election, despite a historic defeat, the Communists and their Socialist allies gathered more than 8 million votes (almost one in three). Some 2 million Italians were members of the party. If Canadian immigration officials viewed Italian immigrants with some disquiet, because they were relatively unskilled and poor, not to say non-English-speaking, the RCMP and the security establishment viewed the prospect of the entry of so many potential security risks with outright alarm. Of course, the two sets of concerns reinforced each other; the results were a huge bottleneck in the processing of applications in Italy and a rate of rejection of Italians on security grounds that well exceeded the normal levels.

The problem was compounded by the fact that the Italian state was much more interested in encouraging the departure of what was deemed surplus population than it was in co-operating in the restriction of that flow. The RCMP officers in the Italian visa operations found that they could put little trust in their police and security contacts in that country. An RCMP inspector reported in 1950 that screening in Italy was "of little or no value". Nevertheless, the RCMP managed to reject a surprising number, reaching 5 to 6 per cent of the total numbers processed in 1956–57, or some 200 a month. In certain cases, involving particular trades where Communist union affiliations predominated, the rejection levels rose to what were called "alarming" heights. For instance, in one scheme to bring in railway track workers, more than 14 per cent were rejected on security grounds. Nor were Communist affiliations the only criterion for rejection. Membership in the Socialist party of Pietro Nenni, which had broken with the Christian Democratic coalition and gone into opposition with the Communists in 1948, would also bar prospective immigrants (and continued to do so well into the 1960s).[15]

By the fall of 1957, the backlog of sponsored cases alone in the Rome office had grown to 52,000 persons, and files were being piled in the outside corridor. An internal report explained, "The Italian temperament is not such that we can examine them and then tell them to go home and wait patiently (and indefinitely) for a decision." The RCMP claimed it was working as efficiently as possible and blamed the civilians; the immigration department tended to view the matter differently. The operation had become an administrative nightmare, and the reluctance to encourage large-scale Italian immigration conspired with the Cold War security mania to worsen the problem. The crowning irony is that there appears to have been no evidence in the government's files to indicate that Italians, whether Communist or Catholic in their homeland, ever constituted much of a security risk after they moved to Canada—even by the exaggerated criteria of the Cold War era.[16]

Anti-Semitism:

"The Good Hard-Working Jew Remains in Israel"

The bleak and depressing story of anti-Semitism in Canadian immigration policy, and of resistance to the admission of the desperate refugees from Nazi genocide, has been well told by Irving Abella and Harold Troper in *None Is Too Many*. Their book ends with Canada's vote at the United Nations in 1948 in favour of the partition of Palestine. They suggest that one motive for this vote may have been a desire to divert Jewish displaced persons away from Canada to the new state of Israel. David Bercuson, in his recent account of Canadian policy towards Israel, does not find any documentary evidence for this in the government records.[17]

Yet the subsequent history of immigration from Israel offers ample evidence of Canadian vigilance against admission of any Jews who attempted to enter Canada through the new state. (Since many Jewish displaced persons had been denied refuge elsewhere, Israel was a potential transfer point for some, as well as a homeland for many more.) The security screening system was at the heart of this vigilance. The story of Israeli immigration in this era thus offers a surprising and ugly twist to the story of immigration security. Born out of the anti-Communist fears of the Cold War, the application of security screening to immigration could be used for other purposes as well: as a cloak for anti-Semitism in immigration policy. The heavy secrecy surrounding security allowed the anti-Semitism to pass relatively unnoticed by those most concerned among the Canadian people.

The first indication that security screening would be employed to bar Jews came as early as 1949, when Laval Fortier indicated in a memorandum to the Immigration Branch that full security clearance would be required for all applicants from former enemy countries, Iron Curtain countries, and Israel. Just to make sure that the significance of the latter inclusion was not missed, Fortier went on to add that all visa applicants in Belgrade, Shanghai, and Stockholm "who are of Hebrew race" would also require full screening.[18]

The real barrier to immigration from Israel was the Canadian government's refusal to accept visa applications in that country, and the subsequent decision that applicants from countries with no visa offices would have to establish residence for two years in a country in which a visa office was located before applications would be considered. The technical justification for not granting visas in Israel was that as a new country Israel had no reliable police records of its residents to be checked; as well, on occasion the RCMP complained that it had difficulty establishing any liaison with Israeli security officials—or of even determining who they were.[19]

These were difficulties of a certain degree, but the picture that emerges from government files is less of technical bureaucratic difficulties than of outright anti-Semitism finding a respectable cover under the sacrosanct rubric of "national security". From time to time the RCMP suggested that the Israelis were far too complacent about Communists, or even that "Israel is being used by Russia to have its agents accepted in democratic countries". This was the stock-in-trade of certain elements of the Western security and intelligence establishments, especially the British. Yet the basis for this thinking seems in retrospect to be laughable, and clearly not innocent of the old anti-Semitic equation of Jews with Bolsheviks. Similarly, bureaucratic problems named by the RCMP were sometimes quite trivial: at one point, the practice of adopting a Hebrew name upon assuming Israeli citizenship was cited as an impenetrable barrier to checking an applicant's past.[20]

When the two-year-residency rule was instituted, Norman Robertson, in his capacity as chairman of the Security Panel, raised the pertinent point: "He did not think that the Panel could recommend a proposal which, although it was in no way intended to do so, would in fact appear to discriminate against Jewish applicants for immigration." It did appear to discriminate, but it was also intended to do so, which may explain why the immigration minister refused to alter the rule when the matter was referred to him by Robertson. Any doubts about the intention are dispelled by the language contained in immigration records. For instance, in a 1953 memorandum to the minister, briefing him for a reply to complaints from the Canadian Jewish Congress concerning the treatment of Israeli immigrants, Laval Fortier quoted approvingly and at length from an official in the British embassy in Tel Aviv:

> What mystifies me is why the Canadians accept such immigrants.... A large proportion of them are agents of the "middleman" type who will certainly never be much good in Canada or anywhere else. The principal country of origin is Roumania...the Roumanian Jew is a kind of standing joke, as being the type of the black marketeer and petty trickster. It has been a shattering experience to interview such people day after day and I shall be very happy to see the last of them.... I can see no end to this stream from Israel to Canada. It is the old "snowball" technique.... Those we are sending now will in turn sponsor someone else: and so on *ad infinitum*. At the present rate there will in a few years be more Israelis in Canada than in Israel!

It would be hard to find a more concise compendium of anti-Semitic clichés than in this dispatch approvingly passed on by the deputy minister to his minister. The dispatch was for private consumption; publicly, the government was at pains to "demonstrate to Jewish groups in Canada that an effort had been made to meet the particular difficulties which immigration from Israel presented", as Jack Pickersgill explained to the Security Panel. An RCMP security officer was sent to Israel to investigate these difficulties. The officer duly reported back that "there are no suitable facilities for establishing the desirability from a security standpoint of any proposed immigration from this country." As evidence for this conclusion he cited his distrust of the Israeli security forces and police, his suspicion that Israel was too soft on Communism, and his doubts about the "type of Jew" who wished to emigrate, as well as alleged fraud among Canadian sponsors. In any event, he observed, "the good hard-working Jew remains in Israel, and is prepared to establish himself in his homeland"—an *obiter dictum* that, if applied across the board, would have had profound implications for the entire immigration program.[21]

By the mid-1950s an RCMP security officer was stationed at Tel Aviv, yet departmental regulations on security screening procedures indicated that "only limited facilities are available" for screening (in this respect, Tel Aviv was unique among visa posts). The immigration department also insisted upon much more stringent investigation and verification of the authenticity of Canadian sponsors of Israelis than was applied to the sponsors of other national groups. As late as 1957, the excuse of "limited facilities" was still routinely being furnished as an official excuse to frustrated sponsors in Canada.[22]

Balked in their attempts to penetrate the security barrier, Canadian Jews tried to attack discrimination in other forms. When they raised the question of the identification of applicants' origin as "Jewish" (a discriminatory categorization since other nationals were not identified by religion), an immigration official sneered: "If a Jewish agency objects to the term 'Jewish' for ethnic origin, they should make representations to have all English dictionaries amended, as the ones we have consulted all state that a Hebrew is a Jew and a Jew is a Hebrew."[23]

That the security argument was merely a pretext for anti-Semitism is plain from the extension of the two-year rule to North African Jews outside Israel. In the mid-1950s increasing numbers of these people sought refuge from governments that were more and more unfriendly to Jews, as anti-Israeli sentiment and Arab nationalism spread through the Arab world. Canada insisted that no security check could be run on North African Jews, and consequently they would have to reside for two years in a country with a visa office. Since their problem was to find a country that would permit them entry at all, this effectively constituted a blanket rejection by Canada. In 1955 some exceptions were allowed, and the following year the political masters of the bureaucracy began to have serious second thoughts about a form of discrimination that was less and less acceptable to liberal opinion. Lester Pearson cited "urgent humanitarian considerations" and added in an unusual intervention that "security considerations are not important enough to seek to follow the normal procedures". Pickersgill, the minister of citizenship and immigration, gave the go-ahead to allow these Jewish refugees to enter Canada on a special basis.[24]

This signalled the first major breach in the discriminatory barriers erected against Jewish immigrants by security screening, which, as one leading departmental bureaucrat frankly recalled, were in fact an "immigration device" using security as a "cover" to "stall" Jewish immigration "in the absence of any legal basis for refusing to deal with such applications." His unusual candour, confined of course to remarks made to his fellow bureaucrats, may serve as a fitting epitaph to a most discreditable episode in the uses and misuses of immigration security.[25]

Yet anti-Semitism was not so easily expunged from the minds of immigration officials who had lived with it so comfortably for so long. As late as 1957 the Hungarian revolt and the special program for bringing Hungarian refugees to Canada served as the occasion for this ancient, ugly prejudice to reappear yet once more within the Immigration Branch. Early in that year the director reported a "rumor" received at second hand "through a very reliable source" to the effect that "many of the refugees were not bona fide ones but persons who had taken advantage of the situation". "These," he added, "were all of the Hebrew race and were in possession of a considerable amount of funds." A member of the branch's medical staff at Halifax "reported that there were a number of Hebrews who he doubted were genuine Hungarian refugees" and about whose presence he "seemed greatly perturbed". On the basis of these overtly racist mutterings (the implicit assumption of which appeared to be that Jews could not be "genuine" Hungarians, and moreover had no right to have money), the Immigration Branch alerted all visa posts abroad and ports of entry to Canada, instructing officers to "closely examine any doubtful refugees", especially those "of the Hebrew race". It is not clear from available documentation whether any further action was taken to preserve Canada against Hungarians who happened to be Jewish; it seems that about 20 per cent of Hungarians who reached Canada in the end listed their religion as Jewish. But once again the cloak of "national security" was being used by public officials for purposes quite different from their public justification.[26]

Yet the walls of anti-Semitism, already breached to a degree in the case of the North African Jews in 1955, continued to crumble. In the aftermath of the Suez invasion and Arab–Israeli war of 1956, Egyptian Jews were under increasing pressure and seeking ways of escape. Jack Pickersgill explained to his Cabinet colleagues that "the Canadian policy in respect of such persons had been quite severe and no applications were processed in

Egypt." Pickersgill argued for a "more liberal policy" and suggested that a small team of an immigration officer and a doctor be sent to Egypt to process some 400 Jews with relatives in Canada, with security screening (and the two-year rule) waived. Cabinet agreed.[27]

In 1958, Treasury Board ordered the Canadian visa office in Tel Aviv closed on the grounds that so few visas were actually issued in Israel that it was uneconomic to maintain the post. The Diefenbaker Cabinet learned that security screening was the problem. Although some Conservative ministers voiced old resentments about Jewish immigration, the new government was not deaf to the pleas of the Jewish community for family reunification. The Tel Aviv office was kept open, and security screening regulations were somewhat relaxed to bring treatment of sponsored applicants from Israel more in line with the treatment of such applicants from other Western countries.[28]

A final chapter in this story came in 1960, under a Conservative government. It had to do with Romanian Jews, the very subject of the viciously anti-Semitic diplomatic correspondence quoted earlier from 1953. The Romanian government had for years restricted the emigration of Jews, but relented late in 1959. The Canadian Jewish Congress had a list of between 150 and 200 Romanian Jews who were ready to come to Canada. There were fears that the Romanian government might not allow this opportunity to last for long, so strong representations were made to the Canadian government. The minister of immigration, Ellen Fairclough, explained to Cabinet that "as there were no security screening facilities in Roumania, the [Canadian Jewish] Congress had suggested that prospective immigrants proceed to Paris for the security check. The Congress undertook to look after those who failed to pass the security check." The government actually went the congress one better by offering to waive security for sponsored Romanian Jews, "provided the sponsors were cleared for security and that applications be endorsed by the Canadian Jewish Congress or Jewish Immigrant Aid Services." There was some grumbling in Cabinet, but it was silenced by the argument that the movement was small and that immigrants of Jewish origin accounted for only 2.2 per cent of total immigration to Canada in 1959. Publicity was to be kept to a minimum. The approach was slightly graceless, perhaps, but it did signal that times were changing for Jewish refugees. It appears that the numbers went well beyond the Cabinet projections, in the end: some 800 Romanian Jews were actually resettled in Canada.[29] Anti-Semitism was certainly on the wane in immigration policy, but it still required end runs around the ubiquitous security screening process.

Greeks and Macedonians:
The Byzantine Politics of Greek Immigration

Greece had been at the centre of the developing Cold War between East and West even before the Second World War had come to a close. Following the defeat of the Nazis, the civil war between the Communist-led insurgents and the rightist government forces became a central issue in the emergence of American leadership of the West in the global confrontation with Communism.

The shift of power was enunciated in the Truman Doctrine of 1947, when America took up the burden of military and material support for the Greek government from the failing hands of the British—a crucial step in the consolidation of the bipolar division of Europe that was at the heart of the Cold War. By 1949 the Communist rebels had been defeated, and in the aftermath of a brutal war, hundreds of thousands were left homeless and destitute. A rightist regime began massive repression of those Greeks believed to have supported the armed left. Tens of thousands of Greeks fled the country (the exact numbers are unclear), many to the Communist states of Eastern Europe and the Soviet Union, others seeking refuge in the West.[30]

Despite the numbers seeking escape from devastation and repression, surprisingly few Greeks were admitted to Canada in the first postwar decade. Although Greeks were to form one of the largest national groups entering Canada by the 1960s, fewer than 15,000 arrived in this country from 1946 to 1955. Canadian immigration officials showed little enthusiasm for Greeks; southern Europeans were not much favoured in this era. But in addition, the superimposition of the security process over the violent left–right politics of Greece itself created complexities and difficulties unique to Greek immigration. In that country, liaison with local security forces meant relying on the winning side in a bitter and brutal civil war, following which the victors showed little generosity to the losers. By the early 1950s, it was evident that reliance on Greek police had combined with the general Cold War aversion to "Communists" to make the numbers of successful Greek applicants smaller than they might otherwise have been.[31]

The bias against left-wing Greek immigrants would likely have gone unremarked had it not been for the intrusion of Greek ethnic conflicts into Canada, specifically the Macedonian question. The question of the Macedonians, a minority even in Greek Macedonia since the influx of Greek refugees from Asia Minor after their expulsion by the Turks in the 1920s, had long been a sore point. The Communists had championed the cause of Macedonian national rights during the last days of the civil war and had been violently attacked by their opponents for threatening Greek national integrity.[32]

Following the civil war, the Greek security police apparently tended to view all Macedonians as "Communists" and thus to issue security rejections of virtually all Macedonians applying to immigrate to Canada. That, at least, was the view of the Macedonian community in Toronto, which found a willing and effective lobbyist in the person of the Liberal MP who represented most of them in Parliament. Charles Henry wrote to the minister, Jack Pickersgill, to suggest that sponsored Macedonians were the victims of "spiteful reports...full of bias" emanating from Greek authorities. Pickersgill admitted to his deputy minister that he himself had "not the slightest confidence" in the information made available for clearing Macedonians. Many who had fought on the "so-called" Communist side were not, he allowed, Communists "at all". In a radical departure from the usual conservative handling of security matters, Pickersgill suggested that perhaps overseas security might be waived for sponsored Macedonian applicants, to be replaced by a security check on the sponsoring relatives in Canada. This suggestion set off a furor when it reached the RCMP.[33]

The RCMP pointed out that Greece was a NATO partner of Canada, and that if derogatory information about applicants came from the "properly constituted Greek security authorities", it was not the RCMP's position "to sit in judgement on the reliability of such information or its source". As for the Greek–Macedonian question, "we do not feel that we are competent to resolve the rights of so complex and baffling a political problem." Instead Canada should receive information through the proper channels and where doubt arose, that doubt "must, as you know, be resolved in Canada's favour." In any event, the RCMP confided, "there has been for a good many years a very active Macedonian fraction [*sic*] in the Canadian communist movement, which has been unceasing in its efforts to control all the Macedonian groups in this country." Commissioner L. H. Nicholson went further yet when he informed the deputy minister that Pickersgill's suggestion "would in effect remove the value of our security screening in Greece. Our security officers would serve no useful purpose as such and I would feel called upon to remove them from Greece."[34]

The RCMP fought against Pickersgill's proposal for over a year, finally putting the matter on the agenda of the Security Panel. While admitting pro forma that this was "clearly a matter for the Minister's judgement", the Security Panel, responding to the deployment of heavy armour by the police, raised half a dozen objections to the proposed change, asserted that it "represented a further reduction in security", and hinted broadly about the danger that "a further weakening of Canadian immigration security might eventually lead the United States to place troublesome restrictions on the U.S./Canada border." No change appears to have been made, as the minister had been isolated by the concerted action of the Ottawa security establishment. By the end of 1957 it was reported within the department that the problems with the Greek authorities had been worked out—although just what this meant is unclear. The flow of immigration from Greece did speed up in the late 1950s, but the records do not show how many of these arrivals were Macedonians.

In the late 1950s Canadian officials in Athens reported that the Greek government was granting amnesties or "decharacterizations" of some Greeks who had been "characterized" as pro-Communist for their activities at the time of the civil war. Ostensibly this was a device for separating the hard-core Communists from those former supporters of the left in the civil war who were now willing to denounce Communism and offer their support to the conservative forces in charge of the country. Security officers were deeply skeptical about accepting "decharacterization" as the equivalent of security clearance for prospective emigrants to Canada—"owing to the potential corruptibility of the poorly paid local police who are suspected of being quite willing to provide a clear conduct sheet for the right price." Moreover, information upon which "decharacterizations" were allegedly based was not made available to the RCMP officers. Canadian officials thought this might cut both ways: an "element of risk is involved in accepting a decharacterization for immigration purposes" since the individual might actually be a Communist; on the other hand, the Canadians also recognized that valid clearances might well be denied by local police "out of spite". Yet despite their acceptance that the latter course was "scarcely fair to those so labelled", the security officials inevitably came down on the side of rejecting any prospective immigrant who had been denied "decharacterization", on the usual grounds that any benefit of the doubt should be resolved in favour of Canada.[35]

Another Cold War issue that affected Greek immigration was the case of some 30,000 Greek children, mainly of pro-Communist parents, who had been forcibly removed by the Communist insurgents to Yugoslavia and Bulgaria during the last year of the civil war. This "kidnapping" handed the Greek government a major propaganda victory, redolent as it was of the Turks rounding up Christian children to be made into janizaries during the Ottoman Empire.[36] Yet Greece's Cold War allies appeared less sympathetic to the well-publicized plight of the captured children when some of their relatives later sought to sponsor their exit from their Communist host countries to join them in the West. Certainly Canadian immigration officials showed reluctance to bend rules that, if followed to the letter, appeared to disqualify any such persons.

The problem was that security screening could not be done in Communist countries, and in most cases it was "practically impossible" (to quote the RCMP) for these young Greeks to leave for visa examinations elsewhere. The RCMP, while fearing that since they were taken when children "it can be presumed [they] will be fully indoctrinated into communist ideologies", nevertheless recognized "humanitarian" considerations and suggested that the children should be offered the chance of being "rehabilitated". The RCMP proposed that such cases be referred to it for individual attention; security screening might be waived "unless the file indicates that unusual close attention is desirable or the applicant is not clear for security." Yet further petty administrative details kept getting in the way, and two years later an RCMP officer, facing more such cases stalled in the bureaucratic machine, reluctantly advised the director of immigration that "while we still feel that there is a definite security risk involved, in view of the political implications we are agreeable to the waiving of the security screening of minor kidnapped children in the Iron Curtain countries."[37]

Two years later, the same RCMP officer was advising rejection of one Greek in Yugoslavia on the grounds that he had been sent there at age sixteen, was now married, and hence did not warrant humanitarian exceptions to the rules. It seems that what played loudly on the Cold War propaganda stage as evidence of Communist atrocities against innocent children came out in rather more muted form when the victims tried to avail themselves of the support of the free world.[38]

CHAPTER FOUR

Refugees from Communism: "The Greatest Threat"

Of all the peculiar deformations of public policy caused by the exaggerated security fears of this era, none is odder than the use of screening to restrict and hinder the flow of refugees to Canada from the very countries cast as the enemy in the Cold War: the Soviet Union, its satellite states in Eastern Europe, and China. This resistance is so odd because it seems to run counter to what one might have thought was the logic of the Cold War. A clever, perhaps machiavellian, Cold War immigration policy might have positively encouraged the entry of large numbers of those fleeing Communism, both to undermine left-wing political associations among certain ethnic groups in Canada (especially the Ukrainians) and to bolster anti-Communism in the population in general through the infusion of dedicated anti-Soviet new Canadians. Objectively, of course, this has been the actual result of East European immigration over the past four decades. But far from seeking to encourage this development, the security establishment in Ottawa spent years doing its best to limit the numbers of refugees from the East who would be allowed into Canada. That it did so in the very name of security considerations is an ironic commentary on just how self-destructive the Cold War hysteria could be when taken to excess.

It was widely believed by the security and intelligence agencies throughout the Western world in the late 1940s and 1950s that persons who left Communist countries were, *ipso facto*, high security risks. This belief appears to have been composed of a number of elements. There was a fear of highly trained agents being deliberately planted for purposes of espionage and sabotage. It was feared that the immigrants would turn out to be Communist agitators, encouraging subversion among ethnic minorities. There was the sense that Communist states were so totally in control of their citizens that if anyone was able to leave, it could only be because the state had some purpose in allowing him or her to leave. Finally, there was the assumption that Communist governments could exercise undue influence over their former citizens in Canada by threatening retaliation against relatives still in the homeland. In 1948, for instance, Premier George Drew brandished in the Ontario legislature a letter purportedly coming from a Yugoslav agency threatening a Toronto Serb that if he did not cease his anti-Communist work there would be no trace left of his family, "not even a rooster to crow". This letter was denounced by Yugoslav diplomatic representatives in Canada as a forgery, but the idea of such control over émigrés was widely held.[1]

This conventional wisdom of the security and intelligence establishments was reflected in media coverage of the threat of Communist agents infiltrating immigrant communities. For example, the European edition of the *Herald Tribune* of April 3, 1950, under the headline "Soviet Strategy Said to Consist of Unleashing Refugee Flood", reported that French and British "political experts" were speaking of a Soviet "strategy of tomorrow". It involved a plan to flood West Germany in an "attack by displacement of the masses", which would include large numbers of agents and Communist sympathizers. The article claimed that half a million "refugees" were scheduled to hit West Berlin on May 27, 1950. This mass movement failed to materialize on the specified date, but when, in the aftermath of the East Berlin workers' uprising in 1953, large numbers of strikers and demonstrators fled the state's retribution by crossing into West Berlin, dark suspicions were raised among immigration security officials about those who applied for admission to Canada and the United States.[2]

Ironically, the one country that had concrete reason to fear the implantation of agents among refugees was West Germany, where East German agents posing as refugees could readily assimilate and penetrate important positions. Spy revelations in the 1980s have demonstrated that indeed this sometimes occurred; yet West Germany was the one Western country that could not afford politically to bar refugees from the Communist East, precisely because of the close ties of language, culture, and family.

Many of these fears seem absurd from our perspective. Agents whose native language was neither English nor French and whose cultural background was alien to that of the countries they were infiltrating seem poor instruments for espionage and subversion. As for agitation among immigrant groups, the record of Communist rule in Eastern Europe has done more to undermine Communism among immigrant groups than these regimes have ever done to promote it. Yet it seems that there was in the late 1940s and early 1950s an inflated sense of the political power of Communism and of Communist states, and thus of the extreme measures that had to be taken to protect people from the otherwise irresistible force of Communist expansion. In retrospect, it appears that altogether too much credit was given to regimes that were actually far weaker and less attractive than the guardians of the West seemed to understand. Ironically, they could have shown a good deal more faith in their own institutions than they actually did. The anxiety about refugees from the East was an extrapolation of this lack of faith, with unfortunate consequences for many seeking refuge from the Cold War enemy: a strange paradox, but one consistent with the often exaggerated fears of a fearful era.

One group of refugees from the Soviet Union and Eastern Europe had relatively little difficulty getting into Canada. These were the refugees from the East found in the displaced persons' camps after the war—those at least who did not bear the misfortune, already indelibly impressed upon them by Hitler's persecutions, of being Jewish. Between April 1947 and February 1948, for example, over 40,000 persons not wishing to return to countries that had come under Soviet domination arrived in Canada, accounting for about two-thirds of all displaced persons admitted to Canada.

From 1947–48 through 1952–53, three-quarters of all refugees and displaced persons admitted to Canada were recorded as having the "racial origins" of Eastern European or Soviet nations. By far the largest national contingents among these were Ukrainians and Poles. (Many of the latter may have been ethnic Ukrainians from the prewar Polish Ukraine.)[3] Since the displaced persons had fled the threat of Soviet Communism, and many had either collaborated with the Germans or even fought against the Red Army during the war, questions concerning their anti-Communist bona fides might have been superfluous. Yet even here there were muted suspicions of Communist infiltration in the refugee camps, as well as in the International Refugee Organization.[4] The main burden of Western suspicion, however, fell upon those who tried to leave Eastern Europe after the consolidation of the Soviet bloc.

As the Soviet take-overs proceeded during the late 1940s, members of the non-Communist political élites fleeing Communist coups could not be ignored by Canadian officials. Exceptions could be made, and some were made for identifiable opponents of Communism. In 1947 Cabinet decided that in "special individual cases" admission on "humanitarian grounds" would be permitted where the individuals might be otherwise inadmissible. The first such case was that of a Yugoslav royalist and opponent of the Tito regime.[5] There was a dark underside to these "humanitarian" exceptions: some of the enemies of Communism had also been the enemies of the Allied war effort; some may have been exactly the kind of "undesirables" that security screening was supposed to filter out. The admission of Nazis and Nazi collaborators will be discussed later; but clearly special exemptions under conditions of total secrecy were an invitation to abuse. That the invitation was not ignored is illustrated by the case of the Czech political and diplomatic refugees.

The Czech coup in 1948 struck Ottawa with particular force. Czechoslovakia had always been viewed as the most "Western" of Eastern European states, there had been personal contacts among Canadian and Czech diplomats, and the memory of the 1938 Munich sell-out to Nazi aggression still smarted among Western policymakers newly sensitive to the signs of Soviet totalitarian expansion. The events of 1948, of which foreign minister Jan Masaryk's "suicide" was a melancholy dramatization, led a number of leading civil servants in Ottawa to propose that their government do something for the thousands of Czech officials caught on the wrong side of the Communist take-over. As one External Affairs official eloquently put it: "The Communists and fellow travellers did a magnificent job in the thirties in organizing public sympathy and support for anti-fascist refugees. If liberalism is to demonstrate that it is a dynamic creed, liberals should show at least the same degree of enthusiasm and ability on behalf of democratic anti-Communists."[6]

The deputy minister of immigration told Lester Pearson, "There is danger in accepting large groups of European manual workers without a leavening of the natural leadership of a democratic intelligentsia." Despite the warnings of Czech-Canadian footwear magnate Thomas Bata (whose family firm was based in Czechoslovakia until the 1930s) that a "considerable number" of Communist agents had been planted among these refugees, the government heeded its mandarins' plea on behalf of liberalism and democratic anti-Communism and launched a modest program to bring in a number of these refugees—and to take care of them once they arrived, since former diplomats, lawyers, and politicians could scarcely be expected to apply themselves to the sorts of menial tasks to which their humbler compatriots were assigned.[7]

The numbers of Czechs were small, but under the reassuring umbrella of liberal democracy, a few highly illiberal and undemocratic figures gathered, including at least two former Vichyite collaborators wanted in democratic France for wartime crimes on behalf of the Nazi occupation. Also among them may have been some former officials of the puppet Slovak "republic" set up under Nazi aegis; their return, ironically, had earlier been demanded by the pre-Communist democratic regime in Czechoslovakia so that they could face charges arising from their wartime activities.[8] So while some genuinely democratic anti-Communists may have benefited from these exceptions to policy, some whose anti-Communism was not in question but whose democratic credentials were highly dubious also benefited.

Refugees of less exalted status had a harder time of it. Some took matters into their own hands. In the late 1940s the first "boat people"—antedating the Indo-Chinese exodus by some thirty years—began arriving on North American shores. Estonia was being incorporated into the USSR, and thousands of Estonians, fleeing Soviet rule via Sweden, crossed the Atlantic in small, overcrowded boats, some perishing at sea. More than 1,500 landed at Canadian ports and asked for refuge. Arrivals were apparently successful in executing an end run around normal procedures, although immigration officials were distinctly ill-tempered about the process. About a dozen would-be immigrants were apparently rejected.[9]

One of the reasons for the desperate measure of proceeding by boat was that Canada did not have any machinery for processing displaced persons in Sweden, where some 25,000 Estonians had gone during the war. The Soviets regarded these Estonians as Soviet citizens and demanded their repatriation. Sweden did not wish to antagonize the USSR by allowing open Canadian processing of the Estonians as "displaced persons". Finally, however, an arrangement was made to allow screening at the Canadian embassy in Stockholm without publicity; the Canadian desire for the utmost secrecy in immigration security thus found a most receptive audience in this case. As it turned out, Estonians were well treated in Sweden, and as fears of a Soviet advance into Scandinavia receded, the numbers seeking admission to Canada were not as great as the original exodus of "boat people" might have indicated.[10]

In the late 1940s it was decided, "humanitarian" exceptions aside, that bearers of valid Soviet passports would not be allowed entry to Canada as immigrants. An External Affairs official expressed the policy succinctly: "As a general rule, the possession of a Soviet passport should be taken to indicate that the bearer is a Communist and...ineligible for an immigrant visa." This policy was further extended to applicants from the countries under Soviet domination. Moreover, posts abroad were notified that while exceptions might be made from time to time for good reasons, the department did not want to be "burdened with having to consider a larger number of special cases than is necessary." There was a certain plausibility to the logic. Inasmuch as the Soviet-bloc countries had fought so vehemently for forcible repatriation of displaced persons at the United Nations and seemed determined to keep their labour forces confined within their borders, it was not unreasonable to conclude as did the Security Panel in 1949 that "any able-bodied worker from Eastern Europe who holds an exit permit from his country of origin should be looked upon with suspicion." Yet this surface plausibility hid a deeper dilemma faced by anyone attempting to get out of Soviet-bloc countries. How could anyone normally exit without a passport? With passports, Soviet-bloc citizens might exit, but then they would find their entry into Western countries barred because they held passports. It was a real catch-22.[11]

The case of the would-be east-bloc émigré was more complicated yet. Even if the passport problem could be somehow resolved, there was the question of the security clearance. The RCMP of course ruled out any liaison with the police in Communist countries; thus security checks, as they were then understood, were impossible to perform in Soviet-bloc nations— and indeed there were no RCMP security officers attached to Canadian embassies and consulates in the east bloc for the purpose of processing immigration or visa applications. As early as 1949 it was departmental policy that sponsored applicants whose security screening had not been waived could only be dealt with if they were first to make their way to Rome, Paris, Salzburg, or Stockholm and there present themselves to the Canadian visa office. That this was no easy matter for an east-bloc citizen was, of course, well understood by Canadian officials. As an External Affairs official readily admitted to the Canadian chargé d'affaires in Prague, the provision meant that immigration from Eastern Europe would be "considerably" curtailed. This was, after all, the point.[12]

This same provision was then extended into the so-called "two-year rule", which required Iron Curtain applicants subject to security screening to reside in a country with a visa post— that is, one where an RCMP security officer was attached—for two full years before their applications for entry to Canada would be processed. After two years' residence in a country where the RCMP could count on the local police, some "record" could be established that would indicate whether an applicant posed a risk to security. As one RCMP officer specializing in immigration security explained to his superior, refugees from the East ("unknown quantities") "present the greatest threat to the security of this country". With the imposition of a residence provision, "the real test of the refugee's bona fides comes when he endeavours to establish himself in civil life in the country which has given him asylum. It is at this time that the various emigree [*sic*] organizations come in contact with him and are thus able to judge his sympathies, etc."[13]

Officials were quite aware of the extreme hardship the two-year rule imposed, how difficult it was for Soviet-bloc citizens to get out in the first place (bribery often being the only means), and how difficult it might be to sustain themselves for two years in a country where they might not be permitted to work. Yet whenever the case for leniency was put forward by sympathetic officials in the field, the policy line—in this case echoed equally by senior officials in Immigration and by the RCMP—was reiterated: "No deviation is possible." Sometimes direct political intervention by the immigration ministers—especially J. W. Pickersgill, who demonstrated a more liberal attitude in the mid-1950s—would gain special exemptions for hardship cases, particularly those that might have more influential Canadian sponsors, but these cases were definitely in the minority.[14]

Applicants originally from East Germany presented special problems in the administration of this procedure, because of the relative ease with which they could slip across to West Berlin (before the erection of the Berlin Wall) and thence assimilate into the Federal Republic, often with little or no security screening by the West German authorities in the *Länder* or provinces where they took up residence. The lack of screening troubled the RCMP, who grumbled about the "considerable volume" of potential security risks who might gain entry to Canada indirectly by the Berlin route. Yet from time to time economic motives could override security concerns. For example, when an acute shortage of farm labour occurred in Ontario in 1956, the steady stream of East German refugees arriving in the Federal Republic offered a source of farm workers who could be "obtained in a few weeks if the immigration procedure could be speeded up", according to Pickersgill. The short cut would consist of dispensing with the normal security screening until the quota of labourers was filled. "No publicity would be given to such an action, of course," Pickersgill assured his Cabinet colleagues, "and the risk of getting planted Communist agents in this short period seemed rather small." And in any event, those who turned out to be politically undesirable could be quickly deported. Cabinet approved this temporary breach to meet the needs of Ontario farmers, but the principle remained.[15]

Increasing friction over Iron Curtain cases was generated between immigration officers and security officers in European posts during the 1950s. At one point in 1955 a high-level meeting had to be arranged at Karlsruhe, West Germany, between the chief of the immigration mission in Europe and two senior RCMP officers. One of the civilian complaints was that east-bloc applicants were often denied security clearance because of membership in the Communist party or in party organizations in their homelands, associations that were in fact "essential to existence or employment." Party affiliation, the chief pointed out, was the equivalent of holding a union card in a closed shop but represented no positive commitment to Communism. The RCMP replied that those who had held "executive positions" or who had belonged to "numerous subversive organizations" (whatever "subversive" was supposed to mean in the context of Communist regimes) were indeed rejected, and that moreover the claims of east-bloc émigrés to be refugees were suspect: "World conditions have changed.... Refugees coming from Iron Curtain countries have had ten years under Communist rule and are a greater threat to our security." Those with valid travel documents, those who were migrating simply for "economic" reasons, should alike be rejected in general. Even "bona fide refugees...can only be cleared when adequate sources of information are available to us in the country where the refugee is located."[16]

Although the RCMP admitted that its officers' occasional tendency to "impersonal rigid uniformity" did little to improve relations with the civilians, it took a strong stand in principle against letting in any more immigrants from the Soviet bloc than it had to, even with maximum use of the various devices open to it. Nor did this resistance stop at the ports of entry. The interdepartmental committee set up in 1951 to review cases of immigrants whose naturalization appeared in doubt because of adverse RCMP security reports had considered 1,874 applications in its first five years: of these, over 81 per cent were from those whose countries of origin were in the Communist world. Of the total applications, 48 per cent were rejected by the committee, but 83 per cent of these were applications from former residents of east-bloc countries.[17]

Jack Pickersgill decided to take on the security establishment directly on this issue. In his memoirs, Pickersgill, who recalls immigration security decisions as "the most distasteful of all the administrative duties of the Immigration Minister", states drily: "I had the greatest respect for the Commissioner, L. R. [*sic*] Nicholson, and frequently saw him about difficult cases, but I did not always take his advice. I knew I was taking a political risk in disregarding the advice of the RCMP, but my occasional decisions not to take it, fortunately, did not get me into trouble."[18]

A meeting was called in the spring of 1955 at which the ministers of external affairs and justice met with leading civil servants and the commissioner of the RCMP to consider a proposal from Pickersgill that "there be a further relaxation of the regulations governing the security clearance of close relatives of persons of Canadian domicile who were still resident in Iron Curtain countries or had departed therefrom and were temporarily resident in another country." Pickersgill was mainly concerned with Yugoslav immigrants, since Yugoslavia was the one Eastern European country that permitted its citizens relative freedom of movement at this time, but the discussion concerned all east-bloc countries. The essence of his suggestion was to shift the burden of screening from the applicant to the sponsor in Canada.[19]

This modest proposal met with a storm of disapproval from the security establishment. RCMP Commissioner Nicholson "did not think the present procedure could be extended any further as it would be misleading for a Security Officer to clear an applicant if that clearance was, in effect, meaningless." He granted that the government could decide to go ahead, but from a "security standpoint" the change was "undesirable". The deputy minister added his voice to the dissenters, claiming that the proposal would give east-bloc applicants an unfair advantage. The Security Panel concluded that "we would be increasing the security risk in this country", that this would be a first step down the slippery slope of laxity in overall security, and that the Cabinet would be duly apprised of this by the panel.[20]

In mid-summer the matter came before Cabinet. Pickersgill confessed, "The Security Panel had considered the problem, and perhaps because he had not been precise in stating what it was intended to do, the Panel had concluded that security would be materially weakened if his proposals were adopted." Pickersgill had consequently modified his proposal to apply security waivers only to east-bloc children and parents of Canadian citizens, and only if their sponsors had received a full and satisfactory security check in Canada. He went on to indicate that there was growing dissatisfaction among Canadians of Eastern European origin about immigration policies: "Many residents in Canada of Slavic origin, of which there were over a million, felt, rightly or wrongly, that Chinese immigrants were admitted to Canada more easily than their relatives." Defensively, Pickersgill went on to deny that he was proposing "a general rule", merely security waivers where "all the circumstances were as satisfactory as possible." Cabinet agreed, and later it extended the same waiver to applicants from North Africa and Israel, who had also faced the two-year rule. In practice, a 1957 report later noted, "the authority for waiver was delegated to the Acting Chief, Admissions Division."[21]

The security establishment attempted to recoup lost ground the following year. The Security Panel became alarmed that following the liberalization in policy a great many more applications were received (as might have been expected). Even more alarming to their suspicious minds was the progress that Soviet applicants had been making in gaining exit permits from their government "through negotiations between the Canadian Embassy in Moscow and the U.S.S.R. Foreign Ministry." Soviet intelligence, the panel believed, might be "substituting agents for the real relatives". After all, a briefing memorandum explained, "In many cases the applicant in Canada has been separated so long from his relatives that he would not recognize them; in other cases the applicant might be put in the position where he could be blackmailed into falling in with a substitution scheme." The members of the Security Panel reminded themselves that they had opposed Pickersgill's liberalization in the first place and hastened to recommend, in light of the "real possibility" that the USSR "could utilize this situation to introduce its agents into Canada through the immigration stream", that the government revert to its former position. Pickersgill was not intimidated. When the recommendation arrived on his desk, he simply scrawled across the document in his own bold handwriting: "I am totally opposed...and would not recommend or support it." The security establishment's counter-attack died at that moment.[22]

Within a couple of weeks, dramatic events erupted far away in Budapest; one of the eventual results was the end of the security mania for keeping refugees from Soviet domination out of Canada. The Hungarian revolt was the most stirring indication of the depth of discontent with Soviet-style rule; the Red Army tanks that crushed the rebels were the clearest indication of the moral bankruptcy of Soviet claims to popular support. The tens of thousands of refugees who fled into Austria in the wake of the Soviet offensive thus constituted a visible reproach to the propaganda claims of the east bloc. Along with the humanitarian appeal of bringing homeless refugees to a prosperous and relatively underpopulated Canada, the propaganda value in Cold War terms of opening up the immigration gates might have seemed overwhelming. Yet the Liberal government and its minister of immigration had to fight yet one more battle against its security establishment. When it was over, the politicians had won a victory for common sense over the security bureaucrats, and Canada became the permanent new home for many of the Hungarian refugees; indeed, of all nations accepting the refugees, Canada welcomed the greatest number in relation to its own population.[23]

The refugees from the East Berlin workers' uprising of 1953 had been greeted with the darkest suspicion by the Western security and intelligence establishments; the Hungarians, too, found that the RCMP had serious doubts about the implantation of agents among the bona fide refugees. Pickersgill, already well alerted to the tenacity of this viewpoint, decided early on to lay down the law. Although security screening was not to be waived altogether, the minister made it clear to the RCMP that following interviews with the refugees in Austria, "unless your Security Officer has serious reason to believe the applicant is a security risk, we would expect him to issue a security clearance." The deputy minister told the RCMP commissioner, "We can properly assume these Hungarian refugees would not present any security risk", and Pickersgill commented in the margin of this communication: "Excellent."[24]

Various alarms were sounded within the bureaucracy concerning possible "subversive elements" among the arrivals (not to speak of continuing alarms about "Hebrews"). Although the RCMP was apparently reconciled to the notion that it would be prevented from carrying out the kind of screening operation it would have liked (a concern partially assuaged by the fact that the Americans also waived security for the refugees), security-conscious police and bureaucrats continued to snipe at the margins of the liberal policy. Concerns were soon raised about refugees arriving in Canada seeking to sponsor relatives still in Hungary. In this case, special instructions were issued that security for those in the close relative category could be waived if the Hungarian refugee sponsors in Canada were subjected to a simple RCMP file check without any "derogatory report". Within a few months the RCMP had sent in unfavourable reports on six refugee sponsors who had eluded their screening net earlier. Immigration officials were unimpressed with the evidence of "subversive" associations. After all, they noted, since the refugees had been working in a Communist country for many years, "this development is not entirely unexpected." The recommendation in these cases was to disregard the RCMP reports.[25]

In 1959 the immigration department recounted for the benefit of the Security Panel the security experience with the Hungarian arrivals:

> There is no doubt that many of the Hungarians who fled Hungary following the October, 1956, uprising had been Communists and that many among them were admitted to Canada, because the emergency created by the refugee problem did not permit the usual security screening. Doubtless, hundreds of those who came to Canada would not have been permitted to do so had strict screening taken place. While, in general, screening did not occur, through interrogation or other means it was learned that some Hungarian refugees had participated in Communist activities prior to the uprising. These persons were not allowed to come forward. Many of them now in Western European countries have close relatives in Canada.[26]

The Security Panel agreed that Hungarian refugees with "a previous Communist association" should continue to be rejected on security grounds.

The Hungarian experience was a watershed in the bizarre history of the security establishment's fear of refugees from Soviet Communism. Not all the Hungarian refugees did equally well in adapting and prospering in their new country, but there is no evidence that among the tens of thousands who arrived here there was any appreciable number of trained agents for Moscow; on the other hand there is abundant evidence that these refugees played a strongly anti-Communist role in the ethnic politics of major Canadian cities such as Toronto. Jack Pickersgill was in no sense pro-Communist or permissive in regard to national security: on the contrary, he took a more enlightened and intelligent view of the Cold War gains to be made by welcoming refugees from the East than did the stolid, unbending police and the security and intelligence bureaucrats. If in the midst of the stream of passionately anti-Communist and anti-Soviet refugees there were a few agents, this was, Pickersgill seemed to feel, a small price to pay for a net gain in the Cold War game—not to speak of the genuinely humanitarian and liberal grounds for generosity. In this he was certainly right, and it is ironic that Pickersgill, a politician, should have known better than the security and intelligence "experts" how to play the game.

Moreover, the treatment received by the Hungarian refugees was a signal to east-bloc applicants in general. Within half a year of the Hungarian uprising, Pickersgill's Liberal government had been defeated and he was succeeded by Conservative ministers, but the trend he had initiated in immigration policy continued. Pickersgill had already noted in November 1956 that Poles could not be treated differently from Hungarians and that "we may soon have to liberalize all of them." Early in 1957, some 500 Poles, including some Jews who were being "encouraged" to leave by the Polish government, were hustled past the security screening barrier on the recommendation of the Canadian Jewish Congress, the Canadian Polish Congress, and the Ukrainian Canadian Committee, all of which, Pickersgill assured his Cabinet colleagues, were "strongly anti-communist". No public announcement was made.[27]

Gradually through the 1960s liberalization did take place. A few visa posts were established in east-bloc countries. Yet even in the 1980s, non-sponsored persons applying from Communist countries experience considerable difficulties in gaining approval. Of course, the main stumbling-block remains the hostility of some of the Communist states to allowing their citizens to emigrate. The USSR itself is the most notorious case, although others, such as East Germany, are strongly opposed as well to allowing even close relatives to join their families in the West. As recently as 1986, a senior Soviet official declared to a Canadian reporter in Moscow, "Many of the Canadian residents who are trying to get their family members out of the Soviet Union are war criminals who fled the country."[28] Soviet rhetoric has apparently changed little since the late 1940s; Canadian attitudes have, to a degree. But the history of security screening of east-bloc applicants demonstrates that not all of the difficulties have been caused by the Communist side.

The case of security screening of immigrants from Yugoslavia forms a coda to the story of east-bloc immigration. Yugoslavia under Tito's independent tutelage offered an uncomfortable affront to the conventional Cold War certainties of the 1940s and 1950s. Representing the only Eastern European Communist regime to have been installed not by the Red Army and the Soviet secret police but by a popular armed struggle against the Nazis under Communist leadership, Tito broke successfully from Soviet hegemony in 1948 and showed that "international Communism" was not quite the slavish monolith that the Western propaganda machine liked to portray. Yugoslavia presented many problems to relatively simple-minded Cold Warriors in Ottawa. Were immigrants from Yugoslavia simply to be treated as "Iron Curtain" cases (when the Soviets themselves clearly did not see matters this way), or was it the case, as Prime Minister Louis St. Laurent apparently believed, that Communists by any name were equally odious, whatever their affiliations?

The issue for the Canadian government was posed in the early days of the Cold War by a reverse movement of immigration: the return to Yugoslavia of thousands of former citizens who had migrated to various countries abroad, including naturalized Canadians of Yugoslav origin. This rather extraordinary event served to cast Canadian Cold War immigration policy in an unflattering light.

The background to the Yugoslavs' return lay in the complicated conflicts between Serbs and Croats and between right and left in the struggle against Nazi occupation during the war. Britain—partly out of realism, partly because of a bargain struck between Churchill and Stalin—had made the decision to back Tito's Communist partisans rather than Mihajlovic's royalists. The Canadian Croatian community had manifested considerable support for Tito, and some left-wing Croatian Canadians had been recruited for special missions behind enemy lines in support of Tito's operations. A Canadian Council of South Slavs emerged as a pro-Tito formation; in the immediate postwar period, it officially endorsed a policy of repatriation to assist in the socialist reconstruction of the homeland.[29]

This movement, strongly supported by the Tito government's representatives in Canada, caught on in Croatian and, perhaps to a lesser extent, Serbian communities across Canada. The historian of Croatians in Canada writes of a "utopian nostalgia of unprecedented dimension. To a generation of immigrants cut off from their homeland by two decades of depression and war, the prospect of contributing to the socialist reconstruction of a society they had been forced to leave seemed overpowering." A fund was established to support repatriation; it eventually raised close to $2 million, and a Yugoslav ship, the *Radnik* (meaning "worker"), made a number of highly publicized voyages to Canada in 1948 and 1949 to pick up a total of 1,869 returnees, of whom about 1,200 were naturalized Canadians.[30]

Canadian government officials and the RCMP watched this movement with growing unease and hostility. Close surveillance was in fact carried out, and the passenger lists of the *Radnik* were scrutinized. This was no idle curiosity. Canadian officials were determined to punish the returnees by revoking their Canadian citizenship. Partly because they expected the returnees to receive "advanced Communist training in subversive activity", perhaps partly out of pique at the negative propaganda spectacle presented by the exodus, the Canadian government was preparing a chilly response to any who might later wish to return. In response to a number of questions, the minister of external affairs, Louis St. Laurent, told the House of Commons on May 23, 1947, that naturalized citizens were governed by the Citizenship Act when they left Canada and could have their citizenship revoked if they resided outside Canada for six consecutive years; further, domiciled immigrants could lose their domiciled status by moving out of Canada with the intention of establishing permanent residence elsewhere.[31]

In fact, the romantic enthusiasm of many of the returnees began to wane almost from the moment they regained their native soil. Even before the end of 1947 the first requests for readmission to Canada were being received, and by the spring of 1948 whole groups were seeking to return to the adopted country they had so recently abandoned.[32] They found no welcome mat out for them.

One supposed security concern alluded to in journalistic accounts was that the passports of the *Radnik* Canadians had been confiscated by the Soviet secret police for intelligence cover.

But little reference is found to this inherently implausible story (why should Tito have thus co-operated with Stalin's agents?) in the government records. As early as 1948, a right-wing Croatian editor had alleged to American diplomats in Canada that the Yugoslavs had been seizing passports from Canadian returnees. When asked why, he said, "You can draw your own conclusions." The *Toronto Daily Star* reported on March 19, 1953, that 120 passports had come into Soviet possession. By the time William Stevenson wrote his highly unreliable book *Intrepid's Last Case* in 1984, the number had grown to "thousands".[33]

A Cabinet directive of May 4, 1950, instructed officials to do nothing to facilitate the return of the *Radnik* people—"except in cases where their return would be useful from the National point of view." External Affairs supplemented this directive with instructions that "no facilities should be given to those who are known to be Communists of the Stalinist school, but that facilities may be given to those former Communists who are known to have recanted their 'faith'." Less generously, the government acted swiftly to amend the Citizenship Act to reduce from six to two years the period of residence outside Canada after which citizenship could be revoked. This was expressly contrived to bar those members of the *Radnik* group whom the RCMP could identify as "strongly pro-Communist or disloyal"; their names were to be reported to the Security Panel. External Affairs continued to agitate for a more liberal interpretation, arguing that not all the *Radnik* expatriates should "automatically" fall under the amended provision of the Citizenship Act, that indeed a "majority" should be readmitted: having been victims of an "intensive propaganda drive", a great many were now genuinely sorry for having left Canada.[34]

The more liberal approach of External Affairs was partly explained by the presentation at the Belgrade mission of some very desperate cases, including Canadian-born children who had innocently accompanied their parents on the *Radnik*, those with close family remaining in Canada, and even a few who had fought in the Canadian armed forces during the war. In addition, External possessed a more subtle appreciation of the significance of the Tito–Stalin split and of the potential for exploiting the schism by treating Yugoslavia differently from other Socialist countries. The RCMP, on the other hand, did not normally deal

in fine distinctions between varieties of Communism. Cases referred to it most often came back with reports that the applicant
had "been an active Communist while in Canada, or was sympathetic to Communism"—even though the applicant's Canadian
experience antedated the Tito–Stalin split. Since it was obvious
that most of the returnees must have harboured some sympathy for Communism in the first place, this kind of report would
eliminate most from readmission.[35]

Moreover, the RCMP attitude was clearly backed by the
immigration department. Indeed, the department interpreted the
amendment to the Citizenship Act reducing the period of external
residence from six to two years as applying only to those who
returned to reside in Iron Curtain countries, a term that expressly
included Yugoslavia; the old six-year rule would continue in
effect for those residing in non-Communist countries. Finally,
in response to External's concerns, Immigration made it clear
that even if External Affairs no longer considered Yugoslavia
an Iron Curtain country, it was "still a communist state" as
far as the immigration department was concerned. "It may be
difficult for Citizenship and Immigration, which is, since the
amendment of the Canadian Citizenship Act, vitally concerned
with domestic reaction to the return of these people, to reflect in
its decisions the important change which has taken place in the
international scene." In other words, External Affairs was free to
play diplomacy abroad, but Immigration insisted that citizenship
and immigration must be ruled by domestic political concerns,
in this case by a rather unsubtle anti-Communism.[36]

As it turned out, however, the RCMP's bark was, as usual,
worse than its bite. When requested to prepare reports on the
entire *Radnik* group, the police refused, citing understaffing. A
second request was answered by a gruff "out of the question".
In the absence of heavy police documentation, Citizenship and
Immigration officials had to rely on the judgement of the head
of the Canadian mission in Belgrade. The registrar of Canadian
citizenship developed abounding admiration for this official as a
"person of exceptional ability in determining whether or not the
persons who approach his office with requests for permission to
return to Canada are non-communists, and great faith is placed
in his judgment in that regard." The Canadian mission head
seems to have applied to his role the broader perspective of his
department rather than the narrower viewpoint of the security

establishment. By June 1951, 313 of the original 1,200 Canadian citizens on the *Radnik* voyages had been granted passports or returning Canadian visas for their return trip, and 40 to 60 more were already authorized.[37]

A year later the RCMP commissioner belatedly acknowledged that External Affairs might well have been right, not only about international affairs but about domestic politics as well: "Due to the benefits which might accrue as compared with the security risk involved, greater leniency could be shown Yugoslav repatriates wishing to return to Canada. The results of the decision are partially evinced by the detrimental effect those already returned have had on the Yugoslav Communist movement in Canada." He also acknowledged that given the time elapsed since the *Radnik* departures, security clearances by the RCMP based on past Canadian activities were of "a very questionable value." Nevertheless, many were rejected as security risks on the basis of interviews at the Belgrade mission (forty-five in all from 1951 through 1955), and others were rejected on the evidence of their Canadian past as gathered in RCMP files. In 1954 a petition arrived from Zagreb for Governor General Vincent Massey signed by twenty-six former Canadians denied readmission. Their plea, resting heavily on equity (others who had belonged to the same organizations while in Canada had been allowed back), found a certain sympathetic ear in the minister of immigration, Walter Harris, who noted, "There are thousands of former citizens of Yugoslavia in Canada who appear to be perfectly dependable citizens here and who simply cannot understand our evasions and explanations of our present policy."[38]

Harris's concerns about "the extremely unsatisfactory situation with respect to immigration from Yugoslavia" encompassed more than the case of the *Radnik* group. He worried about the narrow application of "Iron Curtain" criterion for this Communist but non-Iron Curtain country: "I doubt if we would want to take in any considerable numbers but I would like," he pleaded, "to be in a better position with respect to close relatives." The security establishment thought otherwise. The subtle mind of Peter Dwyer on the Security Panel had discovered yet another ground for rejecting Yugoslavs. Was the Tito regime not anti-Soviet? Then it might be, Dwyer argued, that refugees from that country were "orthodox communist sympathizers rather than anti-communists"; thus, "immigration from Yugoslavia was to be discouraged." Less dialectical and more traditional minds in Immigration used security criteria to clothe some familiar prejudices. Laval Fortier, the deputy minister, reminded Jack Pickersgill, who as Harris's successor had begun to carry out the projected liberalization of east-bloc immigration procedures, that "as I told you verbally, the Immigration Branch reports that the Yugoslavs are not necessarily the best type of immigrants."[39]

In the 1950s, southern Europeans ranked only slightly above Jews, blacks, and Asians in Immigration's hierarchy of "best types". Caught in a double trap, both ethnic and political, Yugoslav immigrants (and Yugoslav Canadians trying to return to Canada) were made only marginally better off than their Eastern European counterparts by Tito's courageous stand against Stalin in the late 1940s. Amid the simple-minded Cold War verities of this era, there was some room, but not a great deal, for more subtle shadings.

For another ethnic group, a Communist take-over in their home-land was only one additional obstacle to overcome on a road already made difficult by Canadian attitudes. The Chinese had always been near the bottom of the racial hierarchy created by Canada's discriminatory immigration policies. Asians had borne the brunt of racism in Canada—along with native people and blacks, they were seen as "unassimilable". The Royal Commission on Chinese and Japanese Immigration concluded in 1902 that Asians were "unfit for full citizenship...obnoxious to a free community and dangerous to the state". Even so liberal an observer as J. S. Woodsworth—later the founding leader of the CCF and the patron saint of social democracy in Canada—concluded flatly in a pioneering 1909 book on immigration, "The Orientals cannot be assimilated." Legislation in 1923 made it virtually impossible for Chinese to continue to immigrate to Canada, and a head tax made it prohibitively expensive for Chinese men to bring in their wives; thus, the Chinese population in Canada was, through the Second World War, overwhelmingly male. Those Chinese who were domiciled in Canada traditionally were treated as virtual non-citizens: until the end of the war, for example, they were prohibited from voting in British Columbia elections, and Chinese Canadians resident in that province (where the majority lived) were prohibited from voting in federal elections as well.[40]

In the aftermath of the war, conflicting currents beset the question of Chinese immigration. On the one hand, the revulsion against Fascism had begun to invalidate a racism that had gone virtually unchallenged throughout earlier Canadian history. Even the wartime hysteria that had led to the forcible removal of the entire West Coast Japanese population to concentration camps in the Interior had abated so quickly following the war that government attempts to deport the Japanese-Canadian population to Japan (including those born in Canada) had to be abandoned in the face of considerable public displeasure. The exclusionary policies towards Chinese immigrants came under attack before Parliament and the Canadian government in the late 1940s. In 1947, Prime Minister Mackenzie King told the House that the government remained hostile to "large-scale immigration from the Orient", but that this was not to be construed as a policy of permanent exclusion. The next day a bill was introduced to repeal the discriminatory Chinese Immigration Act, which had the effect of placing Chinese immigration under the authority of a 1930 order-in-council that was still discriminatory but allowed the sponsorship of wives and children, which had been extremely difficult before.[41]

While this slow liberalization was in process, events were taking place on the Chinese mainland that were to have important reverberations in Canada. The Chinese civil war, which had been raging for years, was now drawing to a close with the sweeping victory of Mao's Communist armies. By the end of 1949 the largest nation on earth had "fallen" (as Western rhetoric of the time had it) to Communism. Just as Chinese Canadians began to sponsor their close family members as immigrants, China itself had become part of the enemy in the Cold War. By 1950 Canadian soldiers serving with the UN forces in Korea were actually in combat with Chinese forces who had intervened on the North Korean side. The triumph of Communism in China had two main effects on Chinese immigration to Canada. On the one hand, there was some agitation for admission of refugees who would not otherwise have been admissible. On the other, the full Cold War security apparatus was deployed to screen Chinese immigration. Not surprisingly, many of the old racist prejudices could continue to operate under the cloak of "national security".

Just as the last remnants of Chiang Kai-shek's battered Nationalist army were retreating to the island of Taiwan, the Canadian

Cabinet was meeting to consider the problem of pressure from the Chinese Benevolent Association to widen the classes of sponsorship to include the families of Chinese residents of Canada who had applied for Canadian citizenship but not yet been granted it. Over the previous year, 2,800 Chinese had filed declarations of intent to become Canadian citizens. If the requested change was made, it was estimated that applications for dependents could average well over 200 per month. The Immigration Branch indicated it was too overworked to deal with such a large number of applications for "some considerable time". Citing "humanitarian" considerations, the immigration minister asked the Cabinet to approve a plan whereby those Chinese who applied for naturalization before December 1, 1949, would be permitted by order-in-council to bring in their wives and children under eighteen years of age—provided that the applicant's family had fled the mainland prior to that date.[42] The date happened to coincide with Chiang's flight to Taiwan.

The Security Panel had already met to ponder the implications of the Communist victory for internal security in Canada. Intelligence estimates were that "a Chinese Communist government might attempt to use native elements in Canada for purposes calculated to strengthen the overseas influence of that regime". External Affairs suggested that one response should be to "tighten our control of immigration from China"; the department also asked the RCMP to "review the measures they should take in order to counter any subversive activities among the Chinese in Canada." The RCMP responded that it had already made a "preliminary survey" of Chinese groups in Canada, which revealed "little positive evidence of discontent". The police considered that "the Chinese community in Canada appeared, on the whole, to be disillusioned with both the Nationalist regime and their Communist successors.... The native elements in Canada seemed to feel that the general confusion in China offered little hope for a happy solution to the problems of that country." The Security Panel, apparently not assuaged by the RCMP's moderate report, asked the police to conduct another survey and also noted with satisfaction that if the panel's general recommendations on security screening of immigrants were approved by the government, Chinese immigration would be more strictly controlled.[43]

One problem that arose immediately was that of requests for asylum from Nationalist government officials. Early in 1950 it was widely believed that Taiwan would fall in its turn to the Red Army, and numerous officials of the old regime were seeking refuge. It was noted by the Cabinet that these people would not have been "normally" admissible, and that it would be even more difficult for them to find gainful employment in Canada than it had been for the former diplomats and officials from Czechoslovakia—an admission of anti-Chinese racism in Canadian hiring. Moreover, External Affairs worried about possible reprisals against Canadians on the Chinese mainland if Nationalists continued anti-Communist political activities on Canadian soil. The Cabinet reluctantly agreed to grant temporary entry permits (six months to a year) to Nationalist officials and private Chinese citizens in Canada who could not be "encouraged" to return to their homeland, but insisted that no other permits to Chinese outside Canada should be given except "on their merits".[44] In the end, of course, Taiwan remained under Chiang's rule as a pretender to the title of legitimate "Chinese" government (a pretence accepted by Ottawa until the 1970s), and die-hard anti-Communist Chinese had a base of their own from which to operate. It is interesting, however, to note that the officials of the regime that the Canadian government publicly praised as "free" China should have been treated so coolly.

Nationalist officials were one thing, but dependents of Canadians caught in a Communist revolution were another. A number of wives and children of Chinese Canadians were reported stranded in Hong Kong without passports or other travel documents that they needed, under Canadian regulations, to enter Canada. Cabinet recommended that the normal provisions be waived "to avoid hardship", and that the superintendent of immigration at Hong Kong be authorized to accept an "affidavit establishing the identity of the holder in lieu of passport." Immigration Branch representatives were further authorized to provide a "fair" screening service, provided the numbers were not too large and "subject to the satisfaction" of the RCMP.[45] The Canadian government was responding to the situation with rather more liberality than might have been expected, judging by its past treatment of Chinese immigrants.

Only twenty Chinese had succeeded in immigrating to Canada in 1947, but the rate rose sharply in the late 1940s and early

1950s. By 1951 the yearly total had reached 2,697, even though the Korean War was in progress. Mackenzie King's 1947 stricture against "large-scale" immigration from Asia was hardly violated by such numbers; yet they did indicate that entire families were being brought together, and that at least was a step up in the sad history of the Chinese in Canada.[46] Yet there were forces lurking in the shadows of the Canadian state ready to counterattack against these modest gains—especially in the security establishment.

One figure who rose briefly out of the security shadows at this time was Insp. John Leopold, the man who had given dramatic testimony at the trial of Tim Buck and other Communist leaders in 1931, revealing his undercover work for the RCMP as a Communist in the 1920s. Leopold had gone on to a long career as an RCMP specialist on Communist subversion; his zeal in this regard was unique, even among Mounties.

Early in 1952 Leopold unveiled the outlines of a Communist conspiracy to substitute trained agents for bona fide sons sponsored by Chinese Canadians. Spiced with allegations of widespread bribery, corruption, and improper procedures in Hong Kong—which were indeed true—Leopold's case of the impostor Chinese sons was not without its bizarre touches, including the apparent implication that the Chinese sponsors might not be able to recognize the impersonators since Chinese all looked alike. Reflecting little more than a blend of ancient anti-Chinese prejudice and more contemporary anti-Communist anxiety, Leopold's "conspiracy" was remarkably short on concrete evidence. Although Supt. George McClellan of the Special Branch backed up Leopold, confiding to Laval Fortier that no less than 85 per cent of all Chinese immigration "would be persons substituted or trained in subversive activities", unmasking a single one of the impostors proved to be beyond the force's capability.[47]

In case the civilians in Immigration might lose interest in the conspiracy, the commissioner of the RCMP wrote a three-page letter to the deputy minister. Commissioner Nicholson indicated that security screening on the Chinese mainland was "practically hopeless" and screening in Hong Kong was "practically impossible". As a result, RCMP investigators in Canada had concluded that "at least a number of the Chinese, now being admitted to Canada as close relatives of Chinese resident in Canada, are in fact impostors.... While it is true", he admitted, "that we have at the moment very few cases in which we could positively prove impersonation, we are satisfied that this practice is widespread." He went on to explain that "investigations into this type of offence are extremely difficult, for we are finding that our contacts among Canadian Chinese are becoming increasingly reluctant to talk."

The commissioner attributed their reluctance to intimidation by the Communists. He seems not to have considered that Chinese parents may have been upset at the RCMP's implication that the sons they had brought to Canada with considerable difficulty were not in fact their sons at all, but clever Communist impostors. Perhaps if their feelings had been considered, their reluctance to talk might have been given a less sinister interpretation. In any event, having raised the spectre of the threat to national security from the admission of "persons who can only be considered enemies of this country", the commissioner concluded his warning with the real policy thrust of the entire impostor affair:

> I realize that there is Government policy dealing with Chinese immigration, but, from a purely security point of view and under present conditions, it would seem to me that complete exclusion is the only thing that will afford complete security. We are not facing individual efforts to immigrate illegally, but a concentrated effort directed by a government inimical to the interests of the country.[48]

"Complete exclusion is the only thing that will afford complete security": there was the security establishment's perspective on immigration in a nutshell. Unhappily for the police, the government already had its own policies regarding immigration, so the quixotic quest for "complete security" through "complete exclusion" did not figure prominently on its agenda. As for the strange case of the impostor sons, the weakness of the evidence did not commend it to the government for immediate action, especially along the precipitous lines suggested by the RCMP commissioner. Yet the police continued to rely on this threadbare fabric for other uses as well.

Among the other fish they tried to bait were two young Vancouver lawyers whom the RCMP suspected of harbouring subversive political ideas. Harry Rankin (later to be the alderman perennially at the head of the polls in Vancouver civic elections) and Ike Shulman had at least one thing in common: both had been called before private inquisitions of the Law Society of British Columbia and required to sign statements that they were not Communists before they were admitted to the Bar in 1950. This inquisition had already claimed one victim, Second World War veteran Gordon Martin, who was barred from practising law in the province (after investing veteran's credits and five years in law school) solely on the grounds that the Benchers considered him to be a Communist—a decision supported by the British Columbia Court of Appeal. Rankin and Shulman signed the statements and commenced careers as practising lawyers. But an unforgiving RCMP was ready in 1952 to carry on the attack against the two.[49]

Commissioner Nicholson informed the deputy minister of immigration in the fall of 1952 that while past investigations of "suspected irregularities" in the admission of Chinese immigrants "were all non-conclusive" because of the lack of "tangible evidence", new facts had been revealed, indicating that a "sizeable racket in the illegal admission of Chinese immigrants does in fact exist." Nicholson revealed a plot by "certain Chinese persons and others". In the latter category were Harry Rankin and Ike Shulman, who were allegedly using their law offices as part of the scheme. Nicholson admitted that his case was "somewhat nebulous" and further that "the information we have obtained does not lend itself to further verification at present." Then he added ominously: "Possibly your Department will be interested in the names supplied so that any Immigration or Citizenship dealings originating with these people can be scrutinized with particular care."[50]

The ethics of exercising secret sanctions on the basis of evidence so "nebulous" as not to lend itself to verification may or may not have swayed the immigration department; certainly when it examined its own records, it gave the RCMP "case" short shrift. Ike Shulman, the department found, had had only one passing connection with a single Chinese immigration case it had investigated. As for the other alleged culprit: "We have no record in our files of Harry Rankin." The Immigration Branch could find little else of substance and concluded, "We have no evidence that an organized racket exists."[51] Like the impostor Chinese sons, Shulman and Rankin eluded the grasp of the police.

Perhaps the impostor Chinese sons were never tracked down because they were, after all, only spectres conjured up by the overheated Cold War imaginations of the security establishment. The immigration department accepted reports from persons with dubious qualifications for political intelligence work, such as a Catholic nun who complained that twenty Chinese on board a ship en route to Canada sang "Communist songs"; it also reluctantly agreed that the majority of young Chinese were "converts to communism" and thus security risks—about whom little could be done.[52]

Later it became known that there was indeed some illegal activity surrounding immigration from Hong Kong to Canada, but there was no evidence of any political content to it. Evidence of illegality in Chinese immigration mounted in the late 1950s, and by the end of the decade the Conservative government, faced with estimates that at least 60 per cent of recent Chinese immigrants had entered illegally, felt compelled to take drastic action. In the spring of 1960 the RCMP carried out one of the most massive searches in Canadian history, raiding Chinese-Canadian homes, businesses, and offices, amid headlines charging that half the postwar Chinese immigration had been illegal. The RCMP's lack of familiarity with the Chinese community was evident in its need to import eleven Hong Kong policemen to act in the investigation; these men were reportedly regarded by many in the Chinese community as "spies". When the furor finally died down, nineteen of twenty-eight persons charged had been given varying but relatively mild sentences. There appear to have been no deportations on security grounds. To the extent that Canadian lawyers were involved, they were certainly not the left-wingers closely watched by the RCMP security branch, but apolitical types interested in turning a few dollars by shady methods. A decade later, the Royal Commission on Security recommended tightening procedures with regard to Chinese immigration, but as the immigration department noted, there was no suggestion in the report that the "admission of Chinese under a false identity is being utilized by persons who represent a security threat."[53]

The last word on the Chinese affair can be given to an official of the US state department who reported on fraud in Hong Kong immigration in 1955. His eighty-nine–page report indicated that intensive American security checks sometimes uncovered various criminal activities but "seldom" revealed anything to do with Communism. If there was a problem of national security, it rarely had to do with impostors, but simply with the general popularity of Communism among young Chinese. Commenting on this report, the director of immigration noted its implications for Canada, which, like the United States, had built up over the years a series of restrictive laws and procedures inhibiting Chinese immigration. "The causes for fraudulent action on their part may be attributed to their eagerness to circumvent the various restrictive measures." This was a rare moment of candour and clarity on an issue that had generated all too much of the opposite.[54]

CHAPTER FIVE

His Majesty's Late Enemies

The immigration security screening process was put in place in the immediate aftermath of the Second World War. Yet the politics of security had far more to do with the incipient Cold War than with the war that had just been fought or with the multitude of His Majesty's late enemies now seeking admission following the defeat of the Axis powers.

Among this multitude were many who had actively espoused the totalitarian ideology against which Canada had fought a bloody and costly war, many who had participated in a process that had encouraged and condoned what the Nuremberg war crimes tribunal called crimes against humanity, some who had had direct roles in organizations the purpose of which was the torture and extermination of large numbers of civilians, and others who had actively collaborated with the Nazi armies of occupation against their own compatriots. All of these categories of persons were excluded in principle as politically undesirable, and applicants of this description were supposed to be screened out through the security process. Many were. Yet some forty years after the screening process was put in place, there was sufficient public disquiet regarding its effectiveness that a royal commission was established to discover whether war criminals had in fact entered Canada despite screening. There is very good reason for this disquiet. The screening process was, in truth, a bird with one wing: an anti-Communist wing.[1]

In the summer of 1946, Cabinet decided not to include a new classification in the Immigration Act to specifically prohibit Nazis, Fascists, war criminals, and other similar categories. "In view of the difficulties in drafting a suitable clause" to add to the legislation, Cabinet decided instead that "the problem could be dealt with by other means." "Other means" clearly meant administrative discretion, an approach that came to inform all subsequent immigration security practices. As indicated earlier, the list of prohibited categories established in 1948 for the use of immigration officials clearly included Nazis, Fascists, SS, non-Germans with the SS blood-mark, Waffen-SS recruited before January 1, 1943, and collaborators "presently residing in previously occupied territories".[2] These categories were, of course, secret. Changes to the categories were also secret. How they were administered and how they were amended were questions that only senior bureaucrats, certain Cabinet ministers, and the top brass of the RCMP could answer—and it was government policy not to answer questions in this area. In the dark and silent space thus created, there was considerable room for shadowy manoeuvres.

One early indication of the potential for arbitrariness in administrative discretion was the inequality inherent in the immigration rules being applied differently to Japanese than to Germans. During the war the entire Japanese population of the West Coast had been forcibly removed to concentration camps in the interior; their property was confiscated and disposed of by the state. This act, arguably the worst Canadian example of minority repression in the twentieth century, was based in part upon alleged public antipathy to the Japanese Canadians in areas where they were concentrated. Although there were some examples of public hostility to German Canadians, there was no similar mass detention of this group, or of Italian Canadians (although certain individuals in both groups who were seen as dangerous to the war effort were interned). The roots of this difference are not hard to find: they obviously lay in racism. Anti-Asian prejudice had always been high in Canada, while Germans—even though they had been the main enemy of Canada in two wars—were, after all, white and European.

Mackenzie King's private thoughts on the day of the atomic bombing of Hiroshima were to rejoice that it had not been necessary to use such a weapon against Europeans. In the same spirit, Cabinet pursued into peacetime a vindictive and racist scheme to deport the entire Japanese-Canadian population (including some 10,000 born in Canada) to Japan. Eventually, in the face of strong public opposition, the government reluctantly backed down; although some were deported, most remained. Yet at about the same time that Cabinet was seriously discussing the mass deportation of thousands of its own native-born inhabitants, it was also discussing a proposal that German prisoners of war located in Canada be allowed to remain to fulfil a demand for skilled labour. Military intelligence vetted about 2,000 prisoners and cleared 745 as "politically reliable". Initially Cabinet agreed to allow 200 to remain, but in the end, none were allowed to stay. The stark contrast in the treatment of Japanese Canadians—against whom the government had proved not a single case of sabotage or espionage—and of German soldiers captured in combat is quite extraordinary, and certainly revealing. Even ten years after the war had ended, the Canadian Cabinet was discussing whether to allow the return to Canada of former naturalized Canadians voluntarily repatriated to Japan.[3]

As for Germans, it was the policy of the Immigration Branch in the immediate postwar years not to encourage the immigration of German nationals, even those who did not fall into "political" categories. As the director of immigration explained to External Affairs at the end of 1946, "The teams we are arranging to send into Germany will be primarily for the examination of displaced persons and it is unlikely they will have the time or the facilities to examine German nationals and it is doubtful whether it would be advisable for them to do so." He was careful to add that "it is not beyond the bounds of possibility that there are some exceptions that will have to be made." Among the exceptions were German scientists and technicians. The Americans and the Soviets were at this time scooping up as many of Hitler's scientists as they could, especially those with special knowledge of rocketry and other important military technology (with little if any regard for possible criminal acts in their Nazi pasts). Canada's own program, called Operation Matchbox, was described to the Cabinet as "very slow…apparently because of delays in the security investigation by the RCMP." Cabinet ordered a speed-up.

(Another reason for the slowness may have been that Canada had very little to offer in the way of scientific and technological research facilities and rewards, compared with her southerly and northerly neighbours.) In 1987 the Deschênes commission recommended further investigation of the wartime activities of fifty-five of the seventy-one German scientists and technicians who had been admitted under the "Matchbox" program.[4]

In general, Immigration continued to state its lack of interest in providing facilities for German nationals through 1949. The so-called *Volksdeutsch* (those of German ethnicity from countries other than Germany, such as Poland and Czechoslovakia) were in a different category and were admissible. These were, after all, mainly displaced persons who either had returned with the retreating German army or had been expelled westward by the Eastern European regimes following the war. Something in the order of 12 million persons took part in this exodus—one of the most gigantic and most harrowing forcible transfers of population in history, with perhaps 2 million (mainly the elderly, children, and women) perishing in the process. Most survivors eventually settled in the two Germanys, the bulk of them in what was to become the Federal Republic. But the capacity of the shattered economy of the Western zones of occupation to absorb these refugees was limited in the late 1940s, and Canada was prepared to offer facilities for processing those who found Canadian sponsors and wished to come to this country. Of course they were subject to normal screening and any in the prohibited categories would, in theory, have been barred.[5]

From the fall of 1949 through the following year, a series of orders-in-council progressively liberalized the treatment of German nationals. By September 1950 all German nationals were in effect removed from the blanket category of "enemy aliens" and brought within the generally admissible classes used to categorize other European nationals. From this point on, Nazis and war criminals would be refused admission on security grounds only on a case-by-case basis—or not refused, if the security net broke down.[6]

The Waffen-SS presented particularly difficult questions. As the military arm of the dreaded Nazi storm-troopers, the Waffen-SS might not have seemed likely to provide promising material for immigrants to Canada. Waffen-SS units in action against

Canadian troops in Western Europe had been particularly ruthless. The sole German charged with war crimes by Canadian authorities had been Waffen-SS officer Kurt Meyer, charged and convicted after the war for having shot Canadian prisoners. Yet the matter was not so simple. Not all Waffen-SS units were in fact made up of enthusiastic Nazi volunteers. After a point conscripts were assigned to Waffen-SS units as well as regular Wehrmacht units. Moreover, apparently for administrative reasons, troops raised among both ethnic Germans (*Volksdeutsch*) and non-Germans in the occupied countries were often organized into Waffen-SS divisions. This fact later became the focal point for what was to become the most contentious issue of postwar immigration security, the decision to allow in former members of the so-called Galicia Waffen-SS division raised in Nazi-occupied Ukraine; this will be discussed in detail in the next chapter.

In the fall of 1950 an unusually large meeting of the Security Panel thrashed out at length the problem of what to do about politically undesirable immigrants who had eluded the security net at entry and were now seeking naturalization. As usual the discussion focused mainly on Communists or those judged by the RCMP to be left-wing sympathizers. There were, however, a handful of applicants of German nationality alleged to be strongly pro-Nazi. Colonel Fortier, citing the recent placement of German nationals on a footing similar to that of other European nationals, indicated that this had "created a special problem for Citizenship and Immigration in that it was necessary to differentiate between German nationals of a desirable type who might apply for Canadian citizenship, and those who might have been actively identified with the Nazi party." An RCMP inspector sitting as an observer on the panel made it known that "Germans who had at any time been members of the SS and the Waffen-SS, the Abwehr [military intelligence], the Sicherheitsdienst [SD, or the SS's own security service], or the Gestapo should be regarded as poor security risks." In the ensuing discussion it was agreed in general that the inspector's listing of dubious organizations was correct, but that "this general ban should not extend to persons in countries occupied by the Nazis during the war who might have become identified with such organizations under pressure from the occupying power." The panel also requested External Affairs to investigate the methods used by the US government in dealing with ex-Nazis and ex-Fascists who applied for American citizenship, presumably as guidance to Canada.[7]

Although former membership in the Communist party, however far in the past, was sufficient grounds for exclusion, the security officers abroad were cabled by the RCMP in the fall of 1950 that membership in the Nazi party "will not in itself be cause for exclusion". Indeed, the immigration department by the 1950s considered that "with very few exceptions", former Nazi party members were admissible. Whatever may be said in support of this approach insofar as it recognizes the ambiguities inherent in membership in the party in a one-party state, the double standard with regard to Communist affiliation is undeniable. In fact, the only ground admitted by the government at this time for changing a rejection for Communism was that of mistaken identity. Moreover, by the early 1950s there were neo-Fascist parties operating in both Germany and Italy. The RCMP apparently used discretion in applying screening to immigrants with these ongoing Fascist associations; the Security Panel decided in 1953 that Fascist party connections should constitute grounds for rejection, but this was considered "more a policy than a security consideration". As the RCMP put it, going easy on Fascists "might present a useful subject for communist propaganda."[8]

Early in 1951 the Canadian Christian Council for Resettlement of Refugees, a major public support group working to bring in European refugees, wrote to the minister of citizenship and immigration to suggest that the government was being unduly harsh on former Waffen-SS; the council's own research indicated that by 1942 enlistment in the military arm of the SS had become less and less voluntary and more a matter of conscription. The minister replied that the government was already treating Waffen-SS enlisted after the beginning of 1943 with some considerable flexibility. In fact a policy decision had already been made that service in the Waffen-SS "in itself should no longer be a blanket cause for security rejection—rejection for such service to be based on the individual case."[9]

Of course the decision to deal with these applicants on an individual-case basis assumed that a certain quality of information would be available to the security officers. Yet this was precisely what appeared to be in question, even in the minds of government officials at the time. External Affairs was asked by the Security Panel to ascertain the value of information available in Germany to Canadian security officers. External's Bonn mission responded with an unusually candid examination of the progress of denazification in the former homeland of Nazism. An Allied Control Directive in the occupied former Reich in January 1946 had decreed the "removal from office and from positions of responsibility of Nazis and all persons hostile to Allied purposes", and to this purpose a universal registration of all adults, with information concerning their past activities, had been carried out. This might have been the basis for a considerable volume of material to be consulted in immigration cases. However, in 1950 the Bundestag had severely modified the original scope of this directive and it had become difficult to obtain reliable information on Nazi party membership or on former membership in the SS.[10]

In any event, the decision to rearm Germany as an integral member of NATO, and the Cold War obsession with the Soviet and Communist threats, had quite turned around the immediate postwar absorption in denazification. As the Canadian mission reported, "For obvious reasons, the Occupying Powers are not interested in maintaining too close an interest in denazification and the main interest of the German authorities is in softening the lot of existing classified Nazis." What was more, the Canadian government could not expect to receive co-operation from Bonn in "such a delicate matter" as passing on information on former Nazi activities. For all except the most flagrant cases of "major offenders", German officials "might even condone an individual's concealment of the fact." Allied sources would have to be relied on; these included the Berlin Documentation Center and information from the American Counter-Intelligence Corps, an organization that was itself deeply compromised by rather intimate dealings with former Nazis and war criminals such as the infamous Klaus Barbie. The Canadian mission confined itself to discreetly suggesting that with regard to Allied intelligence sources, "the benefit of the doubt goes to the persons being investigated." In the light of these limitations, the Canadian response was to take the course of least resistance and gradually widen the screening net so that within a few years all but the more serious Nazi offenders could pass through without impediment.

In the spring of 1952 the Security Panel met to consider a paper refining yet further the criteria to be adopted with regard to former Nazis. Norman Robertson as chairman opened the meeting by suggesting that "an alternative approach to the problem might be an application of, as it were, 'a statute of limitations' to persons who had not in fact been convicted of any war crime." He admitted, subtly enough, that this was "something more than a security problem"—it was a "matter which affected immigration policy as a whole." He may have been alluding to the undoubted fact that public opinion, aroused only a few years earlier to fever pitch over Nazi atrocities, might be less than understanding of an immigration policy that appeared to allow Nazis to obtain Canadian citizenship. (In the late 1940s, former Nazi Otto Strasser—who had broken with Hitler publicly in the mid-1930s and had since been a bitter critic of the Nazi leadership—had been admitted to Canada at British insistence; "strong objections had been raised" from the public, especially in Winnipeg where he had asked to settle.) The time had not yet arrived for a "statute of limitations", at least not one publicly announced.[11]

The RCMP, in the person of security service chief George Mc-Clellan, instantly confirmed Robertson's doubts. "A relaxation of existing regulations", asserted Superintendent McClellan, "might present a useful subject for communist propaganda." The panel went on to agree on specific categories of persons to be excluded. Former members of the SS, SA (Sturm Abteilung, the storm-troopers purged by Hitler in 1934), SD, Abwehr, or Gestapo, and any former Nazi considered by a security officer to have been a "major offender" or an "offender" under the terms of the Allied Control Directive of 1946, would, if detected, continue to be excluded. They also agreed that "particular care should be taken to exclude persons who were responsible for brutalities in concentration or labour camps." Waffen-SS were also to be excluded, subject to an elaborate series of exceptions, mainly on the grounds of age or evidence of coercion or conscription in their enlistment. Former collaborators should continue to be excluded "on grounds of moral turpitude", except "minor collaborators whose actions resulted from coercion."[12]

Later the same year the RCMP raised the question of lifting the exclusion of former members of the Abwehr. The Special Branch, as the RCMP security service was then known, raised the matter with Peter Dwyer as secretary of the Security Panel. The Abwehr, the military intelligence agency, it was pointed out, was not at all like the Gestapo or the SD: "On the contrary it is considered that the Abwehr was fundamentally anti-Nazi and was in conflict with the security and intelligence services of the Nazi party." The RCMP had obviously picked up some signals from its American and British counterparts. Allen Dulles, a leading figure in the OSS (Office of Strategic Services) and subsequently chief of the CIA, later publicly claimed that Admiral Canaris, head of the wartime Abwehr, had been working secretly for the Allies against Hitler; presumably the same story was circulating privately within the Allied security and intelligence networks. The Security Panel considered the matter. George Glazebrook, an External Affairs intelligence expert, intervened to oppose the suggestion: Abwehr officers, "skilled in clandestine operations, might be persuaded to apply these skills to the detriment of Canada." Glazebrook's cautionary note carried the day.[13]

Three years later, in 1955, the government roused itself to clean the slate with regard to all but the most offensive of former Nazis. By this stage all vestiges of the Allied occupation had given way to a Federal Republic of Germany, which now exercised full sovereignty within its territory. The West Germans, moreover, were key military partners in NATO, and the border between West Germany and East Germany was in a real sense the fundamental fault line in the Cold War. Finally, and crucially for immigration policy, the *Wirtschaftswunder*, or "economic miracle" of postwar German prosperity, was well under way: the West Germans were less and less inclined to encourage the outflow of a fully employed and highly skilled labour force. All these factors came together by the mid-1950s to create renewed pressure on the Canadian government to treat German immigrants no differently than other northern Europeans—although the Nazi regime and its genocidal atrocities had come to an end only a scant ten years earlier.

In the course of unofficial negotiations with the West Germans in 1955, it had become apparent to the Canadians that the categories of exclusion they had previously established were something of a nuisance, which they might ease in the interests of good relations with their NATO ally. As Laval Fortier suggested to his minister, Jack Pickersgill, "It is my opinion that now that World War II has been over for ten years and that we are attempting to have better relations with Germany", the time had come to relax restrictions. Consequently, a proposal went before the Security Panel that membership in the SS, Waffen-SS, SA, SD, and Abwehr no longer be considered grounds for automatic rejection, especially for those applicants with sponsoring relatives in Canada or in "meritorious categories"— on the "basis of political and humanitarian considerations". The panel agreed, with the provision that "former members of the Gestapo, concentration camp guards and persons who, in the opinion of an examining officer, would be considered major offenders under Allied Control Directive No. 38 should continue to be automatically rejected as applicants." Ministerial approval was given on November 26, 1955; there was no discussion of this decision at the Cabinet level.[14]

When the idea of relaxing these categories had first been broached by Canadian immigration officials, Canada's ambassador in Bonn, Charles Ritchie, had drawn back in alarm at the mention of former SS or Waffen-SS:

> I am afraid that I cannot agree...that the present ban on the immigration of former members of SS battalions be lifted. I find it hard to believe that we are so short of suitable candidates for immigration that it is necessary to start recruiting in a portion of the German and "Volksdeutsch" population whose war records are of the worst. I think it is doubtful that the Canadian government will be subject to any pressure from the German authorities or the German public to accept former SS members as immigrants, nor do I think that there will be any general criticism of our action in continuing to exclude these individuals. The reaction in Canada to such a change in our immigration policy would also, I think, be of an adverse nature.[15]

Whatever Ambassador Ritchie's moral and political instincts, his detailed knowledge of Canadian immigration practice was somewhat insufficient. Indeed, five years earlier, almost all the surviving members of a Ukrainian Waffen-SS division had been allowed to immigrate to Canada. The head of the Canadian immigration mission in West Germany, J. R. Robillard, felt it necessary to offer the ambassador some enlightenment:

Strange as it may seem, not all former members of SS battalions are inadmissible to Canada. Hundreds of them have migrated to our country since the end of the war. Former members who joined voluntarily are ipso facto inadmissible. Former members who were conscripted before December 31, 1942, are also inadmissible but those who were conscripted after that date and who can otherwise comply with our requirements are eligible. Those, whether conscripts or volunteers, who held a rank above that of sergeant are ipso facto inadmissible. The number of persons who have been refused visas on SS grounds since we started our operations in Germany runs into the thousands; they were mostly Volksdeutsch.

Robillard also noted that the West Germans were by no means as indifferent as Ambassador Ritchie maintained: "Time and time again the German authorities dealing with migration matters...have raised the question of our arbitrary rejection of former members of SS units." Robillard gave Ritchie an example of what he saw as "arbitrary" rejection that would be better reversed. The example is rather revealing of the Cold War political bias so characteristic of immigration officials. It concerned a young man of German ethnicity born in Estonia who had voluntarily joined the Waffen-SS in 1944 as a teenager. After serving on the eastern front he fell into American hands as a prisoner of war. Released by the Americans to work for their armed forces in Germany, he held "several exceptional commendations from the US authorities". In 1949 he joined the French Foreign Legion and for two years "fought against Communist Forces in Indo-China" where he was wounded in action and returned to Germany. "In my opinion", concluded Robillard at the end of this list of credentials, "he would be an excellent type for Canada." Unfortunately, under the old rules he was inadmissible. Under the new, relaxed rules, he and others like him could now pass the security screen.[16] Canadian officials remained uneasy about the potentially embarrassing effect on public opinion of admitting former SS men to Canada. When some publicity was apparently given in West Germany to the new relaxation, and an opposition member of the Bundestag made an enquiry at the Canadian embassy, External Affairs acted very carefully to minimize public notice. An official in the office of the under-secretary of state for external affairs, in a lengthy communication on the subject to the deputy minister of citizenship and immigration, referred to "our mutual understanding that this relaxation of the regulations cannot possibly result in a large influx of ex-members of objectionable Nazi organizations with inevitable undesirable political consequences." The official made it clear that he did "not propose to refer this matter to my Minister for decision." Rather the entire question should be kept under close administrative wraps—in the best tradition of immigration security policy.[17]

In the event, some modifications were made in the new regulations. Those who had enlisted voluntarily in the SS before 1943 would continue to be barred. And even the formerly prohibited categories, it was made clear, would be relaxed only for those applicants who were sponsored by close relatives in Canada or who were especially "meritorious". This change may have assuaged the doubts of those like Ambassador Ritchie who had reacted with revulsion to the idea of former SS storm-troopers being welcomed to Canada. For the Ottawa security establishment, the relaxation presented no problem, because during the course of this minor bureaucratic controversy, a convenient new formula had made its appearance in internal correspondence. The RCMP advised Immigration, which heartily concurred, that decisions about former members of the various Nazi organizations could be handled better by the civilian visa officers than by the RCMP security officers, since "automatic rejection has been largely for political reasons rather than security reasons". This formula, which makes an applicant's Nazi record a "political" rather than a "security" question, is a distillation of the core ideological bias of the entire immigration security process in the Cold War era. The main concern of officials was not to bar former storm-troopers or other minions in the Nazi machinery of oppression, but to avoid any unpleasant "political" backlash from public opinion in Canada. "Security" was a category reserved almost entirely for Communists and left-wingers, not for Nazis or right-wingers.[18]

Nor could it be said that immigration officials were lacking in enthusiasm for receiving some of the applicants newly eligible under the revised regulations. In fact, the department initiated a review through the RCMP of all those cases rejected on the old grounds for the years 1953 through 1955 so that the initial rejections might now be overturned and the applications reopened, at the department's initiative. Thus it would be in no sense unfair to suggest that Canadian immigration officials were actually going out of their way to facilitate the entry to Canada of former Nazi police and military personnel. Such solicitude was rarely shown to those coming from less-favoured national groups, including those who had been allies of Canada during the war rather than her mortal enemies.[19]

In the late 1950s, however, the number of West German nationals immigrating to Canada fell steadily, reflecting booming economic prospects at home. German authorities were particularly reluctant to allow highly skilled workers to emigrate, and Canadian immigration officials in West Germany found them less and less co-operative in processing German applications. There was one exception to this attitude. West Berlin—anomalously a part of the Federal Republic, although geographically an island within the Communist German Democratic Republic—was an arrival point for large numbers of East Germans and, to a lesser extent, other Eastern Europeans seeking refuge in the West. Indeed, West Berlin was a kind of hemorrhage point for East German population until the Berlin Wall stanched the flow in 1961. West German authorities were less interested in retaining all these refugees than they were in holding on to their own labour force, and they continually pressed Canada, as well as other Western countries, to take up some of this burden. This demand, of course, presented the security-minded Canadians with something of a dilemma. As indicated earlier, the security establishment was at this time deeply suspicious of any east-bloc émigrés: if anything, it was doubly suspicious of persons whom the West Germans seemed unenthusiastic about retaining.

The West Germans, for their part, made it increasingly clear that Canadian acceptance of a certain number of these east-bloc refugees, via West Germany, would be a precondition for West German co-operation in facilitating the kind of West German immigration in which Canada was mainly interested, that is, skilled workers. Eventually, by the early 1960s, Canadian officials were congratulating themselves on having achieved a degree of co-operation that they believed to be preferential to that accorded other receiving countries. "It is the consensus", claimed an internal Immigration report in 1964, "that to a great extent this attitude stems from Canada's demonstrated willingness to do what is possible for refugees from Iron Curtain countries, especially those temporarily in Germany." Part of this *modus vivendi* was achieved by the acceptance by Canadian security personnel of West German screening of refugees, as well as much closer liaison with the West German police in processing applications from West Germans from a security standpoint. In short, the criteria for excluding Germans who had been involved in criminal and objectionable activities for the Nazi state were increasingly falling under the control of the Germans themselves.[20]

In theory, at least the "major offenders" or genuine war criminals were still barred from Canada, however. The case of former SD M/Sgt. Albert Helmut Rauca, mass murderer of more than 10,500 Jewish men, women, and children in Lithuania in 1941, extradited from Canada to West Germany as a war criminal in 1983, serves to illustrate the problematic nature of immigration screening. Rauca arrived in Canada in 1950, having passed through the regular screening process; in due course he achieved naturalization as a Canadian citizen. At no point did he appear to have been impeded by the security net. Was this simply inattention, or could it have been something worse? In Rauca's case we will probably never know.[21] There is, however, disturbing evidence that there may indeed have been suspicious elements at play in the postwar immigration process in general as it operated in regard to "major offenders" and war criminals.

In testimony before the Deschênes Commission of Inquiry on War Criminals in 1985, William Kelly, the former head of the RCMP security service and the man in charge of the immigration security screening operation in Europe in the 1950s, raised what appeared to be an incriminating suggestion that indeed, something more than mere inattention or inadvertence was involved in the admission of dubious persons of Nazi background. During questioning, the following exchange took place:

> Q. And now, Mr. Kelly, to your knowledge, based on your years in Western Europe...was there ever in place a program to assist former Nazi officials or military men or women, to immigrate to Canada as a result of

that individual having done something in the interest of Canada?

A. None whatever to my knowledge.

Q. Did it ever come to your attention, sir, while you were in Western Europe, more specifically in 1953, that a country friendly to Canada had introduced into Canada immigrants of European origin through false documents,...individuals who would not otherwise have been approved for immigration into Canada.

A. Yes, but I must say it is quite possible that had they been presented the right way, they might have been cleared for security, might well have been.

Q. And when this knowledge was brought to your attention what did you do?

A. Because the country concerned refused to give us the background of the individuals we refused to handle them.

* * *

Q. And was it brought to your knowledge that nevertheless some individuals fitting the description which I gave of them did actually immigrate to Canada?

A. Yes, I think that before we caught on to what was happening, some of them did pass through the screening based on false information and information which had been established so that when we checked our sources, it would not reveal anything adverse against such people.

Q. To your knowledge, was action taken by the Government of Canada *vis-à-vis* that friendly country in order to deal with that situation?

A. Yes it was.

At this point the commission's counsel broke off this highly intriguing line of questioning by abruptly announcing that commission counsel were of the opinion that any further questions "should be asked in camera because they affect the national security of Canada." Mr. Justice Deschênes agreed to hold such questioning in camera at a later date. David Matas, representing the Canadian Jewish organizations at the hearings, was unhappy with this decision. Names of individuals, he agreed, should not be submitted in open questioning;

> but I think that beyond that restriction, anything else could be addressed in public hearing. I do not believe the security of Canada as it exists today would be affected by answering these questions. It may be that at the time these events occurred, if they were matters of public record, it might have touched on Canadian security at that time, but I assume these are not recent entries, but entries decades ago. I cannot see how this would reflect upon Canada's current security.

The commission counsel responded, "I am privy to information which makes it incumbent on me to say that dwelling on this particular matter, though it may not be of recent vintage, would be harmful to the security interest of this country." Commissioner Deschênes then told Matas, "I have no alternative at this moment but to accept the statement of Commission Counsel at its face value. I think that it would be, therefore, highly imprudent on my part to run foul of his statement and take the risk that obviously would be involved." Despite some further skirmishing, nothing further was allowed on this subject in open session. Not a hint of any of this appeared in the public report of the commission. Some of its findings still remain classified.[22]

What lay behind these cryptic remarks? We know as a matter of public record that certain "countries friendly to Canada", particularly the United States, had been deeply involved in dealings with ex-Nazis, some of them definitely war criminals, as part of the emerging anti-Communist security and intelligence networks set in place in the immediate postwar years. It is known that these dealings involved assistance in smuggling out some persons wanted for war crimes in countries allied to the United States and ensuring their safe passage to refuge in Latin America (the Klaus Barbie model); or, in the case of war criminals from countries that fell within the Soviet bloc after the war, there was complicity in allowing them to enter the United States under false pretences (the Byelorussian, Ukrainian, Romanian, and Yugoslav cases that later ended up in deportation proceedings in the 1970s and 1980s). It is also known that the British had some awareness, at the very least, of these affairs, and that the British advised the Canadian government as early as 1949 not to bother hunting for Nazi war criminals among immigrants.

John Loftus, who wrote a book about war criminals in the United States following a stint in the Office of Special Investigations in Washington, has publicly suggested that Canada was used as a conduit for certain persons to whom the Americans found it inconvenient to offer first refuge. We also know about the highly unequal relationship of reciprocity between the RCMP and the FBI and CIA, in the United States, and M.I.5 and M.I.6, in Britain; might the balance have been redressed by having the RCMP turn a blind eye when someone inadmissible to the latter countries was slipped into Canada? If this traffic was indeed going on, the operation was being kept very secret, so secret that not even the top-level members of the security establishment in Ottawa represented on the Security Panel seemed to be aware of it, judging by their secret discussions of immigration security, which betray not a hint of any clandestine subversion of stated policy.

On the other hand, we have an indication from William Kelly's own truncated testimony that something was going on. Could the operation have been an American and/or British one, with the Canadians as scapegoats? This is possible, but again it seems unlikely that an operation to crack the Canadian security screen could or would have been undertaken without some degree of contact or knowledge at high levels on the Canadian side, especially given the extremely close liaison, almost amounting to integration, between Canadian security and the American and British security and intelligence networks. The truth, for obvious reasons, may remain elusive.

There is, however, evidence—not from documentary sources but from verbal sources—that the truth may lie somewhere between the two extremes of outright Canadian complicity and total Canadian innocence. According to these sources, a high-level, super-secret triumvirate of senior security establishment people in Ottawa acted as liaison with American and/or British intelligence to prepare documentation that would allow certain undesirable or unacceptable persons to slip through the screening process. This triumvirate was reportedly composed of a senior RCMP security service officer, a civilian Security Panel functionary, and Peter Dwyer (who died in 1972), the key civilian in the security establishment at Ottawa after 1952, a man whose previous service for British intelligence in Washington and elsewhere had given him wide contacts among Canada's allies in security and intelligence. According to this hypothesis, it is entirely possible that rank-and-file RCMP security officers were actually unaware of what was happening under their noses. Perhaps even William Kelly, at his post in London, was initially unaware as well. If this is so, the operation was certainly a "dirty" one. Who came into Canada this way, how many, and what eventually happened to them and to the operation remain a mystery.[23]

CHAPTER SIX

Importing Old World Enmities: Wartime Collaborators

On a Sunday afternoon in Toronto in February 1986, a man set himself on fire in front of the American consulate. Canadians were somewhat startled to see photographs of this attempted self-immolation on the front pages of their Monday-morning papers. They might have been even more startled to read that the unlikely cause for which this man had attempted to kill himself was to protest the United States government's extradition to Yugoslavia of an eighty-six–year–old Croatian-American named Andrija Artukovic to stand trial for his part in the wartime extermination of some half-million persons, mainly Jews, Serbs, and gypsies. The protest had taken place during a demonstration by 2,000 supporters of a group calling itself Croatian Solidarity, which alleged in a statement to the press that the US Office of Special Investigations, which had conducted the investigation that led to Artukovic's deportation to his homeland, was a "frightening reincarnation of the SS." The group specifically targeted the Canadian government as the object of its protest, asserting that it would never allow any Croatian Canadian to be extradited at the request of the "very threatening" Deschênes commission, which was conducting hearings about war criminals in Canada and abroad.[1]

A few months earlier, a coalition of Eastern European groups in Canada had sponsored full-page advertisements that appeared in most leading Canadian newspapers. Under the banner headline "Why Discriminate?", the advertisement featured a drawing of a young girl in Ukrainian national costume, with a garland of flowers in her hair, over the question: "How do we explain to our children?" The text of the advertisement asserted that it was discriminatory for the Deschênes commission to focus on war crimes committed only under Nazi auspices; it should also inquire into war crimes committed "in the Soviet Union, Vietnam, Cambodia, Angola, and the Middle East." "It's a tragedy", the advertisement concluded, "that the memory and the history of our homelands are being defiled by Soviet allegations of war crimes in Eastern Europe more than a generation ago."[2] When the Deschênes commission announced its intention (never actually carried out) to travel to the Soviet-bloc countries to gather testimony and information for the inquiry, the indignation from some Eastern European groups in Canada was very deep, and it was given very public and vehement expression. Often heard was the argument that the alleged war criminals to which Soviet evidence pointed were in fact anti-Communist leaders of the Eastern European expatriate communities whom the Soviets wished to destroy. In early 1987 another advertisement warned that a permanent office of investigation would constitute the base for a witch-hunt against entire ethnic communities. Although it had been rumoured to be recommending a permanent office of investigation in Canada, the Deschênes commission—responding explicitly to the very strong pressures being asserted by Eastern European émigré organizations—ultimately disavowed such a recommendation in its report.[3]

Some spokespersons for Eastern European ethnic organizations thus defined the issue of war criminals in Canada in terms of the Cold War. Moreover, any suggestion that there might be war criminals or criminal collaborators, however few and however anomalous, among persons of Eastern European origin who had resettled in Canada after the war was taken by some as an attack upon the integrity of the entire ethnic community in question. With emotions so high, it is worthwhile to examine dispassionately the history of Canadian treatment of former collaborators from the Nazi-occupied countries. Like so much of the record of immigration security, this history has been largely secret. Yet more than most questions, it has spilled out into the public arena from time to time. In fact, the admission or deportation of former collaborators has been at times a very live political issue within Canada, mobilizing various persons and groups on one side or the other to bring pressure on governments.

Admission to Canada of non-Germans who had collaborated with the Nazi armies of occupation had created difficulties from the beginning. The main problem was that a high proportion of those in the displaced persons category had collaborated, in one degree or another, with the invaders. This is not very surprising: collaboration was obviously a leading motive for fleeing westward in advance of the Red Army and the national liberation forces that had fought the Nazis. There were degrees of collaboration, to be sure, and many who had collaborated scarcely answered to the description of "Nazi" or "war criminal" often thrown at them by the Soviet Union and its satellites. A great many had had no choice at all in the matter, having been conscripted as virtual slave labourers by the Nazis. Many had been forced to make a choice of sorts under conditions of violence and duress, and it is surely unfair to make invidious judgements on this choice from the safety of historical retrospect. Indeed, many had made their choice in the light of a record of Soviet rule whose brutality could hardly be distinguished from that of the Nazis themselves. To the Ukrainians of Eastern Poland, for example, the Red Army had been the original army of occupation in 1939, when the Soviets swept into the region to claim their part of the Nazi-Soviet pact. After the Soviets' mass execution of intellectuals and the heavy hand of Stalinist oppression, the Nazi armies that drove out the Soviets in 1941 may even have seemed to some the lesser of two evils.

Unfortunately, the story does not stop here. The unpleasant truth is that the German armies of occupation, thinly stretched as they were over much of Europe, fighting a vast and terrible campaign on the eastern front, in North Africa, in Italy, and by 1944 in western Europe, as well as against partisan forces from Yugoslavia to Poland, were not capable of providing by themselves the administrative infrastructure and coercive machinery for their systematic campaigns to identify, round up, and exterminate Jews and other groups slated for the Nazi death machine. In all countries that fell under the swastika there were locals who, for a variety of reasons, whether out of ideology or racism or simply bloody-minded opportunism, were ready and willing not merely to offer passive support to the Germans, but to take more leading and activist roles in co-operating with the occupation. Certainly there were many non-Germans who actively participated in the hideous campaigns of genocide against Jews and other civilians. There were some ugly fish to be caught in the screening nets, even if most of the applicants were simply innocent persons seeking a refuge from war and oppression. But the screeners were rather inattentive to these kinds of fish; their interest was usually focused elsewhere.

In 1947 Cabinet began to grapple with the thorny problem of non-German soldiers who had served on the Axis side. A report came before Cabinet recommending that such persons be considered admissible "unless they are recorded on the official lists of war criminals and are known to have violated the international rules of warfare." (The reference to "lists of war criminals" is somewhat puzzling in light of the testimony of former RCMP deputy commissioner William Kelly before the Deschênes commission in 1985 that, as the officer in charge of the entire immigration security screening operation in Western Europe in the early 1950s, he had "never" had such lists available; Kelly thought it unlikely, moreover, that his men in the field had access to such lists if he had never seen them.) Cabinet moved slowly on the question, but by 1948 those non-Germans, including Austrians, who had served in their national armed forces against the Allies were beginning to be admitted. As a general criterion, this may well have been acceptable. But there remains a suspicion that the screening net on the ground was not very finely constructed, so that the orders crafted with such delicacy in the rarefied atmosphere of the Cabinet room may have been executed with somewhat less care by the government's agents.[4]

The RCMP, to be sure, had a very decided attitude with regard to collaborators. Those who had assisted the Nazis in the occupation of their own countries seemed to rouse a visceral and very negative response from the police. This was not necessarily the case among Canadian diplomats. In 1951 External Affairs solicited the views of its diplomatic missions in all the European countries that had been under Nazi occupation during the war as to the political effect of lowering restrictions against the immigration of former collaborators. The consensus was that in effect collaborators should be treated in a similar fashion to Germans; that is, the easing of restrictions against minor offenders then in progress should be applied to collaborators as well. As External's intelligence man, George Glazebrook, reported to Norman Robertson, the clerk of the Privy Council:

> Our representatives add, in effect, that for purposes of immigration, collaboration should now be ignored except where "a clear and present danger to Canada and Canadian institutions" are involved, and that, generally speaking, serving a prison sentence which has been imposed should be regarded as wiping the slate clean, with the proviso that there should be a further lapse of several years after serving such sentences in the case of particularly dangerous collaborators.

Certain kinds of collaborators should, nevertheless, continue to be barred, including those who had been convicted of fighting against and harming the well-being of Allied forces; those implicated in the taking of life and of being connected with forced labour and concentration camps; those who had been employed by German security police and who had acted as informers against loyal citizens and resistance groups; and those convicted of treason.[5]

The police reacted angrily to these suggestions. As George McClellan, head of the security service, told Norman Robertson, "We find it difficult to believe that proposed immigrants who are disloyal to the country of their birth would in fact be any more loyal to the country of their adoption". Among the various categories being considered for relaxation, the RCMP assumed that "the collaborator is the most serious from the viewpoint of security risk and it is considered that caution should be exercised in relaxing the restrictions in this class." In a meeting with Immigration, the RCMP reiterated and deepened its objections. "Any large scale migration of collaborators from former German occupied countries would materially increase their [the RCMP's] difficulties should a state of emergency arise." The RCMP representative "clearly stated that the RCMP would accept with great reluctance any large degree of relaxation in the admittance of collaborators." External's recommendation began to draw fire from some Immigration officials as well: the head of the operations division pointed out that under the Immigration Act, the department in fact had no authority to "wipe the slate clean" in cases where prison sentences had been served. The differences were sharp enough that the matter was referred to the Security Panel.[6]

At the Security Panel, the RCMP restated its opposition: Superintendent McClellan made it clear that "from a security viewpoint he considered former collaborators in particular were a long term risk." Moreover, he was reluctant to hand the Communists such a "useful subject" for propaganda. Colonel Fortier added Immigration's objections, noting that "former collaborators were often denied civil rights in their own country and had difficulty in rehabilitating themselves. A relaxation of present immigration restrictions might therefore enable increased numbers of these undesirables to attempt to find better conditions in Canada." External seems to have dropped its advocacy, and the panel concluded that former collaborators should be excluded "on grounds of moral turpitude, except minor collaborators whose actions resulted from coercion."[7]

Such were the outlines of general policy as generated from within the bureaucracy and the security establishment. Yet even while these decisions were being made, there were already a number of precedents in place that suggested a less severe attitude towards collaborators in practice than in publicly stated policy. These precedents seem to have originated from directly within the political realm, at the behest of politicians rather than bureaucrats or police.

One of the most notorious cases of wartime collaborators immigrating to Canada was that of the so-called Count de Bernonville and a small group of other former officials of the Vichy regime in France. This case became notorious because it stirred considerable passions within Canada; the politics that had divided France after the Nazi invasion in 1940 went on to divide Canadians after the war. A man who was by any objective account at the very least a scoundrel and at the worst a war criminal was sheltered by this controversy and ultimately protected from extradition that would have led him to face charges of treason in his country of origin, which had been an ally of Canada in two world wars.

The story began in 1940 with the fall of France after the lightning Nazi blitzkrieg. A so-called French government was set up in the southern two-fifths of the country with its capital in the provincial town of Vichy under Marshal Pétain and his prime minister, Pierre Laval. Until November 1942, when Nazi troops occupied the whole of France, the Vichy regime maintained a pretext of autonomy, while carrying out reactionary, authoritarian, and anti-Semitic policies under the slogan of "work, family, fatherland". Many of the leading figures in the Vichy government were later to stand trial for treason and collaboration after the Liberation in 1944; many were executed or served life sentences for their activities.

One of the most hated elements of Vichy was the *milice*, or military police, who stood in for and assisted the Gestapo in hunting down, torturing, and murdering Resistance members and patriots. Jacques de Bernonville, military governor of Lyons, was of assistance to Klaus Barbie, the "butcher of Lyons" and torturer and executioner of Resistance hero Jean Moulin. Bernonville had been tried in absentia twice and condemned to death in post-Liberation France for torture and murder. Instead of facing the guillotine, Bernonville turned up in Canada. Instead of being deported as soon as he was detected, he became the centre of a major political controversy in Canada, where he turned out to have powerful friends.

The background to this unedifying Canadian story lies in the political attitudes of French Catholic Quebec in this era. There was considerable sympathy within French Canada for the Vichy regime. "Work, family, fatherland" struck closer to the reigning ideology of Catholic nationalism than did the republican trinity of "liberty, equality, fraternity", the motto of the secular France that had grown out of the Revolution of 1789 and that had gone down to apparent defeat in 1940. Even the Fascist and anti-Semitic overtones of Vichy were not without their local echoes in nationalist circles, and within the Catholic church. When Vichy fell, and the Resistance triumphed, feelings in French Canada were by no means unmixed. And when Vichyites went on trial before the courts of a Fourth Republic which, until 1948, actually included Communists in its government, considerable sympathy was openly expressed on their behalf.

It was in this climate that Bernonville found a warm welcome when he arrived in Quebec in 1946, via the United States, having assumed a false name and disguised himself as a priest. Exactly how he managed to elude the screening net is not clear. That he arrived via the US is itself enough to arouse suspicions, in light of the assistance that the Americans gave his former associate Barbie in his escape to South America. That he arrived with the false identity of a Catholic priest arouses certain other suspicions, given the Vatican's known complicity in sheltering some ex-Nazis and Nazi collaborators, and given the fierce lobby on his behalf later mounted by the Church hierarchy and persons close to the Church in Quebec.[8]

The Canadian phase of the scandal began after Bernonville's arrival. He did not arrive alone; three other Vichyite collaborators also slipped into Canada at the same time. Along with Bernonville, one other had been tried in absentia by French courts and found guilty of treason. All were welcomed into Quebec society and especially to clerical circles. One found a teaching position at Laval University, at that time a religious institution. Bernonville in particular was lionized by certain *bien pensants* of Catholic Quebec. When the cry went up in English Canada for his deportation—after all, he was wanted for capital offences in France and had moreover lied to gain entry— the full barrage was unleashed. Premier Duplessis, the mayor of Montreal (himself interned during the war for opposing the war effort), the Catholic hierarchy, the Société St-Jean-Baptiste, the nationalist and Catholic press, and, most influentially, the huge Quebec caucus of the ruling Liberal party in Ottawa all demanded that Bernonville, along with his fellow Vichyites, be granted immunity from French "persecution" and be allowed to stay in Canada. A Quebec MP who also served as a lawyer for Bernonville told the House of Commons, "If it had been Communist Jews who had come here instead of French Catholics we would not have heard a word about them." And Robert Rumilly, the ultra-nationalist Quebec historian who had once been a member of a violent French Fascist group known as the Camelots du roi, which specialized in physical assaults on opponents, preposterously declared that 80,000 to 100,000 persons had been executed in a postwar French purge that was nothing but a "vast political operation, conducted by the Communist party with at least the tacit complicity of pious French ministers...to liquidate the elements of the Right."[9]

As for the insinuations about "Communist Jews", the truth is far different. While the shattered survivors of the Nazi Holocaust were being systematically barred from Canada, Bernonville and his accomplices were literally getting away with murder. In September 1948, Cabinet, acting on a report from the Department of External Affairs that has since mysteriously disappeared from the government records, decided to quash deportation orders and allow Bernonville's three *confrères* from the *milice*— "unobjectionable residents", as they were termed—to remain in Canada, although they had made false statements to gain entry and despite the French charges against them. At the same time, deportation orders were carried out against seven Jews, desperate survivors of the Holocaust, who had similarly relied on forged documents to enter a Canada that continued to keep out as many Jews as it could. Certainly there was a double standard, but it was not the one alleged by the resonant voices of reaction from Quebec.[10]

Bernonville himself was a more difficult case. He had, after all, been the right-hand man to the "butcher of Lyons", and of all the Vichyite collaborators he was the one the French wanted back the most. Cabinet agreed to go ahead with his deportation, two years after his entry. The case must have seemed very clear. Hugh Keenleyside, the deputy minister responsible for immigration at the time, recalled later, "One of the nastiest and also easiest cases of illegal presence in Canada that came to my desk was that of the odious Count de Bernonville." Keenleyside also recalled the massive campaign on his behalf, but seemed unimpressed by it. Deportation proceedings had been launched in Montreal, and the Count himself had to put in a court appearance. Keenleyside remembered: "The Count made no personal contribution to his defence, seeming to feel that it was a gross insult to be forced to submit himself to any court procedure. His grim, closed face and malevolent expression were not such as to invite sympathy."[11]

Yet, remarkably, sympathy was exactly what this unlovely reminder of an unlovely regime did get. Months, then years, dragged by while the government procrastinated before the chorus from Quebec, worrying about "sentencing" him by returning him to France. By the spring of 1950, two years after Cabinet had agreed to deportation, and four years after he had entered Canada, the squalid drama had almost played itself out. Norman Robertson informed the immigration minister, Walter Harris, that "in view of the evidence, it would probably be difficult to avoid ordering deportation" any longer. However, Robertson ingeniously pointed out, he might not have to be deported directly to France, but rather might be allowed to proceed to some other country that would not allow his extradition. Bernonville was duly informed in advance of his impending deportation and, snarling defiance to the end, managed to depart for that last refuge of Nazi war criminals, South America.[12] The final chapter in this story was recorded in 1972 when Bernonville's body was found strangled in his Rio de Janeiro home, the apparent victim of his maid's son, who claimed to be possessed by the voodoo spirit; it was widely rumoured, however, that he had fallen victim to an internecine quarrel among Brazilian Nazis. Perhaps in the end poetic justice prevailed, if no other.

It is not clear whether Bernonville and his relatively well-publicized friends were the only Vichyite collaborators to escape Canada's screening net. There is a curious reference in the government records, alluded to earlier, suggesting that by 1948 at least two French "refugees" had found haven in Canada through the special program set up to aid prominent "democratic" refugees from Communist take-overs in Eastern Europe. Whether these were any of the men in the Bernonville group, or others, is uncertain, since no names were listed.[13]

The most controversial case of admission of non-Germans who had fought for the Axis was surely that of the Ukrainian division raised to fight alongside the Wehrmacht in the uniform of the Waffen-SS. This case in all its complexity, with many unresolved questions and historical shadows remaining, reflects all the moral and political confusions involved in the transition from world war against Fascism to Cold War against Communism—and the degree to which Canadian immigration and its secret security apparatus was caught up in the ambiguities of this transition. The admission of the Ukrainian SS veterans also had a direct, public impact on Canadian domestic politics, especially the politics of Canada's divided Ukrainian community.

Ukraine remains a classic case of a nation lacking a state. Prior to the Second World War, Ukrainians—those speaking the distinctive Ukrainian language and sharing a distinctive Ukrainian culture—were divided between those under Soviet rule in the Ukrainian Soviet Socialist Republic and those in the western Ukraine who were under Polish rule. The Poles were widely perceived by Ukrainian nationalists as vicious and oppressive rulers, but the story was no better on the Soviet side. Here Stalin's brutality had reached a grisly peak in the early 1930s when the great famine—artificially induced and kept going by deliberate Soviet policy—resulted in the excruciating death by starvation of millions of Ukrainian men, women, and children. It was one of the great atrocities of the twentieth century, and one made worse by a lack of recognition by the outside world. Yet however terrible their past, the coming of war would bring only fresh horrors and sorrows to the Ukrainian people.

In September 1939 the Red Army crossed the Polish frontier from the east and seized the Ukrainian (and Byelorussian) lands, while Hitler's Wehrmacht was subjugating the rest of Poland in the blitzkrieg from the west. These moves were in accordance with the Nazi-Soviet pact signed only a week before the Germans invaded and the Second World War began. The arrival of the Red Army was followed by another, murderous assault, this time upon Ukrainian intellectuals and political leadership. By the time the Soviets retreated eastward after the Nazis turned on them in 1941, thousands had been imprisoned, exiled to Soviet gulags, tortured, or butchered. Worse was to follow, for when the Germans arrived it was as the conquering *Ubermenschen*, prepared to crush ruthlessly and even exterminate the "subhuman" *Untermenschen*, the Slavs they found in their path.[14]

During the winter of 1942–43 the Soviets triumphed in the terrible epic battle of Stalingrad, and during the spring and summer of 1943 the Red Army began the vast counter-attack that was to break the back of the vaunted Nazi war machine. With the victory of the Allies in North Africa in May 1943 and the surrender of over a quarter-million Axis troops, it was clear to most that Germany was in retreat. It was in this context of impending Soviet return that a campaign was launched in Nazi-occupied Ukraine for volunteers to enlist in a Ukrainian military formation under Nazi leadership to engage the Soviets. This became the Waffen-SS "Galicia" Division, named after a district of what had been Polish Ukraine. There is considerable controversy surrounding the motives of those who joined this formation. Ukrainian nationalists stress anti-Soviet motives, citing the Soviets as a worse threat to Ukrainians than the Nazis; some suggest that the ultimate goal was a Ukrainian army that would eventually fight for Ukrainian autonomy against both Russian Communism and German Fascism.

Two facts are, however, clear: first, this was a volunteer force, not a conscripted one; second, the context within which the division was raised was one that fairly clearly indicated the prospect of Soviet advances and German losses, and one in which the Nazi policies of Aryan supremacy and brutality towards racially "inferior" peoples, especially Jews but certainly Slavs as well, had been already made abundantly manifest. By 1942–43, it is clear, the population as a whole had turned against the Germans. As Alexander Dallin states unequivocally in his voluminous study of the German occupation, the unique opportunity that Ukraine had presented to the conquering Germans had been "bungled": "However much they may have feared or hated the Soviet regime, the bulk of the population in the occupied East had come to fear and hate the occupying power more."[15] In short, pro-Fascist ideological motives as well as Ukrainian nationalism must have played some substantial part in the motives of those who volunteered in 1943–44.

Moreover, there was another aspect of the world of 1943 that must cast an inevitably sinister shadow over voluntary recruitment to an SS division. The Nazi extermination campaign against Jews was well under way, and elements of the local population in all the countries of the eastern front were, to some degree or other, co-operating with the monstrous machine of genocide: identifying, rounding up, and herding Jews for transportation to the death camps; assisting in on-the-spot exterminations; occasionally carrying out freelance pogroms without German direction; and simply offering the Germans the kind of ongoing administrative and policing infrastructure upon which they could organize their planned slaughter while their own administrative and coercive machinery was stretched thin across vast war fronts.

There was, moreover, the melancholy fact that relations between Christian Ukrainians and Jews had historically been very poor indeed, with sudden and murderous pogroms a not unknown phenomenon of the very recent past.[16] This is not to argue that the Galicia SS Division was therefore guilty of anti-Jewish campaigns or other odious actions against civilian populations, a charge strenuously denied by its defenders on what appear to be plausible factual grounds. It is, however, to suggest that the background of considerable moral ambiguity about an SS division was bound to raise doubts in the minds of many, and especially among Jews who had themselves survived the Holocaust or had relatives who perished. And it helps to explain the inevitability of hot political conflict over the admission to Canada of persons with this kind of background.[17]

In its first action, in 1944, the Galicia Division was severely mauled—in fact, cut to ribbons by the Red Army. Remnants who survived this massacre were then integrated with new recruits and sent to Slovakia, where they took part in the suppression of the Slovakian national uprising and in further actions against partisans. Similar activity followed in western Yugoslavia and against the Soviets in Austria. It seems the Galicia Division was not much of a fighting force, nor did it contribute anything to the Axis war effort. In March 1945, with the Red Army just a hundred miles away, Hitler in his Berlin bunker was startled to learn of this exotic *Untermensch* version of his élite Nazi fighting force. "One never knows what's floating around", he exclaimed. "I've just heard, to my surprise, that a Ukrainian SS Division has suddenly turned up. I know absolutely nothing about this Ukrainian SS Division.... It is idiocy to give weapons to a Ukrainian division which is not completely reliable."[18]

With the German collapse in May 1945 the division, by now numbering some 10,000 men, retreated over the Alps and came to an end in British prisoner-of-war camps in Rimini in Italy. Most insisted they were of Polish rather than Soviet citizenship, thus avoiding falling into the forced repatriation that many displaced Soviets faced in the immediate aftermath of the war while the British and the Americans were still co-operating with the USSR. By the time the Galicians' fate was to be decided, the British were already growing suspicious of the treatment of forced returnees. A few voluntarily returned to the USSR, but the vast majority opted to stay in the West; most were transferred to Britain, where they sought to immigrate to the US, Australia, and Canada.[19]

The Canadian government had its own reasons for maintaining its distance from Ukrainian nationalist groups during the war— some European-based Ukrainian groups had flirted openly with Hitler, and there were suspicions that their Canadian counterparts might harbour such tendencies as well. By the latter stages of the war another concern was felt by policymakers in Ottawa: the demand by Ukrainian nationalist spokesmen in Canada for support for an independent Ukraine was not only hopelessly utopian, but scarcely calculated to endear Canada to its Soviet ally. This hesitancy towards open backing of anti-Soviet nationalist demands continued for a time into the postwar period but began to change with the onset of the Cold War.

In any event, the Canadian government had never been pro-Soviet, even during the wartime alliance; within Canada the full weight of state repression had been brought down upon left-wing pro-Soviet Ukrainian-Canadian organizations, which were declared illegal associations and had their property confiscated, their publications banned, and many of their members interned. After 1945 the domestic Cold War demanded that anti-Soviet Ukrainian organizations be given full legitimation as against their "subversive" pro-Soviet antagonists. This included a relatively friendly attitude towards nationalist demands for the immigration of Ukrainian displaced persons in the camps in Europe. Between 1947 and 1952 more than 27,000 displaced persons of Ukrainian origin immigrated to Canada. Most of this immigration was lacking in controversy. The same could not be said for the Galicia Division members.[20]

Some prominent Ukrainian-Canadian nationalists arrived in Europe in 1946 as a private relief mission to aid Ukrainian refugees, with tacit government support. Soon they were voicing demands for official recognition to work with the immigration teams touring the camps, pointing out that they represented only anti-Communist Ukrainians and would have nothing to do with Communist sympathizers. The Ukrainian Canadian Committee—the umbrella group representing non-Communist Ukrainians that had been set up under direct government auspices during the war—passed along anti-Semitic letters to immigration officials charging that "Jews" were keeping Ukrainians out of Canada, and even that the Immigration Branch was pro-Jewish or in Jewish hands. Constant complaints against the Immigration Branch began to raise the hackles of Director A. L. Jolliffe. (The charge of being pro-Jewish must have especially rankled, given the branch's long record of intransigent anti-Semitism.) The Ukrainian nationalists were not endearing themselves to immigration officials, but by the late 1940s they did play the increasingly powerful Cold War card. [21]

G. R. B. Panchuk, representing the Ukrainian-Canadian mission in Europe, began pressuring the government about the members of the Galicia Waffen-SS division in the summer of 1947. Earlier in the year a Foreign Office spokesman in the British House of Commons had indicated that there were 8,000 such persons in Britain, that they had been screened by a refugee screening committee and earlier in 1945 by the Soviets while they were still in prisoner-of-war camps in Italy, that no war criminals had been discovered among their number, and that His Majesty's Government had no intention of complying with Soviet demands for their forcible repatriation to the East. Panchuk suggested that they should be brought to Canada "in bulk"; after retailing a rather sanitized history of the division's activities during the war, he stressed their strong anti-Communism: "They are now and always have been", he avowed, "FANATICALLY ALMOST, ANTI-COMMUNIST, and would now and always be just as prepared and willing to fight communism, as they were in 1944–45."[22]

The apparent offer of a freelance anti-Soviet commando force did not meet with much approval on the part of the Department of External Affairs, whose diplomatic style was rather more restrained than that of the US Cold Warriors in the CIA and the state department; these Americans were then encouraging Soviet émigrés to form groups to carry on armed sabotage behind the Iron Curtain. Panchuk, who had first tried to conceal the fact that Galicia had been an SS formation, gradually admitted more about its affiliations. Although one government official sympathetically noted that "they were persons under Russian domination, and their struggle against Russia during the war becomes more understandable as time goes on", the general response was highly negative. There was a rule that only those non-Germans who had served on the enemy side by compulsion were admissible; nobody claimed that the Galicia veterans had been anything but volunteers. The Cabinet Committee on Immigration Policy gave a flat no to the proposal. The acting director of immigration made the classic bureaucratic response in the fall of 1948: "The line must be drawn somewhere." To his mind it should be drawn between those who had suffered from the enemy and those who had, "wholeheartedly or not, collaborated". The deputy minister agreed, and so did the full Cabinet, which in 1949 endorsed the decision not to allow the division members into Canada.[23]

Despite this official negative stance, the persistent lobbying on behalf of the division members was already laying the groundwork for a reversal. The indefatigable Panchuk continued to bombard the government with demands that struck an increasingly strident anti-Communist note, at one point even suggesting that the creation of the division under the Russian threat was exactly like the creation of NATO. One card the Ukrainians played with some skill was a Ukrainian-Catholic priest who happened to be a francophone. He was deployed to gather the sympathy of the francophone, Catholic, and very anti-Communist prime minister, Louis St. Laurent. Impressed by these associations, and perhaps impressed as well by a new tack on the part of the Ukrainian lobbyists that emphasized the veterans' qualities as intellectuals and "cultural workers", St. Laurent promised "sympathetic consideration". The negative Cabinet decision that followed this polite promise did not discourage the lobbyists, who merely redoubled their efforts in 1950.[24]

Cold War or no Cold War, immigration officials had their own enduring attitudes to consider. Prominent among these was the long-held belief that Slavs were not the more desirable type of immigrant to encourage. This was the major objection that Laval Fortier as deputy minister raised when the negative 1949 Cabinet decision was put up for review. As he told his minister, Ukrainians constituted the fourth-largest "alien racial group" in Canada (presumably "alien" meant those not of British or French origin). Bringing in a large number more at one time might be a worrisome "precedent." At the same time, Fortier, also a good anti-Communist, could not refrain from noting that the Association of United Ukrainians in Canada, which opposed the entry of the veterans, was a "Communist organization". This certainly put the cards on the table.[25]

Finally it was the Cold War argument that carried the day. In April 1950 Cabinet agreed in principle to making the members of the division admissible, subject to a delay requested by External Affairs to bring forward additional information that might have a bearing on the question. Actually, External was buying time to get intelligence reports from the RCMP and the Joint Intelligence Board of the military. The intelligence reports were confused and confusing, sometimes even contradictory: it was evident that the officers assigned to the task were simply not well enough versed in the intricacies and labyrinths of Ukrainian nationalist politics to make a great deal of sense of what they encountered among the division veterans. Finally Arnold Heeney concluded from the reports that if they were admitted, "it is likely that they would be absorbed into the various politically passive Ukrainian nationalist organizations here who are regarded as loyal to Canada and opposed to Communism." On May 31, Cabinet gave the go-ahead. Each member of the division would have to pass a full security screening individually, but as a group the SS veterans were indeed admissible, by special Cabinet order.[26]

At this point the issue spilled out past the group of Ukrainian-Canadian lobbyists and government officials who had previously been contesting it. Sam Bronfman, national president of the Canadian Jewish Congress, wrote an angry letter in July 1950 to Walter Harris, the minister responsible; he protested the SS connection, citing the revelations of the Nuremberg war crimes tribunal on the activities of Nazi collaborationist groups, and asked that the implementation of the decision be delayed until the CJC could itself carry out a "full and complete investigation". Harris agreeably cabled London to delay processing any of the veterans "for a reasonable time" while the CJC was gathering information. Even A. L. Jolliffe got into the act, surprisingly citing an article from a left-wing Jewish newspaper that claimed that the Galicia Division had taken part in the extermination of Jews. Unfortunately for Bronfman, specific information was very hard to come by, and the one account of an incident that he did cite turned out to be factually incorrect.[27]

By November the CJC had prepared a list of names of ninety-four Ukrainians believed to have been involved in extermination campaigns against Jews. These lists were distributed to the RCMP, which showed interest in a very small number, and to the security screening officers in visa posts. The problem with the list was that it was too vague to establish identities, being not much more than names (transliterated from the Cyrillic) and districts, sometimes only family names alone. The government went ahead with the screening, and the division members began arriving in Canada by the end of 1950.[28]

They arrived to controversy. Jews were bitter, and left-wing Ukrainians carried on hostile propaganda. A left-wing Ukrainian rally at a hall in Toronto was bombed during a children's concert in late 1950. Organizers immediately blamed the "Fascist SS" veterans for the attack, in which a number of injuries were sustained. The nationalists said that the leftists had bombed themselves to create sympathy. The RCMP advised the government that it had arrived at the same conclusion, although publicly the crime remained unsolved.[29]

Gradually the question of the Ukrainian SS division faded from public consciousness, until it was revived in the 1980s with the re-emergence of the war crimes issue and the creation of the Deschênes commission to investigate whether any war criminals had slipped into Canada. The veterans of the division have maintained ties with one another and have on occasion threatened legal action against those who link them with war crimes. The case against the division, as such, does not seem to be supported by any extensive evidence. As Dana Wilgress, who had been Canadian ambassador to the USSR during the war, reported to External Affairs during the delay occasioned by the Canadian Jewish Congress protests: "Although Communist propaganda has constantly attempted to depict these, like so many refugees, as 'quislings' and 'war criminals' it is interesting to note that no specific charges of war crimes have been made by the Soviets or any other Government against any member of this group." Nothing substantive has been made public in the years since to change that judgement. In 1987 the report of the Deschênes commission concluded that charges of war crimes against members of the division "have never been substantiated", either at the time of entry or in testimony or documentation presented to the commission in the 1980s.[30]

Certainly it would have been criminal to have forcibly repatriated these men to what was certain to be a dismal fate in the USSR. Once that was agreed, there was no way that Canada could refuse to take those who qualified otherwise as immigrants. In this sense the outcome of the issue was already determined. Yet the humanitarian considerations were clearly not decisive in themselves; if they had been, they should also have applied equally to all those over the years who have sought refuge in Canada from *right-wing* oppression, but this has certainly not been the case. In the end, it is difficult to escape the conclusion that it was the hard and brittle logic of the Cold War that was decisive: almost anything, even service in the SS, could be sanitized in the name of anti-Communism.

Perhaps the story of the Galicia SS veterans would not carry the same aura of unpleasantness were it not for the notorious fact that the Canadian government acted with flagrant bias and cruelty towards the major victims of Nazi genocide: the Jewish survivors seeking refuge from the unspeakable horrors of the Holocaust. As described earlier, the security screening apparatus itself was used as a cloak for the persistence of anti-Semitic bias in immigration selection. In the name of the same set of Cold War values that permitted this bias to continue, an entire military formation under the sign of the SS was allowed to enter Canada. If Canada had acted with generosity and liberality towards the victims of Fascism, there might have been no need to make invidious comparisons with the treatment of those who had fought alongside Hitler's murderous legions. But in the real world of Canadian immigration practice, such comparisons, however unfair and odious they may be in individual cases, are inevitable.

When the Nazis swept into eastern and south-eastern Europe, they did not always come as military overlords. A series of "alliances" were set up with regimes that were formally autonomous, if hardly so in reality. Some alliances were made with countries such as Hungary, Romania, and Bulgaria; prewar Fascist movements such as the Iron Guards in Romania and the Arrow Cross in Hungary were incorporated into authoritarian and anti-Semitic regimes that did some of the dirty work on behalf of the Nazis and provided armies to fight alongside the Wehrmacht against the "Bolsheviks". In other countries puppet states were set up under German auspices by carving out from pre-existing states sections that contained national minorities: such were the states of Croatia, carved out of Yugoslavia, and the "Republic of Slovakia", carved out of prewar Czechoslovakia, already a dismembered corpse in the wake of the Munich sell-out to Hitler in 1938. As the German defeat drew near, these collaborationist regimes collapsed, all of them ultimately replaced by "people's democracies" backed by Soviet armies (with the exception of Croatia, which became part of independent Communist Yugoslavia). Some of the participants in the odious activities of these states perished in the aftermath, but many fled westward to find refuge eventually in a West that quickly turned hostile to the new Communist states of the east bloc, but friendly to some who just a few years earlier had been seen as collaborators and even war criminals.

Some Iron Guardists and former Arrow Cross members found a haven in the West. These groups had themselves organized exterminations among their local Jewish populations. Some who had participated in these activities may well have come to Canada. For example, recent news reports suggest that a Romanian priest in Toronto, now deceased, may have been a notorious Iron Guard scourge of Jews during the war. Rumours of the involvement of Iron Guard elements surround the assassination of a Romanian-Canadian editor of a pro-Communist Romanian-language magazine in his Toronto apartment in 1986, as well as the earlier shooting of a Romanian diplomat in the Montreal consulate, suggesting that the Cold War continues among old antagonists in the new land.[31]

One particularly interesting case of Canadian complicity in the admission of former collaborators is that of politicians prominent in the Republic of Slovakia. This special interest arises from a number of circumstances. Some very prominent figures came to Canada, despite the official hostility of the Canadian government towards the representatives of the Slovak regime. Some of these persons had been tried and condemned by a postwar Czechoslovak government that was democratic and not yet under Communist domination. And the present-day representatives of Slovakian nationalists in Canada have taken a very prominent role in justifying the wartime regime and its actions.

The Nazi-sponsored Slovakia was not merely a tool of German policy; it represented certain distinctive local roots as well. One of these was Slovak separatism. "Czecho-Slovakia" was an amalgam of two major groups, the Czechs and the Slovaks, who had cohabited, sometimes uneasily, in the same prewar state. The Nazis capitalized on the anti-Czech sentiments of some Slovak nationalists as the prewar state was carved up into the Sudetenland, where Germans predominated; the "Protectorate" of Bohemia-Moravia, predominantly Czech; and the Republic of Slovakia. The latter was ruled, with some autonomy, by the Hlinka People's Party, a clerico-Fascist movement with prewar roots among Catholic authoritarians and Slovak separatists. The clerical nature of this puppet state and its close ties with the Vatican were most strikingly illustrated by its president, Fr. Joseph Tiso, a Catholic priest. Indeed, so close were the links between church and state that the best scholarly account of the regime is entitled *The Parish Republic*.[32]

Slovakia was an "ally" of Nazi Germany and raised troops to fight with the Axis. During its brief life, it also aped some of the characteristics of its Nazi model. Especially odious was its treatment of the relatively small Jewish population. Although later apologists have attempted to magnify the examples of sporadic Slovak or Vatican assistance to Jews, the following facts are indisputable: a Codex Judaicus was enacted that rivalled the most discriminatory features of Nazi Germany's Nuremberg laws restricting the civil rights of Jews. Jewish property was confiscated and handed over to supporters of the Hlinka party. Finally, the regime collaborated in the deportation of the entire Jewish population westward under the pretext that they were being sent to a special district; in fact they were being shipped to their deaths in the gas chambers of the Third Reich. Only a few thousand of the 89,000 Jews in Slovakia survived the Holocaust, and some of these did so only at the cost of converting to Catholicism, thus gaining the solicitude of a Vatican that otherwise showed a relative indifference to their fate.[33]

Canadian policy towards the Republic of Slovakia during its lifetime, like that of the other Allies, was, not surprisingly, extremely hostile. Moreover, Canadian policy as expressed through the Department of External Affairs immediately after the war was also hostile to those who continued to apologize for the regime and to carry on anti-Czech hostilities against the postwar Republic of Czechoslovakia, into which Slovakia had been incorporated and which, until the Communist coup of 1948, was a democratic republic whose government included representation from many parties and leading non-Communist political figures. As early as the summer of 1945, just after the collapse of the Third Reich, Norman Robertson informed the prime minister, Mackenzie King, of an unpleasant visit he had received from a Father Zeman, spokesman for the Canadian Slovak League, with a document demanding that the Canadian government represent the claims for Slovakian independence against the "unjust and unscrupulous" Czechs in the postwar conferences on peace treaties. Zeman made scurrilous and anti-Semitic remarks about Slovaks who did not agree with this position. Robertson was outraged and made it clear that the Canadian government would "not think of transmitting such a document to any other government":

I said I thought the Slovak nationalist movement had, for better or for worse, been badly compromised by its collaboration with the Nazis in setting up Father Tiso's government in the puppet state of Slovakia. No doubt a number of sincere and simple minded Slovak nationalists had supported this movement in all good faith. They could not expect the Allied Governments to have much sympathy for them in their present predicament.... I suggested to Father Zeman that he would be better employed making good Canadians out of his parishioners instead of keeping alive among them old enmities between peoples who had to live together in Europe and whose children would certainly have to live together in Canada. I am afraid he left impenitent.

Mackenzie King scrawled "Many thanks" on the memo.[34]

Later the same year it came to the attention of the Canadian government through the Czechoslovak mission in Canada that a number of persons involved in the government of the puppet state had escaped through Austria and were travelling on passports issued by "Slovakia". The Czechoslovak mission wanted Canada to deny entry permits to such persons. External Affairs agreeably informed Canadian immigration officials to do exactly this, and bearers of "Slovak" travel documents were put on the "look-out" lists at visa posts and ports of entry. The Czechoslovak government had its reasons for this request. Father Tiso had been arrested and was later to be put on trial and executed in 1947. There were others who had to be tried in absentia since they had eluded the Czech authorities.[35]

In 1946 the Czech minister in Ottawa provided the Canadian government with a list of "politically notorious followers of the pro-Nazi Tiso regime" whom the Czech government wished to have returned as "war criminals" if any had succeeded in entering Canada. This more demanding request led to some soul-searching at External Affairs, in the form of a lengthy meditation on the question of war criminals. War crimes, External Affairs surmised, should be taken to include violations of the Geneva Conventions and, more broadly, "the so-called 'crimes against humanity' ". On the other hand, the term "does not include purely political offences within a state; persons who are merely charged with political offences against the state by the Government of the day in their native heath, whatever else they may be, are not 'war criminals'."[36]

Upon checking the Czech list against the lists prepared by the United Nations War Crimes Commission, External found that only one name appeared on both. The rest would have to be regarded by Ottawa as "suspected political offenders". External was dubious about establishing any precedent whereby "political criminals or fugitives were, as such, denied admission to Canada"; Canada's extradition treaty with Czechoslovakia specifically excluded political refugees, and no specific Canadian legislation existed that allowed the handing over of either war criminals or political criminals. In any event, External concluded, there were no cases of Slovaks wanted by the Czech government actually having shown up in Canada: it was thus inadvisable "to take any steps to alter the status quo in advance of necessity."[37] With that fine piece of Mackenzie King–style political wisdom, the matter rested for a few years. When it was raised again by "necessity", much had changed in the world.

In 1948 the democratic government of Czechoslovakia fell victim to a Communist coup with Soviet support. Soon opposition was liquidated and the familiar apparatus of police-state rule clamped down over Czechoslovakian life. This completed the consolidation of a Soviet-dominated bloc in Eastern Europe. The Czech coup was widely viewed in the West, and certainly by Canadian diplomats, as the final straw that rendered the Cold War break with the USSR irreversible. From this point on, the old liberal "Western" Czechoslovakia of Eduard Beneš and Jan Masaryk (the latter a "suicide" victim of the coup), the Czechoslovakia that had been betrayed to Fascist totalitarianism by Britain and France in the infamous sell-out at Munich in 1938, was no more than a memory. The Czechoslovakian government was henceforth a Soviet puppet, the real Czechoslovakia a "captive nation" imprisoned behind the Iron Curtain.

So it was that in 1950, when some of those persons previously labelled "politically notorious followers" of the Tiso regime and condemned by the Czechoslovak government for their wartime activities began turning up as immigrants to Canada, the attitude of Canadian authorities had moderated. Yet it was a mark of how disreputable the Tiso regime had been that the Canadians, although co-operative, were not entirely enthusiastic about accepting Tiso followers, even if they were now being sought by a Communist government on the other side of the Cold War divide. Not even the Cold War could sanitize such persons' past records; it did, however, help make Canada a refuge for them and for their continuing agitation on behalf of their lost cause.

Karol Sidor, a former deputy prime minister of the puppet regime and the leader of the Hlinka Guards, a kind of storm troop used to quell internal dissent by strong-arm tactics, apparently entered Canada in 1950 without a valid passport—and according to one report, quoting Sidor's son, with the direct assistance of the Canadian ambassador to Italy. Sidor had figured prominently on the 1946 list presented to the Canadian government by the Czechs and had been condemned to prison in absentia in Czechoslovakia. Late in 1950 Canada was warned by the British government that Ferdinand Durcansky, who had been minister of the interior and of foreign affairs, had been granted a British visa in Buenos Aires "as a result of an administrative error". Durcansky, described in an External Affairs memorandum as "a leader of the most radical group of the Hlinka People's Party" and a man condemned to death in absentia for his wartime activities, was decidedly not given the "approval" of His Majesty's Government, despite being allowed into the UK. The British suggested that Canada might make a similar disavowal with regard to Karol Sidor and might wish to bar Durcansky from Canada. In fact Durcansky had already been given a non-immigrant visa to enter Canada for three months by the Canadian embassy in Buenos Aires, and before the RCMP could be informed, he had been admitted at Dorval Airport in Montreal.[38]

British intelligence indicated that Durcansky had been tireless in seeking to rally anti-Czech Slovaks under a "Slovak Liberation Committee" in Argentina. They also indicated that Karol Sidor in Canada was "really the main Slovak leader outside Slovakia." Once in Canada on a visitor's permit, Durcansky never left and was able to carry on his political activities from a Canadian base. This was also the case with another former official of the puppet regime, Joseph Kirschbaum, described as the "high priest of Slovakian authoritarianism", who became a leading propagandist for the Slovak cause when he entered Canada. In his history of Slovaks in Canada, Kirschbaum notes with considerable satisfaction that by 1951 some 1,500 Slovaks had arrived in this country without the Canadian government "taking seriously the denunciations of their political adversaries." In Canada, he writes, Slovaks were "able to organize their political struggles against communism and foreign [i.e., Czech] rule in their country of origin."

By 1953 the Canadian Slovak League was honoured at a banquet by the presence of the prime minister and the minister of immigration; a number of former Tiso followers were at the head table. Although later movements of Slovaks into Canada such as the group that came in the wake of the 1968 crisis were less attuned to the cause of Slovak separatism, the North American Slovak Congress, in which Canadian businessman Stephen Roman has been prominent, continues to sponsor literature defending the puppet Slovak government and dreaming of another independent Slovak state.[39]

Despite their initial distaste for the Tiso regime and what it represented, the Canadian government ended by offering both a refuge and a political base for unrepentant former officials of that regime, including some who had been convicted of serious offences by a government that was not yet Communist-dominated. The Cold War once again made all the difference.

There is one last, and somewhat mysterious, element to this story. As was described earlier, a program had been set in motion in the late 1940s to allow into Canada diplomats, bureaucrats, and politicians from countries that had fallen under Communist domination who might not otherwise qualify for admission because of their non-transferable occupational skills. At first these were simply indicated as "humanitarian" exceptions to normal screening, permitted under ministerial order. The first entrant in this category was a Yugoslav royalist. Then in 1948, in response to the Czech coup, a more systematic process was set up to receive "democratic anti-Communist refugees" under the personal guidance of the deputy minister, with a support committee of prominent businessmen and others to ease their transition to Canadian life. As it turned out, this program appears to have ultimately included some whose "democratic" credentials might be considered dubious—for instance, at least two Vichyites. What remains unclear is whether any of the "Czechs" admitted under this high-level program were in fact Slovaks from the Tiso regime. If any were admitted, it would be a considerable irony, considering that whatever else they were, these persons could scarcely be described as "democrats" (even if their anti-Communism was above reproach); moreover, the program was ostensibly launched to assist Czechoslovaks from the pre-Communist postwar government, a government that had condemned these same Slovaks and demanded their return to Czechoslovakia if apprehended by the Canadian authorities. The documentation is not detailed enough to establish the identities of all the "Czechs" thus admitted; the coincidence that the Slovaks were entering Canada at precisely the time that the program came into effect and that they were probably not admissible by old rules leaves a strong suspicion lingering around the affair.[40]

The matter of admission to Canada of those who collaborated with Nazi occupiers is obviously very complex. Sorting out genuine war criminals from those who were pro-Nazi but not directly linked to murders, torture, and other crimes against humanity and the rules of warfare is a delicate task, with which the Commission of Inquiry on War Criminals was officially charged. In the United States, where investigations began much earlier, a number of war criminals have been detected and deported—one in 1987 to the Soviet Union, another to Yugoslavia, and yet another, a Ukrainian, to Israel. The Deschênes commission has identified twenty Canadian residents to be targeted either for citizenship revocation and deportation or for criminal prosecution. It listed another 107 suspects who either had died in Canada or were no longer in the country. There was also a list of 97 persons about whom the commission would like the government to seek more evidence from foreign governments (including east-bloc states). A substantial number of these cases appear to be drawn from the ranks of criminal collaborators.[41]

The controversy that has raged around the inquiry of the Deschênes commission has a number of complicated roots. Some of the wartime collaboration cannot be disentangled from ancient ethnic, cultural, and linguistic tensions in what are now the Eastern European states (these affected, for example, the Slovaks, the Croatians, and the Ukrainians). There is considerable resentment among Eastern Europeans in Canada that the focus has been on them, rather than on Western European immigrant communities. Unfortunately, the historical record is clear enough in this instance: there was far more open collaboration with Nazism in the east than in the west, and particularly of the kind that involved assistance in the extermination of the Jews.

This in turn raises the painful subject of historic tensions between the Jews of Eastern Europe and their gentile neighbours, a history of pogroms and brutalities that is simply not matched in the countries of the west and south of Europe that also fell under Nazi domination for a time. Some of this history even extended into the postwar period, when, as in Poland, the shattered survivors of the death camps and ghettoes found themselves caught up once again in murderous pogroms in the late 1940s. The tensions that have arisen in Canada in the mid-1980s between Canadians of Jewish origin and those of Eastern European extraction over the war criminal investigations are only a melancholy reflection of more ancient tensions.[42]

There is another dimension to the protests of Eastern European groups to the Deschênes commission, which brings us full circle again from the world war to the Cold War. In an article in the *Globe and Mail* in the spring of 1986, two Canadian academics of Eastern European origin argued that "the Soviet Union is as guilty of genocide as Germany" but that "none of the men responsible for [Soviet] atrocities has ever been brought to justice." The mandate of the commission, in their view, should have been to seek out Soviet as well as Nazi war criminals.[43] Apart from the extreme unlikelihood of anyone answering to the description of Soviet "war criminal" living in Canada, having somehow eluded a screening process designed to bar Communists, it is questionable whether there can be any equation between Nazis and Soviets on the matter of "genocide". The brutalities and mass murders that were carried out by the Soviets under Stalin were very real. It is understandable that among Ukrainian Canadians there should be rage and bitterness over the mass deaths and suffering of the famine of the early 1930s. But there is no evidence that the Soviet Union, even in the darkest days of Stalinism, ever contemplated or attempted to carry out the planned physical destruction of an entire people, as the Nazis did with the European Jews. On both counts the equation of Soviet war criminals with Nazi war criminals seems more a symbolic rather than a substantive issue, especially in this country. But of what is it symbolic?

The authors of the *Globe* article come close to uncovering the real point in dispute when they quote, with apparent approval, an editorial in a Ukrainian-Canadian newspaper replying to Canadian Jews supporting the Deschênes commission: "You know and we know that a number of Jews worked willingly with the Soviets.... When will we see your community admit to this?" This charge is more revealing than the authors may understand. Why should Jews not "admit" to having "worked" with the Soviets, when the Soviets were their liberators from the Nazi extermination machine? If the authors imply that this "work" involved atrocities against Eastern European gentiles, they are uttering a serious but unsupported allegation; if they do not imply this, what is the point of the accusation?

The point can only be to spread some extreme right-wing anti-Communist ideology that proclaims the Soviet Union the root of all evil in the world and downplays the evil that was Fascism. This ideology, now given considerable legitimacy by forty years of anti-Soviet propaganda in the mainstream Canadian media and by successive governments, seeks to control Canadians' understanding of the past through the manipulation of the symbols of Cold War rhetoric and thus to undermine an attempt to rectify some of the mistakes made under the rubric of "national security" and bring to justice those who may have used Canada to escape from the consequences of their wartime crimes. Right-wing journalists, publicists, and politicians have joined in the chorus. In the United States, where the process of bringing war criminals to justice has been proceeding much more quickly, these same ideologists have been proclaiming that the Office of Special Investigations is a tool of Soviet disinformation or even an arm of the KGB.[44] This McCarthyite charge, while superficially in tune with Ronald Reagan's Cold War rhetoric about the "evil empire", has not prevented the wheels of justice from turning; it has not stopped Soviet evidence from being carefully sifted and offenders from being extradited. It is to be hoped that the same will happen in Canada.

It is ironic that an investigation of the immigration security process should be caught up within a resurgence of the same Cold War that gave rise to and deeply shaped the process itself, from its inception almost forty years ago. It would be a darker irony yet were this investigation itself to fall victim to the Cold War.

CHAPTER SEVEN

American Controls, Canadian Echoes: The Politics of Travel

In the anxious atmosphere of the early Cold War, there were plausible arguments to be made for controlling the entry into Canada of Communists as immigrants. There were not even plausible arguments, however, behind another aspect of the state's control program over movement of people into Canada. Not all persons abroad seeking to enter Canada had intentions of staying. Many were coming only as visitors: tourists (the target of an entire government advertising campaign); visitors on business or on personal matters; and occasionally persons who had been invited to Canada by private groups to participate in artistic, academic, cultural, or even political events. In the normal intercourse of nations, especially in the present era of relatively quick and cheap international travel, people come and go in large numbers without making any permanent claims on the countries that host them briefly.

Visitors to Canada might, if they came from outside the United States, Britain, France, or the Commonwealth, require non-immigrant visas (this requirement is much rarer now than it was in the 1940s and 1950s). A refusal to issue a non-immigrant visa would effectively prevent a person from visiting Canada. Even those who did not require such visas could still be stopped at ports of entry and refused admission. There may be a number of reasons for refusing entry to a visitor, but we will only be concerned with political reasons. In the first decade and a half of the Cold War era, Canada made extensive use of this form of political censorship over who would be allowed to visit this country.

We should be very clear about the implications of a country exercising this kind of sanction against temporary visitors. Whatever legitimate fears there may have been about admitting certain kinds of people as permanent residents and eventual citizens, the same could hardly be said about temporary visitors. Fears of espionage are ridiculous: surely no hostile foreign power could have been so inept as to employ for espionage a temporary visitor with no access to classified material, who moreover had already become a highly visible target of government surveillance at the point of entry.

When the machinery and the criteria for enforcing non-immigrant controls are examined, it becomes crystal clear that the real perceived threat to Canada in that era was neither espionage nor subversion (whatever that vague and easily abused term might mean). Visitors stopped at the border for political reasons were barred to keep out their ideas, as a prohibitive tariff keeps out foreign imports. Moreover, it was a very specific sort of tariff, used only against ideas from the left. The ideas were sometimes those of Communism, but were not limited to it. Socialism, anti-militarism, advocacy of peace and disarmament, and less definable radical and anarchistic ideas were routinely lumped together as dangerous and presumably "un-Canadian". Of course it was absurd to imagine that a barrier *could* be erected against ideas, or that keeping out certain people could keep out their ideas.

During the so-called McCarthy era the United States became a target for the derision and indignation of civilized and liberal people throughout the Western world for its ham-fisted exclusions of eminent artists, intellectuals, and scholars on grounds of alleged "Communism". People ranging from the novelist Graham Greene to the actor Charlie Chaplin were judged ideologically undesirable visitors. Again in the 1980s, with the renewed burst of Cold War propaganda under Ronald Reagan, the McCarran–Walter Act has been dusted off and used not infrequently to bar or limit visitors—among the more notorious examples being Nobel-prize–winning Latin American novelist

Gabriel García Márquez and the Latin American journalist Patricia Lara, who was invited to attend an awards dinner at Columbia University in 1986 but was instead detained at the airport, thrown into a federal prison cell, and then deported.[1]

Canadians are reminded from time to time that these US controls can be invoked against Canadians. Recently when the colourful writer and naturalist Farley Mowat was prevented from entering the United States to publicize a new book, the outcry was long and loud; it was parlayed by the indefatigable Mowat into yet another book: *My Discovery of America*. Early in 1987, Saskatchewan university professor Jim Harding was prevented by US immigration officials from travelling with his family to Costa Rica via the United States. Officials eventually agreed to issue him a visa that indicated he was a Communist or a member of a Communist front organization. Never in fact a Communist, Harding was told that he was considered a Communist by the US government because he had attended a World Peace Council meeting in the USSR in 1961. A few years ago it became known that Pierre Elliott Trudeau, before he became prime minister of Canada, had been barred from travelling to the United States. And the present attorney general of Manitoba, Roland Penner, must travel on a special diplomatic passport when on business in the US, since he was once, many years ago, a member of the Communist party.[2]

Few Canadians seem to realize that Canada indulged in exactly the same kind of activity; the original American controls were set in place in close consultation and co-operation with Canada, which was at the same time putting its own, similar controls in place. The only real difference between the two countries was that Canada, typically, enacted its controls amid considerable secrecy and under the most discretionary interpretation of general statutory authority, while the Americans, just as typically, enacted theirs under explicit, if illiberal, legislative authority, and with maximum publicity.

Co-operation between Canada and the US on control of the flow of politically undesirable persons across the border seems to have roots that antedate the Cold War. But it is interesting to note that direct co-operation between Canadian police and American authorities, sometimes bypassing official Canadian channels altogether, appears to have been well in place by the end of the Second World War. American diplomatic personnel in Canada, for instance, kept close watch on Canadians whom they considered politically doubtful. John Grierson, the brilliant Scottish filmmaker and founding head and guiding spirit of the National Film Board, was one such person; an FBI file on him in Washington was matched by earlier reports generated by wartime American diplomats in Ottawa who kept notes of his comings and goings and sayings. After falling afoul (for no good reason) of the Gouzenko inquiry in 1946, Grierson was in deep disfavour with Washington and was refused travel visas to the US to pursue film projects there. Within Canada, those who had been associated with Grierson at the NFB fell under suspicion as well. A major witch-hunting purge of leftists was under way by the end of the 1940s.[3]

American access to Canadian police records was well established. This access certainly included direct entry to the RCMP's "subversive indices" and to the materials amassed by the "Red squads" in major cities. For example, in 1948 the veteran Canadian journalist Leslie Roberts attracted the unfavourable attention of the US embassy in Ottawa for having written a book called *Home from the Cold Wars*. It suggested, daringly enough for that era, that America was perhaps not blameless for the growing division of the world into two hostile armed camps and that the Soviet Union was perhaps not always culpable for international tensions. Roberts fell under American surveillance, presumably so that he might be barred from access to the US to pursue his research any further.

The embassy reported back to the state department that Roberts "appears to be at least a fellow traveler, if not a secret Communist." Besides quoting journalistic colleagues of Roberts who described him as a "Pinko", the report also noted that the police departments of Montreal, Toronto, and Ottawa had him "on their books as a Communist" and that the "Toronto office of the Royal Canadian Mounted Police lists him as a Communist also, and states that he has attended LPP [Communist] meetings and is believed to be connected with this political group." The Department of External Affairs also kept a Canadian surveillance file on Roberts, and his movements were watched closely by Canadian diplomatic personnel abroad, especially when he travelled in Communist countries.[4]

What is of particular interest is that the American embassy had direct access to the supposedly secret RCMP Red lists, and that a characterization of "Communism" could be routinely passed on to American authorities with consequences that might be very serious indeed for individuals so labelled. In fact the correspondence passing from the American embassy and consular offices in Canada in the late 1940s and early 1950s to the state department is replete with detailed information and political characterizations of individual Canadian citizens compiled and interpreted by the RCMP for the direct consumption of Americans, apparently unmediated by any responsible Canadian authority. In the case of Leslie Roberts, the Americans finally concluded after a personal interview by the vice-consul in Toronto that he was "calm, fair, reasonable and objective in his opinions and analysis. He criticized both the United States and Russia with equal vigor and conviction, and did not give the impression that he was a member of the Communist Party or a fellow traveler." Roberts was not prohibited from travelling to the United States.[5]

Not so lucky was another Canadian journalist, Margaret Gould of the *Toronto Daily Star*. Gould, a Russian-born Canadian social worker, had first gained notice as a journalist with a series of articles in the *Star* based on a tour of the Soviet Union in the late 1930s. Later she became an editorial writer for the newspaper, attracting the hostile attention of anti-Communist Roman Catholics who were wont to describe the *Star* as the "*Pravda* of King Street". She also attracted the unwelcome attention of the US embassy as early as 1945, when the state department was informed of the "undue influence exercised" by Gould over the policies of a newspaper already suspect in American eyes for its "undiscriminating approval of Russia." In 1949 she was refused permission to travel to New York to board ship for Europe, apparently at the direct order of the attorney general of the United States. This was reported widely in Canada as arising from her association with left-wing ideas, or, as a *Time* reporter suggested to the embassy in Ottawa, her "reputation as having been 'pinko in her younger days' ". In an editorial the Ottawa *Citizen* derided the hypocrisy of an American government that had signed a UN convention guaranteeing open access to journalists at the same time as it was banning Margaret Gould.[6] Canadians were not, however, above hypocrisy of their own on the issue of banning visitors, as events were already demonstrating.

One Canadian echo of the McCarran–Walter Act was that Canadians who fell afoul of American intolerance were sometimes punished further in Canada. In the spring of 1949 police swooped down on 2,000 diners at the Waldorf-Astoria Hotel in New York attending the Cultural and Scientific Conference for World Peace. Three Canadians attending the conference were pulled from their dinners by the police and ordered to leave the United States immediately. They were the distinguished scholar, painter, and writer Barker Fairley, of the University of Toronto, who was at the time a visiting professor at Columbia University; his wife, Margaret Fairley, a left-wing writer; and John Goss, a Vancouver actor and singer. Professor Fairley was allowed to remain until the end of term. (He was still officially barred from entry to the United States until his death in 1986, but once, in his nineties, he slipped over the border into Buffalo, just for "fun".) Margaret Fairley and Goss had to leave or be deported. Upon returning to Vancouver, Goss was denounced in the press and barred from performing at the BC Institute of Music and Drama, where he had been an instructor.[7]

Similarly, after being barred from taking up a teaching post at the University of Washington in 1955, George Woodcock was rejected as editor of an official BC centennial anthology by a committee of "BC worthies", as Woodcock describes them. A Queen's University academic, Glenn Shortliffe, who had been closely watched by US diplomatic personnel for his public statements regarding Soviet–American relations, was barred from taking up a teaching post in the United States after he had resigned his Queen's position. Rehired by Queen's, he was later barred by the Department of National Defence from teaching a summer course at the Royal Military College on the grounds of being an unspecified "security risk".[8]

The most notorious case, however, was that of the "Symphony Six". Six members of the Toronto Symphony Orchestra were refused permits to accompany the orchestra for a scheduled performance in Detroit in 1951. The TSO management fired all six. Sir Ernest MacMillan, director of the TSO and doyen of Canadian music, was in complete agreement with this arbitrary and obsequious act. Despite a public campaign on behalf of the martyred musicians involving the resignation of board members and newspaper advertisements sponsored by persons ranging from Group of Seven painter A. Y. Jackson to the radio broadcaster Gordon Sinclair, the firings were not reversed. The authoritative *Encyclopedia of Music in Canada* concludes, "Sir Ernest MacMillan's stature and the prestige of the Orchestra both suffered." One of the musicians was Dirk Keetbaas, later a celebrated flautist with the Winnipeg Symphony and the CBC. Another was Steven Staryk, who is "regarded as the leading Canadian-born violinist of his generation"; after some time abroad, Staryk eventually returned to the TSO, where he is today its most renowned performer. In retrospect, Staryk's own explanation for his ban and subsequent misfortune is that his childhood teacher had a name similar to that of a Ukrainian-Canadian Communist.[9]

Canadian authorities had no intention of leaving the banning of visitors entirely to the Americans. In 1947–48 a test case was carried out on the basis of which the Canadian government established its ability to exercise administrative discretion in banning visitors. The case had to do with the sensitive matter of labour relations in the northern Ontario gold mining industry. The gold mining entrepreneurs had always been vehemently hostile to trade unions and more than ready to call in the aid of the state against union organizing in the mines, despite their public rhetoric of *laissez-faire*. They were particularly prone to identifying union leaders as "Communists" since this facilitated the intervention of the state.

The Mine, Mill and Smelter Workers Union (known as Mine-Mill) did have Communist organizers and a strong left-wing faction in its international leadership, based in the US. Prominent among this faction was Reid Robinson, who had helped organize the bitter Kirkland Lake gold strike during the war; at the time Robinson was arrested and held for deportation. In the midst of the gathering Cold War in the late 1940s, as the Taft–Hartley Act bit deeply into Communist influence in the American union, the Communist faction looked increasingly to the union's Canadian locals for an escape valve. In 1947 Reid Robinson was "invited" by the Mine-Mill locals in northern Ontario to come to Canada to launch a major organizing drive in the gold fields. The prospect of Robinson's arrival was a veritable red flag before the gold mining capitalists and the anti-Communist politicians and press of northern Ontario. A furor resulted that eventually involved the government of Canada, the non-Communist trade unions, and the CCF (Co-operative Commonwealth Federation, the predecessor of the NDP). When it was over, a precedent had been established for barring at the border persons visiting Canada who were judged politically undesirable.

The government was faced with a broad front of demands that Robinson be barred from Canada. The Department of Mines and Resources, which in 1947 happened to be the ministry that included the Immigration Branch, accumulated a thick file of demands from various individuals and organizations. The file shows that the pressures for barring Robinson came essentially from two sources. The first, which was only to be expected, was the mining magnates and the local chambers of commerce in northern Ontario, along with the usual outriders of anti-Communism such as local branches of the Royal Canadian Legion. Less expectedly, a secondary thrust came from the non-Communist union movement and from CCF politicians. Officials of the Canadian Congress of Labour, with which Mine Mill was affiliated, and CCFers close to the rival United Steelworkers of America (such as the lone Nova Scotia CCF MP, Clarie Gillis of Cape Breton) were vociferous in their anti-Communism and in their demands that the state intervene against "Communist" union organizers. Since trade unionists and the CCF generally opposed any state interventions against union activities, their willingness to join with the mine owners against Communist unionists was welcome assistance to the government in securing a free hand to deal arbitrarily through the Immigration Act with visiting trade unionists—in a country where a very large proportion of the union movement was international.[10]

Robinson was not stopped at the border because the government had not had time to enact its plans. Once he had arrived, pressure began to mount from all sides to deport him. In February 1948, Cabinet was introduced to the problem by the minister of mines and resources, who indicated that while Robinson was in Canada quite legally, he "was known to be a Communist and...had been the cause of considerable trouble in certain industrial areas." Since he had arrived legally, it would be necessary to launch court action for deportation; evidence was being collected. The following week the matter came up again. The minister of justice indicated that a board of inquiry could be set up under the Immigration Act to determine whether Robinson was deportable under a section of the act relating to membership in organizations that advocated the overthrow of government by force.

This was a somewhat sticky matter for a Liberal government: the Liberals had opposed the use of the old section 98 of the Criminal Code by the Conservative government of R. B. Bennett in the 1930s to outlaw the Communist party and imprison eight of its leaders; the Liberals had in fact repealed the section when they were returned to office in 1935. Moreover, they were resisting—for what they believed to be sound reasons—the calls for banning the Communist party in the early, and highly charged, days of the Cold War. James Ilsley, the justice minister, reassured his Cabinet colleagues that "comparable proceedings could not be taken against a Canadian citizen…unless there were an overt act; the Immigration Act provisions respecting deportation applied, of course, only to foreigners." Brooke Claxton, the minister of national defence, always highly sensitive to the Liberals' public image, pointed out that public proceedings based upon the alleged Communist connection of this individual would raise the broader issue of the attitude of the government towards "outlawing" the Communist party. It was to be doubted, Claxton warned, "whether the evidence currently available on the aims of the Communist party would be held sufficient to suggest deportation under the relevant provisions of the Immigration Act." Cabinet deferred decision.[11]

When it returned to the question a few days later, it was to a lengthy discussion of the entire matter of barring "agitators and Communists" from entering Canada. The justice department believed that it had sufficient evidence (based on voluminous reports by an RCMP undercover agent in Mine-Mill) to declare Robinson a prohibited person and to refuse to renew his temporary visa, which was due to expire within days. Moreover, Cabinet directed the justice department to examine the legal position for refusing entry in future "to other persons known to be intending to enter Canada for similar subversive purposes." When it was reported to Cabinet that Robinson had in fact left the country voluntarily, the news was greeted with evident relief, but the general question remained.[12]

To clear up the difficulties of proving that Communists fell under the provisions of section 3 of the Immigration Act regarding prohibited persons, Justice suggested an amendment that would directly prohibit persons who belonged to or were affiliated with "any Nazi, Fascist or Communist party or any organization professing similar beliefs or doctrines." Such an approach would have the advantage of facilitating matters and, as a confidential Justice memorandum candidly put it, "end the present embarrassing situation in Europe where, with dubious legality, we are screening out Communists from the D.P.'s and other applicants for admission to Canada." Cabinet, however, thought it "inadvisable" to openly prohibit Communists by name, preferring to leave the matter to administrative discretion rather than follow the more American route of legislative prohibitions. The ministers went further yet by instructing the minister of mines and the minister of labour to compile a "confidential list of approved U.S. organizers". Immigration officers were to allow into Canada only those on the approved list—any others would be refused.[13] In short, Cabinet was suggesting that all foreign labour organizers were, in effect, subversives unless they were on a secret "kosher" list prepared by the state.

Legal opinion, however, was that a "kosher" list was unenforceable, since mere absence from such a list could not offer evidence upon which a board of inquiry could make a decision on deportation. Instead attention turned to assembling a list of known American Communists, who would be prohibited from entry to Canada. The RCMP was quite happy to provide such lists, which would be based, according to the RCMP commissioner, upon information gathered from the files of the US House Un-American Activities Committee, currently engaged in a witch-hunt in Hollywood, and upon the US attorney general's list of subversive organizations (an official proscription list compiled by the US justice department and the FBI). The preparation and use of such a list of prohibited persons was politically acceptable because, as the minister of labour smugly, but not entirely accurately, told the Cabinet Committee on Immigration Policy, "all Canadian Labour Organizations are against the admission to Canada of Communists." Emphasis was to be placed on exclusion at the border, to discourage the kind of protracted legal proceedings that tended to occur when persons already in Canada were arrested for deportation.[14]

When the new proposal went before Cabinet it provoked a heated debate. Louis St. Laurent, the minister of external affairs, pointed out that the proposal went "substantially beyond" the prohibition originally contemplated by Cabinet, which had been limited to labour organizers. "Adoption of these recommendations", St. Laurent warned, "would involve refusal of admission to known and accepted public figures from certain countries; it might also compel refusal of admission to any USSR national. It might raise the issue of the status of the Communist Party in Canada." The minister of justice indicated that the "legality of prohibiting the entry of Communists" under section 3 of the act "was open to question". In the courts, the "decision might well go against the government." Brooke Claxton added that however desirable it might be to bar "known Communist trouble-makers...care should be taken as to the means employed." In the event of an unfavourable court decision, face-saving legislative amendments might be necessary.[15]

In the face of these objections, Cabinet deferred decision. The clerk of the Privy Council, Arnold Heeney, sent the minutes on to Prime Minister Mackenzie King, who had been absent from the meeting, with an accompanying note indicating that "this discussion was not very satisfactory and the points at issue were not clearly defined." This bureaucratic commentary on the performance of ministers was given further weight by a plea that the prime minister "be present...when the question would be brought up again."[16]

The prime minister was indeed present when his ministers reassembled to try yet again to resolve this thorny problem. By this time there were more cases to be decided. The number of "known Communists" who had already entered Canada as union organizers had grown to four (including Reid Robinson, who had slipped back into Canada). There was also the "special case" of the secretary of the British Communist party, Harry Pollitt, who proposed to visit Canada. The question of whether to bar all known Communists or merely Communist labour organizers had thus been posed concretely. The differences between the ministers on this matter were already clear. Mackenzie King intervened:

> Mr. King drew attention to the fact that adoption of the Cabinet Committee's proposal to exclude all known Communists involved new policy which would inevitably affect the treatment to be accorded the

Communist party in Canada. There were two methods of dealing with Communism, the traditional course which entailed no interference with freedom of speech and suppressive measures which could only be justified by serious emergency. The question for consideration was which of these methods was best to deal effectively with present circumstances.

Like a professor presiding over a fractious seminar, King had ably summed up the two underlying theoretical options. But the students were no better able to decide on a concrete course of action: again Cabinet failed to resolve the issue and deferred action.[17]

The next day they met again, apparently in a tougher mood. After "considerable discussion" (a euphemism for protracted and heated debate, which was unfortunately not reported in the minutes), Cabinet finally approved the hard-line option and declared that "known Communists seeking admission to Canada for the purpose of engaging in subversive propaganda" were considered to fall under section 3 of the Immigration Act, regarding persons advocating the violent overthrow of government, and would thus be barred from entry after the facts were reviewed by a Cabinet committee made up of the external affairs, labour, and mines and resources ministers. In the specific case of Pollitt, this decision meant that an initial approval given by Canada House in London on the advice of External Affairs and the Immigration Branch would have to be reversed. Pollitt was barred.[18]

What the government had done was take a substantial step towards limiting freedom of speech. It must be emphasized that the "threat" to which Cabinet was apparently responding was neither espionage nor terrorism. Instead they were banning persons who they, as Cabinet ministers, believed were "seeking admission for the purpose of engaging in subversive propaganda". There was nothing in Canadian law that defined "subversive propaganda". There was no suggestion that persons barred were likely to commit the criminal offence of sedition or seditious conspiracy. It is quite clear that "subversive propaganda" was simply the expression of ideas of which the government disapproved—yet the same government refused to legislate against the expression of such ideas. Moreover, it was Cabinet that designated which visitors were "known Communists", on the basis of reports from the RCMP that, as one Cabinet memorandum made clear, would not indicate "special sources which would be compromised if…employed in this way": the usual RCMP jargon for protecting its undercover operatives and the foreign security and intelligence services that fed it information.[19] Hearing Mackenzie King's cautious admonition about the choice between "the traditional course which entailed no interference with freedom of speech and suppressive measures which could only be justified by serious emergency", the government had apparently decided in favour of the latter. But was the emergency so serious that suppression of a speaking tour by the leader of the (perfectly legal) British Communist party under the sponsorship of the (perfectly legal) Canadian Communist party was justifiable? Or could it be that the state was actually so unsure of its own support and so afraid of Pollitt's ideas that it had to ban him?[20]

There was little doubt at the time that the state's new policy had substantial support; especially vocal were small business, conservative politicians, and the conservative press. In fact March 1948 saw Red Scare hysteria sweeping across the country, or at least certain sections of it. Boards of trade and chambers of commerce across the country bombarded the government with demands that foreign Communists be barred or deported, that the domestic Communist party be outlawed, and that Communists be banned from holding office in Canadian trade unions. The Ontario legislature, led by the vehemently anti-Communist Tory premier, George Drew, was awash with charges that the Mine-Mill union was a Moscow-inspired conspiracy to "impose on Canada that vile, godless form of slavery" called Communism. The rhetoric spilled over into the House of Commons, where the Conservative House leader moved to adjourn the House to debate the national emergency caused by the Communist menace. Important voices of the press joined in the chorus. In an editorial, the *Globe and Mail* thundered that the government was completely justified in closing the border to Reds: just as the Soviets "deny the right of persons believing in the philosophy of free enterprise to general entry into Russia," argued the *Globe*, "so Canada proposes to treat the enemies of its own way of life. How can that be unjust?" Having thus set Soviet Russia as its standard for political freedom, the *Globe* saw no difficulty in dismissing critics who worried about liberal democracy. "It is the policy of Communist agitators always to hide behind the principles of liberal democracy, while they pursue their destructive ends. The crisis of civilization has now become too acute, however, for temporizing." Apparently Canadians shared the *Globe*'s alarm. When asked by the Gallup pollsters if they supported the government's action in barring Communists from entering the country, 79 per cent agreed while only 8 per cent disagreed.[21]

It is important to situate this moment historically. The Czech *coup d'état*, a crucial event in the consolidation of the Cold War, had just taken place in February. The Berlin crisis was under way. Chiang Kai-shek's armies were on the run before the Chinese Communists. In Italy the Communists were mounting an electoral campaign that threatened to bring them to national office. The international situation was ripe for the American initiative of the Marshall Plan, about to be announced, and for the creation of NATO, which was to follow within a year. In the United States itself, the Red Scare was reaching a crescendo in Washington and across the nation. Canadian policymakers proved reluctant to allow the kind of hysterical witch-hunting in Canada that was already out of control in America, a hysteria that would later produce the sinister figure of Sen. Joseph McCarthy. But the Gouzenko spy affair had already spotlighted Canadian Communists and their sympathizers as followers of Soviet policy and potentially disloyal, and Canadians were not immune to the fear and intolerance sweeping the country to the south.

It was no accident that the flames were being fanned in this country by business and by conservative newspapers and politicians. The attention focused on the Mine-Mill union and its activities in the northern Ontario gold mines, orchestrated by the mining companies themselves and their ideological outriders in the boards of trade and chambers of commerce across the country, was reminiscent of a similar campaign launched in the late 1930s by the same mining interests against the CIO (Congress of Industrial Organizations) in Canada, cheered on by George McCullagh's *Globe and Mail* and the Liberal premier of Ontario, Mitchell Hepburn. In 1937 Hepburn had demanded, unsuccessfully, that the RCMP be sent in to crush a strike at General Motors in Oshawa by the United Auto Workers, a CIO union: behind General Motors had stood the mining interests. During the war a bitter strike had been fought at Kirkland Lake, which the mine owners, in alliance with the state, had won.[22] Now once again the issue was joined, but this time it was fought on the terrain of the Cold War, with the Communists in Mine-Mill as the immediate target.

Whatever reasons there may have been to contest Soviet influence abroad—and there was no doubt that Canadian public opinion strongly favoured Canada's support for an anti-Soviet alliance—that struggle had little to do with the activities of a handful of Communist trade union organizers in northern Ontario. These activities were the main concern of the mine owners and of their business allies across the nation, and in the panicky context of early 1948 they were able to identify their narrowly self-interested demands for state interference in trade unionism with an alleged "crisis of civilization", as the *Globe* had so immoderately put it. The Cold War was a bonanza for business: plain, old-fashioned union-busting could be dressed up in the fashionable and highly saleable language of the defence of Western civilization against godless Bolshevism, and even the Liberal government, with its liberal principles, could be stampeded into the kind of repressive measures that business liked but did not always receive.

The Liberals would not have gone as far as they did in meeting the mining companies' demands if the non-Communist trade union movement, largely pro-CCF in orientation, had not joined in the same chorus. In March the Canadian Congress of Labour in effect declared "full-scale war" on Mine-Mill and on "Communists camouflaged as labour organizers". The Liberal labour minister knew that he could count on the support of the congress in banning Communists. CCF trade unionists tended to take the position that Communists were beyond the pale of normal democratic safeguards; so long as the government took pains to identify Communists precisely as the targets of extraordinary measures, they saw no problem. Any doubts tended to concern the danger that "legitimate" trade unionists might fall victim as well as Communists. Eamon Park, an official of the Steelworkers Union (a Mine-Mill rival) and a prominent CCFer, told a reporter that "while he agreed with the Dominion Government's recent action in barring alien Communists from entry to Canada, he felt the situation should be 'handled carefully'. 'Wrongfully used, this Government order can be distorted to bar legitimate unionists from coming to Canada. My union and the Canadian

Congress of Labour, with which we are affiliated, will insist that there will be no suggestion of a witch hunt in the application of the order.' "23 It was on the basis of just such fine distinctions that Cold War liberalism in the United States played a crucial role in the emergence of a climate in which McCarthyism was to flourish; in the slightly different political culture of Canada, Cold War social democracy was making its own modest contribution to the mood of illiberalism.

How embarrassing it was then to the Cold War social democrats that when the state did act, it acted clumsily and excessively. Robinson was arrested and held for deportation, as the CCL had wished. He was then released on bail after signing a bond that he "would refrain from engaging in any union activities while at liberty". In the words of the Ontario CCF leader, "For pure, unadulterated stupidity this certainly takes first prize. The conditions of the bond are all that could have been asked for by anyone seeking to make a martyr out of Robinson." The congress succeeded in getting the wording of Robinson's bond changed so that "union" became "subversive". But the damage had been done and Robinson and Mine-Mill were soon back on the attack, strongly supported by most Mine-Mill locals. Robinson himself correctly fixed blame on the CCL for his arrest and attacked its leaders for encouraging a "governmental union-busting witch-hunt against foreign-born labour leaders."24

Eventually, however, Mine-Mill was more or less isolated by the CCL leadership. An executive member of the union, Robert Carlin, for many years a CCF member of the Ontario legislature, believed that there was a "deep principle involved—the whole matter of deportation of labour organizers." For failing to support the CCL against his own union, Carlin was expelled from the Ontario CCF. There were many ramifications within Canada of the government's action, as the Cold War came home.25

It did not prove easy to amass the evidence with which Robinson could be deported. In June government counsel expressed the view that the evidence "so far available was insufficient". The minister of justice observed to his Cabinet colleagues that if the deportation proceedings failed, the law would have to be amended. The dossier being assembled drew on some less-than-objective sources, including the Ontario Mining Association, the Royal Canadian Legion, and the Kirkland Lake Board of Trade.

Among the evidence entered against one of Robinson's Mine-Mill colleagues, Harlow Wildman, was the intelligence that in 1942 he had spoken on an Idaho radio station in favour of the Allies opening a second front against the Nazis in Europe ("This was the current popular line of the Communists", the dossier explained). In the end the board of inquiry in Robinson's case was persuaded to agree to his deportation, on the basis of two reports from the House Un-American Activities Committee, the US attorney general's list of subversive organizations, and union documents attacking Mine-Mill.[26]

If the Canadian state showed few compunctions about using the immigration laws as a means of barring left-wing labour union agitators, the same could certainly not be said about its dealings with labour agitators from the other side of the ideological fence. A particularly shocking example of this double standard was the importation of Hal Banks, the American labour racketeer, and his Seafarers International Union (SIU) to help crush the Communist-led Canadian Seamen's Union (CSU). Banks, who had a criminal record, should never have been allowed into the country, according to Canadian law. Far from being barred, he was encouraged and fêted by the Liberal government, and even appointed as Canadian representative to the International Labour Organization in Geneva. Banks' status will be discussed in chapter 8.

In 1949, at the height of the struggle between the CSU and the SIU, an incident occurred that demonstrated the political bias of Canadian immigration policy. During a legal CSU strike at Halifax harbour, a violent confrontation took place that ended in gunfire directed against CSU picketers, six of whom were wounded. An SIU gang of strike-breakers involved in this incident included sixty American strong-arm specialists imported directly, and illegally, from the US. Immigration promised an inquiry, but it never took place.[27]

The case of Reid Robinson and the Mine-Mill union had been very public, very time-consuming, and at times embarrassing. It had been a test case. As the *Toronto Daily Star* headlined, "Others to follow Robinson now precedent set—Ottawa". Just how seriously Ottawa took its duty to stop Communists at the border, and thus avoid protracted deportation hearings, is evidenced by action taken in May 1948 to stop two alleged

Communists, action that actually went beyond the procedures outlined by Cabinet in its March decision.

On May 17, the minister responsible for immigration was urgently cabled by the Vancouver Board of Trade regarding two Croatian Americans scheduled to speak in Vancouver in support of the campaign to encourage Yugoslavs to return to their homeland. "Have good reason to believe both of these men are of communist background and should be denied entry to Canada," the telegram asserted. That was good enough for the Immigration Branch, which, upon gaining quick verbal advice from the RCMP, immediately ordered the men barred at the BC point of entry.[28]

As Hugh Keenleyside, the deputy minister of immigration, admitted, the action "did not conform to the Cabinet directive", which had stipulated that all such cases should come before a special three-member Cabinet committee before action was taken. The reason for ignoring the politicians was simply that "immediate action was essential if the aliens were to be held up at the border". "The circumstances in these cases", Keenleyside observed, "indicate the difficulty in following the procedure laid down by Cabinet directive where the time factor is important." Instead the ministers were asked to retroactively rubber-stamp the action taken by the bureaucrats and the police at the request of the Vancouver Board of Trade.[29]

A further refinement to procedures to allow immediate action at border crossings was the preparation of a list of proscribed American unions, executive membership in which would lead to automatic rejection. If the rejected visitors wished to appeal, the RCMP would then be asked to provide specific evidence against the person to show "that he is a Communist or fellow traveler". If such evidence was lacking, the person would then be let in. The list initially included six unions: besides Mine-Mill, they were the United Electrical Workers, the International Fur and Leather Workers, the American Communications Association, the United Gas, Coke and Chemical Workers, and the Office and Professional Workers. Shortly after the list was endorsed by Cabinet, the international president of Mine-Mill, who was not a Communist but was allied with Communists, was barred. When the RCMP failed to come up with convincing evidence, the case was dropped. The RCMP then went to work and by November had compiled a list of some 100 persons with Communist associations to be stopped at points of entry. It was somewhat more effective than a list of organizations. This was the genesis of the "look-out" list of banned persons that was to become standard operating equipment for immigration officers.[30]

One more twist was added in the early 1950s when immigration officers abroad were requested to forward to Ottawa "advance information about communists or presumed communists who plan to attend meetings or congresses in Canada"; such information was particularly helpful when it concerned British, French, or American citizens, who did not require visas to visit Canada. The point of this procedure was to allow the government to make judgements concerning the political nature of the organizations sponsoring the visitors; if the sponsors were held to be subversive by the RCMP, the visitors would be barred. If the patrons of the visit were considered harmless, the visitors might be allowed to enter (although they might still be barred, if their names already appeared on a look-out list). This procedure meant *de facto* state intervention in Canadian political life, with the police passing secret judgement on the legitimacy of private associations. These decisions could have important consequences for individuals, but the security establishment was in no way made responsible for the accuracy or fairness of its characterizations.[31]

While these events were unfolding in Canada, the Americans were not idle. As early as 1947 the US consul general in Vancouver was writing to his superiors in Washington in admiring tones about Canadian resolve to gather information on American Communists in order to facilitate their exclusion: "Frankly", he added, "I think they are being realistic about it and we are not." Whatever lack of enthusiasm might have existed in Washington was soon replaced by zeal. The barring of Communists at the US–Canada border was in fact essentially a joint Canadian-American operation. The two sides exchanged intelligence information and co-operated in a mutual exclusion of each other's "outside agitators". In a lengthy explanatory circular sent to Canadian diplomatic posts abroad in 1948, External Affairs explained how Cabinet's decision to exclude Communists would work. To gather information on the security risk of an applicant, visa officers could now consult directly the security section of the local American embassy (as well as the UK passport control office). The Americans would consult Washington, thus avoiding having to route such requests through Ottawa. "In principle", the circular admitted, "the exchange of information will be reciprocal, although in practice it is recognized that our contribution will be very small."[32]

In exchange for being plugged into the world-wide network of anti-Communist intelligence over which America presided, Canada could offer information only on Canadians who might come to the unfavourable attention of Uncle Sam when seeking to visit across the "world's longest undefended border". The RCMP threw open its security records to any American diplomat or official who wanted to copy secret police files on Canadian citizens. State department records in Washington concerning Canada in this era are replete with fat dossiers on individual Canadians allegedly associated with Communism (sometimes containing the kind of egregious errors that security services tend to pick up in the course of their snooping).

The warning system was very sensitive. For instance, in June 1948 a Halifax businessman called on the American consul in that city to report that a local trade unionist, whom the businessman described as having "participated in Communist activities", was planning to visit New Hampshire; the consul immediately contacted the local RCMP, which provided him with all the information it held on the man, as well as its assessment that while he was not a card-carrying Communist, he was at least a fellow-traveller. The consul reported to Washington the model and year of the man's car, along with his licence plate number and a general idea of his itinerary, in case the FBI wished to place him under surveillance during his visit. The consul added that he understood the RCMP "habitually reports such cases to Ottawa for relaying to the FBI, and is today so reporting the case under consideration".[33]

It is hardly surprising then that when Queen's University professor Glenn Shortliffe was denied entry to the United States to take up an offer to teach at an American university, the decision was based upon material gathered by US diplomats in Canada with the aid and assistance of Canadian snoopers. Although Shortliffe, a professor of French, was in fact in no way connected with the Communists, his "sin" was to have written articles and broadcast opinion mildly critical of American foreign policy.

The Shortliffe case roused the interest of the CCF in the House of Commons, since the professor was much more of a social democrat than a Marxist, although his views on foreign policy went beyond CCF policy. Shortliffe's plight was a clear case of a non-Communist being snared in a process about which the CCF was generally complacent so long as its targets were confined to those clearly to its left. Late in 1949 the Standing Committee on External Affairs of the House briefly became a forum for questions about Shortliffe and about Canadian complicity in the operations of the American immigration service as they affected Canadians. A Conservative MP asked how the Americans obtained the information on Canadians whom they were barring. Did they get it from the Canadian government or "have they some kind of network in here themselves?" Lester Pearson, the minister of external affairs, played the innocent:

> They do not get it from the Department of External Affairs. They have their own immigration officials in Canada. There are no doubt people in this country who write letters to the United States authorities, who tell them "don't let so and so in, he is a red". I don't know how they get the information.[34]

If Pearson actually did not know where the information came from, he was badly misinformed; but as a former diplomat and senior bureaucrat in External Affairs until he assumed the ministry, it is difficult to imagine that he was as innocent as he appeared. The real answer was that the Americans did have a network in Canada, which included the RCMP security service.

The Americans in the McCarthy era of the 1950s were notoriously heavy-handed in their application of the McCarran–Walter Act to citizens of friendly countries. The barring of Canadians became so notorious that even Lester Pearson was finally spurred to act. In 1956 he launched a formal complaint, asking that liaison be established to ensure that only "bona fide security cases" were barred. Later the Americans apparently agreed to show the RCMP their blacklist of Canadians—although just what might have been accomplished by this formality is not readily apparent.[35]

In any event, spasms of anti-American self-righteousness among Canadians only served to obscure not only Canadian complicity in the American process but, more importantly, Canadian exercise of the same sanctions against Americans. An ugly undertone of this practice was the importation of racism along with political intolerance. The House Un-American Activities Committee, upon which Canada relied for information, was dominated by white Southern racists. The elderly and distinguished black scholar W. E. B. Du Bois (born only a few years after the end of the Civil War and the end of slavery) was barred in 1952 from speaking in Canada, on the word of the RCMP that he was a Communist agitator; earlier Du Bois had been persecuted by the witch-hunters in his own country, although charges were thrown out of court for want of evidence. But as Prime Minister St. Laurent told his Cabinet colleagues, there was after all a "general policy against allowing entry of persons visiting Canada for the purpose of promoting Communist policies."[36]

A more celebrated case of political persecution of a black American was that of the renowned singer Paul Robeson. Robeson not only brought the music of the black gospel to audiences around the world, he was also a fighter on behalf of his people in an America where racial segregation still reigned and black Americans were less than second-class citizens. His quest for equality led him over the years towards definite sympathy for the philosophy of Communism, and to support struggles that were also supported by the Communists; to the witch-hunters, his position was tantamount to Communism. Robeson had performed before large and appreciative Canadian audiences before, sometimes running into local opposition, as he had in Toronto in 1947, when the mayor banned his performance.

In 1948 the special cabinet committee overseeing the barring of visitors came before Cabinet armed with a report from the RCMP that Robeson should be barred from coming to Canada again. According to its secret sources, the RCMP reported, Robeson had in the past used his concerts as a cover; actually, he had "engaged in [unspecified] Communist activities while in Canada". Whatever his politics, more Canadians probably thought of Robeson in terms of his immortal rendition of "Ol' Man River". Cabinet, for its part, decided to let him in, but only with an unusual, mean-spirited rider attached by Louis St. Laurent. National Revenue was ordered to make sure that it collected income tax payable "from such foreign artists."[37]

In 1949 a Robeson concert in Peekskill, New York, was the scene of a violent riot when American Legionnaires and self-appointed vigilantes assaulted cars and buses filled with people, including children, leaving the concert. Hundreds of injuries resulted. This violence was motivated by more than anti-Communist politics alone; anti-black prejudice was strong. The following year Robeson's passport was revoked by the US government. Invited to attend the Canadian convention of the Mine-Mill union in 1952, Robeson was prevented from leaving the US—thus relieving Canada of having to bar him, which it certainly would have done, given the source of the invitation. Robeson dramatized the situation unforgettably by giving a concert just across the border at the Peace Arch Park in Washington state, attended by 30,000 Canadians on the British Columbia side; this event was repeated annually for the next three years.[38]

In 1955, Cabinet considered whether to allow Robeson to enter Canada to sing at the invitation of another labour union. They decided to let him in, so long as he only sang but did not speak. The following year, however, he was not so lucky. Although it was pointed out in Cabinet that "some liberal minded people would undoubtedly object", Robeson was denied entry on the basis that his concert tour was being booked by a "Communist-controlled agency".[39]

Canadians did at least demonstrate slightly more restraint in their banning of visitors than did their neighbours. Canadian officials retained some sense of the ridiculous, a sense notably lacking in American officials. There was, for instance, the case of the colourful and eccentric Rev. Hewlett Johnson, the so-called Red Dean of Canterbury. This singular Church of England clergyman, already well advanced in years but a strikingly tall and energetic figure, long white hair streaming over his clerical collar, tirelessly preached the virtues of Soviet Communism from any platform in the world that would have him. Innocent, enthusiastic, and certainly well-meaning, the Red Dean attempted in the early years of the Cold War to advance the cause of nuclear disarmament—in the inevitable if unfortunate style of that era—by painting the Soviet Union as an exemplar of progress and (stretching a point) Christian charity. The Americans were not amused and barred him from carrying this evangelical gospel to US pulpits.[40]

Taking its cue from the US, the RCMP suggested that the bar might also be lowered in Canada. An official of External Affairs, in a burst of realism rare to this era, advised that a ban on the dean "would be ridiculous". Immigration agreed. Faced with a protest by the Imperial Order Daughters of the Empire, the bureaucrats weighed the dean's reputation as an "eminent cleric" against his "eccentricities" and decided to come down on balance in favour of the "British pattern of free speech", rather than adopt "the more restricted" American way. So the dean brought his eccentric road show to Canada on a number of occasions—usually to capacity audiences, sometimes to verbal abuse and even, on occasion, physical abuse, and always to maximum controversy in press and Parliament. One ornament of the latter institution referred inelegantly to the dean as a "hairy, stinking old goat", and individuals described as "students" once paraded an effigy of the dean hanging from a makeshift gallows on the rear end of a truck through the streets of Toronto.[41]

The guardians of Canada's borders did not always fix their sights on the right targets, even by their own vague standards. Sometimes misfires became public knowledge. Such was the case of a botched attempt to deport American journalist William Reuben from Vancouver in 1955. The attempt fizzled in the courts because it was incorrectly drawn up, but the reasons for the government's action are none the less revealing. Reuben was an investigative journalist who had published a book that year called *The Atom Spy Hoax*, a critical examination of a celebrated series of "atom spy" cases of the early Cold War, including the Gouzenko affair in Canada. On the latter case, Reuben had made a careful and skeptical assessment of the logic of the royal commission report and of the outcome of the subsequent trials, which cast considerable doubt on the seriousness of the alleged espionage.[42]

Perhaps the Canadian government did not appreciate hearing its cherished royal commission report, which it had used as a base from which to launch much of the Cold War in Canada, so rudely and realistically called into question from a Canadian platform. This explanation of the Reuben affair, however, may give too much credit for intelligence (in both senses). The British Columbia district superintendent of immigration, under whose authority the deportation was launched, had a more simplistic explanation for his colleagues in Immigration: Reuben's book talked about "Communists" and "various other subjects relating to communism".[43] In any event, Reuben was an independent left-wing journalist unaffiliated with the Communists.

A curious case concerning a visiting conductor of the Calgary Symphony Orchestra came to the attention of Cabinet in 1955–56. The conductor, a Mr. Plukker, was a Dutch citizen who had arrived with his wife via the United States to take up the Calgary post. Within months Ottawa had been alerted that he was a security risk who should be deported. The matter reached Cabinet no fewer than three times within four months, for there were unforeseen embarrassments involved in taking action against the conductor. For one thing, "he had become quite popular in certain quarters and forcing him to leave would arouse comment and criticism." Worse, Carl Nickle, a wealthy Calgary oilman and Conservative MP, was his "main sponsor". Nickle let it be known that a fund he had been intending to set up "to encourage cultural development in Canada" might be jeopardized if Plukker were deported. These were strange circumstances to surround a supposed security risk, and the censored accounts of lengthy and elliptical discussions in Cabinet only add to the mystery. In the event, Plukker was allowed to stay for another musical season. It seems that at the root of this mystery was a member of the symphony whom Plukker had decided to fire for artistic reasons. The musician had sought vengeance by denouncing Plukker to immigration authorities as a "Communist". Matters then got out of hand, and the Liberals were stuck with a political embarrassment.[44]

Other misfires gathered no publicity, because their victims did not want any. Quiet representations were made on behalf of an unfortunate merchant from the French islands of Saint-Pierre and Miquelon whose business would normally take him on trips to Canada. When he was barred inexplicably, as a threat to Canadian national security, his friends could only surmise that his misfortune arose from having once been a member of the Confédération générale du travail, the French labour federation that was Communist-led. The merchant had, however, left the CGT along with a number of other anti-Communist Socialists years earlier, and had been a candidate for the non-Communist left in elections. Canadian immigration officials were little inclined, it seems, to make fine distinctions among foreign "radicals". When in doubt, the rule in security matters was always to resolve the doubt "in favour of Canada."[45]

There was apparently less doubt about those whose pasts were linked not to Communism but to Fascism. For example, a German industrialist with a Nazi past who was judged "not admissible as an immigrant" even by the relaxed standards of 1958 was nevertheless allowed to travel here as a non-immigrant. Of course, coming to do business in Canada always guaranteed a warmer welcome than coming to share ideas or words or songs. Coming to do business even guaranteed entry to Communists, when they came from Communist countries carrying import orders for Canadian business; security officers were warned not to cause embarrassment by barring visiting Communists who had legitimate business with Canadian capitalists, so long as the RCMP was kept informed of their movements.[46]

What to do with Soviet visitors not on trade business presented recurrent difficulties for the government, especially after exchange agreements between Canada and the USSR were agreed to in the "thaw" following the death of Stalin. In 1956, while Stalinism was being officially denounced by the Communists in the USSR, Cabinet was grappling with a series of embarrassing Soviet visits proposed by various organizations that the government had labelled Communist fronts. The West Coast–based United Fishermen and Allied Workers Union, which had earlier been suspended from the Trades and Labour Congress for alleged Communist leanings, invited representatives from a Soviet trade union to attend its annual convention in Vancouver. In this case, the ministers decided, "It might do more harm than good to prevent these visits.... It would be embarrassing to appear to create an iron curtain after the west had complained for so long of that of the communist world." Yet a week later the same ministers decided to bar a group of Russian women invited by the Congress of Canadian Women (a "communist organization"); in this case Cabinet was armed with a statement from the president of the respectable National Council of Women warning "all responsible women's organizations in Canada to have nothing to do with these visitors should they arrive."[47]

The following year a new Tory government took over the reins of office and was shortly presented with the old problem. A visit by ten Soviet trade and business people was proposed. The new

ministers somewhat reluctantly agreed, on condition that the Soviets did not disseminate propaganda in Canada and that "this
visit did not result in sales of strategic materials to the USSR".
They moreover stipulated that no Cabinet ministers should meet
with these visitors, even socially, since "it was said that attendance by [Liberal] ministers at previous Soviet receptions had
greatly annoyed various ethnic groups." Two years later, the BC
fishermen's union was back with another request to admit Soviet
delegates to its convention. The Cabinet directive barring Soviets
invited by Communist or Communist-dominated organizations
had been reaffirmed in 1958, but on the other hand a precedent
had already been set with this union in 1956. The minister of
external affairs, Howard Green, argued that "the sponsor was essentially a labour organization concerned with the negotiation of
fish prices and the fact that its leaders were Communists was not
the main issue." Cabinet accepted Green's argument as a "special case and without changing the general directive previously
issued on the subject." The Conservatives then demonstrated the
same double standard employed by their Liberal predecessors
four months later when they refused visas to two Soviet "women
professors" invited by a "Communist organization" to celebrate
International Women's Day in Toronto.[48]

In any case, the look-out lists were by no means restricted
to Communists, as such. Among the main targets in the 1950s
were campaigners for nuclear disarmament. Until the latter part
of the 1950s there was only one real organized focus for the peace
movement in Canada, the Canadian Peace Congress, led by the
charismatic and controversial James Endicott, a former United
Church missionary in China who had returned to lead the fight
against the bomb. The Congress was affiliated with the World
Peace Council, which was identified by Western intelligence
as the primary Soviet "front" organization operating within the
Western world.[49]

The Peace Councils were certainly close to the Soviet Union,
although in fact the Canadians were not unalloyed apologists, as
their critical stance towards the Soviet crushing of the Hungarian
revolt in 1956 demonstrated. The issue of nuclear disarmament
was an important one, and no other group in the early 1950s was
addressing the issue from a perspective critical of the philosophy
of nuclear strength. Many Canadians genuinely concerned about
the threat of nuclear annihilation were drawn to Peace Congress

meetings and signed petitions without becoming members of the Communist party or even becoming sympathetic to Communism as such. Unconcerned with such distinctions, the Canadian government declared virtual war against the Peace Congress in the 1950s, seeking thereby to stifle discussion critical of the nuclear policies of our American ally. Part of this repression was the use of immigration controls against speakers the Congress invited from abroad.

One banned visitor invited by the Congress was W. E. B. Du Bois, whose case has already been mentioned. In 1952 Cabinet decided to bar a member of the Belgian parliament from coming to address "the Communist controlled Peace Congress". And in 1953, Monica Felton, a British woman active in local government who had travelled to North Korea during the Korean War and had sympathetic, but by no means uncritical, things to say about the Communist side in that conflict, was banned for what the minister was quoted as calling "Communist sympathies". This set off a considerable flurry of public comment, some supportive, some critical. The *Ottawa Journal* posed the question "Why stop with Monica?", and the rival Ottawa *Citizen* more liberally asked its readers, "Who's afraid of Mrs. Felton?" When a delegation from the Canadian Congress of Labour raised the Felton case with the minister of citizenship and immigration, Walter Harris was unapologetic. He agreed that she was not a Communist "as far as could be ascertained", but she was "perhaps far more dangerous" because of her independence and respectability. "It might be said that by denying her entry, we were tampering with the right of free speech and that the Canadian people could be depended upon to sift the truth from fiction", the minister conceded, but he went on to assert that "it was not felt that facilities for entry must necessarily be granted to one who had no right of admission to Canada and no special claim on Canadian hospitality."[50]

To be sure, Canada was not on the prime circuit for visiting world celebrities, even those associated with the peace movement. It is likely that the state, if given the chance, would have barred some bigger names. The RCMP was expanding and sharpening up its look-out lists for its security officers at visa and entry posts throughout the 1950s. In 1954 External Affairs transmitted to the RCMP and Immigration a document entitled

"Personality Index of Communist-controlled International Organizations", which apparently originated from US intelligence sources. It included more than 700 names that could be used as guidance in preparation of look-out lists. The names included those of well-known Communists, but also of many individuals connected to Communism only by some association with the World Peace Council.[51]

It was quite a star-studded cast. From the world of politics came three future national leaders, Salvador Allende of Chile, Sékou Touré of Guinea, and Cheddi Jagan of Guyana. From the world of science came Nobel-prize–winner Linus Pauling, J. D. Bernal, and the distinguished French atomic scientists Irène and Frédéric Joliot-Curie. From the world of arts and letters came such leading figures of twentieth-century culture as Jean-Paul Sartre, Pablo Picasso, Bertolt Brecht, the Chilean poet Pablo Neruda, the Brazilian novelist Jorge Amado, the Czech writer Jiri Pelikan (today a leading dissident against Communist rule), and the French writer Louis Aragon (later inducted into the Legion of Honour by the president of France). There is no evidence that Jean-Paul Sartre or Pablo Picasso ever sought to sample the cultural and intellectual delights of Canada in the 1950s. If they had, it is likely that the guardians of the borders would have moved to protect Canadians from their subversive influence, especially if a local board of trade or chamber of commerce had alerted authorities quickly to the threat.

One aspect of the banning of visitors that had distinct domestic political ramifications was the device of characterizing the "auspices" under which visitors were invited. On this basis, the same person was sometimes allowed in and at other times barred, as was the case with Paul Robeson. This implied an official judgement on the "subversive" or "Communist" nature of Canadian organizations that were legal and legitimate associations. The US attorney general's practice of keeping a list of subversives was a highly illiberal one for a democratic society, and one that was eventually abandoned; but it did have the perverse advantage of offering a public reference of just who the state considered to be subversive. Canadian practice was in its way no less illiberal, but a good deal more devious. A shadowy, secret version of the attorney general's list was put to use in barring visitors according to who was sponsoring them. Eventually this proved too shadowy even for the bureaucrats, and by the late 1950s the

RCMP was asked to consolidate a list to be officially approved by the Security Panel. This would remain secret, of course, but at least the security establishment itself would have an agreed-upon reference.

In the summer of 1956, the panel had before it a list of "communist-controlled organizations in Canada...for the use of the Department of External Affairs whose missions...would use it to ascertain whether applicants for non-immigrant visas were sponsored by communist organizations in Canada." The bureaucrats judged the list to be too short and requested the RCMP to beef it up. At the beginning of 1957 the list was resubmitted, along with the RCMP's promise to provide up-to-date lists of executive members of the offending organizations. The list was approved, but it was to be provided in two separate versions, the complete version to go to External Affairs and a modified version to immigration officers in view of "the Commissioner's cautionary remarks" (censored under the Access to Information Act). It is unclear just what was at stake here. The full list apparently covered three legal-size sheets, but the entire three pages have been blanked out on the copy released to researchers, under the authority of a section of the Access to Information Act that excludes the release of intelligence material relating to "the detection, prevention or suppression of subversive or hostile activities." In the Citizenship and Immigration records is an undated list, probably the modified version, that lists fourteen "Communist party organizations", eight "front organizations"—including the Peace Congress, the Congress of Canadian Women, and the League for Democractic Rights—and sixteen agencies, such as travel agencies, bookstores, choirs, and a booking agency, allegedly controlled by the Communists.[52]

America in this era had become notorious for its political interference with travel. Canada, on the other hand, tended to escape notice due to its lesser world importance and its secret way of proceeding. The end result, however, was much the same.

CHAPTER EIGHT

Making and Unmaking Canadians: The Politics of Citizenship

If much effort was expended to keep foreign Communists or those associated with them out of Canada, there was also much bureaucratic ink spilled over the more difficult counterpart to that problem: how to keep Canadian Communists inside Canada, or at least prevent them from travelling to places where the Canadian state did not wish them to go. Cold War political controls over the movement of people across borders could not work in one direction only. As the Western allies conspired with one another to control the movements of Communists and other persons deemed to be risks to their national security states, they were faced with controlling the movement of their own citizens as well as blocking the entry of others. These controls raised more acute questions of liberal democratic practice, because citizens, even Communists or security risks, do have rights in liberal democracies, while aliens have few.

The United States showed considerable enthusiasm in tackling this question: passport cancellations and American citizens being forbidden to travel abroad were almost routine aspects of national security policy. The Internal Security Act of 1950 prohibited members of Communist or Communist-front organizations from obtaining or using passports. In 1952 the state department announced that Communist party members, those who supported the party's goals, and those whose activities abroad would further the interests of Communism would be denied passports, formalizing a policy already in place. As David Caute remarks, "It is not possible to estimate how many radicals were effectively denied a passport after 1947, because many of them, recognizing the inevitable, did not bother to apply." A series of court decisions in the late 1950s limited the government's arbitrary power in this field, but before the worst was over, people of the stature of the Nobel-prize–winning scientist Linus Pauling had been told that they had no freedom of movement outside the United States (the exact equivalent to the despised "totalitarian" controls exercised by the Soviets over the movements of their citizens).[1]

Canada could not escape its duties as junior Cold Warrior. In 1950 two cases presented themselves. The first was that of Leopold Infeld, a leading theoretical physicist of Polish origin who had been teaching at the University of Toronto since the beginning of the war. Infeld was active in the cause of peace and disarmament—as was his friend Albert Einstein—and this was itself enough to make him suspect in the atmosphere of the time. But when he announced his intention to spend a sabbatical year in his native Poland, the full fury of reactionary Canada burst forth. Proto-McCarthyites like George Drew charged that Infeld was going to betray atomic secrets to the Communists (a belief shared by the RCMP, although the slightest enquiry into his work would have revealed that he was not a specialist in atomic physics at all). The University of Toronto reversed its earlier view that his sabbatical plans were satisfactory, but Infeld decided to take his leave in Poland nevertheless. Infeld set sail, never to return to Canada. The RCMP noted that Infeld took part in a meeting of the World Peace Council after arriving in Warsaw and concluded that his "disloyalty" to Canada "must be of long standing". In Warsaw, he was told by the Canadian attaché to return his passport; Infeld took this move as tantamount to revocation of citizenship. The persecution of this distinguished scientist surely constitutes one of the worst examples of McCarthyism in this era in Canada.[2]

The second case concerned Raymond Boyer, a scientist who had been convicted of espionage as a result of the Gouzenko affair. Boyer was released from prison after serving his sentence; he apparently had a valid passport, and the government learned that he was about to sail from Montreal "for an unknown destination". Lester Pearson told his Cabinet colleagues that "it was not thought that he had any atomic information that could be of value to the USSR", but "there would undoubtedly be publicity when he left the country and the government would be charged with having facilitated his travel through issuance of a passport.... It seemed desirable", Pearson concluded, "that the passport should be impounded." It was. Boyer subsequently reapplied to travel only to the UK, France, and a couple of other Western European countries. He was then given a passport limited in validity to these specific destinations. Cabinet directed that these countries be notified "in order that they might have an opportunity of determining whether they would grant admission."[3]

The Boyer case was dealt with on an *ad hoc* basis. But what of general policy? The House Standing Committee on External Affairs had recommended that the policy of issuing passports to "known Communists" be examined. Pearson put before Cabinet the following considerations in favour of denying passports to certain persons:

> Passports could be withheld if it were considered desirable and such action would make travel by Communists more difficult. It would also render more difficult their training abroad in subversive activities to be carried out on return to Canada. It would exonerate the government from charges of facilitating their travel.... [A] feasible line of policy might be to withhold passports from persons on a list of avowed Communists compiled by the RCMP. Passports held, at the present time, by persons on the list could be invalidated.

Good liberal that he was, however, Pearson also presented the negative case to his colleagues:

> There were arguments against the policy of withholding passports. At the present time communism was not illegal in Canada and refusal of passports might be regarded as at least a qualified outlawry. The government might be charged with introducing Iron Curtain methods. Moreover, withholding passports would not

prevent travel by communists and would not make it at all impossible to go to the USSR for training. An intermediate line of action might be to require known communists, on application for passports, to indicate the countries for which they wished them to be made valid. The department could then communicate with such countries notifying them that the persons involved were known communists and asking them if they would be willing to allow the entry of such persons. Validity could then be granted only in cases where an affirmative answer was returned.[4]

Prime Minister St. Laurent suggested that it would be desirable to ascertain what other NATO countries did in this regard: "While isolated action by Canada might be the subject of criticism, it would be more acceptable if it were a policy common to NATO countries." When these countries were canvassed, it was discovered that only two, the United States and Fascist Portugal, denied or controlled passports to Communists. Some countries were interested in the idea, however, and France, which for "political reasons" would not initiate action (millions of its citizens belonged to the Communist party or voted for it), indicated that "it would welcome such action if it were taken by Canada."[5]

The liberal case against excessive use of passport controls was ably summarized by Gordon Robertson of the Privy Council Office in a lengthy memorandum. Recent American legislation and "the increasingly firm development of opinion against Communism in Canada" might "force the government to take a position" on this and on a number of related questions, Robertson conceded. There was, however, an important matter of principle that the current Red Scare ought not to obscure:

The Communist party is not outlawed and it is not an offence to be a Communist or to preach Communism. At the same time Communists, or persons suspected of active sympathy with Communism, are not permitted access to positions from which they could endanger the country. In substance, we are opposed to Communism and regard it as fundamentally opposed to our democratic system, but, in line with democratic principles, we are not prepared to outlaw it. That position would appear to provide the basis on which policy...should rest. We should prevent the entry of Communists into Canada or Canadian citizenship, and we should be anxious to get rid of Communists provided that we do not, in so doing, invade what might be regarded as human rights or the rights of citizenship.

The entry of immigrants could, on this principle, "be a point of maximum strictness in dealing with Communists", as Robertson recognized it indeed was. In this view, the dominant one at the time, immigrants were vested with few if any rights. Similar logic could be applied to deportation of landed immigrants on political grounds and to the issuance and revocation of Canadian citizenship. The matter of issuance of passports, however, raised issues of a different order:

A fundamental question is whether a passport should, in general, be regarded as a right of a Canadian citizen or not. Thus far we have, in the facts of our policy, regarded a passport as a right, while in theory maintained that it is not. We do not have any exit permit procedure but to the extent that the passport is the sine qua non of travel abroad, denial of a passport constitutes a refusal of egress and in that degree the application of "Iron Curtain" policy.

Robertson concluded that the denial of passports to persons named by the RCMP as Communists "should be avoided as long as the general policy against outlawing communism in Canada continues."[6]

Cabinet had in its hands a document listing fifteen "known Communists" whose passports the minister of external affairs recommended should be invalidated, and another 101 Communists who should be refused passports if applications were made. An alternative set of proposals was made by Norman Robertson, secretary to the Cabinet, on behalf of a special interdepartmental committee. The committee felt that to refuse passports, as such, was to erect an Iron Curtain "of our own". Instead, a "limited travel control" policy was outlined, whereby Communists would be issued passports with limited validity to countries that had previously been notified of the applicant's intention to travel there and had agreed to this. Such a policy would also allow for strict control and surveillance over Canadians wishing to travel to Soviet-bloc countries as well as for denial of such privileges to Communists. At the subsequent Cabinet meeting, some agreement in principle was achieved, and the ministers decided to have revised legislation drawn up to effect these changes. Gordon Robertson later informed a fellow bureaucrat of a remark made by Walter Harris, the minister of citizenship and immigration, that was not recorded in the Cabinet minutes. Harris had warned of US excesses and stated that "it would be dangerous to go too far". Harris "will want to examine very carefully" any amendments to the legislation, Robertson reported.[7]

The matter remained at a stalemate. Further attempts were made to consult NATO and Commonwealth countries on the subject, but as Arnold Heeney noted, "The results have not been very helpful. The majority of the countries are perplexed by precisely those problems which confront the Government of Canada and no satisfactory solution appears to have been found." By the spring of 1951 Heeney summed up the problems thus: "It would appear that the disadvantages of taking action directed specifically at the travel of Communists outweigh the advantages."

By this time bureaucratic attention was focused almost entirely on the question of Canadian Communists travelling to the Soviet Union "to get instructions on how they are to conduct Communist activities in Canada on behalf of the Soviet Union." The use of Canadian passports for such purposes was "repugnant to us", Heeney averred, but what could one do about it? One proposal was to make it an offence for a Communist to travel to the USSR. There were two objections to this. As stated, these two objections taken together offer a singular comment on the tortured "liberalism" of the civil service mandarins in this era:

> The first is that if the ban were applied only to those who are to be interned at the outbreak of war, the names of the people on the list for internment would by degrees become known to the Communist organization. The second objection is one of principle in that the Canadian Government would be strengthening the iron curtain which divides the Soviet world from the

free world and our declared policy is one of opposition to the creation by the Soviet Union of this iron
curtain.[8]

To fully appreciate the irony of Heeney's argument, it is
necessary to understand what was meant by "internment". In
the two world wars, thousands of persons had been rounded
up and interned in concentration camps under the authority of
the War Measures Act. Most of these had been interned on
ethnic grounds, such as the 22,000 Japanese "relocated" to the
interior from the West Coast during the Second World War.
Some had been interned on ideological grounds, whether as
Fascists sympathetic to the enemy or as Communists or left-
wing radicals, mainly because the state did not approve of their
opinions.

In the brittle atmosphere of the early Cold War, with the clouds
of world war once more dark on the horizon, elaborate plans were
set in motion for the "emergency" internment of those thought
to be sympathetic to the new enemy, Soviet Russia. Plans drawn
up in the early 1950s called for the RCMP to arrest 400 to 500
persons immediately upon the outbreak of war, with contingency
plans to round up five to eight times that number, or even, in
the event of invasion or civil disorder, as many as 18,000 to
20,000. Eighteen detention points were designated at various
locations around the country. Lists were kept up to date of
potential detainees. It was this list to which Heeney was alluding.
The 116 "known Communists" designated by External Affairs
for possible passport controls must have constituted the hard
core of the first group of 400 to 500 internees. The maintenance
in Canada of extensive lists of potential political prisoners thus
adds a piquant irony to Heeney's point about not wishing to
strengthen the Iron Curtain dividing the Soviets from the "free
world".[9]

Cabinet was presented with a modified set of options, short
of refusing passports or issuing travel permits. One device was
to avoid targeting Communists openly, but instead to insist
that all Canadians travelling to the Soviet bloc report their
intentions and movements to the Canadian government. This
could be explained as making it "easier for the Government to
give diplomatic protection" to its citizens in these dangerous
countries. Having to report their movements "might to some

extent inhibit their freedom of action and it would enable the Government to check on the persons concerned. It might also arouse in their minds some doubts and fears as to the use the Government might make of the information about their movement." Cabinet agreed in principle with this approach and within a couple of months authorized a change to that effect in the Canadian passport regulations. As for Communists travelling to "friendly" countries, it was thought useful to inform the countries concerned in advance when this was possible. At the insistence of Prime Minister St. Laurent, a proviso was added that such an arrangement should be reciprocal.[10]

This new "liberal" policy had scarcely come into effect when cries were heard for the government to be tougher. What set off the alarm bells this time was the 1952 voyage of James Endicott of the Canadian Peace Congress to southern China, where he made a broadcast supporting the current charges of the Chinese and North Korean governments that the Americans were employing germ warfare in the Korean War. Endicott returned to Canada, where he gave a series of speeches, beginning with a tumultuous rally at Maple Leaf Gardens in Toronto where 10,000 people filed in past screaming right-wing protesters to hear the charges reiterated. The truth about the charges is still uncertain, but thirty years later there is considerably more circumstantial evidence linking the Americans to bacteriological warfare in Korea than was known at the time.[11]

Few Canadians believed Endicott; most believed he was little short of a traitor, since Canadian troops were engaged against North Korean and Chinese armies in Korea. The rage of the Cold Warriors knew no bounds. Newspapers demanded that Endicott's passport be revoked. In the House of Commons, the Tories vied with one another—his passport should be revoked, said some; his citizenship should be revoked, said others. The well-known civil libertarian John Diefenbaker wanted to know if Endicott's statements were not treasonable under the Criminal Code. In fact Cabinet discussed at length laying a charge of treason against the peace campaigner, finally deciding against it because of the magnitude of the penalty, death; but also because the Americans were reluctant to testify in public that they had not employed germ warfare. Canadians were thus spared the irony of a Canadian being tried for treason in a Canadian court for statements made not against Canada but against the United States.[12]

Reluctant to press treason charges, the government was still mulling over possible ways of barring Endicott from travelling abroad and publicly embarrassing Canada again in the eyes of Uncle Sam. One middle-range official of the immigration department had earlier taken it on himself to concoct, by way of an ingenious technicality, a case for deporting the entire Endicott family to China, where Endicott had been born in 1898 to a missionary family. Cooler counsels were also heard, especially that of Escott Reid in External Affairs, who questioned, as being contrary to "our national tradition", the imposition of "a penalty on a citizen for opinions expressed by him", without any due process in the judicial system.[13]

Pearson sent a long memorandum to Cabinet in the summer of 1952 reconsidering the question of passports for travel to the Soviet bloc. "There are no particularly helpful Canadian precedents upon which to base a decision to refuse passports to Communists", Pearson wrote. Raymond Boyer had had his passport impounded but then returned. "The difficulties encountered with regard to Dr. Endicott", he went on, "have served to emphasize how hard it is to arrive at acceptable decisions in matters of this kind." The British were extremely reluctant to refuse passports. The Australians had tried to control travel by Communists to the east bloc, but that had proved ineffectual and caused inconvenience for non-Communists. In the United States, stern action had been taken: almost 200 passports had been refused or confiscated by 1952.[14]

The Canadian policy, which was just a year old, had proven highly ineffective. There might be many who failed to report their travel to the east bloc; finding "conclusive evidence upon which to base decisions to impound passports" would, in truth, be "a very difficult matter". Yet, Pearson wrote, "we must take into account the fact that there will be from time to time a certain amount of agitation for the government to take more positive steps than it has done so far." Two courses were open: to "resist this agitation" or to accept the desirability of further restrictions, such as a "Red Card" warning system in the passport office to deny passports to those on the RCMP Red list, or placing tighter checks on the movements of Canadians abroad with a view to prosecuting violators.

Cabinet could not decide which way to go. Then Prime Minister St. Laurent intervened in the discussion to point out that "as no person had a right to a passport and as a passport could be withheld at the discretion of the Secretary of State for External Affairs", no specific decision was really required. "It might be best simply to note the intention of the Secretary of State for External Affairs to refuse to issue passports...when the travel abroad of the persons concerned might be a threat to the national security." It was no doubt with evident relief that the ministers immediately accepted this eminently Canadian solution: pure administrative discretion with no formal guidelines in legislation or even in specific government policy.[15]

It seems that no more was heard of this issue from that time on. There have apparently been no cases since 1952 of Canadians refused passports on political grounds. The external affairs ministers from Pearson on have apparently not discovered cases sufficiently alarming to constitute threats to the national security in the foreign travel of Communists or other subversive Canadians. In the United States, court decisions based on the constitutional rights of American citizens severely restricted the government's freedom of action in this area, and the entire process of denying Americans the right to travel freely seems to have eventually disappeared in the face of a general public disapproval. This is one Cold War device that not even the Reagan administration has tried to resurrect. Canada's record in this regard appears relatively clean. However, Canada collaborated with the Americans in their use of passport controls, as was revealed in 1956 by immigration minister Walter Harris when he told his Cabinet colleagues that Canada would discontinue the practice of requiring landed immigrants from the United States to hold a valid US passport. In the past, Harris confided, this requirement had had the "main purpose" of ensuring some security check (that is, American security risks would not have been issued passports). "A recent decision of the Supreme Court of the U.S.", he went on, "has reduced the usefulness of the passport procedure as a security check."[16]

If denying passports to Canadian citizens was altogether too thorny a problem, there was a more pre-emptory method of dealing with citizens who offended politically. In policy discussions, the passport question was usually linked with the more drastic matter of revoking citizenship altogether; the govern-ment thus avoided the difficulty of coming to terms with the rights of citizens. Revocation of citizenship was of limited util-ity in one sense since it could only deal with immigrants who had been naturalized. No one was ever able to devise a means whereby native-born Canadians could be stripped of their cit-izenship involuntarily (although, as we shall see, it could be done to the Canadian-born children of naturalized Canadians who had had their citizenship revoked). But for the long-despised breed of "foreign-born Communists", a cherished target of those Canadians who combined xenophobic nativism with strident anti-Communism, becoming a Canadian turned out to be a reversible operation.

This process of "unmaking Canadians" had a long history be-fore the Cold War. A notable example was the case of the leading Canadian Communist Sam Carr, who had come to Canada from Russia at a very early age. He had applied for and been granted Canadian citizenship in 1931. Later that year, Carr was arrested along with seven other Communists and prosecuted for member-ship in a seditious organization in the famous case of *R. v. Buck et al.* under the notorious section 98 of the Criminal Code, which was later repealed. Imprisoned for his political beliefs, Carr was retroactively stripped of his naturalization by order-in-council. Pleas that he be allowed to regain his citizenship fell on deaf and hostile ears. Carr himself could not help but note that he alone of the naturalized foreign-born defendants had been stripped of his citizenship—and that he alone was Jewish.

In 1940 Carr was once again under a warrant for arrest for being a member of a banned party, this time under the War Measures Act. He went into hiding, later surrendering himself along with other Communist leaders for a symbolic day of internment before being freed to join the Canadian army. After serving his adopted country, Carr was granted citizenship again. In 1946 he was ordered arrested once more under the War Measures Act, this time as one of the accused in the Gouzenko affair. Again Carr went into hiding, but later he surrendered, was tried and convicted of passport offences, and served time in prison again. The Naturalization Branch had no grounds for revoking his 1945 certificate of naturalization (under law, he would have had to have been convicted of high treason). Carr still lives in Toronto, now in his eighties.[17]

The debate about revoking the citizenship of naturalized Canadians was renewed in the early years of the Cold War by the return of Yugoslav Canadians to their homeland to assist in socialist reconstruction under Tito. As we have seen, the departure of more than a thousand Yugoslav Canadians on successive sailings of the Yugoslav ship the *Radnik* galvanized official displeasure at the apparent propaganda coup for Communism—after all, Communism was supposed to create refugees, not attract them from the capitalist West.[18]

The Yugoslav departures were not the only well-publicized case drawing government attention to revocation of citizenship at this time. Another, as described earlier, was that of Leopold Infeld, the physicist whose proposed sabbatical in Poland was blown up into a national security crisis by the witch-hunters. Lester Pearson responded to them by recommending to Cabinet that the proposed two-year rule be reduced further to a one-year period, so that Infeld could be denaturalized on the basis of his planned year in Poland. Six years later, when the Tories came to office, the knife was twisted once more. A vindictive aspect of the 1951 changes had been to remove the right of a child of parents whose naturalization had been revoked to reclaim citizenship on reaching the age of majority. In 1958, Infeld's two Canadian-born children, then teenagers living with their parents in Poland, were notified that their citizenship had been cancelled under this provision by a special order-in-council.[19]

One noteworthy aspect of the 1951 changes was that the section stipulating that citizenship could be revoked for persons who resided at least two years in the country of their former nationality was passed through Cabinet on the express understanding that it would be invoked "ordinarily" in the case of persons from Communist countries—excluding Yugoslavia, since it had already been deemed expedient by 1951 to readmit the politically acceptable among the *Radnik* returnees, even though they had been the original inspiration for the amendment. On the other hand, Cabinet understood that the section would not "ordinarily" be invoked in the case of Canadians who returned to non-Communist countries—"except if there is reason to believe that their conduct is prejudicial to the best interests of Canada."[20]

Even Gordon Robertson, one of the more liberal of the civil servants dealing with these questions in the early 1950s, proved to be surprisingly bloody-minded when it came to revocation of citizenship. In the same memorandum in which he had discouraged withholding passports from citizens, Robertson not only echoed Pearson's call for a one-year rule for residence in Communist countries but added a suggestion that the Citizenship Act should be amended as well to allow "revocation for disaffection or disloyalty of persons in Canada"; he also urged "more active use of revocation against persons who are active Communists and who can properly be regarded as 'disloyal'."[21]

The minister of citizenship and immigration, Walter Harris, took up these suggestions in a presentation to Cabinet, adding the proviso that in the case of persons living in Canada, revocation should take place only "after conviction by a court of law for sedition, espionage, treason, or any other offence involving disaffection or disloyalty." The latter point was related specifically in a Cabinet document to the case of Fred Rose, the Communist MP convicted of espionage in the Gouzenko affair. The existing Citizenship Act was ineffective in stripping Rose of his naturalization, since he had been convicted not of sedition or treason but of espionage, which was not mentioned in it. Harris's suggestion would thus cover Rose. Perhaps the measure specified too particular a target for an act of general legislation, for the change was not incorporated.[22]

Rose solved the problem for the government when he returned to his native Poland in 1953. Ironically, part of the reason for his departure seems to have been that he was being shunned by his former comrades as a political embarrassment. A secret RCMP report in September 1953 stated that since his release from prison, "he has apparently been inactive politically and unable to re-establish himself." Yet his political harmlessness did nothing to weaken the Canadian government's quest for vengeance. In 1956, when Rose had been absent from Canada for over two years, Citizenship and Immigration sent him a notice of intention to revoke citizenship. He was given two months to indicate whether he wished to have objections referred to a citizenship court. Rose's dossier reveals that he wrote "a long letter to complain about the treatment he had received in Canada and to say that he intended to endeavour to keep his Canadian citizenship." His objections were heard but dismissed. In the spring of 1957, Rose was stripped of his citizenship by order-in-council, on the grounds that he had been residing in a Communist country for over two years. Years later, when Rose's daughter was married in Canada, he wrote to the prime minister asking to be allowed to attend the wedding; permission was refused. Again in the 1960s an attempt to visit was denied. Just before he died, his daughter was refused a ministerial permit that would have allowed him to end his days with his family.[23]

Another defendant in the Gouzenko affair, David Shugar, who was acquitted of all charges in court, lost his job as a scientist in the civil service and found it very difficult to work in Canada, since the RCMP had disclosed to private employers that he was a Communist. Eventually Shugar returned to his native Poland. The government threatened to revoke his citizenship, as it had Rose's.[24] But Shugar, a less visible symbol than Rose, benefited from a change in government in 1957 and a slow decline in the intensity of Cold War hostilities in the late 1950s; his citizenship never was revoked.

Early in 1958 the Diefenbaker government brought in amendments to the Citizenship Act that repealed the discretionary two-year residence rule, replacing it with a ten-year rule and adding a provision that revocation could be effected if a person committed a treasonable offence abroad and refused to return to stand trial. When the amending bill was put before the House of Commons, the former Liberal immigration minister, Jack Pickersgill, asked his Tory successor, Davie Fulton, whether he was "at all troubled by the fact that the citizenship of Fred Rose could not have been revoked if this action had been taken earlier?" Fulton replied, "In anything that will be done it will be necessary to take such a situation into account and to ensure that those guilty of such actions as Mr. Fred Rose could not continue to claim the rights and privileges of Canadian citizens."[25]

Another provision "included to deal with such cases as those of Sam Carr and Fred Rose", in the words of a Cabinet discussion, would have allowed the revocation of citizenship if in the opinion of the Governor in Council a person "did not take the oath of allegiance in good faith when he acquired citizenship"; it was strongly opposed by the Liberals as excessively arbitrary. The Tories readily agreed to drop the clause, particularly when it was pointed out in Cabinet that "this provision had some similarities to one which had been used in World War I and which had made the Conservative party unpopular for years with many ethnic groups throughout the country." Yet even after the

1958 changes, the government continued to punish Fred Rose, Leopold Infeld, and Infeld's children.[26]

The last vestiges of the Cold War policies were finally washed away in the new Citizenship Act in 1977. Under present law, citizenship can be revoked only in cases where it was obtained by false representation or fraud. By the 1980s, in the words of the McDonald commission report, "the granting of Canadian citizenship can no longer be considered a privilege bestowed by prerogative of the Crown.... Citizenship is a right which can be claimed after three years by any immigrant."[27] What happened in the 1940s and 1950s was thus a detour from a liberal destination, but in the course of the detour both individual rights and the sovereignty of Parliament were bent by administrative discretion to the prevailing winds of the Cold War.

The screening net at the points of entry to Canada was not, and never could be, foolproof. But a second door could still be closed on an immigrant who roused the suspicions of the security police after he or she had entered the country: citizenship could be denied. An immigrant had to wait five years under pre-1977 law before becoming eligible for citizenship. Although there was never any specific legislative authorization for its role, the RCMP security service was thus provided with the opportunity to legitimately deploy its massive apparatus for the surveillance and infiltration of private associations within Canada, for the purpose of gathering information with which citizenship applicants could be assessed for political trustworthiness. For example, the RCMP security service kept close surveillance over a left-wing Ukrainian group called the Workers' Benevolent Association, and it congratulated itself when in 1948 a county court judge declined to recommend naturalization papers for an applicant who belonged to the WBA, which the judge described as a Communist organization.[28]

A complicating factor was that citizenship was normally granted by citizenship courts, and the kind of information gathered by the RCMP either was not of a quality to be entered in court proceedings or, as the RCMP claimed, could not be entered because its sources could not be revealed. A 1950 amendment to the Canadian Citizenship Act gave the minister of citizenship and immigration discretion not to grant certificates of citizenship, even when the courts had decided in favour of an applicant.

By the fall of 1950 there had accumulated eighty-four cases, approved by the courts, of applicants about whom the RCMP had adverse security reports. Of these, twenty-one were "active" or "known" Communists, sixteen were non-active members of "Communist or Communist-controlled organizations", and the rest fell into a set of miscellaneous categories: subscribers to Communist papers, married to subversive spouses, attendance at a social function sponsored by Communists, speaking "in favour of Communism", working on behalf of Communist candidates in city elections, making monetary donations to "Communist causes", and "has framed portraits of Communist heroes in home". This miscellany offers a revealing look at the kinds of intelligence gathered by the RCMP snoopers and their informants about the private lives and thoughts of individuals.[29]

By the time this list reached the Security Panel for advice on policy one month later, it had grown from 84 to 120 cases. The panel was told that judges must reject for cause, but security was never publicly cited, as a matter of government policy. This was sticky enough, but worse was that "some judges refused to take RCMP reports as evidence, unless offered as sworn evidence, which would place the RCMP in an invidious position to the extent that such action might compromise valuable sources of information." Gordon Robertson, as chairman of the Security Panel, argued that "any person identified with the Communist Party, whether by affiliation with a Communist-dominated group or as an active party member, had proved himself unworthy of enjoying the fruits of Canadian citizenship. He suggested that this fact alone might be accepted as adequate justification for the withholding of a certificate at the Minister's discretion."[30]

The panel recommended that applicants who were active or known Communists be rejected by ministerial order, but that those who were in the category of non-active members of Communist-controlled groups, as well as those who fell into the potpourri of activities considered suspect by the RCMP, should be held for a two-year period provided by the act; these cases would be decided on their individual merits in the interim, by a special committee made up of representatives of the RCMP, Immigration, and External Affairs. The number of applications being held had risen to 160 by the time the matter reached Cabinet three months later. Cabinet rubber-stamped the procedure.[31]

In 1957 statistics were assembled by the interdepartmental committee on its first five years of operation. Of the 1,874 applications reviewed, 971 were accepted and 903 rejected. Of the applications referred to the committee, 81 per cent were from immigrants from Soviet-bloc countries, and 83 per cent of all those rejected were applicants from those countries. Almost a third of the rejected applications were from Ukrainians or from Poles, a category that until 1955 included Ukrainians. Applications by immigrants from non-Communist countries, of which there were fewer, generally had a much higher rate of approval. What is more interesting yet is that almost all the applications referred to the committee were from immigrants who had entered Canada before the war (at least 80 per cent). In other words, the entire procedure became a retroactive application of Cold War screening to those whose entry to Canada had antedated its inception, and it was used mainly against those associated with left-wing ethnic organizations from Eastern Europe. The scope of the security apparatus was rather greater than might appear on the surface, reaching backwards in time as well as shaping the future of Canada's immigrant communities.[32]

Finally, the most menacing spectre of all for those immigrants denied citizenship or awaiting word is deportation. The threat of deportation has always hung over immigrants, especially in the interwar years, when tens of thousands were shipped out for reasons ranging from simply being on relief during the Depression to alleged subversive activities. In the United States during the early years of the Cold War, 163 "subversives" were deported, but many more were arrested for deportation and suffered harassment and severe economic losses while fighting the charges. Intimidation may have been as much the aim as actual deportation. Most of the American deportation cases were of persons who had been living for many decades in America. In his comprehensive survey of Cold War repression in the US, David Caute refers to the "deportation terror".[33]

Canada seriously considered joining in this political persecution. Gordon Robertson, for example, mused about the possibility of deporting all non-Canadians associated with Communism. The argument Robertson had found convincing against refusing passports to Canadian Communists—that the party was a legal entity in Canada—left him relatively indifferent in regard to deportation:

> Our tolerance of communism is a marginal one and based entirely on our conception of the rights of citizens to freedom of thought, etc. Non-Canadians without domicile [those who had lived for less than five years in Canada] do not have the full rights of citizenship. In a sense they are in Canada on sufferance, and we need not suffer them as Communists if we do not wish it. Persons with domicile have a somewhat stronger position and perhaps should not be as strictly dealt with.[34]

Insp. John Leopold of the RCMP security service, the most famous Red-hunter in the Mounties, wanted "all undesirables of the communist type" deported, whether or not they had domicile, and drafted some very sweeping proposals for changes to the Immigration Act to accomplish this end. These were too sweeping for the taste of the government, as it turned out, and Leopold's proposals did not advance very far. But that did not end the matter.[35]

The legislation already on the books gave considerable scope for deportation, if the government wished to use it. It is not possible to specify precisely how many people were deported for political reasons in this period, since security was never cited as the grounds for deportation. From official statistics on deportation presented by the Immigration Branch, however, some idea can be gleaned. From 1947–48 until 1953–54 (the last year statistics were made public), 3,242 persons were deported. When deportations for medical, criminal, and economic grounds are subtracted, 1,956 remain who were deported for "other civil causes". It is unclear what this category described, but it certainly would include deportations for political reasons. Since the main non-"political" causes for deportation in the Immigration Act fall within the medical, criminal, and economic categories, it is likely that many of the "other civil causes" were in fact security cases. If this is so, it is apparent that Canada was still using deportation as a political weapon, perhaps not as much as it had before the war, but with a frequency that rivalled the American use of deportation. In Canada, however—in contrast to the US, with its constitutional safeguards—a greater proportion of deportation attempts were successful, because of the greater use of administrative discretion and the lesser role of our judiciary.[36]

Who was being deported? That question is not easy to answer. That it was not Eastern Europeans is evident from a Cabinet document of 1960, which stated that since 1948 it had been government practice not to deport anyone to Iron Curtain countries for fear of "reprisal and prosecution", although a list of potential deportees was in fact maintained "in the event that deportation becomes practicable". (It was still not considered practicable in the late 1980s.) There were, however, some voluntary repatriations to the East.[37]

One group was discernible by the early 1950s in departmental statistics: about one-third of all deportations were to Britain. This was the inevitable result of one feature of immigration security in this period: the exemption of British immigrants from screening before arrival. It was noted earlier that in the early 1950s British immigrant workers were running afoul of the security screening imposed in defence industries in what the Security Panel felt were somewhat alarming numbers.[38] Such workers would most often be sent back to Britain. Thus a privilege for the "mother country" in immigration screening was being compensated for at the other end by the most direct and brutal of remedies: deportation.

There was at least one case in this era of an individual who had lived and worked in Canada for many years, at a relatively high level of public notice, and was then ordered deported on strictly political grounds. Raymond Arthur Davies, born Rudolph Shohan in Poland, had immigrated to the United States in 1913. At some point he had entered Canada, and in 1936 he obtained a Canadian passport, apparently stating that he was a Canadian by birth. Davies had become a left-wing journalist, associated at one point with the Communist party, who wrote widely about the Ukrainian Canadians in such mainstream press outlets as *Saturday Night* and the *Toronto Star*. In 1943 he had published a book entitled *This Is Our Land: Ukrainian Canadians Against Hitler*, which had roused the vituperative indignation of the anti-Communist publicist and ideologue Watson Kirkconnell. His 1943 pamphlet *Our Ukrainian Loyalists: The Ukrainian Canadian Committee* was in part an attack on Davies. Davies then went to Moscow, where he worked as a wartime correspondent and was sometimes heard on the CBC, as well as the Mutual Broadcasting Service in the United States. Upon his return he embarked upon a national speaking tour in 1946, sponsored by various pro-Communist organizations (and closely followed by RCMP agents).[39]

Davies did not carry on this high-profile political role for long. Apparently disillusioned with Communism, he drifted apart from the party—which, for its part, shortly lost interest in him as a publicist. Working in a small importing business in the postwar years, Davies might have expected simply to fade into obscurity. It was not to be. The RCMP kept him under surveillance, even though the Communists had nothing more to do with him. Then in the early 1950s, during the height of the deportation campaigns in the McCarthy-era United States, it came to the attention of the security people in Ottawa that ex-Communists acting as paid informers for the FBI in the Immigration and Naturalization Service were about to expose Davies' past. "Some kind of hue and cry" might then arise in Canada, it was suggested: would it not be prudent for Canada to do something first, "in order to avoid having to do it after the facts have come to light in the U.S.A."? Still, if he were to be deported it would have to be to the United States, which did not want him. The bureaucrats dithered.[40]

Then Jack Pickersgill wrote Davies' sentence in his own hand on one of his officials' memos: "He certainly should be prosecuted and, if possible, deported. Why should we have to keep him here just because the Americans would prefer not to have him?" Amid sensational and utterly nonsensical newspaper stories about another spy scandal, Davies was arrested and ordered deported. For reasons that remain unclear, the deportation was never carried out. Instead Davies was charged with passport fraud regarding his 1936 application, convicted, and sentenced to the maximum penalty of two years in Kingston Penitentiary. The prosecution at his trial made much of his former Communist activities, and in passing sentence the judge declared, "In these days when passports are used for purposes inimical to Crown and country, obtaining a passport under false pretences is a very serious offence."[41]

If the politically neutered Davies fell into this trap after decades as a Canadian for having lied on a passport application many years earlier, it is an instructive contrast to note the considerate treatment by the same government of another, rather less harmless immigrant who was recommended for deportation to the United States two years later. Hal Banks, the notorious labour racketeer, had been imported into Canada in the late 1940s as a Cold Warrior on the waterfront, to mastermind the smashing of the Communist Canadian Seamen's Union. This he had accomplished with consummate brutality; in the process he had established a reign of terror and corruption on the Great Lakes, eventually broken only when he left the country in the 1960s to avoid criminal charges.

Banks had garnered a criminal record in the United States before entering Canada, and he had also been convicted in this country. This record would normally have precluded his acceptance as a landed immigrant. Yet when he applied, he was given a special application that omitted the usual question about criminal convictions. In 1954 Banks was recommended for deportation by a board of inquiry, but Cabinet stepped in. The minister of citizenship and immigration explained sympathetically that Banks had come in "to clean up a difficult labour situation" and that "he had been of real service to Canada". The record of the Cabinet discussion has been heavily censored (under a provision of the Access to Information Act that supposedly protects the privacy of individuals), but the decision is clear: the board was overruled, and Banks was allowed to remain a Canadian labour boss for another decade. One of the ministers who was particularly strong on Banks' behalf was Jack Pickersgill, the same Pickersgill who had been so tough with Raymond Arthur Davies.[42]

When the Diefenbaker Conservatives came to office in 1957, they were troubled by the deportation question. Within months of the election victory, the new Cabinet was presented with the delicate case of an applicant for citizenship who had joined the Communist party after landing in Canada. A deportation hearing was scheduled before an appeal board. As Davie Fulton, acting minister of citizenship and immigration, explained to his somewhat baffled colleagues, if the government contested his appeal it could only be on the grounds that the individual belonged to the Communist party, yet this party was a legal association in Canada. To make matters worse, his original entry had been quite in order, since his conversion to Communism had occurred after he had arrived. Could a "landed" immigrant— a person whose application for admission as an immigrant had been accepted and who was already in Canada—be deported for carrying on an activity that was legal according to Canadian law? An alternative to this dilemma was to throw the matter to the courts for a judicial opinion on the validity of the previous government's interpretation of the Immigration Act.

The ministers were clearly perplexed at this "anomalous, absurd situation". They decided to let the appeal board go ahead, with the hope (apparently fulfilled) that it would quash the deportation order, thus removing the difficulty. Fulton himself wondered about the "arbitrary and unreasonable" barrier to entry erected against immigrants for associating with a party that was legal in Canada; he mused that "Canada was old enough to allow the discussion of communism within the country without danger to the state." The Cabinet thought it likely that they would have to deal in future with some of the questions of principle involved.[43]

Anomalous and absurd situations kept cropping up. One was that of a Canadian of Yugoslav origin who married a Yugoslav woman on a visit to his native country. She was then ruled an unacceptable immigrant because of her husband's political associations in Canada. Faced with punishing the wife of a Canadian not for what she had done but for something her husband had done—an act that was legal in Canada and could not be used against him since he was a citizen—the government threw up its hands and made an exception. In another case, a Chinese student at the University of Toronto met and married a Canadian woman, who had since given birth to a child. When he applied for landed-immigrant status, the RCMP discovered that he had been an "active Communist" while at university in China, and a deportation order was made. The police refused to make public its security information and told the minister that it "would not stand behind the security aspect of the case in court." Anticipating a public outcry under the circumstances, the government called a halt to the deportation.[44] Exasperation seemed the order of the day in such cases.

Particularly frustrating were the cases where deportations were indicated but impossible to carry out because of the policy of not forcibly removing persons to Communist countries. As the Conservatives discovered, this policy, once it became known abroad, was seen as an open invitation to inadmissible persons from such countries to gain entry as visitors and then stay. Sailors from east-bloc countries such as Yugoslavia and the Baltic states began jumping ship in Canadian ports. After the Cuban revolution, supporters of the former regime began arriving in

Canada with the obvious intention of staying. Grumble as they might, Canadian officials could do little about it.[45]

The most publicized case of deportation during the Diefenbaker years was that of Irene Rebrin. Rebrin was a stateless person, born of White Russian parents in Peking, who had fled to South America with her family at the time of the Communist revolution in China. She had entered Canada from Brazil on a six-month non-immigrant visa, and in the course of her stay had been offered a position teaching Slavonic languages at the University of British Columbia. Armed with the offer of gainful employment, she applied for landed status. The government ordered her deported. Cabinet was told that it was her "personal security record" that was at issue. The public was never informed of the details of the security information allegedly held against her; Prime Minister Diefenbaker read the file and told his ministers that "the particulars of the case could not be revealed to the public because such action would lead to the drying up of the sources of information and might imperil security agents"—the usual excuse. The faculty of UBC offered its enthusiastic support for Rebrin's cause, and numerous questions were raised in Parliament and the press. Cabinet discussed the case on a number of occasions, finally deciding that a statement would be made that it "would be contrary to the interests of Canada's security to interfere with the execution of the deportation order." Brazil agreed to accept her. Rebrin, however, would not give up and took the matter to the courts.[46]

In 1961 the case of *Rebrin v. Bird and the Minister of Citizenship and Immigration* arrived at the Supreme Court of Canada. The justices of that court, taking a narrowly technical view of the matter, ruled that she was a prohibited person on the grounds that she had not entered Canada with an immigrant visa. Security was not mentioned in the decision. Deportation was again imminent. There was one complication, however: Rebrin had brought a libel suit against the Toronto *Telegram* for accusations published about her in that right-wing newspaper. The minister allowed her to stay until the case came to a decision. As time went by, her ties to the university where she taught became closer and the possibility of actually executing the deportation order became ever more remote. Finally in 1963, when a new Liberal government took office, the case was reviewed and the deportation order was dropped. The security reason that had seemed so compelling just a few years earlier (whatever it might have been) had apparently lost its force. Canada, and UBC, gained a teacher and scholar.[47]

CHAPTER NINE

The End of the
Cold War Consensus

Early in 1953 Stalin died. Within months, the newly elected president of the United States, Gen. Dwight D. Eisenhower, had overseen an armistice in Korea. A cease-fire followed in Indo-China, where the French had been defeated by the Communist Vietminh. In 1954, Sen. Joseph McCarthy, whose witch-hunting investigations of "Communists" had driven the Cold War atmosphere in the United States to hysterical pitch, was publicly discredited in the nationally televised "Army–McCarthy" hearings. In 1955 an agreement was concluded between East and West whereby Soviet troops withdrew from Austria in exchange for the official neutrality of that country. Despite some severe ups and downs in the East–West relationship, including the twin crises of the Hungarian revolt and the British and French invasion of Egypt in 1956, the general movement in the late 1950s was towards a thaw in the Cold War.

The 1960s witnessed conflicting trends: on the one hand, there were such shocks as the Cuban missile crisis of 1962, the massive American intervention in Vietnam, and the Soviet invasion of Czechoslovakia in 1968; on the other, there was a gradual movement towards a settlement of outstanding issues in contention between the two superpowers that came to fruition briefly in the 1970s.

The period from the late 1950s through the 1960s was one in which many Canadians gradually disengaged themselves from the fervent Cold War partisanship of the late 1940s and early 1950s, when NATO was born and Canadian troops fought Communist soldiers in Korea. Although the intrusion of the Cold War into Canadian life seemed to reach a peak in the early 1960s, when the debate over nuclear weapons for Bomarc missiles led to direct American intervention in Canadian politics and the collapse and defeat of the Diefenbaker Tory government, the appearance was deceiving. There was a genuine debate between Canadians over the Cold War, a debate that had not really existed in the crucial years of the late 1940s. There was rising opposition to the dominance of Cold War thinking and to American hegemony over Canadian life. Voices of dissent were heard on issues of nuclear armaments and on Third World struggles; the dissenters were no longer simply apologists for the USSR, but instead pointed to a third way, a path of Canadian neutrality and disalignment from the East–West military bloc system. With the growing revulsion against the bloody US war in Vietnam and the rise of left-wing political dissent on university campuses in the late 1960s, these voices acquired sufficient resonance, and respectability, that the government of Pierre Trudeau undertook in the late 1960s and early 1970s a review of Canadian foreign policy that, however modestly and hesitantly, pointed Canada towards a more "national" focus for its efforts abroad.

Yet throughout this period of emergent *détente* and drifting away from strict Cold War discipline, the elements of the national security state, established in the 1940s and early 1950s, did not fade away. Indeed, they were little modified. While the proportion of the Canadian budget spent on defence declined considerably after the end of the Korean War, the ubiquitous apparatus of security and intelligence, surveillance and control—exercised through such agencies as the RCMP security service, military intelligence, and the civilian security establishment in Ottawa—continued to whir and click as it always had.[1] The security screening of public employees continued apace, including a ferocious witch-hunt for homosexual civil servants that peaked in the early 1960s. The Mounties continued to gather information on the private lives, political activities, and beliefs of individual Canadians and to store this information in their vast files. They continued to infiltrate trade unions, political parties, citizens' associations, peace groups, and university clubs with undercover agents, many of them recruited by methods that were sometimes little short of blackmail. And the Cold War establishment continued to offer its privileged counsels within the state against liberalization and against moves to reduce Cold War tensions: after all, they certainly knew which side their bread was buttered on.

Nowhere was this dogged persistence of the thinking and methods of the Cold War establishment more evident than in immigration and citizenship security. A change in government and an attempted internal reform of the process took place in the late 1950s, followed by two external reviews of the entire immigration policy field: the Royal Commission on Security at the end of the 1960s, and a major overhaul of the Immigration Act in the late 1970s. Neither of these did more than scratch the surface of the immigration security process; some never even scratched, despite the growing disillusionment of Canadians with the old Cold War mould and despite some severe external shocks to the old thinking. Among the latter were the collapse of the international Communist monolith of years past, with the Sino–Soviet split and its divisive ramifications throughout the left world-wide, the influx of American political refugees during the Vietnam War, and the challenge of left-wing refugees from right-wing totalitarian violence. None of these developments appears to have had much impact on the thinking of the security establishment as reflected in the practice of immigration and citizenship control. *"Plus ça change, plus c'est la même chose"* appears to be its motto.

By the late 1950s there were ample reasons for the government to reassess the entire immigration program and its administration. The immediate postwar period with its influx of displaced persons was effectively over. Longer-term planning for levels and types of immigration that would be desirable from economic and social perspectives was becoming increasingly necessary. Charges that immigration policies were racially discriminatory (which, of course, was exactly what their framers had intended) and demands that they should be "colour blind" were beginning to gather momentum in some quarters of Canadian opinion. Immigration questions were more frequently coming to the fore in partisan political debate, and public attention was being drawn to problems in administration in ways that were increasingly embarrassing to the government. One such problem was dramatically highlighted by a Supreme Court decision in 1956 that threw the selection and exclusion process into turmoil for a few months.

Under the highly discretionary powers of the Immigration Act, officials of the department were designated as "special enquiry officers" for the purpose of determining who could enter and remain in Canada and who could be deported. This practice came into question in a 1956 case in which a deportation order against an American woman with landed-immigrant status in Canada was quashed by the Supreme Court. More important than the verdict itself was the opinion of the court that in delegating this authority to officials, the government had acted *ultra vires*, or beyond its constitutional power. The effect of the Brent case, as it was known, was drastic. As the minister of immigration at the time, Jack Pickersgill, said later, the Brent case "in effect destroyed the whole administrative basis for the selection, admission and exclusion of prospective immigrants and visitors." At the time Pickersgill told his Cabinet colleagues, "The present state of the law is as bad as it could be. It seemed that anybody, no matter how undesirable, who had been able to get into Canada could remain there provided he had a competent lawyer to take his case up in the courts."[2]

Officials had to scramble during the months following the decision to come up with new regulations that would be acceptable. At the heart of the new regulations was section 20, which specified that "landing in Canada of any person is prohibited" except for four categories of national origin, which were arranged in what amounted to a hierarchy of most to least welcome, beginning with British subjects from the white Commonwealth, Americans, and native French citizens, and ending with a category for applicants from certain unspecified countries. Pickersgill indicated in a secret Cabinet document that the fourth category "will be used to restrict the movement of Asians into Canada." Ease of entry was directly related to these gradations of acceptability. During the Cabinet discussions it was revealingly suggested that section 20 "illustrated more clearly than ever before that the Immigration Act was really a prohibition act with exemptions."[3]

In a "prohibition act with exemptions", the security screening process had a privileged status that was in no way challenged by the new regulations enacted to conform to the Brent decision. Yet even in the highly discriminatory and discretionary terms of the Immigration Act, the security process could be troubling to officials whose liberal consciences were stirred from time to time, however fitfully. It is to Pickersgill's credit that he voiced his concerns publicly, not only later in his memoirs but, much more important, at the time he was the minister of citizenship and immigration.

Speaking in the House of Commons on the eve of the 1957 election (in which the Liberals were unexpectedly defeated), Pickersgill termed the immigration security process "the most complicated, and in my experience, the most painful aspect of the administration of my department." He went on to mount a defence of necessity against suggestions that more rights be given to the subjects of the security process. "In the nature of things, unfortunately, we cannot prove these things", he admitted, referring to security reports that could mean denial of entry to Canada or deportation. We must, he asserted, trust the RCMP: "There has to be an assumption that the people who do it, like our RCMP...are reliable." This was "the only basis" upon which a security screening system could operate. Nor could the government afford to waste its time and tax dollars "getting into debates with the relatives of would-be immigrants" who had been rejected: official silence on security matters would have to be maintained. Pickersgill was putting up a brave front for the security establishment with which he had himself tangled from time to time behind the scenes. As for trusting the RCMP, he noted years later in his memoirs that he did not always take its advice on these matters.[4]

The Brent decision and the growing political clamour over immigration issues did push the government into a quiet, in-house attempt to reassess its security policies and administration, which had already been called into some question by the Hungarian refugee experience.[5] This internal review was begun under the auspices of the St. Laurent government but was cast in a new light when the Progressive Conservatives under John Diefenbaker swept suddenly into office in June 1957 after twenty-two years in opposition. A relatively harmonious and bipartisan approach to immigration in the late 1940s had given way to increasingly critical attacks on the Liberal record by the Tories. Now they found themselves responsible for the policy. As is often the case with new governments who find themselves administering a policy of which they have been critical from the outside, reforming the process proved to be rather more complicated and difficult than they might have anticipated—even when, as in this case, there were elements in the bureaucracy that also wanted reform.

The Conservatives took office in a minority Parliament in June of 1957. The new prime minister appointed as acting minister of citizenship and immigration Davie Fulton, whose main portfolio was Justice. Fulton, who was to remain in charge of Immigration for less than a year, was a once and future Tory leadership contestant who never made it to the top. A Rhodes Scholar and war veteran, Fulton was widely respected as the conscience of the Tory party; in twelve years on the opposition benches he had gained a reputation as one of the more intelligent and liberal spokesmen for the party.

As justice minister, Davie Fulton caused the security establishment in Ottawa some private heartburn by questioning the disregard for the civil liberties of public servants subjected to the security screening process. In his brief tenure in Immigration, he was quickly made aware of the prickly nature of security in that field as well. Less than three weeks after assuming the portfolio, Fulton received a mcmo from the deputy minister, Laval Fortier, on security waivers for Hungarian refugees. Fortier indicated that the RCMP "have always been suspicious" of Iron Curtain émigrés. "I have already indicated to you", he reminded Fulton, "that the security screening of immigrants is one of the main problems that the Immigration Branch is faced with. We have so many different procedures concerning security clearance that it makes it most difficult for the Immigration staff to follow the procedures laid down, and it is quite confusing."[6] If security procedures were confusing to the very bureaucrats who were charged with administering them, things were in a lamentable state indeed. Fortier assured the new minister that a review had already been initiated and that some suggestions for policy changes could be expected in the "near future".

An internal departmental committee had been appointed in the last days of the previous Liberal government to review all aspects of immigration policy and procedures. A subcommittee, made up of three officials not normally involved in security, had been set up to examine screening procedures. It reported just as the new government was taking over. Given the brief period they were given in which to look into procedures that the deputy minister himself had called "confusing", it was no surprise that the subcommittee members were unable to look into the fundamental questions about the security process itself or the possible establishment of criteria "entirely different" from those already in place. As they admitted, "It was not possible to consider and we are not likely to be in a position to determine whether security screening (while desirable) is even effective."[7]

The subcommittee did not question the desirability of screening, but instead looked at the who and the how of the process. On the question of who, they reported, "It is generally accepted that international communism is the chief menace to the internal security of Canada. There are other ideologies or political concepts which are inimical to Canada's way of life but represent no danger by virtue of their lack of cohesiveness among large groups of people throughout the world." That accepted, they did open up a major question when they added, "Although communism in itself is a prime menace, it becomes a question as to whether or not the individual Communist is necessarily a potential source of danger." Flying in the face of the RCMP mentality, they insisted that "it is obvious that not all Communists represent a dangerous subversive element." "Dedicated idealists" and "paid saboteurs" were obviously to be kept out, but "the 'Communist of convenience' who merely supports the party for the purpose of obtaining some immediate and oft-times long overdue improvement in his standard of living—e.g., reform in Italy in the method of holding land—and is essentially democratic in his thinking is not a real danger to the security of this country."

Moreover, it was not possible to simply give the benefit of the doubt to Canada and exclude all Communists by a universal screening of all immigrants without exception, because "it is desirable to take some calculated risks in order to reunite families"; because "it may be desirable to stimulate the flow of immigration even at the hazard of allowing the entry of possible security risks"; and because it "would not be practical or politically expedient" to screen certain nationals, especially those from the British Isles. On the latter point, they admitted that a "British

Communist is just as dangerous as a Communist from any other country." Yet the institution of security screening would "inevitably lead to a slowdown in the movement of immigrants from the United Kingdom", a result that was not "politically sound". Obviously Britain retained its most-favoured-nation status. On the other hand, they recommended continuing the invidious subterfuge whereby French immigrants, "although nominally not subject to screening", were in fact screened. The device was justified on the basis of the small number of French immigrants, and the large proportion of Communists to be found in that country. The unequal treatment of the two "founding peoples" was continued.

The subcommittee also supported the existing practice of not screening American citizens and permanent residents of the US immigrating to Canada, on the intriguing grounds that "for defence purposes, the North American continent is considered a single entity and therefore it would obviously be undesirable and impractical to institute security screening of citizens and residents of the U.S.A." In any event the flow of visitors back and forth across the US border was so heavy that security screening was simply impractical.

The subcommittee affirmed its agreement with waiver categories already in place (children, old persons, widows or divorcees with children, clergymen, etc.) but wished to see the age range for exemption broadened: to include children up to twenty-one years of age rather than eighteen, and to include old persons starting at age sixty, not sixty-five.[8] On the other hand, they also recommended the abolition of special ministerial waivers, which had been used in the Pickersgill years mainly for sponsored immigrants from east-bloc countries who had found it impossible to enter Canada directly, because of the formal security requirements. In these cases, it was the Canadian sponsors who were screened, and waivers were allowed if the sponsors were cleared (in fact, all but one-fifth of one per cent of sponsors in such cases were cleared). Echoing the police view, the subcommittee warned that Iron Curtain immigrants represented a grave threat to Canadian security. Reuniting families was a humanitarian consideration, they conceded, but in a classic formulation of the credo of immigration gatekeepers they asserted that a "line must be drawn somewhere if the national security

is of any importance." Once again it was those who found themselves on the wrong side of the Cold War line who were expected
to pay the price of Canadian national security. Nor did the subcommittee seem much concerned about long delays or about the
requirement for two years' residence in a country where screening could be carried out (even though this made immigration to
Canada virtually impossible for most Eastern Europeans).

In short, the subcommittee urged the simplification of the
security process, but in a way that would only intensify the
inequality of its impact on various national groups, retaining
the bias in favour of English-speaking immigrants and setting
back the position of relatives of Canadians of east-bloc origin.
Although they had suggested in general terms that individual
"Communists" should not necessarily be tarred with the wide
brush of "Communism" in general, this particular point was
neither elaborated nor made specific in the recommendations.[9]

The security subcommittee's report was considered by a joint
meeting of officials of the immigration department and representatives of the RCMP in the fall of 1957. As might be expected,
the RCMP raised objections to any lowering of screening standards, approved the maintenance of existing controls, and even
revealed a hitherto unnoted enthusiasm for extending screening
to British and American applicants.[10] Once more the police were
digging in their heels. The bureaucrats had not in truth proposed
anything very drastic, yet the RCMP was determined that if there
were to be any changes, they would only be changes that increased controls. If there was to be any liberalization, the impetus
would have to come from the top.

Pressure from the top was possible. Davie Fulton as acting
minister of immigration was deeply concerned about the degree
of complexity and of ministerial discretion that had been built
into the immigration process over the years. Two years earlier he
had issued a ringing criticism of secrecy and ministerial discretion from the opposition benches: "When reasons for decisions
do not have to be given, as the government maintains they do
not, and when ministerial discretion, which means in the nature
of things, departmental discretion, is the sole arbiter, then error, corruption, favouritism, and injustice are invited and rights
and liberties are denied in principle as well as in fact." Upon assuming his portfolio, he found himself suddenly facing "large

numbers" of "exceptional cases" (many if not most based on se-curity considerations) that went directly to the minister's office for decision. Fulton brought these cases to Cabinet, which in the course of discussion agreed that "it was impossible for the Cabi-net, or indeed for the Minister to familiarize himself completely with the details of each case." It was, all agreed, a ridiculous sit-uation. Cabinet called for a "thorough review of our immigration laws and practices."[11]

Just before he was to relinquish his temporary portfolio to a permanent successor, Fulton delivered a mammoth, ninety-page memorandum to his Cabinet colleagues on immigration policies and procedures. In it he outlined the problems he had encoun-tered in administering the department; chief among these was security. "Because of the overall impact of security consider-ations on immigration problems", the RCMP had been asked to suggest changes that "could safely be made in this field to 'humanize' or 'democratize' the immigration procedures." Ful-ton bleakly reported that "the results of this study have been discouraging." The RCMP wanted no appeals and no informa-tion released on security grounds for rejection; if there were to be any changes, the police insisted that they should tighten screening and intensify the discretionary aspects of administra-tion. Fulton was obviously moved by the claims of compassion, especially in cases of family reunification, but, lacking any ef-fective counterweight to the arguments of the police (there were clearly no political or bureaucratic elements prepared to con-front the RCMP openly), he was compelled to accept the logic of national security and suggest only marginal changes. For their part the police pointed out that from 1946 through 1958, a to-tal of 29,671 applications for immigration had been rejected on security grounds, "whereas 21,000 is said to be the highest mem-bership the Communist Party in Canada has ever been able to obtain."[12]

Two days later Fulton left Immigration. The new minister was Ellen Fairclough, the first woman Cabinet minister in the federal government. Fairclough, a Hamilton Tory with a United Empire Loyalist background who had been an executive officer of the Imperial Order Daughters of the Empire, was not pleased by the portfolio with which Diefenbaker had entrusted her. It was, she later recalled, a "dirty post. There is not a bit of doubt in my mind that it is the worst post in the government." Four years later she was relieved of the burden in what was generally viewed as a demotion to the post office; Fairclough, however, claims to have been "glad to move out."[13] Immigration officials were kinder in their memories of the minister, recalling her as someone who listened well to her advisers, not necessarily a compliment to ministerial creativity or initiative.[14] In fact the Fairclough years witnessed the abandonment of the initiative of thoroughly reforming the process. A plan to present a new Immigration Act fizzled out amid crises such as the discovery of an illegal Chinese immigration racket and highly publicized RCMP raids on Canadian Chinatowns. These events were taking place against a backdrop of major economic recession and a general decline in immigration, to the point where in 1961 more people left Canada than entered it for the first time in the postwar period.

The one major initiative in this period—coming from the civil servants rather than the politicians, it appears—was the revised immigration regulations presented in 1962. They moved definitively towards the principle of racial non-discrimination, although under them Europeans could still sponsor a somewhat wider range of relatives than could Canadians of Asian or African origin. In addition, the Immigration Appeal Board, established in 1952, was strengthened to deal more independently with deportation orders. Very little was changed in the security process. In the field, old tensions between the RCMP security operation and the civilians of the immigration department remained unresolved.[15]

The importance of the national security dimension in immigration policy and how exasperating it could be to the politicians can be glimpsed in a Cabinet discussion in 1960. Fairclough had received the approval of a special Cabinet committee for her recommendation that a royal commission on immigration be established. Fulton, whose earlier attempts at reform while holding the immigration portfolio had been frustrated, intervened brusquely to oppose the proposal in his capacity as minister of justice.

> The chief difficulties of the Department of Citizenship and Immigration did not arise out of the general policy on the amount of immigration but from procedural questions, especially the security procedure. A Royal Commission would therefore become a forum in

which disaffected groups and subversive organizations would make accusations and sensational statements, which would be hard to answer because of security considerations. He had discussed the subject in detail with the RCMP who had stated that they would be unable to give a satisfactory answer to a Royal Commission on their sources of information. The RCMP would either have to give the appearance of defying the Royal Commission or destroy their security system, and violate undertakings with security authorities in other countries.

Cabinet toyed briefly with the idea of a royal commission whose terms of reference would explicitly exclude security, but abandoned it because it would raise "strong objections" that the commission "was prevented from entering one of the most crucial aspects of the entire subject." Once again the RCMP won. There would be no royal commission.[16]

In 1962 Canadian politics was torn by the divisive issue of installing nuclear warheads for the Bomarc missiles that the Diefenbaker government had stationed on Canadian soil, in place of the projected all-Canadian Avro Arrow jet interceptor that had been cancelled in the late 1950s. It was this issue that eventually split the Diefenbaker Cabinet and led directly to the defeat of the government in the House of Commons in 1963; the Tories were defeated in the general election that followed. Earlier, the Cuban missile crisis of 1962 had brought the world closer to nuclear midnight than at any time in the postwar period—and it had led to bitter contention within the Canadian government.

After the Liberals' return to national office in 1963, the nuclear threat seemed to fade somewhat from the front pages, but it was replaced by the Cold War in another guise. The growing American intervention in the Vietnam War under presidents John Kennedy and Lyndon Johnson began to loom larger in the consciousness of Canadians, although Canada was not involved militarily, as it was in Korea, nor was public opinion strongly supportive of this Asian campaign against Communism. There were sections of Canadian opinion that shared the official US perspective, but there were many who rejected it. In America itself, Vietnam was the most divisive war in the country's history; as antiwar protests erupted and grew across America, angry Canadians went out into the streets as well. Even the Liberal prime minister, Lester Pearson, who had won the 1963 election with the support, both directly and indirectly, of the US government, was moved to publicly criticize US Vietnam policy at an American university. And by the end of the decade, Pearson's successor, Pierre Trudeau, was ordering a general review of Canadian foreign policy, including a reassessment of our commitment to NATO. The simple Cold War verities of the late 1940s and early 1950s were no longer uncontested.

The 1960s also witnessed a more clamorous level of public debate and contention about many issues and causes, from Quebec independence to Canadian nationalism to women's liberation. University campuses became centres of protest, and "counter-culture" life-styles emerged among the young. In this atmosphere of questioning traditional authority, it was inevitable that immigration policies would come under more critical public scrutiny than in the past. And so they did—but not necessarily in a coherent manner.

Canadians did not enjoy anything near a consensus about immigration and its role and meaning in Canadian life. On the one hand, the 1960s saw a growing and sometimes strident clamour to eliminate discriminatory barriers, particularly those of a racial or national kind, along with demands that the civil rights of immigrants be given recognition. These demands reflected the more liberal climate of the decade and could flourish in an economic context of prosperity and relatively full employment. By the mid-1960s the greatest postwar boom was in progress, and the flow of immigration increased dramatically. In 1967 the number of immigrants reached almost a quarter of a million, more than three times what it had been in 1961 at the trough of the earlier recession. But most of these immigrants were very different from the earlier wave in the 1950s. There were many more Asians than before, as well as blacks. Among the Europeans, there were more southerners than northerners. Whereas almost one in three immigrants to Canada in the first postwar decade had been British, the proportion had fallen to less than one in five by the end of the 1960s.

On the other hand, while loud voices were being raised in some quarters in favour of more liberal and generous treatment of immigration and of immigrants, it was by no means clear that public opinion in general was becoming more liberal. In fact the evidence suggests the contrary. In 1947, when a Gallup poll asked whether Canada needed more immigration, 51 per cent had responded affirmatively, with only 30 per cent saying no. By 1971 when the same question was asked again, opinion had dramatically reversed: only 26 per cent remained in the affirmative, while 66 per cent were negative.[17] The question had been asked a number of times in the intervening years, and through the 1950s and 1960s the negative response had been growing steadily. As immigration became more a matter of public contention, the level of consensus declined. In 1966 a Gallup poll asked Canadians if they approved or disapproved of government immigration policy. Opinion split almost evenly down the middle, with the "don't knows" almost as numerous as those with opinions.[18]

If immigrants were coming in more colours and cultures than in the past, it was also true that political criteria for admitting them were becoming more complex. In the 1940s and 1950s the ostensible targets of security screening had been Communists and Nazis, who had few vocal supporters in the Canadian population. In 1968 there was an influx of Czech refugees after the Soviet intervention in Prague, recalling the pattern of the Hungarians in 1956–57. Throughout the late 1960s there was also a movement of a very different kind of political refugee: young Americans fleeing military service in Vietnam, among whom there were many genuine opponents of American Cold War policies.[19]

These refugees presented an ideological challenge to the entire security process. A screening net that had been devised to filter out left-wing immigrants, developed in the closest liaison with the Americans, was now faced with an influx of Americans who refused, some on firm principle, to heed their government's order to fight against Communism. Worse, some were actually deserters from the US military. There was no systematic Canadian security screening of either visitors or immigrants from the US, although look-out lists were maintained of those to be barred, and grounds were available for turning back Americans at the border. There were also ways of handing back Americans in Canada wanted by the US authorities for violating US statutes. Finally, for those landed in Canada who applied for Canadian citizenship, there were security screening procedures; here the politics and past behaviour of applicants could be considered. At all these points negative controls could be exercised against American draft resisters.

On the other hand, these immigrants had many more claims on Canadian support and sympathy than the luckless left-wing refugees and would-be immigrants of the past. In a sense, there were historical antecedents to this refugee movement with very positive connotations for Canadians. English Canada had itself been born out a movement of American political refugees in the late eighteenth century: the Loyalists who had trekked north after the victory of the American revolutionaries over British rule. These same refugees had defended the British North American colonies against a US invasion in the War of 1812. Later Canada became a haven for black slaves who escaped to freedom in the years leading up to the Civil War. Given the sympathy with which the antiwar movement in the US was viewed by many Canadians and the sense of disillusionment with America engendered by the bloody spectacle of Vietnam on the nightly television news, by the riots in the black ghettoes of American cities, and by the political assassinations and other forms of violent instability that seemed to be gripping the US in that era, there was ready-made public support for the new American immigrants. It quickly flared into loud public criticism at any evidence that the Canadian government was impeding or blocking the flow on behalf of its American ally.

Informal support groups to welcome American "war resisters" (as their supporters called them) or "draft dodgers" (as their detractors preferred) grew up around the country. But there was no question of the Canadian government itself offering official sanction and support to "refugees" from its closest external ally. Sympathetic Canadians began in the middle and late 1960s to air charges that RCMP and immigration officials were harassing and in some cases stopping war resisters at the border. In response to such criticism, the immigration minister told the House of Commons in 1968, "The Canadian Immigration Act and Regulations contain no reference to an individual's military draft status and consequently this is not a factor in determining admissibility to Canada."[20]

Being subject to military service did not constitute valid grounds for being barred at the border, but the case of American deserters was apparently more difficult. Deserters were not covered under NATO agreements (since they had not been stationed in Canada previous to their application to immigrate), but Canadian practice through January 1968 had been to prohibit deserters of any foreign military force from acquiring landed-immigrant status. In the face of growing public revulsion against the Vietnam War, this secret restriction was relaxed, albeit somewhat grudgingly, through 1968. In the end, thousands of young Americans (exact numbers are impossible to determine) immigrated to Canada in this period to avoid military service. With the eventual American retreat from Indo-China and the subsequent termination of the peacetime draft, the flow came to a halt. Many returned to their homeland, but many others stayed in Canada where over the years they have made their own contributions to Canadian life.

Developments on the other side of the Cold War gulf also came home to Canadians in 1968 when democratic reform in Czechoslovakia had a brief flowering in the "Prague Spring" before the brutal intervention of Soviet forces. Under the leadership of reform elements of the Czech Communist party, the possibility of "socialism with a human face" leading to a general liberalization throughout the Soviet bloc was broached. Hopes were quickly dashed when Soviet troops poured into Prague; the real masters of the fate of Eastern Europe dismissed and purged the reformers and replaced them with a neo-Stalinist regime more to Moscow's liking. Thirty years after the West had sold out Czechoslovakia to Hitler at the Munich conference, twenty years after the Communist coup that had closed off Eastern Europe to democratic pluralism, and a dozen years after the Soviet repression of the Hungarian uprising, the world saw again the familiar scenes of protesters helplessly and hopelessly confronting the implacable steel of tanks and gun barrels. And as the Prague Spring withered and died, there were once again refugees.

As some Czechs and Slovaks fled into Austria, the office of the United Nations High Commissioner for Refugees appealed to potential host countries to absorb the flow. Canada responded with a special government program including travel assistance and a large-scale adjustment plan to help the refugees establish

themselves in Canadian life. Almost 12,000 Czechoslovaks settled in Canada under this program, about one-third as many as
the Hungarians who came here after the 1956 uprising. (Since the
Soviet invaders had met no armed resistance in Czechoslovakia
and had exacted less bloody punishment of the resisters than
they had in Hungary, there were many fewer refugees.) From the
self-interested Canadian point of view, the Czechs selected were
"good" material: predominantly young and well educated, and a
high proportion had technical and professional skills. The total
cost to Canadian taxpayers was approximately $11 million, less
than $1,000 per refugee.[21] Given the productive use to which
most of them were put by the Canadian economy, there is little doubt that the return has far outweighed the modest initial
investment.

The RCMP was involved in the planning from the beginning,
along with Immigration, External Affairs, and Health and Wel-
fare. There appears to have been somewhat less concern about
security considerations than the Ottawa security establishment
had shown at the time of the Hungarian inflow. In part the Hungarian experience had already deflated some of the exaggerated
anxieties previously held by the security establishment about infiltration of agents. In 1956–57 Pickersgill had simply overruled
the security people, and he had been proved right. In addition
the general criteria applied to Soviet-bloc immigrants had eased
somewhat by 1968. Criteria that usually would have excluded the
Czech applicants, such as membership in the Communist party
or participation in a Communist government, were not necessarily made barriers to their entry as refugees. After all, it did not
require vast sophistication of analysis to realize that the targets
of the Soviet invasion had been reform elements of the Czech
Communist party apparatus.

The issues of immigration are often dramatic, involving, as they
so often do, compelling human stories of separated families, es-
capes from oppression, and the fundamental rights and freedoms
of individuals in contest with the sovereignty of the state and the
rights of the community. This was certainly so during the 1960s.
Yet the state's method of dealing with these issues, and especially of devising better machinery for processing immigration
problems, is most often faceless, bureaucratic paper-pushing.
There were numerous attempts during the 1960s to assess and

reform immigration processing, including its security aspects; these attempts took the form of internal reports, published papers, inquiries by parliamentary committees, and even that most Canadian of responses to problems, a royal commission. The concrete results of all this paper production were not overwhelming, but the bureaucratic apparatus was at least showing clear signs of administrative indigestion—if nothing else, a prelude to greater changes.

First off the mark under the Pearson Liberal government was the minister of immigration, René Tremblay, who announced a sweeping series of reassessments of policy and proposed reorganizations of the administrative apparatus in the summer of 1964. He stressed, laudably, that long-term objectives of the immigration program must be formulated and the appropriate administrative means put in place, but he did not last more than a year in the portfolio (before being shuffled off to the post office to deal with the first national postal strike). One of Tremblay's objectives had been a revised immigration act; it was to be more than a decade in the making.

Short-term problems always seem to crowd out the long-term questions. Just as Tremblay was gearing up for a major review, headline-grabbing stories of the threatened deportation of illegal immigrants (mainly Greek seamen who jumped ship and subsequently married Canadian women) led to an official inquiry. An eminent Toronto lawyer of impeccable Tory credentials, Joseph Sedgwick, was asked by the Liberal government to inquire into allegations from the press and the parliamentary opposition that "certain aliens have been unlawfully detained and deprived of access to counsel", as well as to examine the general procedures for the arrest and deportation of those illegally in the country. The terms of the inquiry were later widened to include the question of ministerial discretion under the Immigration Act.

In the course of his investigation, Sedgwick touched on the problem of security, a matter familiar to him throughout his long legal career.[22] Sedgwick was bluff and to the point:

> The matter of security is a vexed problem and seemingly incapable of a truly satisfactory solution. At least I could find none. The difficulty arises in that the gathering of security information is an extremely delicate and sensitive process—particularly abroad—and it is

an undeniable fact that the obtaining of this intelligence would be completely frustrated if sources were disclosed and, in many instances, if even the nature of the information were disclosed.[23]

Sedgwick agreed that it was "both necessary and proper that every effort should be made to exclude aliens who are undesirable for security reasons". He added that "while the word security immediately brings to mind the struggle with Communism" it covered other kinds of "totalitarian causes" and criminals as well. He recommended that in certain cases those in Canada temporarily but seeking permanent status should be subjected to security screening while in Canada. An adverse security report would have to be taken into consideration by the Immigration Appeal Board, but security could not be cited as grounds for refusal:

> The result will be that in some cases where an appellant might otherwise have been successful he will fail without having had the opportunity to challenge the grounds upon which the adverse decision is based. As a matter of general principle this is not a desirable course of action, but in the context of national security I am convinced of its necessity and justification. One point that must not be lost sight of is that the Board will be dealing with aliens seeking the privilege, not the right, to remain in Canada permanently and any doubts concerning security and the methods of dealing with it should be resolved in favour of Canada.

Sedgwick's recommendations concluded with this general proposition:

> I think the Act should state clearly that admission to Canada, either as an immigrant or a non-immigrant, is a privilege and is not to be construed as a right. Flowing from that, it should be made clear that the mere physical presence of a person in Canada gives him no special privilege; he is, or should be, in the same position as if he had applied in his country of residence for a landing in Canada as an immigrant.

As I have said, coming and then staying here illegally should not confer on him any rights, no matter how long he has been here.

The Sedgwick report can be viewed as a strong restatement of the traditional conservative view on national security and the rights of the state as overriding the rights of individuals, especially if they are not citizens. It was to be reiterated by other official or quasi-official statements of policy in the latter half of the decade.

While the Sedgwick inquiry was under way, the immigration bureaucracy was itself in the process of producing an internal study of its policy and objectives. This report, suitably rewritten for public consumption as a White Paper called *Canadian Immigration Policy*, appeared in 1966, just eleven days after the department had been effectively reorganized into the Department of Manpower and Immigration (a juxtaposition of functions that in itself indicated a new economic priority in immigration policy). The new deputy minister was one of the senior mandarins of the Pearson era: Tom Kent, a principal policy adviser and political strategist for Pearson while the Liberals were in opposition in the early 1960s. The new departmental structure had been imposed upon a surprised and not very pleased Immigration Branch as a kind of coup originating in the Prime Minister's Office. At the time, this massive reorganization rendered the White Paper on immigration policy, which had come up through the old bureaucracy, rather superfluous and irrelevant. In fact, it was largely devoted to a single *idée fixe*: greater control over sponsored applicants for immigration.[24] It had little else of substance to say about other longstanding problems.

Among these longstanding problems, of course, was security. Here the White Paper was relatively taciturn, although somewhat more liberal than past official statements. For one thing, the barring of non-immigrant visitors to Canada on the basis of their alleged "subversive" associations was attacked as an "embarrassment for all concerned". Moreover it was argued that "these provisions are difficult to administer" and "repugnant to the cherished beliefs of many Canadians". Yet the authors of the White Paper were aware of the political aspects of this practice. Even if denying entry to visitors was not a "major deterrent" to subversives and spies, it "at least avoids the appearance of an open invitation". The authors cut through to the real core of the problem of banning visitors when they wrote, "It is important that recognition be given to the fact that the holding or expression of unpopular opinions, or sympathy with such opinion, is not in itself indicative of subversive activity."[25] Twenty years after the policy of barring visitors for political reasons was instituted, there was at last on the record an official statement that distinguished between the expression of dissent and the practice of subversion.

Security screening was itself identified in the White Paper as the "most troublesome feature of selection and control procedures". This was no more than had been readily admitted by Jack Pickersgill as minister of immigration a decade earlier. As for solutions to the problem, the White Paper deferred to the pending Royal Commission on Security, which the department hoped would settle the vexed issue—with one specific exception. In regard to immigration from Communist countries, the White Paper suggested a modest change in emphasis. The authors admitted that immigration from these countries had been "narrowly confined", because of security considerations, to very close relatives, where sponsors were involved, and to "negligible" numbers of unsponsored immigrants. The White Paper indicated that Canada should open the doors wider to sponsored relatives "wherever they may live", thus ending a long-standing practice that discriminated against Canadian families with relatives in Communist states. However, it did not propose to open the doors to unsponsored applicants from countries "where screening cannot be carried out" (which meant, in practice, mainly Communist countries).[26]

Security concerns were still an issue of public concern as well, as evidenced by debates in the House of Commons on a bill to establish a new Immigration Appeal Board in 1967. Along with the perennial issue of sponsored immigration and family reunification (always taking pride of place for MPs with large numbers of immigrants in their constituencies), security questions received unusually serious attention. Especially contentious was the question of the rights of would-be immigrants rejected on security grounds to be informed of the nature of the case against them and to have access to a judicial hearing. Opposition MPs did succeed in amending the bill to force the appeal board to give reasons for its decisions, and to allow "compassionate or humanitarian considerations" to be taken into account in deportation cases. They failed, however, to convince the government that judicial hearings should be mandatory in cases where rejection was based on security grounds. Instead the bill expressly provided that security cases, as well as cases involving criminal records, would not be heard by the board if the minister of manpower and immigration and the solicitor general jointly declared in a certificate that it would be against the national interest.[27]

A second Sedgwick report was commissioned by the government in 1970 to consider the administrative backlog resulting from the large number of visitors to Canada whose applications for landed-immigrant status had been rejected and who then filed appeals with the Immigration Appeal Board. In his recommendations, Sedgwick urged that the appeal board's jurisdiction no longer extend to security cases at all, with or without ministerial certificates. In support of this change he cited a recommendation of the Royal Commission on Security, which had made its report by this time. Among its findings was a proposal for a special security review board to deal with all appeals against security decisions involving public servants or immigration or citizenship applicants.[28] This proposal to bypass the Immigration Act appeal process altogether in security-related cases offered the government a possible way out, in the face of increasing criticism of the state's arbitrary exercise of its near-absolute discretion when it assumed that national security was at risk in immigration and citizenship cases.

This recommendation, from a royal commission specifically charged with investigating national security questions, could have been a significant one, but it was to have a long and very tortuous career in the limbo of governmental good intentions before expiring unaccountably. But it was later resurrected by yet another royal commission and finally fixed in Canadian law in the mid-1980s. Tracking the course of policy changes in this area sometimes seems more like following underground streams and rivulets, which mysteriously vanish and then just as mysteriously reappear, than the theory of public policy-making in a democratic country would indicate.

The Royal Commission on Security was appointed in 1966 after the Pearson government had weathered a number of security scandals: a Vancouver postal clerk was found to have been passing information (gathered mainly in public libraries) to the Soviets; a Tory Cabinet minister was retroactively declared a security risk, in an inquiry called by the Liberals, for having conducted a liaison with a prostitute who had once worked on behalf of the Soviets in Germany; and—although this was not known to the public at the time—former prime minister John Diefenbaker had threatened Lester Pearson with exposure of an American security file from the 1950s that associated Pearson himself with alleged Communist espionage (Pearson coolly stared his antagonist down on that threat, and the allegation did not become public until the 1980s, when both men were dead).[29]

Pearson appointed Maxwell Mackenzie to chair the commission, which was to "make a full and confidential inquiry into the operation of Canadian security methods and procedures"; other commissioners were Yves Pratte, later chairman of Air Canada, and M. J. Coldwell, former leader of the CCF. The commission reported two and a half years later, not to Pearson, who had retired, but to a Liberal government headed by Pierre Trudeau. The report, in abridged (that is, censored) form, was published in June 1969. Immigration security questions attracted some of the commission's attention, but its treatment of the problem did not turn out to be much to the government's liking, on the whole. Ironically, just when it appeared that a federal government was willing to move in a more liberal direction, a royal commission produced a report that was notable for its philosophical reversion to the kind of hardline conservatism characteristic of discussions of national security matters in an earlier era.

The seriousness with which the Liberal government considered the national security question in immigration is underlined by the close attention it paid to the Mackenzie commission's deliberations in this policy area. Early in 1967 Cabinet became involved in the process when the minister of manpower and immigration, Jean Marchand, outlined for the benefit of his ministerial colleagues some of the problems concerning security screening of immigrants and made recommendations for changes. A record of what transpired in Cabinet was not available at the time of writing, because of the twenty-year rule of secrecy regarding Cabinet deliberations and documents; but a letter written shortly after the Cabinet meeting by the deputy minister, Tom Kent, "with the express approval of the prime minister", set down the "complete precis of the Minister's remarks and recommendations" to Cabinet. In this letter, sent to Maxwell Mackenzie, the government was making available to the chairman of a commission inquiring into security questions the most up-to-date statement of its own thinking on the matter. This letter offers a remarkably frank and revealing glimpse into the government's own disillusionment with a process that it had itself set in motion some twenty years earlier.[30]

Above all, Kent stressed the excessively arbitrary features of the system, and the consequent lack of consistency in administration:

> At present we are unable to deal with potentially admissible sponsored immigrants from many countries [i.e., mainly Communist states] simply because the facilities to make inquiries about them are lacking. On the other hand, we accept immigrants from some countries (notably Britain) without a general screening. Also, in relation to applicants from other countries, various exemptions and waivers have been developed over the years. The result is that the operative security screening rules have little logic. In their varied impact on Canadians wishing to sponsor relatives, the rules are distinctly inconsistent. Consequently, so much resentment has been generated within the public, Members of the House of Commons, ethnic organisations and other interested groups that defence of the system by this Department has become virtually impossible to sustain.

The department was disturbed about the grounds for security rejection employed by the RCMP in posts abroad:

> There are various grounds for rejection, but the one that concerns us is that, if this check produces evidence of any communist political association, the application is automatically refused and no review is conducted unless representations are subsequently made in Ottawa to the Minister or senior officials in the Department. Thus we now exclude people from Canada—including, in the case of sponsored immigration applications, the relatives of Canadian

citizens—on evidence reported by foreign agencies. These are security agencies but the reports often deal purely with political opinions and actions and the evidence is frequently of a purely hearsay or unsubstantiated nature.

It should be added that, since the sources cannot be identified publicly, we cannot in any way explain our adverse decisions.

This was a startling enough indictment of policy and practice to issue from a deputy minister, with the apparent blessing of the minister and the prime minister. But Kent went on to point to a "deeper issue" yet:

Even if the facts are certain, there is a great deal of variation, according to circumstances, in the extent to which some communist sympathy or association makes a man in any proper sense a "security risk" as an immigrant. Obviously, such depends on the nature of his past activities, his personality, and his intended employment in Canada.

Even more important is the environment in which the man has supported a Communist party in the past. The present criteria make no distinction between countries. But, while a communist from Britain has made a deliberate choice of an extremist position, a communist from Italy or France may have been simply a man who supports the same political party as his neighbours. A communist from Yugoslavia or Poland may have simply been a conformist. It could be argued, indeed, that his desire to migrate from behind the Iron Curtain...is, in normal circumstances, prima facie evidence that he is not ideologically oriented to communism in a way that makes him a danger to our society.

The impact of the present screening process, however, is exactly opposite to these considerations. An immigrant from Britain or the United States is admitted without our having taken any steps to find out whether he is a communist. There is virtually no chance for anyone, communist or anti-communist, to come from behind the Iron Curtain. And the Italian cannot come if he is reported to have attended Communist meetings.

Having made these rather devastating criticisms of the standards and criteria of the immigration security process as it had been practised for a generation, Kent then went deeper yet to undermine the ultimate rationale of the process:

> We do not believe that any immigrant security screening system imposed on a large volume of immigration can provide significant protection against the skilled, professional subversive. Canada is wide open to the entry of non-immigrants. There is no need for an agent to make application as an immigrant, and it is therefore impossible to regard the screening of immigrants as a means of detecting foreign agents.

Kent hastened to add that he was not arguing against the usefulness of "some close check of immigrants, especially for criminal activity." But "what we question is the relevance to security of the present kind of political screening." That said a lot.

If the department's thinking, "with the express approval of the prime minister", was along these lines, the government was clearly signalling the Mackenzie commission in the strongest terms that it favoured new directions in immigration security policy and a departure from the old hardline orthodoxy. If so, the appeal seems to have fallen upon deaf, if not hostile, ears. The thrust of the commission's findings in this policy area, as it was generally in all aspects of national security, was very hardline indeed, reminiscent of the conventional thinking of the Ottawa security establishment in the early 1950s. Although the RCMP and its supporters had initially distrusted the allegedly liberal influence of M. J. Coldwell, the CCF/NDP representative among the commissioners, they had little to fear in fact. Coldwell turned out to be what John Sawatsky later described as the "conservative anchor on the commission" who "often argued against some of the more liberal proposals of his two fellow commissioners."[31]

As it turned out, the RCMP was enraged at the commission's report and even attempted to have its publication suppressed, but not because of any philosophical disagreement with the commission's attitude towards national security. Rather it was because the commission struck at the vital interests of the RCMP at a level more sensitive than philosophy or ideology: it recommended that the security service be removed from the jurisdiction of the RCMP and be "civilianized". Apart from that blow at the RCMP's organizational integrity and self-esteem—a blow that was motivated by a desire to create a more effective instrument for implementing the logic of the national security state—the report of the Mackenzie commission, or those parts of it that were published (some sections remained secret), tended towards advising a general tightening of Cold War controls over Canadian life.

The chapter on immigration security opened with what amounted to a veiled repudiation of the content of Tom Kent's letter to Maxwell Mackenzie two years earlier. A royal commission is in theory independent and in no way obliged to follow the suggestions of government. It is obvious that the commissioners must have explicitly rejected the logic of Kent's critique of security practice in immigration, even though that critique apparently bore the imprimatur of both the minister and Cabinet as a whole. The report cited the pre-eminent importance of excluding immigrants who represented a "potential danger in the fields of subversion or espionage". The commissioners went on to urge a drastic simplification of the complex patchwork of exemptions and loopholes that had developed over the years, in terms of both classes of immigrants and nations of origin, but it was a simplification that would have had the effect of widening the screening net enormously.

If there were inconsistencies in the screening process as applied in different countries and in different classes of immigrants, the Mackenzie commissioners concluded that all applicants should be subjected to the most rigorous screening "irrespective of relationship, sponsorship or country of origin." The special arrangements that had been worked out in the 1950s under Jack Pickersgill for transferring the screening of east-bloc dependants to their Canadian sponsors were rejected out of hand: "We cannot understand why the state should deny itself the use of available means of inquiry concerning an immigrant merely because he is sponsored." They were deeply suspicious as well of the "leniency" with which the rejection criteria were allegedly being applied in the case of close relatives, and particularly of any discretionary intervention in the process by civilian officials of the immigration department acting against the advice of the RCMP. Although they reluctantly granted that formal authority rested with the civilians, even when security was at issue, they insisted that "the significance to be attached to an adverse security report would be best evaluated in conjunction with specialists in security"—presumably the RCMP and the Ottawa security establishment.[32]

The commission dismissed the existing rejection criteria as "unnecessarily complex and somewhat illogical...obscure and outdated". The report advocated a single set of criteria to be applied as rigorously as possible to all applicants, regardless of national origins, sponsored or unsponsored. Four classes of applicants were to be rejected: first, persons "who are believed on reasonable grounds" to have held "at any time" an official position in a Communist (or neo-Fascist or other "subversive or revolutionary") organization or to have held any senior position or appointment known to be given only to "reliable members of such an organization"; second, persons believed to have been members within the past ten years of such an organization, "unless the applicant can demonstrate that membership was for trivial, practical, non-ideological or other acceptable reasons"; third, "persons believed to have at any time been agents of such organizations, or to have taken part in sabotage or other clandestine activities or agitation on behalf of such an organization"; and finally, those who, "for unexplained reasons", significantly misrepresented the facts in their applications.[33]

The Mackenzie commission came down particularly hard on the gradual trend towards more liberality with regard to Communist-bloc emigrants. Grudgingly acknowledging that there might be some humanitarian considerations to be taken into account in cases of family reunification, they nevertheless stressed their reservations—reservations that precisely echoed the ancient security establishment fear of the infiltration of agents. Sponsors should continue to be screened, and an adverse report "balanced against the humanitarian considerations". They reiterated the necessity of the rule requiring two years' residence in a country with screening facilities for independent applicants from the East (although they would waive their own rule in the case of a "communist scientist of international repute"). But the principle must be maintained, they asserted, for its regular violation would lead to the most calamitous consequences:

> [It] would cast doubt on the value of the entire security screening programme. It would encourage communist governments to make use of an obvious opportunity to infiltrate persons into North America, and, when combined with the current [ease] of entry into the Canadian public service, would eventually invalidate (or at least call into question) the basic governmental security programme.[34]

This was perhaps less alarming than alarmist: it certainly seemed to be making a national security mountain out of an immigration molehill.

Nor was Chinese immigration forgotten by the commissioners. They wished to see "some years" of residence in Hong Kong made a requirement. Inspector Leopold's impostor Chinese sons had not been lost from sight. Fingerprinting of Chinese applicants was a "clear requirement", "the only sure method of establishing identity", to be applied first at the visa post abroad and then rechecked at the port of entry with the fingerprints of "the person who actually arrives". Fingerprinting was discussed in detail only in relation to Chinese immigrants, but the proposal was extended in a later sentence—almost as an afterthought, apparently—to cover all immigrants to Canada. This recommendation was not taken up by the government.[35]

On the question of citizenship, the commissioners were less conservative. They reported an "element of unfairness" in a citizenship application procedure under which citizenship could be denied to someone resident in Canada for five years "when his actions have not been illegal and represent no immediate and direct threat to the security of Canada". They recommended as a general rule that citizenship be withheld only for "actual illegalities or criminal acts; in the area of security, these would include espionage, treason and similar offences. Membership in communist organizations or even of the Party itself, however, should not constitute causes for rejection", although discretion in security risk cases would still rest with the minister.[36] In cases where deportation was ordered on security grounds, the commission proposed a security review board that would act as an independent body to hear appeals; it would also offer an appeal procedure for rejected applicants for immigrant visas already in the country, and for sponsors of rejected applicants for immigration from abroad. These were liberal proposals, and they rested somewhat incongruously beside the generally conservative and security-conscious recommendations that characterized the Mackenzie commission's report as a whole.

Taken together (the citizenship proposal excepted), these recommendations would have had the effect of greatly extending the scope of the security screen, and of considerably tightening the mesh. The politicians were not anxious to introduce more inflexibility in the face of a rising tide of public complaints, especially from constituents of Eastern European origin seeking family reunification. The Mackenzie commission had produced a report that was predicated on an overriding concern for national security, reflecting the conventional wisdom of the Ottawa security establishment. But in immigration, the overriding concern with national security had always been the problem, not the solution.

Ironically, the commission's concern with national security led it to question the efficacy of the major instrument of security policy enforcement in the postwar period, the RCMP, which it wished to see replaced by a civilian security and intelligence agency. This in turn led the commission into head-on conflict with the RCMP security service and the RCMP brass, themselves key elements in the security establishment. The ensuing fight not only weakened much of the commission's influence but tended to disperse whatever political energies there may have been for reform of the security process in Ottawa.[37]

A new deputy minister of manpower and immigration, Louis Couillard, had succeeded Tom Kent after the Trudeau government's landslide victory in the 1968 election. Although internal department documents indicate that the immigration bureaucracy itself was not particularly keen on this renewed emphasis on security controls, nor on the greater rigidity and backlog in an already overloaded process that the recommendations would undoubtedly encourage, Couillard seems to have made a tactical decision to play along with the commission for the purpose of bagging an elephant that Immigration had long wanted brought in: the RCMP. At a meeting of the Security Panel on the eve of the tabling in Parliament of the abridged report, the RCMP made a last-ditch attempt to head off civilianization, even citing the last refuge of the security police, the alleged support of "all friendly security services" for a Canadian security service "within the police structure". Couillard confronted the police directly:

> [He] expressed the view that there was a basic difference between the police function and the security function, in that the former was guided by law and the latter permitted a wide discretionary power. He gave as an example the fact that the Visa Control [security] Officers at Canadian immigration posts abroad, who were members of the R.C.M. Police, did not have an intimate knowledge of the social and political scene in source countries necessary to do an effective job. Without intending to be unduly critical, he had observed on a recent visit to a number of posts that the Visa Control Officers were deficient in training, basic education, adaptability, and use of the local language. They tended to operate independently and in isolation from other Canadian officials, making decisions based on ad hoc information obtained from security services in host countries, and sometimes providing more information to local police and security authorities than to Canadian officials. This lack of consultation and of "committee competence" in the selection of immigrants was, to his mind, quite unsatisfactory, and had been justifiably criticized by the Commissioners.... He was particularly concerned that steps be taken to improve the Visa Control service, and integrate it more closely with Immigration and External Affairs officials at posts abroad.[38]

Deputy RCMP Commissioner William Kelly, a former head of the security service and once in charge of the overseas visa security operations headquartered in London, was wheeled in by the top RCMP brass to defend their position. More articulate than some of his colleagues, Kelly made pointed use of the authority of the Western security and intelligence network:

> There were established and agreed criteria by which Visa Control Officers made their decisions, and...it

was their responsibility to get information from anyone prepared to give it to them. Although some of
it came from Interpol, the bulk of the information
was provided by other security services for RCMP
use alone; if it were known to them that the information was used for immigration purposes, much of it
would be denied. Although the number of security rejections based on such information was relatively low,
the deterrent effect of the process was valuable.

In fact the RCMP brass were able to mobilize considerable
support for the maintenance of their organizational position from
the other civil servants on the Security Panel. The argumentation
on their behalf was usually weak, sometimes amounting to not
much more than expressions of trust, but the numbers were there
to head off endorsement of the full civilianization recommendation. Realizing that the indictment of the RCMP was sufficiently
severe that some gestures would have to made in the direction
of improvement, the Security Panel, under the able chairman-
ship of Cabinet secretary Gordon Robertson, moved towards the
compromise notion that civilianization could be partially carried
out under RCMP organizational jurisdiction.

The advice was followed: at the beginning of 1970 the government responded minimally to the Mackenzie recommendation by
appointing a civilian head of the RCMP security service to oversee a greater role for non-police personnel. The man appointed
was John Starnes, a very hardline Cold Warrior and son of a former RCMP commissioner, who had spent a quarter of a century
as a security and intelligence specialist in External Affairs. Despite his solidly conservative credentials, Starnes was resented
and opposed by the Mounties; he finally left in 1973, having
achieved little in the way of fundamental reorientation of the security service. The immigration bureaucracy would have to wait
more than a decade before the RCMP was finally removed from
the security scene.

One other recommendation of the royal commission was pertinent to immigration. As mentioned earlier, the commissioners
called for the creation of a security review board, an idea endorsed by Prime Minister Trudeau in the House of Commons.
This was seen at first as an independent body to hear complaints

from public servants regarding security clearances; tens of thousands of investigations were being carried out by the RCMP each year on public servants with access to classified materials and on employees of private companies with government contracts in defence or other security-related areas. Initial discussions centred on these workers, but the question soon arose of whether cases of security rejections of immigrants, citizenship rejections, and deportation cases on security grounds might usefully be added to the jurisdiction of such a board, as the commission itself had proposed.

A review board might have been a significant innovation in the field of national security. It had always been a characteristic of the Canadian way of dealing with security matters that natural justice for individuals affected—the right to be heard in one's own case, to understand the nature of the evidence used against one, to present evidence on one's own behalf, and to cross-examine and contest hostile sources of information—had been at best only imperfectly guaranteed by institutional safeguards and at worst ignored altogether. An independent review board did offer the possibility of an institutional focus for introducing a semblance of natural justice into the otherwise highly arbitrary procedures.

These kinds of considerations, however, did little to commend the proposal for a review board to the bureaucrats and politicians, who had always tended to look at such civil liberties-oriented ideas in terms of the threat they posed to administrative discretion and efficiency. At first Immigration was attracted to the idea, for the more mundane reason of interbureaucratic rivalry: such a board might offer a means of counteracting or bypassing that ancient antagonist of the civilian immigration officials, the RCMP. The Mounties routinely withheld pertinent information on security rejections from the immigration officers in the field; they also withheld information from appeal boards, a self-defeating practice since it meant that many appeals were successful.[39] A security review board could take such difficult matters off the immigration department's plate. Although it was not spelled out in such bald terms, the implication was that Immigration might prefer to have someone else deal with the RCMP in these cases.[40]

While this shift might have made life easier for Immigration, it offered little prospect of allaying the misgivings of civil libertarians or of those who found themselves on the wrong side of security decisions. As an internal *aide-mémoire* frankly recognized, "If [a] person is ordered deported simply on the basis of a document submitted by the RCMP...this would probably be deemed to be a highly arbitrary procedure and contrary to the Bill of Rights." On the other hand, if the RCMP documentation were open to cross-examination, the RCMP would not submit it in the first place, and "we would continue to be in a position where no effective action can be taken to refuse or remove persons who are a security risk." Moreover, it was also the judgement of the department's legal experts that rejected applicants in Canada or at ports of entry would still have "recourse to the courts by means of prerogative writs."[41]

The RCMP would agree to a review board only if it was toothless and unable to compel the force to submit its evidence from confidential sources. Couillard, the deputy minister, advised his minister, the wily Cape Breton politician Allan MacEachen, to oppose the police recommendations: "It is a matter of judgement whether their recommendations are politically palatable." Couillard had in his hand departmental advice that "it was doubtful whether Parliament would enact, or the Canadian public would accept, legislation denying the right of appeal to a special group of persons, which would seem to deny any semblance of natural justice. Moreover, such a law might well be contrary to the Bill of Rights." MacEachen agreed, and Couillard informed the Security Panel that "the underlying principle governing the position we have adopted is that persons ordered deported concerning whom no factual evidence has been presented should not arbitrarily be denied a review of their cases or have no recourse to appeal."[42]

The Security Panel saw things differently. The secretary to the panel, Don Wall, argued with brutal clarity that any legislation establishing a review board must make clear that review could not be a substitute for judicial appeal when national security ruled out such appeals:

> Indeed, the whole purpose of establishing the Board by a special Act of Parliament...is to seek legislative sanction for the withdrawal of one of the basic requirements of natural justice, that a person be given "a fair opportunity to correct or controvert any relevant statement brought forward to his prejudice." In other

words, the function of the Board is to provide a kind
of "honest broker's" assurance, to the individual concerned and to the public at large, that its scrutiny of
governmental decisions in the sometimes murky area
of "security" provides the best available substitute for
the fulfillment of the requirements of natural justice in
circumstances in which it is not in the public interest
to make available to the individual, and to the public
in general, all of the relevant information.[43]

Even the security establishment was becoming concerned
about public appearances, if only for cosmetic purposes. This
development was something of a turning-point in discussions of
national security questions in immigration. Indeed, public opinion was a factor in a surprising number of internal government
discussions at this time. In the 1940s and 1950s, public opinion
had rarely put in an appearance. When it did, it was usually in
the unexamined guise of alleged public intolerance of left-wing
immigrants, almost never in terms of public displeasure over violations of civil liberties or natural justice in the name of national
security. When public opinion began playing a major role in policy deliberations in the late 1960s and early 1970s, it weighed in
the balance against the overriding authority of national security
and on behalf of greater liberality—and against the power and
influence of the RCMP within the counsels of state.

Invoking public opinion on their behalf, some leading officials
in the immigration department questioned the rationale for the
security review board as laid out by Don Wall. Would the transfer
of security appeals out of the jurisdiction of the Immigration
Appeal Board—where unsupported assertions from the RCMP
that national security was at stake were sometimes given second
place behind humanitarian and compassionate factors—to a
review board that would ignore humanitarian considerations
not be "interpreted by certain segments of the public as being
regressive", or as a removal of a right previously granted by
Parliament?[44] Such concerns were now vying for attention with
the older concerns for national security and for administrative
efficiency.

Despite an official endorsement by the prime minister and
the support that the proposal had garnered from the various
interested bureaucratic actors (albeit for varying reasons and

motives), the review board kept falling short of realization. In 1972 the Trudeau government suffered a near-defeat at the polls, and for the next two years it found itself in a minority position. Its agenda was out of its own control in this period, and such matters as security review boards fell by the wayside. But major changes in immigration law lay ahead.

CHAPTER TEN

Terrorists, Scholars, and Refugees

In 1974 the Liberals won another majority government. In 1976 a bill for a new Immigration Act was introduced in the House of Commons, the first major revision of the immigration law for a quarter of a century. By the time it became law in 1978, the context within which the issue of immigration security was understood had changed once again.

By the late 1970s, the domestic threat of international Communism, once so menacing, seemed much shrunken; the United States had withdrawn from its lengthy and self-destructive war in South-east Asia, and the superpowers moved into a short-lived era of *détente* during the Nixon–Kissinger period and later under Democratic president Jimmy Carter.

Yet national security continued to be a matter of great public concern during the 1970s. One element of this concern was the threat of terrorism, which had replaced that of Communism, to a degree. Terrorism had reared its head in the national trauma of the October Crisis in Quebec. In October 1970, the Front de libération du Québec (FLQ) kidnapped a British diplomat, then kidnapped and murdered the Quebec minister of labour, Pierre Laporte. The state's response had been to invoke the extraordinary powers of the War Measures Act against an "apprehended insurrection". Canadians witnessed the army in the streets, peacetime censorship of the press, arrests without warrant and without charge, persons held and interrogated without counsel and without habeas corpus. Although public opinion of this hardline response may have soured to a certain extent in retrospect, the Trudeau government enjoyed unprecedented public approval of its actions at the time, in Quebec as well as in English Canada. The threat of subversion and of the violent overthrow of the state, which in the guise of international Communism had begun to fade like an old photograph, suddenly took on a new and urgent life.

Throughout the 1970s an external dimension was added, that of international terrorism. Aircraft hijackings, airport massacres, terrorist bombings of random civilian targets, attacks on diplomatic missions: such incidents increasingly dominated the headlines and were brought into the living rooms of the electronic global village in the vivid and horrifying images of the nightly television news. As always in such times of fear and anxiety, conspiracy theories were rife. Some were suspiciously close to the old international Communist conspiracy theory: there was a terror network operating throughout the world under the careful direction of Moscow. Other theories recognized that there were indigenous non-Communist bases for terrorism—such as the displaced Palestinian people, the Ulster Catholics, and other aggrieved national minorities—but still saw international connections and shadowy networks linking the explosions of violence. International terror networks, real or apprehended, had profound implications for national security in relation to the movement of people across national boundaries. In short, the political alarms of the 1970s focused the attention of states, including Canada, on immigration and travel and crystallized national security concerns around points of entry—in an age when the technology of air travel, as well as instant electronic communication, had already raised the problem of controlling border flows to entirely new levels of complexity.

If this context seems to imply a new hardening of official attitudes and a resurgence of the protection of national security as the standard for judging public policy, the decade was not without opposing pressures from the other direction. Out of the trauma of the October Crisis came not only the anxious feeling that "it can happen here" and the realization that Canada was not immune to the bloody afflictions of the outside world, but as well a revulsion against the excesses of state repression and the assault on individual liberty that had been undertaken in the name of national security and under the authority of the War Measures Act. One part of this reaction was a dawning realization on the part of many—especially among opposition politicians who had been stampeded into near-unanimity at the time by the hysteria orchestrated by the government—that the federal, Quebec, and even Montreal municipal governments had manipulated public perceptions to their own advantage by exaggerating the real threat posed by the FLQ. The seeds of suspicion concerning what was done in the name of national security were thus planted.

Suspicion was to grow throughout the decade concerning the main agency charged with protecting the national security of Canada, the RCMP. The RCMP security service had not been well prepared for dealing with terrorism that acted in the name of Quebec independence, since its attention had traditionally been focused on the Red Menace. The force attempted to catch up by infiltrating and disrupting the activities of Quebec *indépendantiste* movements—in the process, failing to distinguish between terrorist groups and legitimate political expressions of *indépendantisme*, like the Parti Québécois, and resorting to illegal methods, "dirty tricks", and even some violent acts of their own such as burning barns. The Musical Ride had been replaced by the RCMP Follies, and the media in the early and middle 1970s were agog with revelations of Mountie wrongdoing. These embarrassing exposés eventually led to the creation in 1977 of the McDonald Royal Commission of Inquiry Concerning Certain Activities of the RCMP, a much more serious and critical examination of national security than the Mackenzie commission of a decade earlier; a second result was the civilianization of the security service in 1984 under the Canadian Security Intelligence Service Act, which would change the basic rules under which all national security matters were to be handled.

Canadian concern about international terrorism and transborder traffic was dramatically highlighted by the staging of the 1976 Olympic Games in Montreal. With painful memories of the murder of Israeli athletes by terrorists at the previous games in Munich, and aware that publicity-seeking terrorist groups would be attracted to an event where world attention was focused, the planners of the games organized massive security operations.

Parliament was asked to pass a special law, the Temporary Immigration Security Act, which allowed visitors to be turned back at ports of entry at the discretion of the government or to be deported without a formal inquiry. This was, as its name indicated, a temporary measure to deal with a specific situation, but it had a lasting effect on immigration security policy. The government argued that the old immigration procedures involved too many cumbersome appeal procedures when national security demanded quick and effective action against terrorists or potential terrorists. When it came time to introduce a new Immigration Act, later in the same year as the Olympics, some of the provisions of the Temporary Immigration Security Act had apparently commended themselves to the drafters of the bill, for they were incorporated into permanent immigration procedures.

Even before the Olympics, there were indications that the government was changing its position with regard to immigration security. Part of the run-up to the new Immigration Act had been the Green Paper on immigration policy, published by the immigration department in 1974 under the title *The Immigration Program* as a discussion paper to raise various important issues in the policy field. On security matters, the Green Paper reflected and brought into sharper focus some of the ambivalence that had characterized the White Paper of the previous decade.

On the general question of controls and enforcement, the authors of the Green Paper tried to strike a reasonable balance:

> So long as Canada does not choose to extend its hospitality to all comers, and continues to operate a selective immigration policy, there will be a need to prevent the entry of the unwanted immigrant and undesirable visitor, and take action against abuses of immigration law and policy.

The problem was that controls in the age of mass tourism were based on the Immigration Act of 1952: "It is scarcely an exaggeration to say that jet-age traffic is still largely governed by steamboat law." Yet the scope for controls was limited by the values and opinions of the Canadian people:

> Canadians have always enjoyed a free and open society, and this forms no small part of Canada's attraction

for people in other lands. Canadians wish to preserve the freedom and openness of their society, and
therefore immigration control activities have always
shunned any general practice that would infringe on
these qualities.[1]

The authors cited practices such as regular reporting to police
and fingerprint controls prevalent in other democratic countries that would presumably be unacceptable to Canadians (the
Mackenzie commission had recommended that all immigrants
be fingerprinted).

The Green Paper was particularly concerned about possible
security threats from visitors, reflecting the growing fear of
international terrorism. Yet the system once in place requiring
visas for travellers was now largely dismantled. Even in cases
where visas were still required, formal security screening was
"not conducted except as a post-factum audit". The focus was
now on ports of entry, where the ultimate decision rested with
the examining officer (these officers were now the first control
point for 99 per cent of traffic), but of 560 official ports, only 43
were staffed permanently by immigration officers.[2]

The old system of "look-out" lists, dating back to the end of the
1940s, was still in operation. There were cumulative lists available in all offices of 5,000 persons "whose presence in Canada
would constitute an immediate and serious danger to public
health, public safety or national security." This information was
being computerized, to be readily and quickly accessible.[3] In
fact, while the Green Paper was being prepared, there were a
number of notorious cases of visiting academics being barred
from entering Canada to give lectures or engage in other scholarly activities, apparently because of their presence on a look-out
list. Public protests had been loud, but the Green Paper did not
comment on them.

On the vexed question of the legal definition of a subversive
threat to Canada, the Green Paper was reticent. If "subversives"
were to be treated as a prohibited class, there was a problem of
identification. Subversive activity was open to many different interpretations: "One must guard against classifying as subversive
what may amount to no more than innocuous dissent." Yet the
Green Paper insisted:

Great care is taken by the Government to ensure that the criteria for determining whether an organization or an individual is subversive relate directly to the security of Canada and Canadians, and that they are fair, relevant to current conditions, and conscientiously observed.[4]

On the actual screening process abroad, the authors somewhat misleadingly reported that "selection officers normally accept RCMP officers' opinion on questions of subversive activity": in fact, officers in the field had no authority to overrule RCMP rejections—that could only be done in Ottawa. The time involved in screening varied considerably from country to country, but the "present global average is 70 to 75 days" on security case delays, which they claimed to be even shorter than those for medical reasons (they cited no statistical evidence for this comparison).[5]

The authors made much of the significance to liberal democracy of the Immigration Appeal Board and the "exceptionally progressive appeal philosophy introduced in 1967". At the same time they claimed that a "very liberal selection policy" had proven "unmanageable in practice"; this result was cited as justification for the legislative changes made in 1973 that restricted the jurisdiction of the board. Nevertheless they showered praise on the board; hearings were conducted "in an atmosphere of solemn dignity"; natural justice was scrupulously followed; the attitude towards appellants "has consistently been one of patience and understanding.... The Board's concept of natural justice has always taken precedence over considerations of expediency or expense."[6] The authors remained silent about the denial of natural justice that was manifested by the lack of appeals in security cases.

All in all, the Green Paper was not a decisive statement pointing the way forward—whatever way that might be. Even academic specialists who were enlisted in preparing background papers pronounced themselves unimpressed. This was certainly the view of Freda Hawkins, the most distinguished scholarly analyst of immigration policy. She scornfully described the Green Paper as "a disappointing and inadequate document which is, for the most part, best forgotten."[7]

In the early 1970s a number of foreign scholars were barred on security grounds (and attempts were made to bar others) from entering Canada to take up academic positions offered by Canadian universities. Widely seen as an attempt to infringe upon academic freedom and freedom of expression through the immigration laws, these incidents roused considerable anger in some influential quarters of Canadian opinion and served to bring the immigration security process into public ridicule.

During the height of the Cold War in the late 1940s and early 1950s, American universities had been the site of some of the bitterest struggles over the issues of disloyalty and McCarthyism. Many American scholars lost their jobs, and some fled the country. In Canada there were few notable Cold War conflicts on the campus; there were fewer universities in this period in Canada than there are today, the existing ones were small, and there was little tradition of radical politics among faculty. One mathematician, Israel Halperin, arrested in the Gouzenko spy affair in 1946 and later named in a royal commission report as a Soviet espionage agent, was allowed to keep his position at Queen's University after he was acquitted in criminal proceedings. Moreover, a number of American academics who had been fired on political grounds or whose jobs were threatened came to Canada to take up careers at Canadian universities. Immigration security controls did not appear to have impeded this small-scale but significant movement of political refugees into Canada, despite the ideological cloud under which they left the US.[8] Given this background, it was somewhat odd that the Cold War hit the Canadian campus, through the immigration route, a decade or two later.

The troubles arose out of an unusual conjuncture. During the 1960s, Canadian universities had proliferated and expanded at an unprecedented rate. Lacking sufficient qualified teaching staff graduated from Canadian universities, they widened their recruitment to include many foreign academics, especially Americans. New universities sought to attract leading scholars and scientists, mainly from abroad, to build up the prestige of new faculties and departments and lay the groundwork for future strength. These were the same years when political protest on American campuses exploded into sometimes violent confrontations with the forces of law and order. Beginning at Berkeley in the mid-1960s, speeded by the rising tide of protest against the

Vietnam War, left-wing protests spread around the country, culminating in such events as the student take-over of Columbia University and the notorious massacre of student demonstrators at Kent State University in 1970.

Around the world as well, students were rising up. In France, a massive student revolt in conjunction with a general strike came close to toppling the Fifth Republic in May 1968. These events had echoes in Canada: there were well-publicized student protests at Simon Fraser University and at Sir George Williams in downtown Montreal, where students took over and destroyed the multimillion-dollar computer centre. In Quebec, campuses became hotbeds of separatist sentiment, while the FLQ was bombing and building up to the ultimate confrontation with power in the October Crisis. Canada's universities, once largely ignored by the security establishment, were beginning to be seen by that establishment as targets for subversion and as possible breeding grounds for violence and revolution.

Nor were faculty immune from the suspicions with which radical student movements were viewed. The late 1960s were the era of the "new left" in North America, and the movement had many theorists and enthusiasts among faculty. Moreover, some of the younger faculty members being recruited in the United States for Canadian universities were themselves graduates of new-left campus politics. All the warning signs were out for the immigration security people. The criteria for rejecting immigrants on security grounds had not changed much from the early days of the Cold War, but when these criteria were applied to the academics coming into Canada in the late 1960s and early 1970s, the numbers barred suddenly shot up. As an immigration department document of 1969 put it: "One of the most difficult problems we have had to face in recent years has been the influx of radical students, professors and others concerning whom the RCMP had furnished adverse security reports."[9] It seems that the security establishment was not prepared for the reaction that followed.

The RCMP was singularly unprepared to deal with academics. Few members of the security service had university educations. A program begun in the 1960s helped security service officers take time off to gain degrees. Over the long haul this effort may have had some effect, although many of those who did gain degrees later quit the force for work that they found more satisfying. The RCMP had little appreciation of the concept of academic freedom and exhibited a definite tendency over the years to confuse dissent with subversion. Moreover the RCMP was in bad odour on campuses after the discovery in the early 1960s of undercover agents monitoring lectures. This operation was called off after formal protests by university administrations and pressure by the Canadian Association of University Teachers, who denounced such intelligence-gathering as inimical to academic freedom.

In the late 1960s the RCMP was raising the issue of national security in relation to the universities with greater frequency. In the spring of 1969 Deputy Commissioner William Kelly told the Security Panel, "The current unrest at universities posed both a police and a political problem, and one province was considering establishing an intelligence unit to look into the matter. RCMP liaison with such units would be of great importance in the future."[10] It does not seem that such units were actually created, but that universities represented "both a police and a political problem" was accepted in many circles in Ottawa.

Around this time cases of academics either barred from entry or put through various degrees of difficulty in coming to accept teaching posts began to surface in the media. In procedural terms, the RCMP could not bear sole responsibility for these decisions. It was official immigration policy that university teaching staff were treated in security matters in the same way as sponsored dependants. If adverse information was received, their applications would be forwarded to Ottawa for review by the Interdepartmental Committee on Immigration Applications.[11] In other words, all cases of barred academics would have been considered not merely by the security service, but by civilian officials in Immigration and other departments represented on the committee. This procedure involved more red tape than usual, and complaints about delays in getting final approval for incoming academics were frequent.

More serious were the outright rejections. It is impossible to know the exact number of those rejected, for the non-arrival of academics was not always news and the government did not publish figures. Delays were probably more common, and in some cases the delays alone discouraged the individuals in question from coming to Canada. What is clear in every case of which details are available is that the scholar in question seems to have had some connections, either overt or even distant and indirect (through family relationships, for instance), with the political left. Communism as such was not necessarily at the root of the connection, although some variation on the Communist theme seems to have been in the background of most of the European scholars who were barred. Scholars of the American new left often had no connections with the Communist left of a generation earlier, but in some cases association with the new left seems to have been the only visible basis for negative security reports. This political bias, so typical of the immigration security process, was bound to create a debate about state interference in academic freedom and freedom of expression when applied to the highly sensitive culture of the university campus—especially at a time when there were relatively large left-wing student movements.

What made matters worse, angering faculty and university administrators who had no particular sympathy for left-wing ideas, was that some of the scholars, especially some from Europe, were of world renown. The academic world is a more international one than many professions; word passes quickly across borders. Canadian scholars began to speak of the actions of their government as an "embarrassment", even a "great national humiliation" that was threatening to make Canadian universities the "laughing stock of Europe".[12]

A number of universities, including the University of British Columbia, Simon Fraser, and Queen's, found that the foreign academics they invited were barred or delayed at the border. But the university that seemed to suffer the problem with the greatest frequency was York. Located in the northern suburbs of Metropolitan Toronto, York was by far the most ambitious of all the new universities that came into being in the 1960s in English Canada.[13] Starting from scratch, the university pursued an aggressive and imaginative recruitment policy; unhappily for York, this drive coincided with the Canadian government's own drive to step up the security measures applied to imported academics. The result was a series of at least eight cases from 1968 to 1973, ranging from delays and difficulties resolved by RCMP interviews to attempted barrings fought by the individuals in question. At least one invitee was kept out of the country.

Among the more prominent York cases was that of Andreas Papandreou, who had been a minister in the reformist Greek government of the early 1960s led by his father, George Papandreou.

The younger Papandreou, a noted economist, was incarcerated in the colonels' coup of 1967 that brought a temporary end to democracy in that country. After his release, he was offered a position in the economics department at York. The university experienced considerable delays and difficulties in getting clearance, difficulties that were apparently ended by a direct and lengthy discussion in 1968 between Prime Minister Lester Pearson and John Saywell, York's dean of arts. Saywell made an undertaking that, in effect, Papandreou would not use his university position to organize resistance to the military dictatorship, while insisting that what he might do in his own time, outside his university duties, was of course his own affair.[14] With that agreement, permission was granted.

Papandreou spent a few years as an eminent figure at York. What he did in his spare time was precisely to organize against the Greek junta; he laid the groundwork for a non-Communist party of the left. When the junta crumbled in 1974, Papandreou's Canadian teaching career ended abruptly, and he flew back to a tumultuous welcome at Athens airport. In 1981, Papandreou's PASOK party won a landslide victory in a general election, and the one-time Canadian academic became the prime minister of Greece, an office he continues to hold today. Canada had offered a temporary haven for a leader of a democratic movement opposing a brutal dictatorship that imprisoned and tortured its opponents; ultimately this earned us a certain amount of gratitude from the restored Greek democracy. Why, one may ask, was the Canadian government so concerned to keep out Papandreou, who was in any case admissible under the government's own guidelines?

Shortly after the resolution of the Papandreou case, the York economics department was faced with another immigration case. A Polish economist, Kazimiercz Laski, had been offered a position and then refused entry to Canada. Laski had apparently been a member of the Polish Communist party since 1945—the year that a Communist Poland was established—and had held relatively prominent state positions. Both these affiliations would have placed him within the inadmissible category, according to the secret guidelines used by the government for Soviet-bloc applicants, except for the fact that he had had a falling-out with the regime and had left Poland for Vienna, where he was working for the Austrian government. This did not sway the security judgement: Laski was considered a threat to Canada's national security. Laski refused to pursue the matter and never came to York. Explaining why he did not fight his designation as a threat to Canada, the Polish economist replied, memorably: "Who needs to run from one police state to another?"[15]

In 1970 another well-publicized York case involved Gabriel Kolko, a brilliant and productive young American historian. Kolko had already acquired a reputation as one of the leading revisionist historians, who were challenging conventional accounts of the origins and meaning of America's role in the world conflict with the Communist bloc through a series of books that radically reinterpreted American history. Naturally his views made him a contentious figure in an America torn apart by the Vietnam War. When Kolko accepted an offer to teach history at York, the Canadian government refused to issue an entry permit. Kolko decided to come to Canada to fight. An applicant physically present within the country could pursue certain avenues of appeal that could not be followed from abroad. Press publicity followed, and high-level representations to the Trudeau government were made by York on Kolko's behalf. Immigration officials finally claimed that it was not a security problem at all, but cited a medical question that could easily be resolved with a medical certificate. It was produced and Kolko was admitted.

The claim of medical grounds is not to be taken at face value.[16] There can be little doubt that the real obstacle was political objections passed from the FBI to the RCMP. No other explanation makes sense in the context. That Kolko came and fought—and won—was a significant victory in the struggle to protect academic freedom from the meddling of the security police. Kolko himself remains at York, where he continues to publish important work. Recently he was made a Fellow of the ultra-establishment Royal Society of Canada.

York was not yet through with immigration security. In 1972 the most infamous case of all hit the press. The university had appointed István Mészáros to teach in the Social and Political Thought Program. Mészáros was considered a major addition to the York faculty, for he is among the most distinguished contemporary Marxist philosophers. By birth a Hungarian, and associated in his work with George Lukacs (one of the leading figures in twentieth-century Marxist thought), Mészáros had left Hungary in 1956 along with many of his compatriots when the Soviet army crushed the Hungarian revolt, which he had supported. He eventually settled in England, where he acquired British citizenship.

Mészáros was teaching at the University of Sussex when he decided to accept the York offer. Having resigned his Sussex position, he then discovered, after the usual lengthy delays, that the Canadian visa office in London would not accept his application for landed status. In the usual unspecific fashion, it was indicated that his entry into Canada would be "contrary to the Canadian public interest". Mészáros, unlike Laski, was not prepared to accept this apparent slur on his name. On legal advice from those who understood how best to deal with Canadian immigration laws, Mészáros flew to Canada, entered the country as a visitor, and prepared to fight on Canadian soil.

The minister of immigration at the time was Bryce Mackasey, a garrulous politician from the streets of Irish Montreal who knew a great deal about old-fashioned ward politics but apparently little about Hungarian philosophers or university scholarship. No impression appears to have been made on Mackasey when the president of York University, David Slater, wrote him shortly after Mészáros's unauthorized arrival to "request the urgent and sympathetic review" of the Mészáros application.[17] Slater made the point that "Dr. Mészáros' ideological views are not hidden but are given careful, open exposure in his writings and are therefore open to the criticism of all. Ideological views are not, we understand, a basis for judging the national interest as it applies to entry." Slater also pointedly questioned the credibility of security screening in such a case: "We have no assurance that the interviews carried out with Dr. Mészáros have been by highly experienced officers who have a great deal of expertise in dealing with such matters." Moreover, "Dr. Mészáros was well known as an opponent of the Stalinist regime in Hungary and a defender of civil liberties."

This latter observation touched upon what may have been the RCMP's real difficulty with Mészáros: he had been a Communist who had broken with the regime and come to the West, but who retained a Marxist philosophical perspective—indeed, who criticized the practice of Communism in the East from a Marxist point of view. Subtle distinctions between Marxism and Communism were not the forte of the RCMP. Yet this was the real point of the affair: Mészáros must have been barred for his ideas, because in the circumstances there could have been no evidence of subversive activities on behalf of Soviet Communism. When all is said and done, barring a distinguished philosopher from teaching in Canada because of his ideas is state interference with freedom of expression.

Personal interviews by Slater and other York officials with Mackasey and his aides did little to clarify the situation. It was admitted that a "security report" was involved, and Mackasey maintained to Slater that he had personally reviewed the case and regarded "the allegations seriously and the evidence as weighty"—but no evidence or details were ever produced.[18] The impression grew that "the case against Dr. Mészáros is based on scant materials and may evaporate when further checking is done", as a university document put it. Worse followed. In the absence of evidence, beleaguered government officials blurted out innuendoes that reflected on Mészáros's character.[19] In a convivial moment, Mackasey allowed that as a "compassionate man, I hope he's not guilty", but he refused to specify what Mészáros might be "guilty" of.[20] A Mackasey aide told the press, among other things, that the philosopher was "no golden-haired boy".[21] Mészáros sued the aide. That officials of the government should make innuendoes based on privileged access to secret documentation was surely to bring the whole process into contempt. All the while, the government seemed determined to block every attempt by Mészáros's lawyers to bring the matter to court, leaving the clear implication that it had no defensible case after all.

Mészáros was offered a ministerial work permit but declined, because his lawyers suggested it was merely an attempt by the government to avoid exonerating him on the security matter. According to Mészáros, it was suggested by a ministerial aide that he should return to Britain and refile for landing, on the "95% assurance" that everything would go ahead if the minister were thus allowed to "save face".[22] To Mészáros himself, and to his wife, who had remained in England with their children, it had understandably become a matter of clearing his own name, not saving Bryce Mackasey's face. But going through the necessary legal channels was of course costly. York itself funded Mészáros's case up to $5,000, but the Association of Universities and Colleges of Canada, which had publicly supported the professor in representations to the government, either would not or could not offer additional financial assistance. Like Gabriel Kolko, Mészáros himself was left to pay for much of his own defence; the prospect of similar legal costs would prove to be an additional barrier that would discourage other applicants with immigration problems.

Within York University itself, there was strong support for Mészáros and sharp condemnation of the government among both faculty and students. A large contingent of faculty from the Osgoode Hall Law School termed the government's action an "offence to the Canadian Bill of Rights and our professed adherence to the Rule of Law." The student newspaper made a telling editorial point: "security" was a screen used by the state. "The individual, powerless to know what's hidden by the screen, is a victim of psychological warfare."[23] Across Canada, thirty-two faculty associations and the Canadian Association of University Teachers made representations to the minister.

If the Canadian reaction did not embarrass the government sufficiently, the Mészáros case quickly became an international *cause célèbre.*   American academics and intellectuals condemned the government. Members of Britain's National Council of Civil Liberties denounced a "flagrant intellectual witch-hunt" by the Canadian government. Asa Briggs, the eminent British scholar and former colleague of Mészáros, cancelled a scheduled lecture at an Ontario university as a protest. The British sociologist Tom Bottomore, who had once taught in Canada himself, wrote that Mészáros had "come up against that strong illiberal element in Canadian society which I also encountered in a more moderate way...and [which] had some part in affecting my decision to return to Europe." Isaiah Berlin, a celebrated British political philosopher of pronouncedly anti-Marxist views, added his voice to the protests. And in the French newspaper *Le Monde*, under the headline "Les sorcières d'Ottawa", Pierre Vidal-Naquet headed a list of prominent Parisian scholars and intellectuals signing an open letter of protest to Prime Minister Trudeau. This was an international humiliation for Canadian universities. Bryce Mackasey may not have felt it, but it was beginning to touch others in government. On October 25, Senator Donald Cameron wrote Mackasey, "While I have no brief for Dr. Mészáros' views...a grave injustice has been done to the man as well as to York University."

Yet in mid-November a special inquiry officer made an order to deport Mészáros. After a personal interview with the minister of external affairs, Mitchell Sharp, a university representative reported that Sharp was "privately ready to concede that there was not a substantial charge against Professor Mészáros, [but] he confessed to being puzzled, as we are about the case. While Mr. Sharp thought the Minister might have been provoked to take a hard line, what remains unexplained is who is responsible for the original refusal and for what reason."[24]

If it had become a case of saving the minister's face, the problem was solved when Mackasey was dropped from Cabinet following the Trudeau government's near-defeat in the fall election of 1972.[25] The new minister, Robert Andras, less colourful but more reasonable than his predecessor, began the slow process of bringing the government down off the limb upon which Mackasey had left it. Eventually Mészáros was able to take up his teaching post at York when the mysterious evidence of a "security risk" just as mysteriously evaporated. Scarred by the experience, however, Mészáros, along with his wife and children, could no longer give his heart to a country that had treated him as Canada had. After a couple of years he returned to Britain, where he continues to teach and write today. It was a sad end to a discreditable affair.

Did the government learn anything from it? In the spring of 1973, the Mészáros affair was raised by an NDP member of the House of Commons Standing Committee on Immigration. What were the criteria for determining "security risks"? The new minister blandly replied, "I was never aware that he was in any way described as a security risk." Under further questioning, Andras granted that his entry had been described as "not in the Canadian public interest", but would go no farther. He also bristled at the suggestion that academics had been treated any differently than any other category of would-be immigrants. The minister did, however, allow that "an individual is always at a disadvantage in dealing with large organizations such as governments."[26] That might serve as a fitting epitaph for the Mészáros affair and for the role of immigration security in Canadian academic life.

Perhaps the Mészáros affair did teach the government something, for there have been no similar cases since the final messy resolution of his case. However, before any credit is given to the

Canadian state, a few other contributing factors might be mentioned. By the mid-1970s university funding had begun to slow down and higher education in Canada entered a phase of fiscal crisis and restraint from which it has never recovered. In this context, the heavy volume of recruitment characteristic of the late 1960s, especially of relatively high-priced senior scholars from abroad, has largely dried up. Thus there have been few invited scholars to fall afoul of security. Secondly, by the early 1970s the scare about revolutionary activities on the campus had dissipated and then vanished, in Canada and other countries. The Ottawa security establishment turned its attention elsewhere and left university professors once again to their books and lectures. It would be foolish to assume that there could be no recurrence of a Mészáros-type affair in the future. The machinery is still in place.

The large international refugee movements of the 1970s put Canadian immigration to the test. One of the first trials came in September 1973, when tragic events unfolded in Chile that were to demonstrate far more clearly than bureaucratic memoranda and official government statements the political and ideological biases that continued to underlie Canadian immigration policy. The Fascist coup that brought down the democratically elected Socialist-Communist government of Salvador Allende began an onslaught of brutality and torture against Allende supporters and created a flood of refugees. For the first time Canada was confronted with the mirror image of the refugee movements it had faced in the past. Unlike the displaced persons refusing repatriation to the Soviet-dominated East, or the Hungarians and the Czechs and Slovaks fleeing Soviet tanks, the Chileans were left-wing refugees, including Communists, fleeing a right-wing totalitarianism allied to the United States and tied closely to Western economic interests (including some Canadian interests).

Faced with this challenge, Canada failed the test of political even-handedness. Although Canada had moved within a generation from an immigration policy that had been openly racist and unashamedly biased in favour of certain nationalities to a policy that was officially blind to the colour of an immigrant's skin, the Chilean military coup demonstrated that the politics of immigration were anything but colour-blind: red and even shades of pink were still like the proverbial flag to the bull of the Ottawa security establishment and, it seemed, to the Trudeau government as a whole.

The political bias in Canada's treatment of the Chileans was cast into even more striking relief by the welcome given only the year before to another group of refugees, a welcome that had seemed to indicate that Canada's ancient racist biases had been much diminished. In 1972 the Ugandan despot Idi Amin decreed the expulsion from his country within ninety days of some 50,000 persons of Asian origin who held British passports, precipitating a major international refugee crisis. Where were they to go? Britain, whose citizenship they held, was reluctant to add to what was perceived as a growing economic and racial problem with its own Asian and black minorities. An appeal was sent out to other countries.

In Canada no significant racist backlash appeared to develop, and public opinion, at least as expressed through newspaper editorials, tended to emphasize humanitarian responsibilities. The government announced its intention to help some of the refugees to come to this country; eventually Canada accepted 5,600 Ugandan Asians. By getting an immigration team into Uganda very quickly Canada was able, in effect, to skim off the cream of the crop. Gerald Dirks concludes, "In terms of age and educational qualifications, the Ugandan Asians comprised one of the most desirable groups ever to gain admittance to Canada."[27] The Ugandan Asians, like the Czechs and Slovaks a few years earlier, became self-supporting and economically productive members of Canadian society in an extraordinarily short period of time. For the first time a relatively large number of non-white refugees were resettled in Canada, and in a relatively painless and cost-effective manner.

A year later, Chile showed the other, political side of Canada's refugee policy. Chile was a sad case of what happens to indigenous forces for change in the underdeveloped world when they become ensnared in the ruthless politics of the Cold War. Since the triumphant arrival in Havana of the Cuban revolutionaries under Fidel Castro on New Year's Day 1959, successive United States administrations have labelled all left-wing movements to overthrow conservative regimes in South America as "Communist" and have used all means, up to direct military intervention, to enforce their will. Just as the USSR has maintained hegemony over Eastern Europe, reserving the "right", as enunciated in the so-called Brezhnev Doctrine, to intervene militarily against opposition, so too under the nineteenth-century Monroe Doctrine the United States claims the "right" to intervene wherever it feels its interests threatened throughout the entire Western Hemisphere. In both cases the superpowers justify their overlordship as defence against subversion allegedly directed by the other side. Direct military intervention is undertaken only in desperation. A more common weapon of American hegemony is a covert war against the left and the direct and indirect support of repressive and reactionary regimes throughout the continent.

Chile posed perhaps the sharpest challenge ever to the American position. Salvador Allende led a coalition called Popular Unity (majority Socialist, minority Communist) to a victory in a free election in 1970. Without jailing opponents or in any way impeding the opposition's freedom of expression, the Allende government began a program of profound social and economic change, including an attack on the holdings of the huge landowners and the nationalization of foreign (mainly American) companies operating in Chile. After Allende's coalition won an unprecedented increase in public support in mid-term congressional elections, the Chilean military carried out a military coup on September 11, 1973. Allende himself died defending the presidential palace. The coup set in motion a veritable bloodbath that would claim many thousands of victims and created a military police state under Gen. Augusto Pinochet, who is still ruling with an iron fist as this is written, fourteen years later.

As the army and the police swept through Santiago, dragging victims to their fate, some sought routes of escape. There were many non-Chileans residing in Allende's Chile who had themselves fled repressive right-wing regimes in other Latin American countries such as Brazil; they now became targets of Pinochet and were recognized by the UN High Commission for Refugees as legitimate recipients of assistance. But there were also many Chileans—supporters of the Allende regime, people of leftist views, trade union organizers, and so on—who were in immediate physical danger. Some sought refuge in foreign embassies in Santiago, including the Canadian embassy.

The immediate Canadian response was markedly different from that which had greeted the Hungarian and Czechoslovakian revolts. Then, maximum Cold War propaganda effect had been wrung from the Soviet interventions, and Canada's humanitarian concern for resettlement of the refugees from tyranny had been stressed. Canada recognized the Chilean junta with alacrity and showed deep reluctance to consider the claims of the refugees from that junta. Those who had sought refuge within the Canadian embassy compound were the immediate concern. Canada refused to recognize formally any right of diplomatic asylum, a common convention in Latin America. Dispatches from the Canadian ambassador to External Affairs, indicating overt hostility to the refugees, were leaked to the press. Eventually about fifty persons were grudgingly given temporary shelter in the embassy while they sought safe passage out of the country. But that left the broader question of assistance to allow Chilean refugees to resettle in Canada.

Voices of considerable resonance were raised within Canada in support of a special program. The Canadian Council of Churches appealed to the government on "humanitarian, and not political" grounds:

> Since these refugees are in danger of their lives, under a very repressive military regime, we have only one option: to do what we can to save these lives. Canada opened her doors to refugees from Hungary, Czechoslovakia and Uganda. If we refuse to open our doors to people who are in danger under another type of political regime, this would mean that we had acted from political rather than humanitarian motives.[28]

It was a very pointed appeal—and one that signalled the emergence of a new coalition of public interest groups with an interest in promoting refugee claims on humanitarian grounds. The churches were advised by their own missionaries and the World Council of Churches on conditions in Chile. They were soon joined by other groups such as the Canadian Association of University Teachers and the Association of Colleges and Universities of Canada, who had not previously made representations on refugee questions. The churches have in fact remained active throughout the 1970s and 1980s in monitoring refugee policy and acting directly to assist resettlement of refugees, forming the nucleus of a kind of humanitarian public interest lobby on behalf of persons who otherwise lack any effective voice.

In 1973–74 these voices were heard but not always listened to by the Liberal government. As Dirks remarks with some understatement, the government demonstrated "greater caution and reluctance to adopt a liberal refugee policy than on earlier occasions."[29] No special waivers were granted and no relaxation of normal standards was initiated, as had been done for the Hungarian, Czechoslovak, and Ugandan refugees. There were no immigration officers in Chile, and it was not until late November 1973, almost three months after the coup, that a special immigration team arrived in Santiago. When it set to work, independent Canadian observers were outraged at what they saw. Processing was agonizingly slow. By Christmas, a mere 184 applicants out of 1,400 had received visas. Three months later the number of visas had grown to only 780, yet in the summer of 1974 Canada decreased its immigration personnel in Chile and in neighbouring states where other Chileans were making applications. Canada's record was judged by the observers to be one of the worst of the Western countries processing refugees in the country.[30]

The main reason for the delay was the old bugbear of immigration processing: security screening. This was of course where the political and ideological bias was focused, and the contrast with past refugee experiences was glaring. First, the real refugees from Pinochet were exactly the sort of persons that the security screening system had been devised to filter out: left-wingers, socialists, and, worst of all, avowed Communists. There were others wanting to leave Chile who were either politically centrist or apolitical "economic" refugees. These could, and did, pass through the security screen, but they were not the ones in pressing physical danger from the junta; for those truly threatened, it was catch-22. In the Hungarian case the RCMP had pressed the government to put national security concerns above humanitarian motives, but the Liberal minister of immigration had decided to waive security, despite the RCMP's objections. In the Chilean case, neither the minister of external affairs, Mitchell Sharp, nor the minister of immigration, Robert Andras—nor the prime minister, Pierre Trudeau—appears to have had the courage shown by Pickersgill two decades earlier.

But in addition, there was a wider context to consider. The Hungarians were mainly anti-Communists fleeing a state ruled by Canada's Cold War antagonist. Chile, however brutal and distasteful its new regime may have appeared to idealistic Canadian observers, was firmly anchored within the anti-Communist American alliance; moreover, it was seen to be protecting not only specific American economic interests (ITT, for instance, had insisted that the US government bring about the overthrow of Allende and had offered its own services to the cause) but the general interests of North American investment in Latin America (Canadian businesses, especially banks, have considerable stakes in Latin America). In the Hungarian case, security could be set aside temporarily because Pickersgill recognized that the larger cause of anti-Communism would thereby be better served—even if the security police, with their narrower vision, failed at first to appreciate this. In the Chilean case, both the short-term and the long-term Cold War logic of the security system dictated that humanitarian considerations should get short shrift. And so they did.

There was another, sinister dimension to the security aspects of the Chilean case. The security problem in the Hungarian case was that local screening could not be done; that is, the RCMP did not contact the Hungarian secret police to inquire about applicants. In the Chilean case, the strict security screening being applied would normally have involved referring names of applicants to the local authorities; but it was precisely this type of official attention that the genuine political refugees were fleeing. It is not clear whether local screening of Chileans was actually carried out; the relevant internal documents were not available at the time of writing. It is a reasonable assumption, however, that the RCMP had some liaison with the Chilean police. If the Americans were contacted, it would have been no better for the refugees, since the CIA had been gathering lists of leftists during the Allende years for possible use by anti-Allende forces, and it was working hand-in-glove with the junta following the coup. So no matter where the RCMP did its screening investigations, the cards were stacked heavily against the political refugees. Indeed, many Chileans may have been deterred from even applying to emigrate to Canada out of fear of being brought to the hostile attention of the junta's secret police.[31]

By early 1975 a total of 1,188 Chileans had reached Canada. It was widely rumoured among the pro-refugee lobby groups that many of these were non-political or political moderates. These immigrants were of course welcome, but their acceptance reduced the number of refugees in genuine physical danger with a chance of reaching safety in Canada; it is not known how many refugees fell into these categories. A broad coalition of church, labour, and public interest groups sharply criticized the government:

> Expressed humanitarian concern by the Canadian government has been contradicted by lengthy processing and excessive security interrogations.... Canada is hardly humanitarian if in the execution of its policy, an adequate and speedy response to human need is superseded by time consuming procedures, partial measures for the oppressed, and out of date and inappropriate security interrogations.[32]

The government seemed unimpressed by criticisms from the public. At most it displayed a degree of irritation from time to time. The Green Paper, for example, was uncharacteristically defensive and snappish on the Chilean question. Although the authors had previously patted the Canadian government on the back for its "generous" treatment of refugees, describing in glowing terms the Hungarian, Czech, and Ugandan experiences, Chile called forth much vague rhetoric about the situation in the wake of the coup being "grave and complex...confused in the extreme". Not denying the danger to individuals, the authors nevertheless generated clouds of bureaucratic squid-ink to obfuscate a reality that was not difficult for most observers on the scene to grasp: "Reports differed as to the numbers of people in immediate danger.... Reliable information was hard to obtain.... Consistent and responsible policy demanded energetic efforts to get at the facts, and the development of a program to process those people who most needed and deserved attention." The Green Paper even slipped into special pleading when it maintained that the Chileans were actually the objects of a special program "provided they complied with basic health and security requirements"—a proviso that blatantly missed the point.[33]

The melancholy example of Chile led Gerald Dirks to end his fine 1977 study of refugee policy with the following reflections:

Ideological considerations may have overshadowed race, at least temporarily, as a determining factor for refugee admission. If the experience of the Chilean refugees of 1973 and 1974 reflects official Canadian attitudes, it is clear that in future other right wing regimes will compel citizens holding left of centre views to forsake their homelands. Only then will it become clear whether ideological considerations have replaced racial criteria as a discriminatory factor in determining Canada's refugee admissions policy.[34]

The continuing problems experienced by refugees from right-wing regimes in Central America in the 1980s, to be discussed in the next chapter, show that Dirks' speculation of a decade ago was not far off the mark.

At the end of the decade dramatic stories of a new refugee problem caught the attention of the world media. Vietnamese, Kampucheans, and Laotians were fleeing in unprecedentedly large numbers from the Communist regimes established in the wake of the historic defeat of American arms in the Vietnam War and the subsequent collapse of the pro-American South-east Asian states before the Communist armies in the mid-1970s. Many of these refugees were fleeing in small boats, prey to rough seas and to pirates who raped and murdered their victims. Those who survived the waters found themselves in desperate straits in grim camps in countries such as Thailand and Malaysia. An appeal went out around the world, and by the summer of 1980 close to 900,000 had been resettled, well over half of whom had fled by boat. They were resettled in many countries: in Asia itself, in Europe, and in North America. The United States, whose armies had shot, bombed, napalmed, defoliated—and bled—in South-east Asia for over a decade, in a vain but enormously destructive war against the Communists, took the greatest number of the refugees: 389,000, or 44 per cent of the total. The People's Republic of China, whose armies had themselves invaded Communist Vietnam briefly in 1979, took over a quarter of a million, or 30 per cent. France, which had been the original colonial power and whose armies had been defeated by the Communist Vietminh in the early 1950s, accepted about 66,000, making it host to the third-largest group.

Close behind was Canada, which alone among the large host countries had had no official connection with the cataclysmic events that had convulsed the region. Canada took in more than 60,000 Indo-Chinese refugees in a short period of time, the single most generous record of any major country in proportion to its population.[35]

The sheer humanitarian appeal of people adrift at sea at the mercy of fate was no doubt at the heart of the public response in Canada. The ideological dimension, is, however, rarely absent in the response to political refugee movements. Right-wing Canadians did not miss the opportunity to score anti-Communist points off the backs of the refugees. In the United States, a factor in the positive initial response on the part of the government was clearly an attempt to steal some justification retroactively for a traumatic and divisive, not to say unsuccessful war: the fact of the boat people showed the Communist states to be exactly the sort of brutal totalitarian regimes the Americans had claimed to be opposing. One cannot deny that the Communist states were doing their best to live up to this label; certainly any state that drives its citizens to such desperate lengths to escape must be doing something terribly wrong. Yet the simplistic anti-Communist perspective in which the refugee movement was so often viewed fails to come to terms with some important realities.

First and foremost, the refugee movements were not merely the result of the imposition of a particular ideological regime; they were also the direct result of war. The Vietnamese had been at war for four terrible decades: against the Japanese, against the French, against the Americans, and against one another. Even with the collapse of the South Vietnamese government in 1975 and the reunification of the country under Communist control, war did not come to an end: Vietnamese armies invaded neighbouring Kampuchea to overthrow the Khmer Rouge regime established in that country, and they had to defend Vietnamese territory against invading Communist Chinese armies at the end of the decade. Constant war had exacted a profound economic, social, and human toll. Far more bombs were dropped on Indo-China than had been dropped by all sides in all theatres of operation in all of the Second World War. Much of the countryside had suffered terrible ecological damage, and as a result of chemical warfare unborn generations were fated to suffer severe genetic malformations. The United States had agreed in secret peace negotiations with the North Vietnamese to pay reparations for the damage its military operations had cost—and then reneged on the promise.

War had brought about, as it always does, massive relocations of people. In fact, the largest movement of people by far was within Indo-China, inside existing states and among the states of the region. The movement of boat people out of the region was a small proportion of the overall forced migration. All this upheaval was further complicated by the ancient ethnic and cultural divisions underlying a crazy quilt of state antagonisms, superpower rivalries, and intra-Communist quarrels. Communist fought Communist with as much enthusiasm, and as much brutality, as Communist had fought American.

Kampuchea had been taken over by what appears to have been one of the worst regimes of the left ever seen. Estimates vary, but it seems that the Khmer Rouge government of Pol Pot exterminated its own citizens in numbers that probably reach into the millions. This nightmare was finally ended not by the intervention of Western democracy but by the Communist armies of Vietnam, which invaded and set up a pro-Vietnamese puppet regime that at least was milder in its treatment of Kampucheans than its indigenous but bloodthirsty predecessor. Refugees fled Kampuchea, but it is difficult to superimpose a simple Cold War schema of left and right upon this tragedy.

Within Vietnam the largest movement of refugees was among the ethnic Chinese minority. Much of the problem here stemmed from majority–minority tensions that had little ideological or political significance; they were exacerbated, however, by external political events that did not conform in the least to Cold War assumptions. The split in the Communist world between the USSR and China divided the Communists of Indo-China. The Vietnamese, who had much to fear from Chinese domination, sided with the Soviets, who had supported their long struggle against the Americans with material assistance, and soon found themselves at blows with the Chinese. When the Chinese invaded Vietnamese soil, the ethnic Chinese minority in Vietnam fell, rightly or wrongly, under suspicion. It is interesting to note that the second-largest contingent of refugees went not to the West but to the largest Communist state in the world, China.

The political implications of the refugee movement out of Indo-China were thus anything but simple. Nevertheless, when the appeal went out in 1979 it seemed to fall into a pattern familiar to Canadian ears: once again refugees were fleeing Communist tyranny, and once again Canada was being asked to open its doors. Once again Canada did so—this time with a generosity that outshone the response to all previous appeals of the same kind. It was an extraordinary example and is a genuine tribute to this country. Praise could be unalloyed were it not for the uncomfortable comparison with the Chileans before and the Central Americans later, a comparison that can be understood only in the light of a certain political bias—a bias in favour of refugees seen as fleeing Communism and against those who are associated, rightly or wrongly, with support of Communism. The Indo-Chinese movement once again showed that Canadians had indeed become colour-blind with regard to race. After all, just thirty years earlier an explicit goal of Canadian immigration policy was to keep Asians to a minimum in the Canadian population; now tens of thousands of Asian refugees were being assisted and welcomed into Canada amid considerable popular enthusiasm. But political colour-blindness was another matter.

There can be no doubt about the significance of the Indo-Chinese movement in the postwar refugee experience. The 60,000 Indo-Chinese refugees accepted within two years represent almost one-fifth of all refugees accepted in Canada over the thirty-five years following the end of the war. As a single movement they far outnumbered the Hungarians of the late 1950s, who had previously been the largest single group. And excluding the ten-year-long movement of displaced persons from Europe, the Indo-Chinese constituted an astonishing 40 per cent of all special refugees accepted up to that point.

A major difference between the boat people and previous large groups of immigrants was that 54 per cent of the Indo-Chinese applicants were privately sponsored (43 per cent were government sponsored, and 3 per cent were sponsored by relatives). In fact the entire plan was predicated upon the massive involvement of Canadian volunteers, both groups and individuals, in the process. The Conservative government of Joe Clark, which had come to office in 1979, had placed considerable emphasis in its program on the involvement of voluntary agencies in the policy process, as part of its desire to reduce the role of the state in Canadian life. The emergence in the 1970s of private refugee-support groups was seized upon by the government; it is-sued them a challenge, in effect, to privatize and decentralize the resettlement process. The response actually exceeded realistic expectations. Throughout the country groups were formed spon-taneously to organize sponsorship and support. In some cities mass rallies were held, where the atmosphere was not unlike that of the concerts to aid African famine victims in the mid-1980s. When the first refugees arrived at Canadian airports they were greeted by crowds waving welcome banners amid a crush of television cameras and reporters.

The refugees, almost three-quarters Vietnamese, were unusual in many ways. Three-quarters had left Indo-China by small boat, hence the term "boat people" was largely accurate. They were re-markably young: 80 per cent were under thirty years of age, and just under half were under twenty. Over 90 per cent knew nei-ther French nor English upon arrival.[36] Not surprisingly, given the large numbers involved and the cultural and linguistic gap, assimilation into Canadian life has not been as easy as it was for such earlier special movements as the Ugandan Asians or the Czechs and Slovaks in 1968–69. Unemployment, especially among the young, has become a problem, and the inevitable as-sociation between urban poverty and crime has been observed in Indo-Chinese communities in large cities like Toronto and Montreal. In the United States, Indo-Chinese refugee communi-ties have been subjected to open ethnic discrimination in some areas, and tensions have resulted, for instance between the Indo-Chinese and the anti-Castro Cuban émigrés in Miami. Entering under the auspices of anti-Communism does not apparently of-fer invulnerability to lingering racial biases and problems in assimilation.

The political context of the refugee movement has some distant echoes within Canadian life. Just as the displaced persons from Eastern Europe often brought with them a mil-itant anti-Communism, so too a minority of the Indo-Chinese have imported a bitter and intolerant anti-Communism that has been manifested on a few occasions in threatening counter-demonstrations against peace marchers in Canadian cities. To be sure, there is no reason to deny any new Canadians the right to demonstrate their political opinions; what is worrying is a tendency to intimidate other Canadians of different views. The point is made only because one of the "security" arguments made against admitting refugees from right-wing oppression (Chileans and some Central Americans, for example) was that they would use Canada to continue political activity against the states they had fled. To apply this argument with political bias is sheer hypocrisy. Refugees from political oppression, of whatever kind, are highly unlikely to abandon the strong opinions formed in the course of their oppression at the moment they step onto the soil of their adopted country. This may be a price that Canada must be prepared to pay for opening its doors to political refugees. It is no solution to invoke national security against one set of ideas, while apparently offering quasi-official sanction for another.

The Trudeau government, after recapturing a majority in the election of 1974, drafted a long-overdue new Immigration Act. Over the course of the quarter-century since the passage of the Immigration Act of 1952, there had been much dramatic change both in the content of immigration policy, such as the shift from racial discrimination to colour-blindness, and in its procedures and processes. Moreover, much had changed in the structure of Canadian society, not least as a result of postwar immigration itself. The new act was intended to update comprehensively the statutory basis of this changed set of policies and practices. In the matter of national security, the drafting of the new act and the subsequent debate was the focus for a temporary resolution of the conflicting trends that had been developing throughout the 1960s and into the 1970s.

In contrast to the quiet progress of the 1952 act, there was actually a debate in 1976 around the issue of immigration security, which was at least partially public. Even behind the closed doors of government, there was more contention than there had been the last time around. The RCMP and elements of the Ottawa security establishment continued to press their familiar case for strict security controls—now buttressed by the appearance of new threats to national security, especially the threat of international terrorism. On the other side, there were arguments for introducing more liberality and more recognition of individual rights into the process—arguments that could now be supported by displays of public protest against excessive administrative discretion in the name of national security. The protest was expressed by groups such as refugee-support organizations and civil liberties associations, which were not even in existence in

1952. Some of the details of the closed-door discussions can only be inferred, since restrictions on access to Cabinet discussions and Cabinet papers make documentary reconstruction too difficult at this time. However, the public portion of the debate is interesting and suggestive.

During the Green Paper inquiry, the views of interested groups had been solicited about desirable features of a new act. The British Columbia Civil Liberties Association presented particularly thoughtful views on security questions. The association did not challenge the basic need for security screening, but it did challenge the lack of rights available to applicants, especially those abroad. It was reasonable, the association believed, to refuse applicants who had been convicted of espionage, treason, or sabotage against "basically democratic states", but the provisions for prohibiting persons about whom doubt exists were more dubious:

> Such provisions as these, involving the assessment of probable future activities rather than the judging of past acts, seem to require a different sort of determination altogether than many "legal" questions. None the less it would be bizarre and inconsistent to deprive a person "reasonably suspected" of being likely to endanger national security, of the hearing which is afforded one charged with having done so in fact in the past.

The group suggested that the Bill of Rights (that is, the Diefenbaker bill of 1960) put this procedure in question—not only because of the lack of an applicant's right to a hearing, but also because of the lack of judicial review of decisions. They recommended that the new act should recognize legitimate dissent and protest (freedom of expression) for political organizations as for individuals; that persons should be distinguished from organizations with which they have associated; and that the ministerial role of "fact-finding" be excluded from tribunals determining immigration status, an exclusion that would restrict the state's capacity to introduce evidence based on privileged security information not revealed to the applicant.[37]

The same group also pinpointed a crucial element in the immigration security process: secrecy. The association called for one key reform: recognizing that standards of refugee determination will "sometimes" be affected by the political complexion of a host country's government, equity demanded that the standards nevertheless be publicized. In this regard it raised the question of the Chilean refugees and of the Canadian state's control of information. The civil libertarians contrasted unfavourably the generous treatment of Ugandan Asians with that of the Chileans, "whose personal danger in many cases would seem to be greater than that of the Ugandans" but who "have been processed slowly and with considerable severity." Presenting their views shortly after the coup, they noted the difficulty of verifying the actual number of refugees admitted from Chile:

> Of course it is the Department, rather than groups of private citizens, which is in possession of most of the facts, which might explain why treatment of refugees at times seems open-handed and generous and at other times grudging and inflexible. However, a person not party to the Department's deliberations and instructions might be forgiven for concluding that those fleeing conservative or reactionary regimes for political reasons are unlikely to find the stringency of our immigration barriers relaxed in their favour.[38]

The implication was pointed: if the government rejected criticism of its security policies in immigration as exaggerated and unfounded it had only itself, and its obsessive devotion to secrecy, to blame. The answer was to throw open the windows and let in some light. As the Canadian Civil Liberties Association put it succinctly, in a submission to a special parliamentary committee on immigration policy in 1975, "Governmental secrecy encourages public suspicion."

The new act seemed to temper the traditions of administrative discretion with greater recognition of individual rights, to some extent, leading one observer to suggest:

> [The act] attempts to strike a balance between administrative efficiency and respect for civil liberties. It accords the government increased power to deal with terrorists, subversives, criminals and those seeking to circumvent immigration laws; at the same time,

it offers increased protection to the individual in a number of areas—refugees, the adjudication system, alternatives to deportation, and arrest and detention.[39]

On the liberal side could be cited the removal of the ban on homosexual immigrants (which had proven not only illiberal but largely unenforceable); the official statement of the rights of refugees, following Canada's belated signature to the UN Convention Relating to the Status of Refugees in the late 1960s; and the strengthening of some procedural protections for individuals in hearings.

On the other side, it must be said that the drafters of the new act outdid themselves in offering the government the most sweeping statutory authority to exercise administrative discretion in national security matters. Section 19(1) defines inadmissible classes; item (d) refers to "persons who have engaged in or who *there are reasonable grounds to believe are likely to engage in* acts of espionage or subversion against democratic government, institutions or processes, as they are understood in Canada, except persons who, having engaged in such acts, have satisfied the Minister that their admission would not be detrimental to the national interest" (emphasis added). The emphasized clause gives extraordinary leeway to the state since it deals with perceptions of intentions in the future rather than with actual acts in the present or past. Another point to be noted is that persons could be judged inadmissible for possible subversion against any democratic government, not just the Canadian government.

The same language is continued in other sections. Item (f) in section 19(1) adds to the list of inadmissible classes "persons who there are reasonable grounds to believe will, while in Canada, engage in or instigate the subversion by force of any government." And item (g) refers to "persons who there are reasonable grounds to believe will engage in acts of violence that might endanger the lives or safety of persons in Canada or are members of or are likely to participate in the unlawful activities of an organization that is likely to engage in such acts of violence."

Resident non-citizens can be removed for possible use of force against any government and for possible subversion against the Canadian government according to section 27 (1), items (a) and (c). Under these items, visitors can be removed for falling under any of the above clauses or for actually engaging in or instigating subversion of any government; this was an innovation carried over from the Temporary Immigration Security Act passed to deal with the Olympics.

The range of discretionary power is breathtaking. "Subversion" is left undefined, as are the concepts of "reasonable grounds" and "democratic government, institutions or processes, as they are understood in Canada." It is possible to interpret these sections to mean that refugees might be removed from Canada for working against the governments from which they have fled, such as Sikhs in regard to India, Tamils in regard to Sri Lanka, or Salvadoreans or South Africans in regard to their governments.[40]

Just before the passage of the new act, a case came before the Federal Court of Appeal in which it was decided that the government did not have to prove that a particular organization was actually subversive; in the face of evidence of non-subversiveness presented by the appellant it had only to demonstrate "reasonable grounds for believing the fact". In another case, before the Immigration Appeal Board in 1972, the government, having refused landing to an applicant because of membership in an organization advocating subversion, refused to name the organization; the appellant could not introduce evidence to disprove a case that the government refused to specify.[41] This kind of Kafkaesque procedure would not be eliminated by the new legislative framework.

In fact the Immigration Act of 1976 lays out procedures for dealing with appeals against security rejections and for removing security risks from the country that could certainly find a place in Kafka's *The Trial*. The problem that had so bedevilled the RCMP in appeals—how to have appeals of security cases rejected without having to introduce security information—and that had set off the long and tortuous process of trying to devise a security review board was dealt with under the new legislation in a manner that must have pleased the police.

Section 39 deals with the safety and security of Canada in relation to visitors and persons other than permanent residents. Under this section a person believed by the minister of immigration and the solicitor general (the minister representing the security service), on the basis of security intelligence reports, to be inadmissible under section 19 or section 27 (quoted above) may be so described in a certificate. This certificate is considered conclusive proof to be presented before an adjudicator at an inquiry. If such a certificate is filed, the adjudicator has no task beyond establishing that the person before him is the same as the one described in the certificate; the certificate is a sufficient basis for deportation. In other words, no evidence whatsoever need be filed other than the simple assertion, stated in a certificate, that the minister has "reasonable grounds to believe" that the person is "likely to engage in" certain activities.

In the original act, a hearing was possible beyond this level for permanent residents. Sections 41 and 42 provided for the establishment of the Special Advisory Board, which might advise the minister on matters relating to the safety and security of Canada and could hear reports on specific security cases involving permanent residents that might be filed by the minister. This was the long-awaited appearance, in a shrunken and misshapen form, of the security review board first suggested in 1969. It was not an appeal board, since security rejectees could not themselves appeal. According to section 40, the minister and the solicitor general, after receiving security or criminal intelligence reports, "may make a report to the Special Advisory Board." If they do so, the board would give the individual in question the "opportunity to be heard." Just what this opportunity might accomplish is unclear, for the act goes on to indicate that the person would not be allowed to see the confidential evidence upon which the certificate was based or to cross-examine sources of information. After receiving a report, the Cabinet could then proceed with a deportation order—against which there was no appeal.

The Special Advisory Board was set up, but by 1981 the McDonald commission reported that it had actually heard only a single report involving an individual case, confining itself almost entirely to advising the minister in general.[42] Eventually, as a result of the McDonald recommendations and the Canadian Security Intelligence Service Act of 1984, the sections of the Immigration Act concerning the Special Advisory Board were repealed and replaced by references to the new Security Intelligence Review Committee, with much broader jurisdiction than immigration alone. It will be discussed in the next chapter.[43]

Under certain circumstances, based on rights arising out of non-security sections of the act, appeals in deportation cases are possible even when security is involved. At this stage, however, even when security has not been mentioned or entered by the minister in earlier proceedings, a security certificate may be entered at the Immigration Appeal Board hearing. The effect is to cause the board to dismiss the appeal. The minister and the solicitor general simply indicate that "in their opinion...it would be contrary to the national interest for the Board to do otherwise." This opinion is not open to examination; it is conclusive. Moreover, under sections 83(1) and 83(2) the act specifically grants a ministerial prerogative to deprive the board of the right to consider humanitarian or compassionate reasons to dismiss an appeal against a removal order or against refusal of a sponsored application.

If the Immigration Act of 1976 represents an attempt to balance administrative efficiency with respect for civil liberties, this balance is not in evidence in the sections on national security. In the end, national security overrode civil liberties and individual rights to a remarkable extent, actually providing a tougher basis for enforcing security than had existed in the earlier legislation. The raising of civil libertarian concerns in the public debate does not seem to have weighed in the balance to any appreciable extent. The perception of a renewed threat to the national security emanating from international terrorism and other causes provided the background for what amounted to a famous victory for the Ottawa security establishment—even in an era of international *détente* and declining salience of the old Red Menace, which had been so important in laying the groundwork for the security apparatus in immigration in the first instance. At the same time that the RCMP security service was falling under public suspicion and ridicule because of revelations of illegal bugging and barn burning, the Trudeau government was arming it and its civilian allies with increased arbitrary powers in immigration.

In the summer of 1978 the immigration department furnished Ted Finn, assistant secretary to Cabinet for security, intelligence, and emergency planning, with a lengthy document describing the situation in immigration security following the implementation of the new Immigration Act.[44] By this stage, Immigration had followed the Mackenzie commission recommendation of a decade earlier in abandoning the patchwork of special exemptions and waivers for security screening that had been built up over the years: "Currently, all prospective immigrants are subjected to a security check." In countries where security screening facilities existed, the security decision was to be made by the RCMP officer. Where such facilities did not exist (particularly the east-bloc countries), screening was to be conducted by the immigration visa officer, "but it should be noted that where full screening facilities do not exist independent immigrant applications are not accepted." In other words, the practice continued of accepting only sponsored or nominated applications in Communist countries, with the sponsors in Canada being screened. "All sponsored applications refused on security grounds are reviewed in Ottawa before the final decision is released." Non-sponsored applicants from these countries were normally accepted only at visa posts in countries where screening facilities existed—that is, they had to leave their own countries first to apply. However, the department did not enforce any residence requirement in these cases (the old two-year rule was long gone). Chinese applicants in Hong Kong were not being treated any differently than applicants from European Communist countries, despite the Mackenzie recommendation for special procedures, which was rejected as being based on "discrimination that could not be defended on security risk grounds."

Officials in the field were armed with guidelines that interpreted the "inadmissible classes" clauses somewhat more specifically for application in particular cases. In some cases they seemed to widen the criteria. For instance, rejection might be based not only on reasonable grounds for believing that such acts as espionage, sabotage, terrorism, or the violent overthrow of government were likely to take place, but on "the use of or the encouragement of the use of force, violence or any criminal means, or the creation or exploitation of civil disorder." The addition seemed to suggest that officials might refuse entry to people on the expectation that they might advocate certain acts without actually carrying them out themselves. Communism was not mentioned, nor was any other particular ideology named, but persons were to be considered inadmissible who "hold, or have held, positions of executive responsibility in any organization, group or body which promotes or advocates the subversion, by force or violence or any criminal means, of democratic government, institutions or processes, as they are understood in Canada."

Interestingly, the minister and the solicitor general (on behalf of the RCMP) were "authorized to prepare lists", in consultation with External Affairs, "of organizations in which, because of their history and the nature of their activities, membership in itself would constitute reasonable grounds for determining that a person should be refused." The practice of maintaining a sort of secret attorney general's list of subversive organizations, which was begun in the 1950s, was still followed at the end of the 1970s. The list itself cannot be obtained. It is very likely that the Communist party still headed the security establishment's unwanted list. It is possible for applicants who have held executive office in such organizations to sanitize themselves: "The length of time since holding of such position and the circumstances involved would be considered with a view to satisfying the Minister...that admission in some cases would not be detrimental to the security of Canada."

Finally, the memo stated, "These criteria are to be applied in all cases regardless of sponsorship for immigration, country of residence or citizenship status of the applicant for immigration to Canada." The discriminatory patchwork of special exemptions that had led to the highly unequal incidence of security screening discussed in earlier chapters was now formally at an end, replaced by a universal application of similar criteria to all prospective immigrants of whatever national origin. Of course, there was still a discriminatory barrier against independent applicants from countries where no screening facilities were available (that is, where the RCMP had no liaison with local police). Apart from this category, the application of security screening appears to be more equitable under the 1976 act, at least formally. However, this improvement was not mirrored by equity in the application of selection criteria. Ideological colour-blindness was still not part of the Canadian immigration process.

CHAPTER ELEVEN

The Second Cold War: Old Wine in New Bottles

The 1980s have seen a renewal of the Cold War at a level of rhetoric and superpower animosity not witnessed since the 1950s, especially after the accession of Ronald Reagan to the US presidency in 1981. Events in Poland, Afghanistan, Grenada, Nicaragua, and Libya, the shooting down of a Korean airliner off course over Soviet airspace, and various spy arrests and scandals on both sides have punctuated the troubled decade, over which looms the threatening spectre of nuclear war, made more pressing and alarming by an arms race out of control and the thickets of missiles growing on both sides. In North America, the popular culture seems to have turned decisively to Cold War bellicosity: Rambo splatters Asian Communist blood across movie and television screens, which also host lurid fantasies of a future America under the ruthless heel of Communist rule. But at the same time the peace movements of the West have reached levels of popular participation and energy unprecedented in the postwar world. The Cold War may be resurgent but it has also encountered passionate opposition. Unlike the 1950s, the 1980s are an era of little consensus, imagined or real.

Moreover, despite the best efforts of the Reaganites to paint the world in the Manichaean colours of the Cold War, some of the most troubling features of the international scene in the 1980s are much more complex than the official American view would suggest. International terrorism has assumed the proportions of an obsession in the Western media. Yet despite grandiose conspiracy theories linking every terrorist act to Moscow, it is evident that terrorism grows out of many disparate roots. The PLO, the IRA, the Sikh separatists, the Tamil rebels, the Shiite kidnappers of Lebanon, and the African National Congress may have certain things in common, but a disciplined devotion to the Soviet Communist party line is simply not among them. Moreover, the terrorist activities of the Contras in Nicaragua are openly sponsored by the government of the United States, as the terrorist operations in Mozambique and Angola are backed openly by South Africa and covertly by the United States.

At the same time the world economic crisis has deepened suffering on a global scale. It is manifest in such dramatic problems as Third World debt, famines, the increasing numbers of refugees, and the pressures of forced migration. At the same time developed countries are growing more restrictive and more fearful of outsiders because their own economies are suffering stagnation, high unemployment, and a fiscal crisis in state services. The refugee movements are often precipitated by war—sometimes by Cold War clashes, like the upheavals in Central America or the Soviet war in Afghanistan, sometimes by local Third World conflicts, like the Iran–Iraq war, sometimes by internal clashes of majority and minority nationalisms, like the civil war between Tamils and Sinhalese in Sri Lanka, or the violence between Sikhs and Hindus in India.

Many of the advanced industrial countries have been gearing up for increased and often repressive controls over immigration, especially now that the fear of terrorism has been added to the existing concerns to protect jobs and services from aliens. The US Immigration and Naturalization Service has become a major police, surveillance, intelligence, and prison operation handling millions of illegal migrants (many of whom are fleeing the devastation of US-sponsored wars or brutal US-backed dictatorships). In France the conservative government elected in 1986 enacted severe police-state laws against foreigners, giving the authorities the power to deport simply on the basis of a police decision, and it now demands visas for all visitors entering the country. West Germany has considered amending its constitution to permit it to exclude refugees at its borders. And behind these developments there is the unsettling fact that travel between countries has itself become a battlefield: aircraft and ship hijackings and airliners blown out of the sky by bombs remind the world of the dangers of travel.

Canada has been an ambivalent participant in these developments. Certainly not immune to the winds of the Cold War, nor insulated from the popular revulsions against the dangers of nuclear war, Canada has itself been a contested terrain in the 1980s between anti-Soviet pro-Americanism and the peace movement, between support for Ronald Reagan's global confrontation of the "evil empire" and protest against American intervention in Central America and elsewhere. Canadian government policy has reflected this division in public sentiment. The Trudeau government of 1980–84 incurred the wrath of the peace movement by agreeing to test the US cruise missile on Canadian soil and supporting the deployment of cruise and Pershing missiles in Europe. Then Trudeau attracted the enmity of the Reagan administration by embarking on his quixotic global peace mission in his last days in office. The Conservative government of Brian Mulroney has energetically pursued a pro-American policy in continental trade and intergovernmental relations, a direction symbolized by the Shamrock Summit between Mulroney and Reagan. Yet the Tories have not been such enthusiastic Cold Warriors as might have been expected: they rejected Canadian participation in Reagan's "Star Wars" program, and they have even been mildly critical of US interventionism in Nicaragua. In domestic politics, there have been few signs of a return to the stultifying atmosphere of political repression characteristic of the first Cold War—signs that have been discernible in Reagan's America.

Nor has Canada moved as sharply as its Western allies to restrict the movement of people across borders and to step up controls over non-citizens within its borders. In immigration and citizenship policy, Canada appears to be pursuing its own unique course. Although it is buffeted by many of the same pressures as its allies, Canadian responses have not followed the same patterns. This final chapter will look at the ambiguous legacy of the Cold War apparatus of immigration controls in the face of this changing reality.

The McDonald commission called to investigate evidence of RCMP wrongdoing in the late 1970s expended little of its time and energy on the question of national security in immigration and citizenship. Only about 25 out of some 2,000 pages of its final report were devoted to this subject. However, the McDonald commission's 1981 recommendations did lead to the civilianization of the RCMP security service and its re-emergence as the Canadian Security Intelligence Service (CSIS), with a more precise legislative mandate than its predecessor and a formal definition of threats to the security of Canada embodied in the legislation establishing the agency. The CSIS Act also created a review committee before which all security cases in immigration and citizenship may be heard. In short, some of the basic context of immigration security has now been changed.

According to the McDonald commission's report, "The screening of aliens crossing a national frontier can still be considered the first line of defence in any country's security programme, but in today's fast-shrinking world it is a decreasingly effective barrier." The commissioners insisted that a screening process was nevertheless necessary, especially in light of the Canadian government's low level of internal security controls over residents, as compared with those of some other Western states.[1] They made a series of specific recommendations for improving and in most cases tightening the administration of the process, such as the introduction of a more flexible system of limited non-renewable visas, to maintain stricter controls over visitors who required visas, and greater security controls over refugees who had come in under special waivers and relaxed screening. They also wanted amendments to the Immigration Act regarding security criteria, to bring them into line with the new criteria of "threats to the security of Canada" that they were proposing for the civilian security agency's legislative mandate. They also wanted new appeal and review procedures.

Most interestingly, the commission commented with thinly veiled alarm on the old question of the trustworthiness of the RCMP's sources abroad. There is, they suggested,

> a danger in the immigration screening process of placing too great and uncritical reliance on foreign agency information. The information received must always be carefully analysed in the context of the political circumstances of the country providing it. No foreign agency should be considered a "reliable source" in the

sense that its reports can be accepted uncritically. The interests and perceptions of foreign nations will often differ from those of Canada, and their interpretation of data may well reflect those differences. The security intelligence liaison officers and the analysts at Headquarters must be sensitive to the shades of difference between foreign and Canadian concerns. One of the reasons an effective and knowledgeable review body is needed to review the evidence supporting denials of security clearance in immigration cases is the fact that frequently the evidence will be based on reports from foreign agencies.[2]

On citizenship security screening, the commission was of two minds. On the one hand, the commissioners admitted that the security risk in granting citizenship was "marginal", considering that permanent residents without citizenship encountered little restriction on their activities, and given the state's reluctance to deport to many countries. On the other hand, they approved the principle of screening and thought that its existence might have some deterrent effect on those who might have reason to fear security rejection. After noting that the RCMP had no formal authorization to do what it had been doing for forty years or more, and after describing the present procedures for screening some 130,000 citizenship applications each year as "cumbersome", they recommended that "the discretionary power of the Governor in Council to reject citizenship on security grounds be retained." They added a few specific recommendations for speeding up the process and making it more effective, as well as for bringing the security criteria and the appeal procedures in line with the commission's other recommendations.[3]

The work of the McDonald commission, like that of almost all royal commissions, had a mixed fate. Much of the specific evidence of RCMP wrongdoing was never satisfactorily dealt with, by the government or by the courts. No officer has ever been jailed for activities that broke the law. But the long and difficult effort to civilianize the security service finally came to a successful conclusion in the wake of the pressure generated by McDonald. And with it came a new legislative and institutional framework for immigration security.

The Canadian Security Intelligence Service Act was proclaimed on June 30, 1984, just hours before Pierre Elliott Trudeau finally left the office of prime minister, which he had held for the best part of sixteen years. Trudeau had been quietly concerned about the activities of the Western security and intelligence network, with its global reach into small countries like Canada.[4] The CSIS Act, following an extraordinarily vociferous public debate, a series of amendments, and major changes recommended—unusually—by a Senate committee (chaired by Trudeau's former clerk of the Privy Council, Michael Pitfield), suggested some new approaches in national security practice. Most dramatic and controversial was the civilianization of the security service. But there were other, equally significant features of the CSIS Act.

For the first time there is a statutory mandate for security investigations. CSIS is mandated to investigate activities that "may on reasonable grounds be suspected of constituting threats to the security of Canada" (section 12). Threats are defined as follows:

(a) espionage or sabotage that is against Canada or is detrimental to the interests of Canada or activities directed toward or in support of such espionage or sabotage.

(b) foreign influenced activities within or relating to Canada that are detrimental to the interests of Canada and are clandestine or deceptive or involve a threat to any person.

(c) activities within or relating to Canada directed toward or in support of the threat or use of acts of serious violence against persons or property for the purpose of achieving a political objective within Canada or a foreign state, and

(d) activities directed toward undermining by covert unlawful acts, or directed toward or intended ultimately to lead to the destruction or overthrow by violence of, the constitutionally established system of government in Canada.

But the term "threats" does not include "lawful advocacy, protest or dissent, unless carried on in conjunction with any of

the activities referred to in paragraphs (a) to (d)." The last clause
could be very important for the protection of civil liberties and
freedom of expression. For the first time the security agency has
been told what it can investigate and what it cannot investigate.
It is still too early to assess the effect of this mandate in defining
the targets of CSIS investigations. CSIS is empowered under
section 14 of the act to advise the government and provide
information relating to security relevant to government functions
under the Immigration and Citizenship Acts (that is, CSIS takes
over the old security functions of the RCMP). It is possible that
the security criteria employed in immigration screening may
have to be brought into line with the CSIS mandate, and as a
consequence some of the activities that previously led to adverse
security reports may no longer be valid grounds for refusing
entry to Canada.[5]

Significantly, the CSIS Act created the Security Intelligence
Review Committee (SIRC), which was to oversee the operations
of CSIS and to hear individual complaints against it or against
the effects of its security assessments.[6] The Immigration Act
and the Citizenship Act were amended to provide for hearings
before SIRC in cases of security rejections in immigration and
citizenship applications. As with the late and unlamented Special
Advisory Board (which disappeared with these amendments),
the legislation merely provides that the minister and the solicitor
general may make reports to the new review committee. When
reports are made, notices are to be sent to the individual concerned. SIRC will then hold a hearing into the matter, at which
the individual will be represented. SIRC itself claims that an individual judged a security risk in immigration or citizenship is
"now accorded the opportunity of a thorough review of the case
by an independent body."[7]

SIRC is required to furnish the individual concerned with a
"statement summarizing such information available to it as will
enable the person to be as fully informed as possible of the
circumstances giving rise to the report". There is a wealth of
meaning in those two small words "as possible". They are the
Trojan Horse through which all the secrecy and governmental
discretion associated with the term "national security" can once
more be smuggled back into a process that is supposed to
afford the individual an idea of the case against him or her. The
ancient imperative of security services, that their information and

sources be confidential and never divulged to individuals or the public in general, remains quite intact. There is already some evidence to this effect from hearings held by SIRC.[8]

By the fall of 1986, thirteen citizenship cases and two immigration cases had been referred to SIRC. In one of the immigration cases, the review committee upheld CSIS and Immigration in ordering the deportation of an Irish visitor associated with the IRA. One citizenship case has already attracted some media attention. It involved an Argentinian, Alberto Rabilotta, who has been a landed immigrant in Canada since 1970 and helps operate a small news agency in Montreal, which provides stories to Prensa Latina, the official Cuban news agency. His 1977 application for citizenship had been ignored for a number of years until he was suddenly served in 1986 with a certificate declaring him a threat to the security of Canada. Was it the business relationship with the Cubans that had drawn the unwelcome attention of the CSIS, or was it something else? As usual in such cases, rumours began flying. One Montreal newspaper cited alleged Canadian intelligence sources as saying that Cuba had used the agency to funnel Communist money into the terrorist FLQ. Rabilotta dismissed this accusation by pointing out that his agency had only been founded in 1975, when the FLQ was already practically dead.[9] In this case SIRC advised against the government's ruling, indicating that the security reasons were not continuing grounds for rejection. Rabilotta's application is still pending at the time of this writing. In another case, involving two Chilean applicants, SIRC refused to uphold a government security assessment and found in favour of the applicants. There is reason to think, therefore, that appeals to SIRC—despite the inherent limitations—are not merely pro forma but may actually overturn government rulings from time to time. But it must be remembered that SIRC's findings are advisory and can be rejected by the government.

The civilianization of Canada's security service has been accomplished with suitably little fanfare. The name has changed, the ranks and designations have changed, the red serge and the riding boots have gone, but 95 per cent of the men (and very few women) who woke up and started the day on July 1, 1984, as agents of the Canadian Security Intelligence Service were exactly the same people who had gone to bed the night before as members of the Royal Canadian Mounted Police Security Service. But their transition to civilianization has not been a smooth one. CSIS has suffered widely reported identity and morale crises. By the summer of 1986, at least 131 CSIS agents had taken advantage of a "bridge-back" provision to return to the RCMP. CSIS has had difficulties gaining access to the voluminous records of the Canadian Police Intelligence Centre.[10] There have even been rumours that the cherished liaison links with American security and intelligence sources were being weakened as the Americans question to what extent they can entrust secrets to the new agency, especially since it is subject to a civilian oversight agency like the Security Intelligence Review Committee.

It is precisely in this area of liaison with the American and other Western intelligence networks that pointed questions have been directed at CSIS. The review committee asked for information on arrangements with "friendly powers" and was told that they fall into three categories: formal agreements with other countries, which are explicitly documented; informal arrangements, in which general understandings of co-operation are exchanged; and *ad hoc* arrangements at the operational level (which may never come to the notice of anyone other than the security agencies themselves). SIRC asked for copies of the agreements CSIS had inherited from the RCMP, including those in the first category, some in the second, but not necessarily any in the third. What it got was four to five feet of documents—thousands of pages. SIRC argued that "these arrangements should all be reviewed in light of the new [CSIS] Act and renegotiated." This recommendation was made in the first annual SIRC report to Parliament, then reiterated in the second. This second time around, SIRC commented laconically: "CSIS' lack of action to date suggests that it does not agree."[11]

The international dimension is particularly pertinent to any understanding of the role of CSIS in immigration security. Various aspects of this question have been explored in this book, and some of the implications of liaison with dubious forces abroad, not least its implications for Canadian citizens, as well as for immigrants to Canada. The review committee raised a point that had been troubling Canadians since the 1950s:

We inquired into the provision of information by the Canadian government to the United States Immigration and Naturalization Service (USINS) and found that before 1980, the RCMP Security Service provided USINS with information that may, in some cases, have been used to place individuals on a USINS "Lookout List" which is kept at border crossings. This is a list of individuals to be refused admission into the United States. The Canadian government cancelled this agreement in 1980 and asked the U.S. government to purge from USINS files all information previously provided.[12]

SIRC expressed its concern that the INS has not complied with this request, "offering various legal and administrative reasons". The service has agreed only to review files on a case-by-case basis. In effect, this means that individual Canadians on the US look-out list because of information supplied by the RCMP before 1980 can apply to CSIS to ask the INS to have the information withdrawn. If they are not satisfied that CSIS has forwarded their request, they may complain to SIRC, which will in turn complain to CSIS. However, even if the request is made to the Americans, the US Immigration and Naturalization Service will agree only to review the case and "may comply".[13]

Another concern has been raised recently by the House of Commons Committee on Labour, Employment and Immigration. In a report on the state of family-class immigration—a report that strongly urged the adoption of policies favouring family reunification—the committee pointed to the same difficulty to which the McDonald commission had devoted some concern: the reliability of information on immigrants supplied by some sources abroad.

The Committee has a major concern that, in some countries, the information used by CSIS to evaluate immigrants on security grounds may not be trustworthy. Canadian officers rely on the good graces of the police and security agencies in the host countries, whose priorities, methods and loyalties may be quite different from Canada's. The Committee does not have the expertise to advise CSIS in detail on how best to assess potential immigrants but we do recommend that the security service re-evaluate its methods.[14]

The committee coupled this with a plea that what it called "rote screening" of all applicants—the universal screening instituted in the 1970s—be reduced in the case of family-class (that is, sponsored) applicants:

> In this age of international terrorism, it is important that Canada take whatever measures possible to protect itself. Yet, past experience has shown that very few family class immigrants are refused on the basis of security. In fact, since 1982 only 12 family class applicants have been refused on security grounds. These checks are often a major delaying factor in processing and in some posts the security check can take up to a year.[15]

The committee noted that CSIS itself has recently begun a streamlining process in some posts, allowing those family-class applicants who have been rejected on security grounds to be "profiled" and those applicants likely to present difficulties to be targeted for full scrutiny, while others have been processed more quickly. The committee approved this procedure and suggested that it be extended to all posts. If this were done, time would then be available to CSIS to pursue "avenues of inquiry that might yield more reliable and useful information" than the current reliance on sometimes dubious foreign sources.[16]

A screening system with a permanent list to the right, backlogs caused by screening delays, doubts about links with external security and intelligence networks: some things never change. But it can be argued that the political and ideological bias in the immigration process has at least been redirected in the 1980s, shifting from the traditional area of security screening (which is still important) to the question of refugee determination—that is, the criteria used by the state in deciding who is a "real" refugee.

The emergence of the refugee question at centre stage in the 1980s is due to a number of elements: the rise in the numbers of refugees seeking resettlement, coupled with much tougher admission requirements in other Western states; the rise in the number of false claims to refugee status, and the resultant pressures on the system and on the patience of Canadians; the political roots of many of the refugee movements and the connection of political refugees to continuing political struggles against their former governments, sometimes through terrorism and armed struggles; and finally, but of particular significance to Canadians, the emergence of a new language of legal rights for refugees and for non-citizens in general. Taken together, these factors have created an entirely new context for Canadian immigration policy.

From 1945 until the close of the 1970s, about one-tenth of all immigrants to Canada came as refugees fleeing oppression, war, or civil disorder in their homelands. In the 1980s, that proportion has risen dramatically. The government's forecast for 1985 was that about one-fourth of that year's immigrants would be accepted either as members of the refugee and designated classes or under rules allowing special humanitarian considerations. This projection turned out to be an underestimate, as reported to Parliament by the minister of immigration only midway through 1985. For 1987 the projection is for one in five.[17]

Canada was once relatively hard-hearted about refugees, especially if they came from minority ethnic or religious groups, who were shunned or discriminated against by the white Christian majority. This was notoriously the case with the Jews attempting to flee the Nazi Holocaust, as chronicled in Irving Abella and Harold Troper's *None Is Too Many*. In 1939 the ship *St. Louis*, carrying 907 desperate German Jews ("the voyage of the damned"), tried to find refuge in any country in the Western Hemisphere. None, including Canada, would accept them and eventually the ship sailed back to Europe and to the crematoria and gas chambers of the Third Reich.[18] In 1986 when 151 Tamils were found in lifeboats off the Newfoundland coast, they were immediately granted landing until their refugee claims could be processed. When it was discovered that they had come not from Sri Lanka, as they had originally claimed, but from refugee camps in West Germany, there was considerable public backlash—said by some to represent covert racism against Asians, by others to be merely a reaction against claimants lying to take advantage of Canadian generosity. But the response of the Canadian government, expressed by both the prime minister and his immigration minister, was to stress Canada's humanitarian commitments to the dispossessed, even though much of the backlash was being expressed through the Conservative party's own backbenchers in Ottawa.[19]

In November 1986, in a gliterring ceremony at the National Arts Centre in Ottawa, the United Nations High Commissioner for Refugees presented to the Canadian people the Nansen Medal for their generosity towards the world's refugees. The commissioner praised Canada for the "humanitarian impulse which lies behind the welcome traditionally extended to refugees", which has "kept the door open" to refugees at a time when many other countries have been closing their doors.[20] In the past, the medal has been awarded to outstanding individuals such as Eleanor Roosevelt, or organizations such as the Red Cross. This was the first time in its more than thirty-year history that the award had been given to an entire people. In accepting the award on behalf of all Canadians, the governor general, Jeanne Sauvé, told the four hundred guests, "this celebration cannot allow us to forget the harsh reality of the millions of displaced people and their tragic journey through solitude and abandonment." The medal, she said, "is not an invitation to smugness but something I am sure will inspire even greater generosity on our part."

The Nansen Medal is given in honour of the memory of Fridtjof Nansen, the Norwegian philanthropist who was the leading figure in refugee resettlement under the League of Nations in the interwar period—the very period when Canada's own refugee record was most deplorable.[21] Yet only three months after the ceremony, the Canadian government abruptly put the lie to Governor General Sauvé's fine words. The sound of doors being slammed shut in the face of desperate people fleeing oppression and death was becoming all too familiar in the late 1980s in Europe and the United States. Canada, which had become for a time a modest but important refuge for at least a few of the world's dispossessed, began shutting its doors as well. New regulations in February 1987, and major amendments to the Immigration Act regarding refugee determination introduced in Parliament in May the same year, signalled a sharp reversal of policy. The erratic trajectory of Canadian immigration policy in the 1970s and 1980s—from increasing liberality to sudden backlash—has been charted by the ambiguous politics of the refugee issue.

Canadians are alternately pleased to be seen as international "good guys" and displeased to pay the costs. Moreover, refugee resettlement remains one of the focal points of Cold War politics.

Canada, caught up as always in the rivalry of the superpowers, seems unable to maintain an autonomous role independent of American foreign policy. The anti-refugee backlash of 1987 is intimately related to the way in which the Cold War has distorted the response of Western nations, including Canada, to the growing world refugee crisis of the late twentieth century.

That there is a growing world refugee crisis is not in doubt. Writing half a century ago, in the late 1930s, American journalist Dorothy Thompson already discerned the growing spectre of humanity uprooted: "A whole nation of people, although they come from many nations, wanders the world, homeless except for refuges which may at any moment prove to be temporary."[22] Thompson was reacting to the existence of some 4 million refugees, left homeless in the years following the First World War. In the four decades since the Second World War it is estimated that at least 70 million people have been forced to move because of political conditions.[23] In 1987 this "nation" of refugees is believed to number 21 million, about 10 million of whom are displaced across national borders.[24] The refugee "nation" is almost as large as Canada.

What was once largely a European phenomenon has become a world-wide crisis. One of every two refugees in the world today is in Africa. The Middle East has been racked by an apparently permanent refugee crisis for the past four decades. The refugee explosion propelled out of South-east Asia a few years ago has abated, but may again erupt. More recently, millions of refugees from Afghanistan have been crowding into Pakistan, while in Central America millions have been displaced, some across borders, some as far as North America.

Occasionally refugee movements are generated by natural disasters in countries too poor to cope effectively. But people are more often made into refugees by deliberate persecution and violence exerted upon them by other people who happen to wield *power*—either state power or military power. Refugees are a product of the modern nation-state, and of warfare (internal or external) as an instrument of the state. They can be offered refuge only by other states, and thus they become the objects of international politics and interstate rivalries. Nor are international organizations such as the United Nations High Commission for Refugees autonomous, as they are sustained by individual states, and therefore their operations are inevitably coloured by these same international antagonisms.

Why do states generate refugees? They may be authoritarian regimes which persistently deny basic political freedoms; some people flee such regimes, when possible. However, since these states tend to deny or restrict exit to dissidents, the numbers of refugees from them tend to be relatively small, except for brief periods of upheaval; Soviet-bloc nations are the obvious examples. According to one authority on refugee movements, Aristide Zolberg, large refugee movements are more often caused by social revolutions (or attempts to suppress revolutions) or by Third World nationalist movements that seek to force unity upon new nations by excluding or repressing some ethnic, linguistic, religious, or other minority groups.[25] Both kinds of transformation are typically linked to wider regional or international conflicts, often extending to global superpower rivalries. It is within the context of this complex web of forces that refugee movements must be understood.

When the Cold War is superimposed upon refugee crises, as it has been for the past four decades, a certain pattern emerges. Communist states produce refugees of their own but rarely receive those produced by other states; it is the Western states that are the main host countries for resettlement. While Communist states control movement of people across their borders much more than do Western states, the latter are selective about what kind of refugees they will accept. The result is that refugees from Communist states tend to fare much better than refugees from anti-Communist regimes backed by the West. Most refugees are simply fleeing war, violence, or oppression; only a relative few deliberately choose sides in the Cold War. Yet where they happen to find themselves in relation to the superpower conflict may have a decisive effect on their fate.

The United States has shown a dramatic ideological bias in its treatment of refugees. In the postwar era, well over 90 per cent of all refugees welcomed to American shores have been from Communist states.[26] Would-be refugees unlucky enough to come from the "other side" have been treated much more harshly. Those fleeing American-sponsored counter-insurgency and destabilization campaigns in Central America not only are virtually barred from achieving refugee status but are subject to deportation back to the very regimes they fled, if they enter the

US illegally and are caught. Attracting refugees from the Soviet bloc provides a weapon in the Cold War: mass movements from East to West score mighty anti-Communist propaganda points, and even provide the human raw material for destabilization campaigns and "roll-back" operations (such as the Cuban exiles whose US-backed attempt to invade Castro's Cuba was destroyed at the Bay of Pigs in 1961, or the US-funded Contras currently attempting to overthrow the Sandinistas in Nicaragua).

Canada has never joined in the more offensive operations of the Americans, but it has shared in many of their Cold War assumptions, including the ideological double standard applied to refugees. From 1945 to the early 1980s, about 80 per cent of refugees accepted in Canada were from Communist states. In the past few years that proportion has fallen somewhat, although "anti-Communist" refugees continue to account for a clear majority. What has happened in the late 1980s is that there has been a change in the kind of refugees arriving at Canada's doors: fewer have been arriving from behind the Iron Curtain or the Bamboo Curtain; more have been arriving from countries subjected to American-backed repression and war in Central and Latin America. This change has created a new refugee crisis in Canada and has helped inspire a reversal of the liberalization trend in refugee policy in the 1970s. Yet at their most liberal, Canadian governments have justified their refugee policies on humanitarian as well as ideological grounds. Canadians who responded to such humanitarian appeals may not have been convinced by the sudden shifting of policy gears into reverse in 1987. It is against this shifting backdrop that current refugee policies must be assessed.

Although Canada has been a leading host country for refugee resettlement since the end of the Second World War, it has shown some reluctance to enter into international agreements specifying its obligations. It only acceded to the 1951 United Nations Convention Relating to the Status of Refugees in 1969, although it had abided by its provisions and had actually functioned as a member of the executive committee of the Office of the UN High Commissioner for Refugees since 1958.[27] But when the new Immigration Act of 1976 was drawn up, these obligations and some others were given statutory basis.

This act explicitly recognizes that immigration policy, rules, and regulations shall be designed and administered "to promote the domestic and international interests of Canada" (section 3). The same section speaks of fulfilling "Canada's international obligations with respect to refugees" and upholding "its humanitarian tradition with respect to the displaced and the persecuted." Section 6 specifies eligibility for refugee admission: those legally entitled to enter or remain in Canada include any person falling under the UN Convention definition of refugee: anyone "who by reason of a well-founded fear of persecution for reasons of race, religion, nationality, membership in a particular social group or political opinion, (a) is outside the country of his nationality and is unable, or, by reason of such fear, is unwilling to avail himself of the protection of that country, or, (b) not having a country of nationality is outside the country of his former residence and is unable or, by reason of such fear, is unwilling to return to that country."

"For the first time", Gerald Dirks writes, "Canadian legislation gave explicit recognition to duties and responsibilities toward refugees."[28] Previously refugees were dealt with in an *ad hoc* manner, by orders-in-council and ministerial permits; statutory recognition meant permanent machinery and procedures for determining refugee claims. Rabbi Gunther Plaut made the same point more decisively in a 1984 report to the minister of immigration: refugees in Canada "must be dealt with in the context of our international obligations which are part of Canadian law, and a person who is a refugee as defined by the Convention may not be returned to his/her country of persecution." Canada has thus "voluntarily limited its sovereignty in this one respect." He goes on to argue that the reference to "humanitarian tradition" alongside international legal obligations in the Immigration Act thus "adds an ethical imperative to our legal obligations." To put it differently, the Immigration Act, 1976 avers that Canada considers itself both morally and legally bound not to return Convention refugees who are within its borders to the land of their persecution. Declaring a claimant to be a refugee is, then, "not a privilege we grant, but rather a right we acknowledge."[29]

As a right, it is not without restrictions. As always, national security is at the root of the limitations. According to section 55 of the Immigration Act, refugees may be forcibly returned to the country in which they fear persecution if national security is believed to be endangered by their presence.[30] Nor does Canada depart from its international obligations by imposing such restrictions, for the UN Convention provides escape clauses for signatory states that wish to override refugee claims for reasons of national security.[31]

The question of the rights of refugees is an important one. In the past, immigration and citizenship policy was always based upon the principle that immigration to Canada and the acquisition of citizenship are privileges and not rights. This was certainly the philosophical basis upon which the government justified the extraordinary controls and denials of natural justice in the name of national security that have been described in this book. But since the recognition of international obligations and humanitarian tradition in the Immigration Act of 1976, there has been a fundamental transformation in the very constitutional fabric of Canada in relation to the rights of individuals because of the coming into force of the Charter of Rights and the jurisprudence already being built up around it.

Part of that jurisprudence, directly relevant to the treatment of refugees and to immigration in general, is the case of *Singh et al. v. Minister of Employment and Immigration*, which established a very important legal precedent in the matter of the rights of immigrants in the Supreme Court of Canada in 1985.[32] The Singh case was an appeal by a number of persons who had been ordered deported, with the Federation of Canadian Sikh Societies and the Canadian Council of Churches as intervenors. All the appellants had claimed Convention refugee status, but the minister of immigration had refused to accept these claims. They had appealed to the Immigration Appeal Board, but that body refused to hear the cases on the grounds that success was "improbable"; in effect, the board said it did not wish to waste its time. The appellants then turned to the courts. The Supreme Court agreed with counsel for the appellants that the procedures for determining refugee status under the Immigration Act were "inconsistent with the requirements of fundamental justice" as provided for under section 7 of the Charter of Rights.[33] Specifically, the refusal of the appeal board to hear deportation cases was incompatible with that section.

What was vitally important about the Singh case was the impact of the Charter of Rights on immigration law and practice. The coming into force of the Charter has obviously opened up whole new vistas for the protection of individual rights against the intrusions of the state, but the Charter might have had little effect on immigrants if the traditional interpretation of their status *vis-à-vis* Canadian citizens had been reaffirmed by the courts. Instead, the Supreme Court ruled that the term "everyone" in section 7 must be understood to include "every person physically present in Canada and by virtue of such presence amenable to Canadian law". As a consequence, the applicants in the Singh case, although not Canadian citizens, were "entitled to fundamental justice in the adjudication of their status."

In addition to the fundamental judicial rethinking about the rights of non-citizens that it has engendered, the refugee problem has given rise to other issues that are highly pertinent to our questioning of the political and ideological bias inherent in the security screening process. In the 1976 legislation Canada actually went beyond the UN Convention Relating to the Status of Refugees by authorizing the government to create "designated classes", by means of orders-in-council, to extend the criteria for refugee admission to include individuals or groups who did not fall within the fairly rigid UN Convention definitions. For instance, Canadian criteria were to include those who were still within the country of persecution but might be assisted to depart. The extensions represented laudable enthusiasm on the part of the Canadian government, and it is certain that many thousands of genuine refugees have been able to find resettlement in this country under the protection of the designated-class provision. Unfortunately, the implementation of this provision is not without a certain bias—in fact, the familiar political bias that has always characterized the immigration process.

Three designated classes have been created sine the 1976 act came into effect. One is for refugees from Soviet-bloc countries, another is for Indo-Chinese fleeing their countries since the series of Communist victories in 1975, and a third category, much smaller, is for certain Latin Americans. Latin Americans are allowed to apply for refugee status within their countries but still have to demonstrate that their fear of persecution if they remain is well founded. Applicants from Soviet-bloc countries and Indo-China need not demonstrate that they are personally targeted for political reprisal in their homelands; in effect, the existence of special categories for them is an acknowledgement of their claims.

A glance at the figures is revealing. In 1984, the leading ten countries of origin of refugees settled in Canada accounted for 12,809 admissions. Of these, 8,589, or 67 per cent, were from countries under Communist governments. Just under 20 per cent were from countries with right-wing dictatorships engaged in repression of the left (El Salvador and Guatemala). In 1985 the comparable figures among the leading fifteen countries of origin were 67 per cent from Communist countries and 17 per cent from right-wing countries.[34] Refugees from El Salvador and Guatemala accounted for 54 per cent of those admitted as Convention refugees in 1984, while those from Communist countries accounted for a mere 6 per cent of this category. Under the designated-class category, however, the proportions were sharply reversed: refugees from Communism accounted for 87 per cent; refugees from right-wing dictatorships for 3 per cent.[35]

In 1985 well over half the refugees assisted to come to Canada were from Eastern Europe or South-east Asia. It was projected that 53 per cent of federally sponsored refugees in 1987 would be from Eastern Europe and South-east Asia.[36] These figures are no accident. These regions, both areas under Communist rule, account for two of the three designated classes of refugees currently recognized by Canada (the other is for political prisoners and oppressed persons, and accounts for much smaller numbers than those in the other two classes). The point is that to fall under a designated class is to enjoy a great advantage over a refugee who must claim Convention status. The latter have far more hoops through which to jump and more difficult hurdles to pass. The former are almost assured of achieving refugee status by virtue of where they come from. But it is quite possible that many Eastern European refugees, for example, have been economic refugees rather than political ones. The imposition of martial law and the crushing of the Solidarity movement in Poland in 1981–82 led to a large increase in the number of legitimate political refugees from that country who were resettled in Canada; but under the designated-class provisions, some Poles whose motives for emigrating had more to do with bettering themselves economically have probably been admitted easily on the assumption that they were political victims of Communism. In short, Canada has created two unequal classes of refugees, and this inequity has helped confirm the longstanding bias in favour of refugees from Communist countries and against refugees from right-wing dictatorships.

In the 1980s the main area of the world producing so-called "left-wing" refugees is Central America. The United States, backing right-wing dictatorships and opposing both left-wing guerrilla movements and the left-wing governments of Cuba and Nicaragua, is virtually closed to the people displaced by war and by counter-insurgency drives under American tutelage. Reagan administration hostility to Latin American refugees and new legislation in 1986 and 1987 restricting entry of illegal aliens have led to increased pressure on thousands of Salvadoreans and Guatemalans living illegally in the United States. A number of them have begun to show up as refugee claimants at the Canadian border. Their flight to Canada is in every sense a genuine refugee movement, since the US government will deport them to their country of origin if they are apprehended—and in many cases that means certain death.

Early in 1986 the Conservative government, citing the alleged swamping of the refugee process by a tidal wave of claims, many of them fraudulent, acted to shut the doors on refugees. It did so with a degree of bureaucratic officiousness not seen since the 1930s. What was the threat to Canada to which the immigration department was responding? In the first two months of 1987 just under 2,300 Salvadoreans and 600 Guatemalans crossed into Canada at the US border. About 1,000 Chileans arrived by air. These people constituted about two-thirds of the 6,000 refugee claimants who entered Canada in this period. (Tamils and Iranians together accounted for another 15 per cent of the total.)[37]

It is true that the problem of processing refugee claims has become something of a nightmare. Claimants abroad are administratively manageable, but that is not the case for those in Canada. The numbers of claimants to refugee status presenting themselves at ports of entry or making such claims after arriving in Canada as non-immigrants has risen precipitously, reaching over a thousand a month by mid-1987, with a backlog of over 30,000 unprocessed claims. Bogus claims—such as those of the so-called Jehovah's Witnesses (many wearing crucifixes) citing religious persecution in their native Portugal—have angered Canadians. The backlash against the Tamil boat people was given maximum coverage in the media. Unscrupulous immigration "consultants" were advising clients to take advantage of Canada's lengthy appeal process by making phoney claims and then awaiting an eventual amnesty when a future government would simply clear the backlog.

All these attempts to undermine the legitimate refugee process have been disgraceful enough. Yet critics are quick to point out that much of the administrative nightmare was of the government's own making. For example, the Portuguese "Jehovah's Witnesses" could have been stopped quickly by the simple expedient of imposing a visa requirement on Portuguese travellers to Canada. This was eventually done, in fact, but not before a lengthy delay by a government concerned about alienating Portuguese-Canadian votes added a few thousand phoney claimants to the backlog. In any event, when the Tories did apply the brakes, it was apparent that the real targets of their wrath were the Central and Latin Americans, whose claims were legitimate by any reasonable measure—except the old and not-so-reasonable measure of the Cold War.

The initial impact of the new regulations was felt mainly by Salvadoreans and Guatemalans illegally in the United States who had been crossing the Canadian border and claiming refugee status. Now they were told that they had to apply from the United States, where they already faced deportation to their violent homelands. Soon refugee camps began to form around border towns such as Plattsburgh and Buffalo, New York. Some refugees began slipping illegally across the border. There was talk of another Underground Railroad like the one that led black slaves to freedom before the Civil War.

Salvadoreans and Guatemalans were stopped at the US border and told to wait in the US while immigration inquiries in Canada were arranged. Canadian authorities explained that they had an agreement with the US that no one awaiting a Canadian inquiry would be deported. US Immigration and Naturalization Service officials scoffed at this and stated flatly that anyone who had a criminal record or "derogatory information" on his file would be deported. "Derogatory information" is a code term for "national security risk". This is truly a vicious circle, since the US defines virtually anyone who flees one of its right-wing client states as a Communist.

The new rules also ban persons arriving by air from claiming refugee status upon arrival (except for Soviet-bloc arrivals who are, of course, exempted). Airlines are being forced to deny passage to persons who lack valid travel documents for Canada. This measure is directed particularly against Chileans fleeing General Pinochet's dictatorship. According to our government, Chileans are free to claim refugee status at the Canadian visa office in Santiago—free, that is, if they can brave the swarms of Pinochet's secret police in the lobby of the building where the visa office is located. Moreover, church groups in Chile helping targets of the Pinochet police to escape do not recommend that applications be made to Canada: the success rate for political opponents of Pinochet is simply too low.

Refugee support groups—most of them church-based—and a number of lawyers who represent legitimate refugee claimants have raised severe criticisms of the new policy, criticisms that have also been taken up by the Liberal and New Democratic opposition in Parliament. But to those who have been closely following events in the Tory immigration department, it is apparent that the senior civil servants and key ministers have been determined for some time to attack the liberal and humanitarian direction that refugee policy had been taking. Amendments to the Immigration Act dealing with refugee determination had been promised for two years. Successive drafts had run into the internal criticism that they might require Canada to renounce its international commitments on refugees. But in May 1987 the amendments were finally given first reading in the House of Commons.[38]

The main thrust of the amendments is to restrict access to Canada for refugees and, for those who arrive from so-called "safe" third countries, to provide for deportation back to those countries. Cabinet is to draw up a list of such "safe" countries, and since it is extemely doubtful that the Canadian government will declare its closest ally, the United States, an "unsafe" country, the prospect looms of Central and Latin Americans being sent to the US, where they will then be deported to the original country of their persecution. In short, Canada may use the US as a means of subverting the UN Convention. The new amendments would also shift the burden of proof onto claimants, deny them the ability to work or attend school while in Canada, and severely restrict their right of appeal against a promised quick decision on their claims by a two-member board. Whether some of these amendments can withstand a challenge based on the Charter of Rights remains to be seen. In many ways the proposed amendments read as if the government is trying to roll back the implications of the Supreme Court Charter decision in the Singh case.

It should be noted that all of these amendments are directed towards Convention refugees only. Refugees from Communist states who fall under the designated-class provisions are not directly affected. The double standard for the two classes of refugees is even further accentuated by the legislative changes. It is obvious, in fact, that the Tory government is attempting to slam the doors very selectively and in a highly discriminatory manner.

Indeed the government's entire presentation of the issue to the public is redolent of ideological bias. The prospect of a few thousand Salvadoreans, Guatemalans, and Chileans knocking on Canada's doors has once again called forth the classic bureaucratic formulation used to keep out Jewish refugees in the 1930s: "A line must be drawn somewhere." Yet the actions of an earlier Conservative government in 1979 in regard to the Indochinese boat people were altogether different, even though that earlier movement far overshadowed the present numbers of Latin American claimants. At that time 60,000 refugees were welcomed and actively assisted to settle in Canada; the Conservatives reached out to appeal to the more generous and humanitarian impulses of the Canadian people and received an overwhelming response. This time it seems that the same party has chosen instead to appeal to the more selfish and mean-spirited elements of public opinion. There is, of course, only one real difference between 1979–80 and 1987: the Indo-Chinese were fleeing Communist oppression, while the Central Americans are fleeing the oppression of "our" side. It is not a distinction that lends much credit to Conservative motives in refugee policy, but it is in keeping with Canadian traditions.

Canada has certainly been more generous to these refugees than its southern neighbour, but its generosity can be seen to have distinct limits when compared with the real generosity accorded refugees from Communism. As the immigration department states its position in regard to Central American refugees: "Resettlement outside the area is the most practical option for a relatively small number of persons.... Repatriation or local resettlement is preferable."[39]

It is not clear what criteria Immigration bases this judgement upon. Resettlement in the area is hardly a solution for people whose camps have been brutally attacked. And repatriation is no solution for those who fear the death squads or the bombers or the army patrols. As Gerald Dirks concludes, in his recent study of refugee policy:

> Regardless of the prevailing Immigration Act, refugees from Latin America have never been the recipients of as prompt or as liberal treatment as individuals from such regions as Eastern Europe. This state of affairs has been and continues to be attributable to political, administrative and ideological considerations on the part of various Canadian governments rather than to any discriminatory features of immigration legislation.[40]

It would of course be an inadequate response to this persistent political bias to propose that the relatively favourable treatment enjoyed by refugees from Communist persecution should be reversed, that the generosity that Canada has shown over the years to refugees—particularly those from the Communist states—should be levelled down to a mean-spiritedness equitably shared all around. Canadians ought to be proud of their assistance to the oppressed of the world, especially at a time when doors elsewhere are closing. What should be instituted is a policy of ideological colour-blindness similar in principle to the policy of racial colour-blindness that was formally embedded in the immigration process in the 1960s. A refugee is a refugee, and persecution is persecution, whether exercised by governments of the right or of the left, in the name of freedom or in the name of socialism—or in the name of national security, a claim that all states, including our own, make for their actions.

There is one more dimension of the relationship between national security and immigration in the 1980s that can be touched upon briefly before closing this book. International terrorism is the great *frisson* of the decade, not unlike the great fear of international Communism that gripped the Western world, and especially the United States, in the late 1940s and early 1950s. Terrorism presents, of course, a real threat to security and public safety. But as in the earlier case, there is also much exaggeration about it, much panic, and much talk of extreme measures. There is no shortage of self-proclaimed "experts" on terrorism prepared to sell their nostrums to a fearful public. And there is no shortage of voices counselling the abandonment of liberal freedoms and the need for stern repressive measures.

Sen. William Kelly moved in the upper chamber in early 1986 that a special committee on terrorism be struck. Citing unnamed "expert" sources, Senator Kelly spoke of the threat to Canada posed by terrorists and pondered such measures as media censorship and controls over travel: "We face a fundamental conundrum posed by the basic and inalienable freedom of speech and association. A similar conundrum would occur should the Canadian government wish—as the Reagan administration has done for Americans—to restrict Canadians from travel to or working in certain tourist 'hot spots' around the globe." When Senator Kelly's committee got under way in late 1986, its closed-door hearings aroused strong reactions from some representatives of ethnic minorities because it was learned that the committee was devoting special attention to groups it considered "terrorist-prone": the Irish, Bulgarian, Sikh, Moslem, and Armenian communities in Canada.[41] The committee's 1987 report, while generally restrained and moderate in tone, did identify the refugee determination process as a security problem. It recommended that CSIS and RCMP officers be allowed more discretion in rejecting applications on security grounds.

At a Quebec conference on terrorism that attracted an audience of military, security, and police officials, its implications for immigration and refugees were spelled out. A "world-renowned terrorism expert" from Israel said Canada's biggest terrorist threat came from such ethnic communities as the Sikhs, the Armenians, and native Indians. He maintained that some of these were being trained in Palestinian terrorist camps. John Starnes, former head of the RCMP security service, argued that Canada's immigration laws needed tightening to prevent terrorists from claiming refugee status. "My understanding", he was quoted as saying, "is that if someone like Abu Nidal [a wanted Palestinian terrorist leader] came to Mirabel Airport and declared himself to be a refugee, he would get exactly the same treatment as someone from the east bloc who also claimed political asylum. To me, that's silly."[42]

It may well be that the government will come under increasing pressure to increase the discretionary powers of the bureaucracy and the security apparatus in response to the terrorist threat.[43] By now one point should be tolerably clear, however, to the reader. The discretionary powers that can be exercised by the Canadian state in the name of national security need no expansion. As is true of the nuclear arms race, adding more discretionary powers to the existing armoury can only constitute overkill. And the history of the exercise of these powers in immigration and citizenship—once secret, still largely hidden—should form a salutary warning about what is likely to happen when states have the opportunity to act arbitrarily, outside the overview of public scrutiny and outside the restraints of liberal safeguards. A genuinely free society ought to have the courage of its own convictions.

Afterword:
In the Name of
National Security

"Canada's immigration policies", two writers tell us in a recent work, "remain among the most open of all western societies. An important consequence of this has been that since the Second World War, Canada's electorate has grown more quickly than that of any other liberal democracy except Israel."[1] Canada is truly a nation of immigrants. The Canadian identity is constantly being redefined by the arrival and acceptance into the community of new Canadians. Citizenship is thus a more open-ended concept in Canada than in most other Western countries.

Much attention has been paid to the political and cultural barriers with which immigrants of certain national origins have been confronted. Prejudice against certain ethnic groups, especially visible minorities, is at the centre of this issue. But close scrutiny of immigration security policy reveals another set of barriers. Canada has set selective political and ideological standards for those who wish to immigrate to this country (or even for those who would visit it). Canada, a liberal democracy, has in effect proscribed certain kinds of political views and certain kinds of political associations among those applying to enter it—even though those views and associations are not unlawful among those already enjoying full rights of citizenship in Canada. There is a distinct ideological bias, documented throughout this book, to this selectivity. Yet the standards have never been spelled out. Political controls over immigration in the name of national security have been created within the broader framework of immigration policy. But this policy within a policy has been so shrouded in secrecy that its very contours have been unclear. There is much more here than meets the eye.

The American journalist Thomas Powers, writing about the CIA, tells us that the people who run that intelligence agency have a belief in secrecy "which is almost metaphysical":

> In their bones they believe they know the answer to that ancient paradox of epistemology which asks: If a tree falls in the forest without witnesses, is there any sound? The CIA would say no. It would agree...that history is not what happened but what the surviving evidence says happened. If you can hide the evidence and keep the secrets, then you can write the history.[2]

As befits an agency with a mission to guard the Canadian national security, the RCMP has tried over the years to keep its secrets. "The Security Service is one of the most secret institutions in Canada", John Sawatsky noted at the beginning of a book that went a long way towards lifting the veil on that institution.[3]

The security operation in immigration is among the most secretive of the ongoing activities of Canada's security service. Yet the tree has not fallen silently in the forest. Security agencies write a lot of their own rules, but they are also bureaucratic organizations with a zeal for amassing information in carefully ordered and cross-referenced files.

> "The horror of that moment", the King went on, "I shall never, *never* forget!"
>
> "You will, though," the Queen said, "if you don't make a memorandum of it."

Alice's White Queen was quite right. There will always be some under-secretary or clerk who will dutifully take down the details and file them. According to Max Weber, the sociologist of bureaucracy, it is characteristic of bureaucratic organizations that everything they do must be put in writing. Even when it is a matter of state secrets, of decisions taken in the shadows behind the bulwark of "national security", there are always memoranda that linger in dusty archives, sleeping witnesses to be awakened and led into the light of day. However much attention may be paid to protecting the record from prying eyes, some of it will eventually get out. And when the security service operations are sheltered within the broader operations of a government department, as immigration and citizenship security screening has always been, the spread of documents originated by the security service is even more difficult to control—especially now that the Access to Information Act has come into effect. The paper trail that has been followed in this book is a tribute both to the record-keeping propensities of modern bureaucracy and to the value to scholars and journalists of that legislation.

The civilian officials joined the security service in the secrecy campaign, as did the ministers of immigration and Cabinet as a whole. There was nothing surreptitious or improper in the behaviour of the security service or the immigration bureaucrats. In covering the tracks of the security process they were acting as good, conscientious public servants, under the highest authority in the land. Maintaining secrecy was public policy. Here is a central paradox of this history: should *public* policy in a democracy be made and administered in *secret*?

Of course secrecy is always present to some degree in the process of policy making and administration. Cabinet deliberations are always conducted out of the public eye, and great efforts have been made by successive governments to maintain this privilege. Policy planning within the bureaucracy is similarly protected from the scrutiny of press and Parliament. The administration of laws and government programs involves elements of secrecy that are generally accepted as reasonable and appropriate.

In the formulation of public policy, elements of secrecy and publicity are normally mingled: internal government deliberations are carried on behind closed doors, but at the same time there is opportunity for interested sections of the public to make their views known. Parliament is a forum for marshalling opposition and seeking modification of government policy. Beyond Parliament, liberal democratic governments recognize an obligation to maintain freedom of the press and freedom of discussion. An electorate must be able to gain some reasonable sense of government policy and its execution if it is to be able to pass informed judgement on that government at the polls. Secrecy has its traditional place within this process, but if it becomes an end in itself it can threaten liberal democracy.

Immigration security policy has gone beyond this framework of everyday secrecy. Policy here has been made in secret and administered in secret. Secrecy has not been seen merely as an element of a process that would be partially secret and partially public. Instead, very elaborate efforts have been made to insulate the process as a whole from any public scrutiny. These efforts have not been entirely successful, of course. But this has always been the aim of policymakers: minimal public information and discussion, and maximum administrative discretion. Moreover, governments have sought—with considerable success—to insulate the process from the courts as well. Both Parliament and the judiciary are expected to defer to the executive in all matters relating to national security.

Essential to the Canadian state's success in its pursuit of secrecy has been its power to treat the objects of immigration policy as persons without claims to full democratic citizenship. Under the oft-repeated dictum that "immigration to Canada is a privilege, not a right", policymakers have categorized immigrants as inferior to citizens. Citizenship has both rights and obligations; immigrants have many obligations but fewer rights. This approach has allowed the government to ignore or devalue various liberal principles in its dealings with immigrants, including natural justice and the rule of law. There has been an erosion of the principle underlying policy, however: immigrants have acquired more rights over the years, and the gap between Canadian-born citizens and immigrants has narrowed. Yet during most of the postwar era, the government has been able to justify shrouding its activities in immigration security in such secrecy because immigrants were deemed to have no right to know the basis upon which decisions about them were made—even though those decisions were sometimes matters of life and death.

When public policy is made and administered in secret, certain consequences result. Responsible government gives way to irresponsible government. In the case of immigration security, there is clear evidence that publicly proclaimed government policy has been deliberately undermined at times by what is done in secret. Since the criteria for screening have been secret, those outside the process have had little opportunity to evaluate their realism—or their political bias. Injustices have been done to individuals, but seeking redress has been nearly impossible. Moreover, evaluation of the effectiveness of the policy requires access to information that has been routinely denied to "outsiders".

Secrecy can cover a multitude of sins. It is not surprising that the parliamentary opposition and the public have developed the suspicion that a government that takes such efforts to maintain secrecy must be trying to cover something up. That suspicion is inevitable—and, as this book shows, it is often justified. Secrecy is the front line of defence for incompetence and malfeasance in government. A Cabinet directive on government security policy issued in 1986 states boldly, "In no case is information to be classified in the national interest in order to conceal violations of law, inefficiency or administrative error, to avoid embarrassment, or to restrain competition."[4] Who knows what might be revealed if this admirable principle were to be applied retroactively to the records of the past four decades of the administration of immigration policy?

In the name of national security, secrecy has shrouded some motives that had less to do with security than with prejudices on the part of the policymakers—such as the camouflaging of anti-Semitism. Similarly, the ideological bias that favours refugees from Communism over those fleeing right-wing oppression has been deliberately obscured—although it has not escaped notice.

The damage done by secrecy is not limited to these relatively obvious examples, however. Administering a secret policy imports a deep bias into the very structures of government. Secrecy is a much sought-after good *within* government; possession of it gives considerable advantages in bureaucratic infighting over control of resources and jurisdiction. The process of immigration policy has been skewed in favour of those forces that hold the secrets. This is evident first in the inability of the political masters of the bureaucracy to control and reform the system. A strong and persistent minister like Jack Pickersgill was able to make some headway, although he lost some rounds to the bureaucrats. A reform-minded minister like Davie Fulton was stymied and left frustrated. Most ministers have not even tried to intervene. In all cases the bureaucracy has held a strong hand because it can call upon secrecy as self-justification.

Within the bureaucracy, the same displacement of influence is evident. The immigration officials, with their mandate to administer the flow of immigration, have often found themselves fighting the security service; usually it is the department's officials who have had to back down because the security service has controlled pertinent information and refused to share it on grounds of secrecy. When civilian appeal boards or the courts threatened to open up individual security cases, the police claimed privileged status for their information; the RCMP's successor, CSIS, can do the same. And when laws have been rewritten, the Ottawa security establishment has been able to maintain and in some instances even strengthen its privileged hold over information. In short, within government, those who have most closely controlled secrecy have been able to exert an influence beyond their limited status as public servants.

In the name of national security, a state within a state has grown up in the administration of immigration policy. This secret state has set its own agenda, followed its own rules, and paid little heed to the principles of liberal democracy. The Cold War has exacted a price from Canadians. It is time that an accounting be made.

Notes

Introduction

1. Paul Knox, "Guatemalans seek refuge in Canada from political terror", *The Globe and Mail*, 26 Dec. 1985. Even a Canadian diplomat who had just processed a particularly urgent refugee case was shot at by unknown assailants while driving in his car that same night. The diplomat was immediately withdrawn to Canada.

2. Jim Christie, "Ihnacak granted special permit", *The Globe and Mail*, 3 Jan. 1986; James Davidson, "Leafs assign star's number to new Czech", *The Globe and Mail*, 4 Jan. 1986.

3. Canada, Royal Commission on Security, *Report* (Ottawa 1969), 45-6; Freda Hawkins, *Canada and Immigration: Public Policy and Public Concern* (Montreal 1972), 329-33; Gerald Dirks, *Canada's Refugee Policy: Indifference or Opportunism?* (Montreal 1977), 168-71; Alvin Finkel, "Canadian Immigration Policy and the Cold War, 1945–1980", *Journal of Canadian Studies*, 21:3 (Autumn 1986), 53-70; Canada, Commission of Inquiry Concerning Certain Activities of the Royal Canadian Mounted Police, *Second Report*, v. 2 (Ottawa 1981), 813-38.

Chapter One

1. Michael R. Marrus, *The Unwanted: European Refugees in the Twentieth Century* (New York 1985), 299-300.

2. L. W. Holborn, *The IRO: A Specialized Agency of the United Nations* (New York 1956), 197-8.

3. Canada, Manpower and Immigration, *Immigration and Population Statistics* (Ottawa 1974), 31, 6; Leroy Stone, "Canadian Population Growth—Past and Future",

Proceedings of the Conference on Future Immigration Policy (Toronto 1974), 61, table 1.

4. On the Jews, see Irving Abella and Harold Troper, *None Is Too Many: Canada and the Jews of Europe, 1933–1948* (Toronto 1983); on ethnic discrimination in general, see Gerald Dirks, *Canada's Refugee Policy: Indifference or Opportunism?* (Montreal 1977).

5. Donald Avery, *"Dangerous Foreigners": European Immigrant Workers and Labour Radicalism in Canada, 1896–1932* (Toronto 1979), 63-4, 92-3, 118, 136-7; statistics on deportation are from K. A. H. Buckley and M. C. Urquhart, *Canadian Historical Statistics* (Toronto 1965); on the Second World War, see Reg Whitaker, "Official repression of Communism during World War II", *Labour/le Travail: Journal of Canadian Labour Studies* 17 (Spring 1986).

6. See Reg Whitaker, "Fighting the Cold War on the home front: America, Britain, Australia and Canada", in Ralph Miliband, John Saville, and Marcel Liebman, eds., *The Uses of Anti-Communism* (London 1984), 23-67.

7. Reg Whitaker, "Origins of the Canadian government's internal security system, 1946–1952", *Canadian Historical Review* 65:2 (June 1984), 154-83.

8. See J. L. Granatstein, *A Man of Influence* (Ottawa 1981) and *The Ottawa Men* (Toronto 1982).

9. Robert A. Divine, *American Immigration Policy, 1924–1952* (New York 1972), 116, 177-8; see also Milton R. Konvitz, *Civil Rights in Immigration* (Ithaca, NY, 1953); Anthony T. Bouscaren, *The Security Aspects of Immigration Work* (Milwaukee 1959); and David Caute, *The Great Fear: The Anti-Communist Purge under Truman and Eisenhower* (New York 1978), 224-66.

10. Nicholas Bethell, *The Last Secret: The Delivery to Stalin of Over Two Million Russians by Britain and the United States* (New York 1974). Particularly controversial views on the issue of forced repatriation, charging Sir Harold Macmillan with conspiring with the Soviets, have been argued by Nikolai Tolstoy in *The Minister and the Massacres* (London 1986), but see Robert Knight's critique of Tolstoy in "Harold Macmillan and the Cossacks: was there a Klagenfurt conspiracy?", *Intelligence and National Security* 1:2 (May 1986), and his review of Tolstoy in *The Times Literary Supplement* (June 1986), 639-40.

11. John George Stoessinger, *The Refugee in the World Community* (Minneapolis 1956), 60-84.

12. "Evolution of policy and procedures: security screening", documents submitted to the Commission of Inquiry on War Criminals by the Department of Manpower and Immigration, 1985 (hereinafter referred to as EPP), A. L. Jolliffe to J. A. Glen, 16 Oct. 1945. "Memorandum by the Second Political Division", 3 Jan. 1946, *Documents on Canadian Foreign Relations* 12:1946 (Ottawa 1977), 353-4.

13. Abella and Troper, *None Is Too Many.*

Chapter Two

1. Irving Abella and Harold Troper, *None Is Too Many: Canada and the Jews of Europe, 1933–1948* (Toronto 1983), 200; Gerald Dirks, *Canada's Refugee Policy: Indifference or Optimism?* (Montreal 1977), 124. Public Archives of Canada (PAC), Department of External Affairs (DEA), A12, v.2116 f.AR41812, H. Wrong to V. Massey, 10 Mar. 1945; Rivett-Carnac was back in London on a similar mission in 1947 with Paris, Brussels, and the Hague added to his itinerary: ibid., L. B. Pearson to Massey, 5 June 1947.

2. Privy Council Office Records (PCO) RG 2 Accession No. 83-84, f. R-100-M (1946-47), Security Panel Minutes, 19 Aug. 1946. PCO 18, v. 103 f. S-100-1 (v.2), A. L. Jolliffe confidential memo, 5 July 1946; Secretary of Security Panel to J. A. Glen, 23 Sept. 1946; ibid., v.82 f.I-50 (1945-46), 13 June 1946. Dirks, *Canada's Refugee Policy*, 145.

3. Abella and Troper, *None Is Too Many*, 239-40. J. L. Granatstein writes that Keenleyside had been passed over for the post of permanent head of External Affairs at the end of 1940 because he "had blotted his copybook in the Prime Minister's view by supporting the Japanese Canadians too enthusiastically": *The Ottawa Men* (Toronto 1982), 95.

4. Hugh Keenleyside, *Memoirs*, v.2: *On the Bridge of Time* (Toronto 1982), 298-301.

5. John Holmes, *The Shaping of Peace: Canada and the Search for World Order, 1943–1957*, v.1 (Toronto 1979), 100. Freda Hawkins, *Canada and Immigration: Public Policy and Public Concern* (Montreal 1972), 238-40. Abella and Troper, *None Is Too Many*, 190-285. Leonard Dinnerstein, *America and the Survivors of the Holocaust* (New York 1982), has much interesting material on the American experience in processing displaced persons, especially on the slipshod and discriminatory security screening (192-6).

6. Brief from the Association of United Ukrainian Canadians, 7 June 1947, reprinted in Bohdan S. Kordan and Lubomyr Y. Luciuk, eds., *A Delicate and Difficult Question: Documents in the History of Ukrainians in Canada, 1899–1962* (Kingston 1986), 149-51; John Kolasky, *The Shattered Illusion: The History of Ukrainian Pro-Communist Organizations in Canada* (Toronto 1979), 88-101; "Report of the repatriation poll of displaced persons in UNRRA Assembly Centers in Germany for the period 1-14 May 1946: analysis of negative votes", May 1946, reprinted in Yury Boshyk, ed., *Ukraine During World War II: History and Its Aftermath* (Edmonton 1986), 209-19.

7. B. Heydenhorn, "The Left in Canadian Polonia", *Polyphony* 6:2 (1984), 57-8; Dirks, *Canada's Refugee Policy*, 132, 141-2; Abella and Troper, *None Is Too Many*, 218.

8. PAC, Immigration Branch, Department of Mines and Resources (IB), v.800 f.547-1 (pt.1), A. L. Jolliffe "for file", 24 Jan. 1947, and Jolliffe to J. A. Glen, 27 Jan. 1947.

9. PAC, William Lyon Mackenzie King Papers, Memoranda and Notes series (WLMK/M&N), v.419, Cabinet Conclusions, 29 Jan. and 5 Feb. 1947, v. 420, Cabinet Document No. 387 "Security examination of prospective immigrants", 4 Feb. 1947. PCO Acc. No. 83-84, f.S-100-M (1946-47). IB, v.960 f.SF-S-129(1). "A brief résumé of the arrangements for security examination of immigrants", January 1967. Note that the figures in the text refer only to applicants, not to spouses and dependent children, so the total numbers of persons involved were actually much higher. The reference to criticism from the public should be placed in context: Gallup polls conducted in the late 1940s indicated that Canadians believed, by a three-to-one margin, that Canada needed a much larger population. In 1947 51 per cent agreed that Canada needed more immigrants, while only 30 per cent disagreed. Thus, serious backlogs in immigration processing would almost certainly have roused popular displeasure with government performance. See Nancy Tienhaara, *Canadian Views on Immigration and Population: An Analysis of Post-War Gallup Polls* (Ottawa 1974), 8-9, 18.

10. WLMK/M&N, v.419, Cabinet Conclusions, 5 Mar. 1947, v. 420, Cabinet Document No. 405, J. A. Glen "Security screening for immigrants", n.d. PAC, Louis

St. Laurent Papers (LSTL), v.225 f.I-17 (1937-54), meeting of Cabinet Committee on Immigration Policy (CCIP), 27 May 1947. IB, v.800 f.547-1(1), C. E. S. Smith to Deputy Minister, 15 Oct. 1948, L. H. Nicholson to L. Fortier, 12 Nov. 1948, S. T. Wood to A. L. Jolliffe, 3 July 1948, and Jolliffe to Wood, 5 July 1948, joint declaration of 12 July 1948. A Cabinet directive in 1949 declared that the disclosure of any information regarding security rejections resulted in "serious embarrassment to the immigration authorities and to the police" and concluded that "under no circumstances" should a rejection be attributed to security reasons. PCO v.139 f.C-20-7 (1947-54), Circular No. 14, 28 Oct. 1949.

11. House of Commons, *Debates*, 1 May 1947; Hawkins, *Canada and Immigration*, 91-5; J. W. Pickersgill and D. F. Forster, eds., *The Mackenzie King Record*, v.4 *1947–1948* (Toronto 1970), 33-6.

12. PCO 18, v.103 f.S-100-M, Security Panel Minutes, 2 Apr. 1948; v.189 f.S-100-1(1) (1949-50), F. W. T. Lucas to A. D. F. Heeney, 26 Jan. 1949.

13. Malcolm J. Proudfoot, *European Refugees, 1939–52* (London 1957), 401. PCO Acc. No. 83-84 f.S-100 (1946-49), G. C. Crean to Secretary, Security Panel, 14 Apr. 1948; C&I, v.164 f.3-18-17(1), L. Fortier to A. L. Jolliffe, 22 Apr. 1948. In the fall of 1949, only 2.5 per cent of the staff of the IRO were nationals of Communist-bloc countries; by contrast, Canadians alone accounted for 2.7 per cent, and the British and Americans together for just under half the total: L. W. Holborn, *The IRO: A Specialized Agency of the United Nations* (New York 1956), 100 (adapted from table).

14. United States National Archives, Washington DC, RG84, State Department Records, v.710 f.1948-49 59A543, US State Department, Nanking, to US Ambassador, Ottawa, 10 Mar. 1948. IB, v.801 f.547-5-54, Vice-consul, Shanghai to DEA, 18 Aug. 1948. On 16 Mar. 1948 the readers of *The Windsor Star* learned that "seasoned veterans of Red revolution in many lands are entering Canada secretly to lead a nationwide offensive of sabotage and terror scheduled for the immediate future." Even a handful of agents among the DPs could "be more dangerous than their weight in T-N-T" (Don Cameron, "Loopholes in law admit Europe's Red saboteurs"). Cameron particularly cited the dangers of Communism among Jewish refugees whose admission was advocated by Joseph Salsberg—a Communist MPP in Ontario. See also *The Chicago Tribune*, 3 Sept. 1948, "Canada moves to halt influx of reds as DPs" and *The Detroit Free Press*, 3 Sept. 1948, "Canada wary of DPs". The minister of labour, on the other hand, hastened to assure reporters after visiting Europe that "these people don't want Communism, they have seen too much...they should be a great bulwark against Communism spreading in this country," *Labour Gazette* v.48 (1948), 1343.

15. C&I, v.164 f.3-18-17(1), H. Keenleyside to S. T. Wood, 28 Apr. 1948, and Wood to Keenleyside, 10 May 1948 (Wood's letter has been heavily censored under the Access to Information Act). Fortier may have been operating on a hidden agenda. For one thing, his trip to Europe and his charges of Communist infiltration followed the embarrassing disclosure in the media that IRO officials had revealed an anti-Semitic bias practised by Canadian immigration agents in selecting prospective immigrants from the refugee camps (Abella and Troper, *None Is Too Many*, 254-5). Perhaps Fortier considered that the best defence was an offence. The IRO was much more liberal about finding homes for Jewish survivors of the Holocaust than were immigration officials in countries like Canada where anti-Semitism still reigned. Pro-Jewish sentiment was often characterized in this era as "Communistic".

16. C&I, v.169 f.3-32-1(1), L. D. Wilgress to L. B. Pearson, 14 May 1948.

17. PCO 18, v.189 f.S-100-1(2), "Screening of applicants for admission to Canada", 20 Nov. 1948; IB, v.166 f.3-25-11(2), memo from Associate Commissioner

to the Commissioner for Immigration, 7 Feb. 1949. In the evidence given by former RCMP commissioner William Kelly before the Deschênes Commission of Inquiry on War Criminals, references are made to a document that appears to be an office consolidation of the various categories dating from the early 1950s, which I have not been able to obtain: transcript, Commission of Inquiry on War Criminals, hearing of 8 May 1985 (thanks to Ms. Alti Rodal of the commission's research staff for making this transcript available). IB 83-84/347, box 5 f.SF-S-118(1), "Chapter 7: Security screening procedure", 7.01(b).

18. EPP, W. H. Hickman to P. T. Baldwin, 17 May 1951, and C. E. S. Smith to the Deputy Minister, 18 May 1951.

19. IB, v.800 f.547-1(1), "Security screening", 7 Feb. 1951; PC 2856.

20. Ibid.

21. 1 Eliz.II c.42: note especially "prohibited classes" 5(l), 5(m), and 5(n).

22. Hawkins, *Canada and Immigration*, 102-3.

23. *Attorney General of Canada v. Brent* [1956] SCR 318; PC 1956-785; J. W. Pickersgill, *My Years with Louis St. Laurent: A Political Memoir* (Toronto 1975), 240.

24. Philip Girard, "From subversion to liberation: homosexuals and the Immigration Act 1952–1977", draft paper. Thanks to Professor Girard for making this paper available and for sharing his ideas.

25. Hawkins, *Canada and Immigration*, 105.

26. Statutes of Canada 1946, c.15, s.10(1)(d). Commission of Inquiry Concerning Certain Activities of the RCMP, *Second Report* v.2 (Ottawa 1981), 829-33.

27. See the interesting essays by R. Kenneth Carty and W. Peter Ward, "The making of a Canadian political citizenship", in Carty and Ward, eds., *National Politics and Community in Canada* (Vancouver 1986), 65-79; and Alan Cairns and Cynthia Williams, "Constitutionalism, citizenship and society in Canada: an overview", in Cairns and Williams, *Constitutionalism, Citizenship and Society in Canada*, v.33 of the studies of the Royal Commission on the Economic Union and Development Prospects for Canada (Toronto 1985), 1-50.

28. Hawkins, *Canada and Immigration*, 30.

29. PCO Acc. No. 83-84, f.S-100-M (1946-47), Security Panel meeting, 5 Apr. 1949, RCMP memo "Security screening of immigrants—present problems", SP 40, 31 Mar. 1949. PCO 16, v.17, Cabinet Conclusions, 24 Aug. 1949, Security Panel Report (Cabinet Document No. 1022), 29 Sept. 1949, citing the danger of compromising "counterespionage activities" if security grounds for rejection were to be disclosed. PCO 18, v.189 f.S-100-1(2), R. A. S. McNeil to E. F. Gaskell, 11 July 1950.

30. C&I, v.803 f.547-5-645, H. Allard to Director of Immigration, 15 Dec. 1952; Belgrade Embassy to Secretary of State for External Affairs, 29 Nov. 1952; IB 83-84/347, box 5 f.SF-S-118(1), "Chapter 7: Security screening procedure", 7.05(d)(2).

31. C&I, v.894 f.591-I(5), C. E. S. Smith to Deputy Minister, 25 Mar. 1952; f.591-1(7), Operations Division to posts abroad, 17 Apr. 1956.

32. C&I, v.119 f.3-25-15, L. Fortier to the Minister, 26 Feb. 1953; P. M. Dwyer, draft memorandum to Cabinet, "Immigration security policy", 23 Feb. 1953.

33. IB 83-84/347, box 5 f.SF-S-118(1), "Chapter 7: Security screening procedure", 7.01(b)(i) and (iii) and 7.00(c) and (d).

34. *Winnipeg Free Press,* "Pickersgill to get bar committee's immigration data", 3 Sept. 1954. C&I, v.166 f.3-25-11(2), Fortier to Pickersgill, 17 Jan. 1955; v.167 f.3-25-11-13(1), Minutes of meeting on security, 6 Dec. 1954. As late as 1956 the deputy minister was writing to such eminently respectable organizations as the

Canadian Council of Churches, the Canadian Jewish Congress, and the Canadian Christian Council for Resettlement of Refugees, reviewing reasons for rejections on criminal, medical, and occupational grounds, but scrupulously avoiding any mention of security: v.110, f.3-24-12(1), L. Fortier to J. W. Pickersgill, 1 Feb. 1956.

35. Pickersgill, *My Years with Louis St. Laurent*, 231.

36. EPP, J. R. Robillard to C. S. A. Ritchie, 22 Apr. 1955. IB, v.800 f.547-1(3), K. W. N. Hall to C. E. S. Smith, 9 Aug. 1955, admitting that "visa officers have had a very legitimate complaint in that certain very minor offences, which could under no circumstances be considered as serious in this country, have been included in the [forms] forwarded by our Security Officers"; v.801 f.547-5-513, Robillard to Chief, Operations Division, 30 Sept. 1955; v.802 f.547-5-575, A. M. Mont to Officer-in-Charge, 13 Oct. 1955; R. Brunet to Director of Immigration, 20 Oct. 1955; G. R. Benoit to Brunet, 28 Oct. 1955.

37. Hawkins, *Canada and Immigration*, 282-3.

38. IB, v.800 f.547-1(1), "Meeting on immigration matters", 22 Jan. 1954. This meeting is reported at greater length by Alvin Finkel, "Canadian Immigration Policy and the Cold War, 1945–1980", *Journal of Canadian Studies* 21:3 (Fall 1986), 58-60.

39. C&I, v.168 f.3-25-13(1), L. H. Nicholson to L. Fortier, 15 Mar. 1954; v.103 f.3-18-14(1), Report to the Annual Meeting of the Canadian Bar Association, 9 July 1954. IB, v.800 f.547-1(3), Undersecretary of State for External Affairs to Fortier, 24 June 1955. LSTL, v.236 f. "Immigration (1952-56)", Canadian Labour Congress to Government of Canada, 15 Dec. 1956. Jack Pickersgill in his memoirs claims that the bar association complaints were entirely attributable to one law firm specializing in Chinese immigration, whose interest was in gaining ministerial backing in specific cases in exchange for calling off its "agitation": *My Years with Louis St. Laurent*, 233-6. Be this as it may, the bar association's case was certainly not lacking in substance on its own merits.

40. PAC, Department of Labour Records (DL), v.835 f.1-28-1(1), A. MacNamara to R. Haddow, 4 June 1948, Haddow to MacNamara, 5 June 1948, S. T. Wood to Mac-Namara, 8 June 1948. My thanks to Gary Marcuse for drawing this correspondence to my attention.

41. DL, S. T. Wood to MacNamara, 8 June 1948.

42. C&I, v.166 f.3-25-11(2), J. J. Deutsch to L. Fortier, 13 June 1955; draft report on European immigration activities of Canadian government, Dec. 1955; v.164 f.3-18-17(1), L. H. Nicholson to S. Garson, 7 Apr. 1955 (this letter has been censored under the Access to Information Act).

43. Secretary of State for External Affairs, "Summary of instructions sent out on April 22, 1948", 1 Nov. 1949.

44. C&I, v.119 f.3-25-15, Security Panel Document No. 151 "Immigration security policy", 25 Feb. 1953; draft memorandum to Cabinet, "Immigration security policy", 23 Feb. 1953; Security Panel Minutes, 2 Mar. 1953; L. Fortier, memorandum for the Minister, 3 Mar. 1953. Even the motives of friendly local police authorities might sometimes be doubted, as former commissioner William Kelly was later to recall in regard to the West Germans, whom the RCMP suspected of discouraging the outflow of skilled labour in the 1950s: see Deschênes Commission of Inquiry on War Criminals, transcript, 935-6.

45. PCO 1952, f.S-100-5-B, G. A. Sincennes to Officer-in-Charge, Security Section, London, 18 Dec. 1951; Secretary of State for External Affairs to Washington Embassy, 20 Mar. and 25 Apr. 1952. IB, v.153 f.1-18-14, K. W. N. Hall to E. F. Gaskell, 2 Feb. 1952. DEA, f.50207-A-40, Security Panel Minutes, 11 Mar. 1952. EPP, T. C.

Davis, "Immigration security arrangements", 6 Mar. 1952. Sol Littman, *War Criminal on Trial: The Rauca Case* (Toronto 1983).

46. Deschênes commission, transcript, 943-5, 972. Information on Gehlen and the CIC can be found in John Loftus, *The Belarus Secret* (New York 1982). On the flagrant collaboration of the CIC with Nazi war criminals see Magnus Linklater, Isabel Hilton, and Neal Ascherson, *The Fourth Reich: Klaus Barbie and the Neo-Fascist Connection* (London 1985).

47. C&I, v.153 f.1-18-7(1), Security Panel minutes, 20 Nov. 1953.

48. C&I, v.164 f.3-18-17(1), L. H. Nicholson to S. Garson, 7 Apr. 1955. Ironically, the very discussion of the question by the RCMP commissioner in the 1955 document has been so heavily censored under the Access to Information Act at the RCMP's insistence that is impossible to know what, if anything, was actually done about it thirty years ago. Some examples of Canadians who have been barred by the United States are discussed in chapter 7.

49. This is a point made by Richard Hall, *The Secret State: Australia's Spy Industry* (North Melbourne 1978), 67.

50. See, for instance, Ronald Williams, "How to keep Red hands off our new Canadians", *The Financial Post*, 12 Mar. 1949. A study of opinion surveys regarding immigration notes that since 1949 "business executives and professionals are found at the favourable end" of a continuum of occupational categories regarding the need for more immigration: Tienhaara, *Canadian Views on Immigration and Population*, 26-7. British immigrants were exempted altogether from screening, and in the early 1950s they represented a large proportion of those skilled trades that were often employed in defence industries. Some defence contractors were reluctant to employ British workers on the grounds of political unreliability since all defence industries were required to screen employees with access to secret work: see chapter 8.

51. PCO Acc. No./83, box 16 f.S-100-5, P. M. Dwyer to N. A. Robertson, 7 Mar. 1952, and Dwyer to L. Fortier, 20 Mar. 1952.

52. Tienhaara, *Canadian Views on Immigration and Population*, 64-5.

53. Dirks, *Canada's Refugee Policy*, 180-2.

54. Ibid., 186-9; Hawkins, *Canada and Immigration*, 18-20.

55. PCO 16, Cabinet Conclusions, 5 May and 15 June 1955.

Chapter Three

1. On the background to Quebec concern, see Freda Hawkins, *Canada and Immigration: Public Policy and Public Concern* (Montreal 1972), 213-27; Jacques Brossard, *L'immigration: les droits et les pouvoirs du Canada et du Québec* (Montreal 1967); Paul-André Linteau, René Durocher, and Jean-Claude Robert, *Histoire du Québec contemporain: de la Confédération à la crise* (Montreal 1979), 46-9.

2. PC 2743, 2 June 1949; amendment of PC 4851, 26 Nov. 1947. The Ontario episode is noted in Hawkins, *Canada and Immigration*, 201-5.

3. C&I, v.167 f.3-25-11-13(1), L. B. Pearson to J. A. MacKinnon, 15 Oct. 1948 (this letter can also be found in LSTL, v.56); IB, v.801 f.547-550(1), C. E. S. Smith to Deputy Minister, Mines and Resources, 20 Sept. 1948; v.894 f.591-1(1), de Miffouis to O/C, Special Branch, 30 Aug. 1948.

4. LSTL, v.56, memorandum (Jolliffe and Chance) for J. A. MacKinnon and L. St. Laurent, 28 Oct. 1948.

5. IB, v.801 f.547-5-550(1), "AWB" to G. R. Benoit, 3 June 1952; Acting Chief, Operations Division, to Director of Immigration, 4 Oct. 1956.

6. IB, v.801 f.547-550(1), P. Fortin to Director of Immigration, 28 July 1955; Director, Immigration Branch, to A/Chief, Operations Division, 4 Oct. 1956; v.894 f.591-1(1), G. G. Congden to Assistant Commissioner of Immigration, 3 Nov. 1948; v.167 f.3-25-11-13(1), J. W. Pickersgill to L. Fortier, 23 June 1955, W. R. Baskerville to Deputy Minister, 17 July 1957. EPP, Methods and Procedures Section to Acting Chief, Operations Division, 24 Sept. 1957: "Many a French immigrant is aware that the procedure set up in the United Kingdom...does not require British immigrants to wait as long."

7. Hawkins, *Canada and Immigration*, 79.

8. C&I, v.164 f.3-18-17(1), S. T. Wood to H. Keenleyside, 10 May 1948 (as censored under the Access to Information Act).

9. DEA, f.50207-A-40, Security Panel Minutes, 27 Apr. 1950 and 3 May 1951. Retrospectively, the RCMP claimed that it had been in favour of screening British immigrants, but that this had been administratively impossible: IB 83-84/1347, f.SF-C-35, Committee on review of immigration policy and procedures, Subcommittee on security screening policy, 28 June 1957, appendix "D".

10. PCO 18, v.188 f.S-100-D, Security Panel Document No. 9, "Security of defence contracts", 24 Apr. 1951. Deportation statistics are from Citizenship and Immigration Department annual reports. The number of Britons deported in the early 1950s was averaging between 100 and 200 per year: see chapter 8.

11. PCO, Acc. No. 83-84/213, Security Panel Minutes, 18 Sept. 1952, and Security Panel Document No. 127, "Security screening of British immigrants", 5 Sept. 1952.

12. C&I, v.167 f.3-25-11-12(1), L. H. Nicholson to L. Fortier, 26 Oct. 1955. IB, v.803 f.547-5-645, "review of immigration security screening", 28 June 1957. Americans, of course, could enter as freely as Britons, but as the level of American emigration to Canada in this era was negligible, the issue was rarely raised. One security issue that did arise among British immigrants was membership in the IRA, although the low level of activity on the Irish front in this period coupled with the obsessive attention to Communism made this a relatively marginal concern: IB, v.803 f.547-5-636, Undersecretary of State for External Affairs to Director of Immigration, 31 Aug. 1956.

13. Hawkins, *Canada and Immigration*, 114; PCO, Cabinet Minutes, 7, 21, and 28 Feb. 1956.

14. Hawkins, *Canada and Immigration*, 60-61. Over 400,000 Italians immigrated to Canada from 1946 to 1967. The equivalent figure for Britons is well over 800,000. For the first postwar decade, Italians accounted for 10.7 per cent of all immigration, while Britons accounted for 29.3 per cent (adapted from table 12, 58-9).

15. IB, v.802 f.547-5-575, Director of Immigration to G. Benoit, 13 Nov. 1950; W. Milligan to Director of Immigration, 10 June 1957 (this letter was heavily censored under the Access to Information Act but was restored in full upon appeal to the Information Commissioner).

16. IB, v.800 f.547-1(3), Milligan to Director, 29 Sept. 1957; PCO Cabinet Document No. 283/57, "Immigration to Canada—1958", 6 Nov. 1957; EPP, Methods and Procedures Section to Acting Chief, Operations Division, 24 Sept. 1957.

17. Irving Abella and Harold Troper, *None Is Too Many: Canada and the Jews of Europe, 1933–1948* (Toronto 1983), 278-9. For the ambiguities of Canadian policy with regard to the creation of Israel, see David Jay Bercuson, *Canada and the Birth of Israel* (Toronto 1985).

18. IB, v.800 f.547-1(1), L. Fortier, "Security", 20 June 1949.

19. PCO 1952, box 4 f.S-100-I-M, Security Panel Minutes, 15 May 1952; f.C-20-5, Cabinet Document No. 180-52, 6 June 1952; f.S-100-I, G. McClellan to P. M. Dwyer, 31 May 1952.

20. C&I, v.199 f.3-25-15, Fortier to Minister, 20 May 1952. According to Professor Bercuson, governing circles in Britain tended to think of Israel as an instrument of Soviet expansion, but US State Department and Canadian External Affairs officials "did not consider this theory to hold much truth" (personal communication to the author from Professor Bercuson, 4 Dec. 1985). Apparently some members of the Ottawa security establishment did.

21. PCO 1952, box 4 f.S-100-I-M, Security Panel Minutes, 15 May 1952. C&I, v.119 f.3-25-15, L. Fortier, memorandum to the Minister, 26 Feb. 1953; Security Panel Minutes, 2 Mar. 1953; G. H. Ashley to Fortier, 25 May 1953. PCO 16, v.18, Cabinet Conclusions, 24 Sept. 1953, where "increasing pressure" concerning "alleged" close relatives of Canadian Jewish sponsors was cited as coming from the Canadian Jewish Congress, and 29 Sept. 1953, when Cabinet decided that no discrimination was involved, merely the application of security considerations—since it was "not unlikely a certain number of Communist agents might gain access" through Israeli immigration.

22. IB 83-84/347, box 5 f.SF-S-118(1), "Chapter 7: Security screening procedure", 7.26 Amend. No. 494 (1-8-55), Acting Chief, Operations Division to District Superintendents, 11 June 1957.

23. IB, v.801 f.547-5-550(1), J. R. Robillard to G. R. Benoit, 23 Mar. 1955.

24. C&I, v.181 f.3-3-37, L. Fortier to the Minister, 20 Sept. and 14 Oct. 1955. IB, v.801 f.547-5-500(1), Director of Immigration to the Deputy Minister, 27 July 1956, Fortier to Minister, 31 July 1956.

25. C&I, v.181 f.547-5-550(1), G. R. Benoit to Chief, Administration Division, 13 Jan. 1954. Late in 1958, sponsored Israeli applicants were finally placed on the same basis as those from other "Stage B" European posts (that is, visa offices with security officers): IB 83-84/347, f.SF-S-1188, A. W. Boulter to Acting Chief, Operations Division, 23 Sept. 1958.

26. C&I, v.167 f.3-25-11-40, Director, Immigration Branch, to Acting Chief, Operations Branch, 14 Jan. 1957; L. Fortier to Director, 15 Jan. 1955; Acting Chief, Operations Division, to all district superintendents and all posts abroad, 16 Jan. 1957. Gerald Dirks, *Canada's Refugee Policy: Indifference or Opportunism?* (Montreal 1977), 203.

27. PCO, Cabinet Minutes, 31 Jan. 1957.

28. Ibid., 14 and 17 July 1958.

29. Ibid., 1 Apr. and 21 July 1960; Cabinet Document No. 107/60. "Re: Roumanian immigrants of Jewish origin", 30 Mar. 1960; Hawkins, *Canada and Immigration*, 137.

30. Constantine Tsoucalas, *The Greek Tragedy* (Harmondsworth 1969), 114-5; Dominique Eudes, *The Kapetanios: Partisans and Civil War in Greece, 1943–1949* (London 1972), 357-60.

31. Hawkins, *Canada and Immigration*, from tables on 56-9. In 1952 departmental officials were discussing whether they should rely on American information, apparently containing Red lists on Greeks that dated back to 1941, in preference to reports from the Greek authorities, which were described as "corrupt and dishonest": IB, v.802 f.547-5-552, G. R. Benoit to Commissioner of RCMP, 3 July 1952; J. M. Knowles to Director of Immigration, 11 June 1952.

32. Lawrence S. Wittner, *American Intervention in Greece, 1943–1949* (New York 1982), 271-2.

33. C&I, v.167 f.3-25-11-14(1), L. Fortier to L. H. Nicholson, 9 Dec. 1954; Charles Henry to J. W. Pickersgill, 18 Jan. 1955; Pickersgill to Fortier, 27 Jan. 1955; Fortier to Nicholson, 31 Jan. 1955.

34. C&I, v.167 f.3-25-11-14(1), J. R. Lemieux to L. Fortier, 1 Mar. 1955; L. H. Nicholson to Fortier, 9 May 1956.

35. EPP, "Review of present grounds for rejection of applications for immigration", 1 Apr. 1963.

36. Tsoucalas, *The Greek Tragedy*, 111. Wittner, *American Intervention in Greece*, 162, cites US state department knowledge of the "flimsiness of the 'kidnapping' charges, as well as the double-standard with which it was applied" (15,000 children were removed from their homes by the Greek government while the American authorities remained silent). What Wittner calls "utilizing child abduction as a propaganda issue" was brought back to public attention in 1985 by the perfervidly anti-Communist film *Eleni*, which purports to depict the "history" of the Greek Civil War, from a singularly one-dimensional point of view.

37. IB, v.803 f.547-5-645, G. McClellan to P. T. Baldwin, 17 Sept. 1952; v.802 f.547-5-573(1), G. H. Ashley to Director of Immigration, 24 Sept. and 28 Oct. 1954.

38. IB, v.803 f.547-5-645, Ashley to Director of Immigration, 17 May 1956. The procedures for dealing with such cases were laid out in "Chapter 7" regulations, which covered a full page and a half of the 26-page document: IB 83-84/347, box 5 f.SF-S-118(1), 7.28 Amend. No. 170 (2-2-54).

Chapter Four

1. US National Archives, State Department 710, f.1948-49 59A543, box 1745, American Ambassador to Secretary of State, 11 May 1948; editorials in *Ottawa Journal*, 19 and 30 Apr. 1948.

2. IB, v.801 f.547-5-551(1).

3. PCO 18, v.127, Immigration Branch, IMP Document No. 43, 1 Mar. 1949, Statement for the Calendar Year 1948. Citizenship and Immigration, *Annual Report 1954*, 38.

4. PCO 18, v.183, Security Panel Minutes, 2 Apr. 1948: Laval Fortier insisted at this meeting that greater co-operation with the CIC and British intelligence was the answer to the "communistic elements...trying to introduce undesirables into the immigration scheme".

5. C&I, v.131 f.3-33-37, A. D. P. Heeney to C. D. Howe, 23 May 1947, H. Keenleyside to A. D. P. Heeney, 23 June 1947.

6. IB, v.784 f.541-1. L. Chance to H. Keenleyside, 18 Mar. 1948 (same letter sent to G. G. Crean and Escott Reid); Keenleyside to L.B. Pearson, 25 May 1948.

7. Ibid., Thomas Bata, memorandum on file in London immigration office, 26 May 1948; H. H. Wright to J. G. Levy, 27 Mar. 1950; W. E. Harris to J. W. Pickersgill, 18 Apr. 1950. PCO 18, v.83, Cabinet Conclusions, 14 May and 23 July 1948; Cabinet Document No. 711, PC 3371, 28 July 1948.

8. Ibid., Escott Reid to Secretary of State for External Affairs, 30 Sept. 1948.

9. PCO 18, v.83, Cabinet Documents Nos. 745 and 746, 15 Sept. 1948; E. Reid to Secretary of State for External Affairs, 21 Sept. 1948, Cabinet Conclusions, 29 Sept. 1948; v.95 f.R(12)(1940-49), memo for Acting Secretary of State for External Affairs, 7 Apr. 1949; Gerald Dirks, *Canada's Refugee Policy: Indifference or Opportunism?* (Montreal 1977), 64-6; Karl Aun, *The Political Refugees: A History of the Estonians in Canada* (Toronto 1985), 25-6.

10. Aun, *The Political Refugees*, 27. Other Baltic peoples came by boat: on Lithuanian immigration, see Milda Danys, *DP: Lithuanian Immigration to Canada* (Toronto 1986).

11. PCO 83-84, f.S-100-M(1946-47), Security Panel Minutes, 5 Apr. 1949. IB, v.894 f.569-1(1), Secretary of State for External Affairs, "Summary of instructions", 1 Nov. 1949.

12. IB, v.800 f.547-1(1), draft memorandum of meeting between RCMP and Immigration Branch officials on problems of security screening, 28 July 1949; v.802 f.547-5-573(1), Secretary of State for External Affairs to chargé d'affaires, Prague, 3 Mar. 1950.

13. IB, v.167 f.3-25-11-13(1), G. H. Ashley to Officer-in-Charge, RCMP Special Branch, 9 Mar. 1955.

14. IB, v.800 f.547-1(2), L. Fortier to N. A. Robertson, 23 Apr. 1952, and to Director of Immigration, 7 May 1952; v.802 f.547-5-575, Acting Director to Officer-in-Charge, RCMP Special Branch, 20 Oct. 1953; f.547-5-5731(1), Central District Superintendent, Toronto, to Director of Immigration, 3 Feb. 1953; Chief Operations Division to Central District Supervisor, 6 Feb. 1953; Fortier to J. W. Pickersgill, 30 Aug. 1955, Pickersgill to Fortier, 6 Sept. 1955; v.801 f.547-5-513, Officer-in-Charge, Linz, to Director of Immigration, 28 Apr. 1955, Minutes of meeting in Director's Office, 8 June 1955; C&I, v.119 f.3-25-15, draft memorandum for Cabinet, "Immigration security policy", 23 Feb. 1953.

15. C&I, v.167 f.3-25-11-13(1), G. McClellan to L. Fortier, 15 Apr. 1953, with attached extract (censored under the Access to Information Act); PCO, Cabinet Minutes, 5 Apr. 1956.

16. C&I, v.167 f.3-25-11-13(1), G. H. Ashley to Special Branch, 9 Mar. 1955 (censored under the Access to Information Act). In some cases, the immigration officials complained that security officers were flouting Cabinet directives—refusing to waive security for east-bloc wives of Canadian sponsors, for example: IB, v.801 f.547-5-513, Chief, Operations Division, to Immigration Mission, Karlsruhe, 9 Sept. 1955.

17. C&I, v.153 f.1-18-7(1), W. M. Haugan, "Cases submitted to the interdepartmental committee", 2 May 1957.

18. J. W. Pickersgill, *My Years with Louis St. Laurent: A Political Memoir* (Toronto 1975), 240-41.

19. C&I, v.131 f.3-3-37, L. Fortier to J. W. Pickersgill, 14 June 1955.

20. Ibid., L. H. Nicholson and Fortier to Pickersgill, 16 June 1955; Fortier to Pickersgill, 30 June 1955; v.153 f.I-18-7(1), Fortier to Pickersgill, 5 July 1955.

21. IB, v.800 f.547-I(3), "Security screening of immigrants", 27 June 1957; 83-84/347 box 5 f.SF-S-118(1), "Security screening procedure", 7.31. PCO 1955, Cabinet Conclusions, 11 July and 21 Sept. 1955.

22. IB 83-84/347, box 4 f.SF-S-22(4), Security Sub-Panel Document No. SSP-79, "Soviet interest in Canadian immigration matters", 27 Sept. 1956; Security Sub-Panel Minutes, 28 Sept. 1956; C. E. S. Smith to Deputy Minister, 11 Oct. 1956; Smith to D. F. Wall, 16 Oct. 1956.

In the mid-1950s the USSR and its satellites stepped up a program to encourage repatriation of their former citizens from the West, a campaign that was scrutinized with intense interest by Canadian diplomats abroad and was put under close police surveillance in Canada. Few naturalized Canadians responded to the siren call; the campaign found its only successes in Latin America. Then the events of 1956 in Hungary and Poland sharply diminished whatever dim attraction may have existed for most East European expatriates. See IB 83-84/347, f.SF-I-10 and v.920 f.586-8-573 with correspondence indicating that Canadian officials were for a time fearful that east-bloc immigrants had been only "pseudo-immigrants" planted for the purpose of later returning to the East accompanied by a propaganda campaign.

23. Dirks, *Canada's Refugee Policy*, 176-92; Freda Hawkins, *Canada and Immigration: Public Policy and Public Concern* (Montreal 1972), 114-7; David Dewitt and John Kirton, *Canada as a Principal Power* (Toronto 1983), 249-51. Canada ultimately accepted over 37,000 of some 200,000 who had reached Austria.

24. C&I. v.167 f.3-25-11-40, L. Fortier to L. H. Nicholson, 6 Nov. 1956; Fortier to J. W. Pickersgill, 26 Nov. 1956.

25. C&I, v.167 f.3-25-11-40, Acting Chief, Operations Division, to all district superintendents, 3 Jan. 1957 (warning that "there is a possibility that among recent Hungarian refugee arrivals there may be some...who have been affiliated with communistic organizations" and asking that such persons be "reported forthwith" to the RCMP); C. E. S. Smith to L. Fortier, 7 Jan. 1957; Fortier to Minister, 9 Jan. 1957; Acting Chief, Operations Division, to district superintendents, 17 July 1957; IB, v.802 f.547-5-573(1), Supt. Hall to C. E. S. Smith, 18 Apr. 1957; Inspector Milligan to Smith, 3 July 1955; Smith to Deputy Minister, 20 Dec. 1957.

26. EPP, Security Panel Document No. SP-198, "Immigration security policy—review of present grounds for rejection", 8 Apr. 1959.

27. C&I, v.167 f.3-25-11-40, L. Fortier to J. W. Pickersgill, 26 Nov. 1956, with the latter's comments dated 27 Nov. 1956; PCO, Cabinet Minutes, 21 Mar. 1957. Pickersgill, in *My Years with Louis St. Laurent*, recalls that "of the thirty-five thousand Hungarian refugees, about six hundred turned out badly, a few of whom were Communists, and most of the six hundred eventually went back to Hungary" (245). On the role of Hungarian refugees in right-wing anti-Communist ethnic politics in Toronto, see Peter Oliver, *Unlikely Tory: The Life and Politics of Allan Grossman* (Toronto 1985), 150-5. That the hand of security did sometimes fall upon Hungarians who may never have deserved to be screened out is suggested by journalist Victor Malarek: "Denied entry, bitter man fights on", *The Globe and Mail*, 2 July 1985, concerning a 1956 refugee and survivor of a Soviet gulag who is still barred from entering Canada to join his wife and family on mysterious "security" grounds.

28. Lawrence Martin, "Soviets firm on emigration", *The Globe and Mail*, 25 Sept. 1986.

29. For Croatian-Canadian wartime contributions, see Roy MacLaren, *Canadians Behind Enemy Lines, 1939–45* (Vancouver 1981).

30. Anthony W. Rasporich, *For a Better Life: A History of the Croatians in Canada* (Toronto 1982), 167-80.

31. RCMP surveillance is evident in reports in the RCMP Special Branch *Monthly Bulletin*, a secret internal communication circulated among members of the security service, obtained by the author under the Access to Information Act: see especially 1 June 1946 and January-February 1948; C&I, v.131 f.3-33-37, C. H. Coghlan to C. D. Howe, 18 Mar. 1948; L. B. Pearson to Deputy Minister of Mines and Resources, 29 May 1947. Canada, House of Commons, *Debates*, 23 May 1947.

32. Rasporich, *For a Better Life*, 178.

33. US National Archives, State Department 710, box 1745 f.1948-49 59A543, American Ambassador to Canada to Secretary of State, 11 May 1948; Rasporich, *For a Better Life*, 189 n.65; W. Stevenson, *Intrepid's Last Case* (New York 1984), 203.

34. C&I, v.131 f.3-33-37, L. Fortier to the Minister, 21 Apr. 1951; A. D. P. Heeney to Fortier, 27 June 1951; Fortier to J. E. Duggan, 20 June 1951. PCO 16, v.24, Cabinet Conclusions, 27 Apr. 1951.

35. C&I, v.131 f.3-33-37, Fortier to Heeney, 10 July 1951; Duggan to Fortier, 10 July 1955.

36. Ibid., memorandum "Implementation of Section 19(1)(d) of the Canadian Citizenship Act", 23 July 1951.

37. C&I, v.131 f.3-33-37, J. E. Duggan to L. Fortier, 8 Aug. 1951. PCO 18, v.138 f.C-20-5(1951), Cabinet Document No. 283-51, L. B. Pearson and W. E. Harris, "Revocation of citizenship", 5 Oct. 1951; PCO 16, v.27, Cabinet Conclusions, 31 Oct. 1951.

38. IB, v.803 f.547-5-645, Commissioner to C. E. S. Smith, 13 Sept. 1952, K. W. N. Hall to Smith, 24 Oct. 1952. C&I, v.131, f.3-33-37, J. E. Duggan to Deputy Minister, 13 June 1955; Martin Kasumovich *et al.* to the Governor General, 4 Feb. 1954; Harris to the Deputy Minister, 22 Mar. 1954.

39. C&I, v.164 f.3-18-17(1), P. M. Dwyer to L. Fortier, 13 Mar. 1953; v.131 f.3-33-37, W. E. Harris to Fortier, 22 Mar. 1954; Fortier to J. W. Pickersgill, 14 June 1955.

40. On Chinese immigration in general see E. B. Wickberg *et al.*, *From China to Canada: A History of the Chinese Communities in Canada* (Toronto 1982). Woodsworth, *Strangers within Our Gates* (new ed. Toronto 1972), 155. Patricia E. Roy, "Citizens without votes: East Asians in British Columbia, 1872–1947", in Jorgen Dahlie and Tissa Fernando, eds., *Ethnicity, Power and Politics in Canada* (Toronto 1981), 151-71.

41. Ann Gomer Sunahara, "Deportation: the final solution to Canada's Japanese problem", in Dahlie and Fernando, *Ethnicity, Power and Politics in Canada*, 254-78; *The Mackenzie King Record*, v.4, 34-5, indicating Mackenzie King's Cold War argument for not permanently excluding Asians; Hawkins, *Canada and Immigration*, 89-95.

42. PCO 16, v.18, Cabinet Conclusions, 22 Dec. 1949.

43. PCO 83-84, f.S-100-M(1946-47), Security Panel Minutes, 19 Sept. 1949.

44. PCO 18, v.137 f.C-20-5(1950), Cabinet Document No. 29-50, 25 Jan. 1950; PCO 16, v.19, Cabinet Conclusions, 1 Feb. 1950.

45. PCO 16, v.19, Cabinet Conclusions, 8 Feb. 1950; v.20, Cabinet Conclusions, 23 May 1952. The question of possession of passports was a somewhat artificial one. As the Immigration Branch explained to External Affairs, Nationalist passports were no good, since they were not recognized by the Communist government, which effectively ruled the mainland; on the other hand, the Communist government was not recognized by Canada, so People's Republic passports were no better: IB, v.894 f.591-1(3), Acting Director of Immigration to Secretary of State for External Affairs, 23 June 1950. This was, of course, a self-imposed dilemma.

46. Figures from IB, v.801 f.547-5-54.

47. C&I, v.168 f.3-25-13(1), memo for file, Director of Immigration, 13 Jan. 1952; C. E. S. Smith to L. Fortier, 22 Mar. 1952; Fortier to Director of Immigration, 6 May 1952. The reference to "sons", whether impostor or otherwise, was not inaccurate. From 1946 to 1953, 3,229 sponsored children from China were male and only 517 female: IB, v.801 f.547-5-54.

48. C&I, v.168 f.3-25-13(1), L. H. Nicholson to L. Fortier, 12 June 1952. The RCMP was not blessed with many internal resources for understanding the Chinese community. There were no officers of Chinese origin in the force at the time of

the Communist revolution, and after the revolution, employees with relatives on the Chinese mainland were excluded from the force as security risks. This was the point at issue in a judicial case in 1981 in which the Supreme Court unanimously upheld the right of the government to refuse a security clearance—in this case for an RCMP employee—without having to give reasons: *Lee v. Attorney General of Canada* [1981] 2 SCR; on the RCMP's difficulties with counter-intelligence against the Chinese, see John Sawatsky, *Men in the Shadows: The RCMP Security Service* (Toronto 1980), 185-6.

49. Harry Rankin, *Rankin's Law: Recollections of a Radical* (Vancouver 1975), 61-72.

50. C&I, v.168 f.3-25-13(1), L. H. Nicholson to L. Fortier, 17 Nov. 1952.

51. Ibid., C. E. S. Smith to Fortier, 8 Dec. 1952.

52. C&I, v.168 f.3-25-13(1), L. Fortier to the Minister, 13 Feb. 1953.

53. PCO, Cabinet Minutes, 10, 17, 19, and 20 May, 1960; 8 Nov. 1962. Wickberg *et al.*, *From China to Canada*, 213-7; Hawkins, *Canada and Immigration*, 131-4; IB, v.960 f.SF-S-129(2), Director, Home Services Branch, to Assistant Deputy Minister, Immigration, 13 Nov. 1970.

54. C&I, v.168 f.3-25-13(1), A. M. Congen to Department of State, 9 Dec. 1955; C. E. S. Smith to L. Fortier, 6 July 1956. Hawkins, *Canada and Immigration*, discusses the actual Chinese immigration scandal (131-4), as does Edgar Wickberg, in *From China to Canada*.

Chapter Five

1. Reg Whitaker, "Canada used loose screen to filter Nazi fugitives", *The Globe and Mail*, 1 Mar. 1985.

2. WLMK/M&N, v.419, Cabinet Conclusions, 5 Aug. 1946. PCO 18, v.189 f.S-100-1(2), "Screening of Applicants for admission to Canada", 20 Nov. 1948 (see chapter 2). The SS blood-mark was a tattoo placed under the armpit of SS volunteers, hence not removable; Josef Mengele, perhaps foreseeing eventual retribution, reportedly refused to have the blood-mark tattooed on himself.

3. WLMK, 6 Aug. 1945. (Note that this revealing reflection of the Prime Minister was not recorded in the published Mackenzie King Record); WLMK/M&N, v.419, Cabinet Conclusions, 10 and 19 Dec. 1946, and Cabinet Document No. 346, 9 Dec. 1946. On the Japanese deportation policy, see Ann Gomer Sunahara, "Deportation: the final solution to Canada's 'Japanese problem' " in Jorgen Dahlie and Tissa Fernando, eds., *Ethnicity, Power and Politics in Canada* (Toronto 1981), 254-76. Public opinion on the question is usefully summarized in the tables in Nancy Tienhaara, *Canadian Views on Immigration and Population: An Analysis of Post-War Gallup Polls* (Ottawa 1974), 56-8. The American ambassador to Canada noted the paradox that the political élites (with the exception of those from the CCF) were united in support of the deportation policy, yet "public opinion is being aroused against it all over Canada": US National Archives, Department of State, Decimal files 842.12.1.1945, J. Atherton to Secretary of State, 1 Dec. 1945; PCO, Cabinet Minutes, 20 Apr. 1955. A year after this discussion Cabinet approved the issuance of passports to Canadians of Japanese origin living in Japan, which had previously been denied on what the Cabinet itself admitted were racially discriminatory grounds: 15 Mar. 1956.

4. PC 2047, 29 May 1947; WLMK/M&N, v.419, Cabinet Conclusions, 9 July 1947. On the American operation to enlist German scientists and its sinister implications for the entry into America of war criminals and concentration camp "doctors", see

Tom Bower, *The Paperclip Conspiracy* (London 1987) and Clarence G. Lasby's earlier *Project Paperclip: German Scientists and the Cold War* (New York 1971). Commission of Inquiry on War Criminals, *Report* (Ottawa 1987), 51-2, 273-4.

5. EPP, form letters to answer inquiries of Germans and *Volksdeutsch*, 1 Jan. 1949. On the background to the appalling human tragedy of the *Volksdeutsch* expulsions, see A.M. de Zayas, *Nemesis at Potsdam: The Anglo-Americans and the Expulsion of the Germans* (2nd ed. London 1979), 1-130, and Michael R. Marrus, *The Unwanted: European Refugees in the Twentieth Century* (New York 1985), 325-30; on the Canadian response, see Gerald Dirks, *Canada's Refugee Policy: Indifference or Opportunism?* (Montreal 1977), 159-64.

6. PC 1606, 28 Mar. 1950, and PC 4364, 14 Sept. 1950, concluded the liberalization process; from 1946 to 1955 over 169,000 immigrants to Canada were classed as of "German ethnic origin" and over 132,000 were of German citizenship: EPP, "Briefing paper: immigration from Germany", 7 May 1964.

7. DEA, f.50207-A-40, Security Panel Minutes, 27 Oct. 1950.

8. EPP, Director of Immigration to Officer-in-Charge, Canadian government Immigration Mission, New York, 1 Dec. 1950; Director to Deputy Minister, "Security recommendations for discussion at Security Panel", 18 May 1951. PCO 1952, box 16 f.S-100-5; box 14 f.S-100-I-M, Security Panel Minutes, 15 May 1952. C&I, v.153 f.I-18-14, Security Panel, 44th meeting, 1953, Minutes.

9. IB, v.801 f.547-5-551(1), Canadian Christian Council for Resettlement of Refugees to W. E. Harris, 17 Apr. 1951; Harris to T. G. F. Herzer, 11 July 1951. EPP, Chief, Admissions Division, memorandum for file, 19 May 1951.

10. PCO 18, v.139 f.C-22-1(1951), G. de T. Glazebrook to R. G. Robertson, "Restriction of immigration from Europe", 29 Nov. 1951. EPP, the Head of the Canadian Mission, Bonn, to the Secretary of State for External Affairs, "Restriction of immigrants from Germany", 15 Aug. 1951.

11. DEA, f.50207-A-40, Security Panel Minutes, 15 May 1952. PCO 16, v.16, Cabinet Conclusions, 28 Apr. 1949.

12. DEA, as in n.11, above.

13. PCO 18, 1952, box 16 f.S-100-5, G. H. Ashley to P. M. Dwyer, 16 Sept. 1952; Acc. No. 1983-84/213, box 15 f.S-100-I-M, Security Panel Minutes, 18 Sept. 1952.

14. IB, v.166 f.3-25-11(2), L. Fortier to J. W. Pickersgill, 16 Nov. 1955, with attached memorandum from the Director of Immigration to the Deputy Minister, 15 Nov. 1955 (also found in EPP).

15. EPP, C. S. A. Ritchie to L. Fortier and to J. R. Robillard, 20 May 1955.

16. EPP, J. R. Robillard to C. S. A. Ritchie, 7 June 1955.

17. EPP, R. M. Macdonnell to L. Fortier, 29 Dec. 1955; C. E. S. Smith, responding on Fortier's behalf, agreed that it was "not necessary to refer this matter to our respective Ministers" (5 Jan. 1956).

18. EPP, C. E. S. Smith to Administration Division, 24 Jan. 1956; Smith to J. W. Pickersgill, 2 Feb. 1956; Smith to Administration Division Director, 24 Feb. 1956.

19. EPP, C. E. S. Smith to Commissioner L. H. Nicholson, 24 Feb. 1956; Acting Chief, Operations Division, to posts abroad, 21 Mar. 1956; "Notes on security to be discussed with Commissioner Nicholson", 18 Apr. 1956 (noted by Deputy Minister).

20. EPP, "Briefing paper: immigration from Germany", 7 May 1964. (This is an updated version of a paper first written 30 June 1957 for the general review of immigration procedures launched that year); C. S. A. Ritchie to L. Fortier, 20 May 1955, where the agreement of the West Germans to screening "some 90 per cent of

the persons coming from the East Zone and other countries behind the Iron Curtain" is first indicated.

21. Sol Littman, *The Rauca Case: War Criminal on Trial* (Toronto 1983), 128-31 and 154-9, suggests at least circumstantial evidence of complicity at some level.

22. Commission of Inquiry on War Criminals, transcript of testimony of William Kelly, 922-9. The commission's public report points to the presence in Canada of a number of possible war criminals but shows an extraordinary lack of interest in how they arrived here in the first place—especially when their entry raises questions about government security practices.

23. The evidence upon which this paragraph is based comes from sources that, for obvious reasons, are strictly confidential. Since some of the activities may have been illegal, and some of the persons involved are still alive, the issue is highly sensitive.

Chapter Six

1. "Man sets himself ablaze at Croatian Solidarity protest", *The Globe and Mail*, 24 Feb. 1986. Artukovic had been the minister of the interior (in charge of the police) during the wartime reign of terror of the puppet Croatian "republic" created by the Nazi invaders. He had first been ordered deported from the United States as early as 1953 but was given a two-decade reprieve by the US attorney general not on grounds of innocence, but simply because the US refused to extradite people to Communist countries.

2. *The Globe and Mail*, 28 Sept. 1985.

3. Murray Campbell, *The Globe and Mail*, 1 Mar. 1986. Commission of Inquiry on War Criminals, *Report* (Ottawa 1987): "Creating an OSI in Canada would be courting dangers which must be avoided at all costs: internal peace between the various ethnic groups which form now such an important part of the population of Canada is more important, in the long run, for the good of this country than results which may be more spectacular in the short run, but are likely to inflict serious and possibly incurable wounds" (829).

4. PCO 18, v.82 f.I-50-D(1946-8), H. Keenleyside to Cabinet Committee on Immigration Policy, 25 Aug. 1947 (Imp. Doc. No. 9); L. B. Pearson to L. St. Laurent, 27 May 1948; f.I-50-M(1), Cabinet committee meeting, 26 Sept. 1947; WLMK/M&N, v.421, Cabinet Document No. 538, memorandum to Cabinet Committee on Immigration Policy, 7 Oct. 1947; Deschênes commission transcript, W. Kelly testimony, 8 May 1985, 913-4, 940.

5. PCO 18, v.139 f.C-22-1(1950), G. de T. Glazebrook to N.A. Robertson, 29 Nov. 1951.

6. PCO 1952, box 16 f.S-100-5, G. McClellan to N. A. Robertson, 24 Jan. 1952. EPP, W. Hickman to P. T. Baldwin, "Restriction of immigration from Europe", 23 Jan. 1952; Baldwin to L. Fortier, "Restriction of immigration from Europe", 4 Mar. 1952; Fortier to Robertson, 19 Mar. 1952; Chief, Operations, to Director of Immigration, 12 May 1952.

7. DEA, f.50207-A-40, Security Panel Minutes, 15 May 1952.

8. On American and Vatican complicity in the "rat line", which hustled Nazis and Nazi collaborators out of danger in Europe, see Magnus Linklater, Isabel Hilton, and Neal Ascherson, *The Nazi Legacy: Klaus Barbie and the International Fascist Connection* (New York 1984), 132-96. On Bernonville's relationship to Barbie, see Erna Paris, *Unhealed Wounds: France and the Klaus Barbie Affair* (Toronto 1985), 91.

9. Accounts of the campaign to back Bernonville and his friends can be found in Pierre Savard, "L'ambassade de Francisque Gay au Canada en 1948–49", *Revue de l'université d'Ottawa*, 44:1 (1974), 19-25; Lorne Slotnick, " 'A war hero': Barbie was the darling of Quebec's conservatives", *The Globe and Mail*, 11 Feb. 1983; Thomas Walkom, "Nazi count: St. Laurent advised war criminal to leave country, papers show", *The Globe and Mail*, 24 Jan. 1984; David Vienneau, "King cabinet approved order to let alleged Nazis stay in Canada", *The Toronto Star*, 21 Mar. 1985. The most recent account of the postwar purges concludes that just over 2,000 death sentences were passed on collaborators, but only 768 were actually carried out: Herbert R. Lottman, *The Purge* (New York 1986).

10. WLMK/M&N, v.419, Cabinet Conclusions, 1 Sept. 1948; "Claim influence gave collaborator suspects Canada haven—Ottawa", *The Toronto Daily Star*, 15 Oct. 1948; missing documentation on the Bernonville *et al.* case is discussed in David Vienneau, "Ottawa's files missing on Nazi collaborators", *The Toronto Star*, 26 Dec. 1985.

11. Hugh Keenleyside, *Memoirs* v.2, *On the Bridge of Time* (Toronto 1982), 302-3.

12. C&I, v.130 f.3-33-34, N. A. Robertson to W. E. Harris, 11 Apr. 1950, referring to Cabinet discussion 5 Apr. 1950.

13. See chapter 4.

14. Orest Subtelny, "The Soviet occupation of Western Ukraine, 1939–41: an overview", in Yury Boshyk, ed., *Ukraine During World War II: History and Its Aftermath* (Edmonton 1986), 5-14; Alexander Dallin, *German Rule in Russia 1941–1945: A Study of Occupation Policies* (2nd rev. ed. Boulder, Colo. 1981), especially 107-67.

15. Dallin, *German Rule in Russia*, 166. See also Bohdan Krawchenko, "Soviet Ukraine under Nazi occupation, 1941-4", in Boshyk, *Ukraine During World War II*, 16-37.

16. Philip Friedman, "Ukrainian–Jewish relations during the Nazi occupation", in Friedman, *Roads to Extinction: Essays on the Holocaust* (New York 1980), 176-210.

17. Defences of the Galicia Division can be found in Wasyl Veryha, "The 'Galicia' Ukrainian Division in Polish and Soviet literature", *Ukrainian Quarterly* 36:3, 253-69; Lubomyr Luciuk and Miroslav Yurkevich, "Ukrainian division 'Galicia' defended", *Ukrainian Echo*, 7:4, 6 July 1983, 3; L. Luciuk, "Ukraine's wartime unit never linked to war crime", *The Globe and Mail*, 26 Mar. 1985. Accounts that raise certain doubts are Jock Ferguson, "Ukrainian veterans expect investigation by war crimes study", *The Globe and Mail*, 12 Apr. 1985, and "SS veterans in Canada centre of furore", *The Globe and Mail*, 13 Apr. 1985.

18. Quoted from stenographic transcript in George H. Stein, *The Waffen SS: Hitler's Elite Guard at War* (New York 1966).

19. On the scandal of forcible repatriation see Nikolai Tolstoy, *The Minister and the Massacres* (London 1986), and *Victims of Yalta* (rev. ed. London 1979), Mark R. Elliot, *Pawns of Yalta: Soviet Refugees and America's Role in Their Repatriation* (Urbana, Ill. 1982), and Nicholas Bethell, *The Last Secret* (London 1974).

20. The RCMP had an undercover agent operating within various Ukrainian organizations at the outset of the war who was reporting on their activities: I have obtained a copy of his report "Ukrainians in Canada", 1 Oct. 1939, from the RCMP through the Access to Information Act. External Affairs records and the William Lyon Mackenzie King papers contain numerous references to the wartime activities of Ukrainian nationalist groups; postwar relations with the USSR and Canadian Ukrainians are explored in Samuel J. Nasdoly, "Changing perspectives:

the Ukrainian-Canadian role in Canadian-Soviet relations" in Aloysius Balawyder, ed., *Canadian–Soviet Relations, 1939–1980* (Oakville 1981), 107-27; on the wartime attack on left-wing Ukrainians see Reg Whitaker, "Official repression of Communism during World War II", *Labour/le Travail: Journal of Canadian Labour Studies* 17 (Spring 1986); on immigration of Ukrainian displaced persons in general, there is an unpublished paper by Myron Momryk of the Public Archives of Canada, Ethnic Archives division, "Ukrainian displaced persons and the Canadian government 1946–1952" presented to a conference at St. Michael's College, University of Toronto, 5 Nov. 1983.

21. IB, v.656 f.B53802(1) on the Canadian Relief Mission to aid Ukrainian refugees; v.856 f.7554-33, A. L. Jolliffe to J. D. McFarlane, 20 Nov. 1947, memos to file, 9 Oct. 1947 and 17 Mar. 1948.

22. Statement by Sir Hector McNeil in House of Commons, 18 June 1947. IB, v.656 f.B53802(1), Panchuk memorandum to Canadian government, 4 Aug. 1947; Panchuk to Canadian High Commissioner, London, 7 Aug. 1947. See also Panchuk's own memoirs, *Heroes of Their Day: The Reminiscences of Bohdan Panchuk*, Lubomyr Y. Luciuk, ed. (Toronto 1983).

23. PCO 18, v.82 f.I-50-M(1), Cabinet Committee on Immigration Policy, 15 June 1948 and 7 Nov. 1947. IB, v.656 f.B53802(1), B. Panchuk, memorandum 31 May 1948; A. W. Boulter to Deputy Minister, 19 Nov. 1948; C. E. S. Smith to Deputy Minister, 1 Oct. 1948; H. Keenleyside to C. Gibson, 12 Aug. 1949; Gibson to Keenleyside, 13 Aug. 1949; confirmed by Cabinet, 13 Sept. 1949. Although the Canadian government, as such, was not interested in contributing to commando operations behind the Iron Curtain, this is not to say that some of the Ukrainians who came to Canada did not associate themselves with organizations that did have interests in such operations, such as the international Anti-Bolshevik Bloc of Nations and the Canadian League for Ukrainian Liberation: see McKenzie Porter, "Hero of the hunted men", *Maclean's*, 1 May 1952.

24. LSTL, v.56 f.I-20-29-P, J. Jean to L. St. Laurent, 31 Mar. 1949; St. Laurent to Jean, 7 Apr. 1949; Ukrainian Canadian Committee to St. Laurent, 21 Apr. 1949; St. Laurent to B. Kushnir, 25 Apr. 1949.

25. C&I, v. 130 f.3-33-34, L. Fortier to W. E. Harris, 23 Mar. 1950 (also in IB, v.656 f.B53802[2]).

26. PCO 18, v.166 f.I-50-2(1)(1949-51), Cabinet Document No. 110-50, 4 Apr. 1950; Cabinet Conclusions, 5 Apr. 1950; Brooke Claxton to L. B. Pearson, 17 Apr. 1950; A. D. P. Heeney to W. E. Harris, 26 May 1950; Cabinet Conclusions, 31 May 1950. A screening report done in the Italian camp in 1947 is reprinted in Boshyk, *Ukraine During World War II*, 233-40.

27. IB, v.656 f.B53802(2), S. Bronfman to W. E. Harris, 4 July 1950; A. L. Jolliffe to A. D. P. Heeney, 9 Aug. 1950; Harris to Bronfman, 15 Sept. 1950; Bronfman to Harris, 25 Sept. 1950.

28. Ibid., P. T. Baldwin to J. R. Stirling, 7 Nov. 1950; K. W. N. Hall to Director of Immigration, 24 Nov. 1950; F. B. Cotsworth to Hall, 29 Nov. 1950.

29. John Kolasky, *The Shattered Illusion: The History of Ukrainian Pro-Communist Organizations in Canada* (Toronto 1979), 105. See " 'Mass murder' plotted in bombings", *Toronto Telegram*, 11 Oct. 1950. Earlier instances of attacks on left-wing Ukrainians by displaced persons elicited no sympathy or interest from the RCMP: C&I, v.130 f.3-33-34, S. T. Wood to A. MacNamara, 23 Jan. 1950; when Ukrainian displaced persons broke up a meeting in which left-wing Ukrainians were holding forth on life in the USSR, immigration officials concluded, "while it is, of

course, undesirable that displaced persons or any other residents of Canada should resort to fighting as a means of enforcing their views, it would appear that the displaced persons in this instance were subject to extreme provocation. As the RCMP evidently do not consider that the conduct of the displaced persons called for any disciplinary action...this Department can safely leave the matter in their hands": Acting Director to Deputy Minister, 22 Feb. 1950.

30. IB, v.656 f.B53802(2), L. D. Wilgress to Secretary of State for External Affairs, 14 Aug. 1950. Commission of Inquiry on War Criminals, *Report*, 249-61. It is interesting to note that there is no specific allegation against the Galicia Division in the forty-two volumes of the Nuremberg war crimes tribunal.

31. David Vienneau, "Toronto priest was pro-Nazi, papers say", *The Toronto Star*, 14 Feb. 1985. On the role of the Iron Guardists in anti-Semitic atrocities in wartime Romania, and on continued political activity in America after the war, see Allan Ryan, *Quiet Neighbors: Prosecuting Nazi War Criminals in America* (New York 1984), 218-45.

32. Yeshayahu Jelinek, *The Parish Republic* (New York 1976); see also Jozef Lettrich, *History of Modern Slovakia* (New York 1955), written by the former leader of the non-Communist Democratic Party of Slovakia.

33. In a book published in 1983 in honour of Joseph Kirschbaum—a minister in the Slovak regime and a leading apologist for it in Canada, where he later emigrated—edited by his son, there is an essay on the "Political programme of President Tiso" by Lisa Guarda Nardini that, in attempting to whitewash the Tiso regime, skates perilously close to virtual apologetics for its complicity in the Slovak Jewish Holocaust: Stanislav Kirschbaum, ed., *Slovak Politics: Essays on Slovak History in Honor of Joseph M. Kirschbaum* (Cleveland 1983), 221-51.

34. DEA, f.7899-40, N. A. Robertson to W. L. M. King, 17 July 1945.

35. IB, v.617 f.916207(10), Acting Undersecretary of State for External Affairs to the Director of Immigration, 17 Oct. 1945; District Superintendent, Circular to all Immigration Inspectors-in-Charge, 14 Nov. 1946.

36. IB, v.617 f.916207(10), Dr. F. Pavlasek to N. A. Robertson, 16 Apr. 1946; memorandum, "Political adherents to Tiso regime in Slovakia—admission to Canada", 27 June 1946.

37. Ibid., N. A. Robertson to Dr. F. Pavlasek, 28 June 1946.

38. DEA, f.7899-40, A. D. P. Heeney to the Director of Immigration, 15 Dec. 1950; Director of Immigration to Heeney, 22 Jan. 1951. Catherine Bainbridge, Howard Goldenthal, and Albert Nerenberg, "Sinister secret", *The McGill Daily*, 11 Apr. 1985, and Howard Goldenthal, "Ottawa allowed Hitler's puppets to operate here", *The Ryersonian*, 12 Apr. 1985. According to Bainbridge *et al.*, there was one other former Slovak official who had entered Canada as early as 1948 with the connivance of the Canadian ambassador in Italy.

39. DEA, f.7899-40, High Commissioner in London to Secretary of State for External Affairs, 13 Dec. 1950. Kirschbaum, *Slovaks in Canada*, 164; A. X. Sutherland, *The Canadian Slovak League: A History* (Toronto 1984), 65-6. Among apologetics, see Kirschbaum, *Slovakia: Nation at the Crossroads of Central Europe* (New York 1960); Joseph Mikus, *Slovakia and the Slovaks* (Washington 1977), and Sutherland, *Dr. Jozef Tiso and Modern Slovakia* (Cleveland 1978). A controversy over the kind of history exemplified in the magazine *Slovakia* broke out in the columns of *The Nation*, 18 May, 22 June, and 6/13 July 1985.

40. WLMK/M&N, v.419, Cabinet Conclusions, 21 Apr. 1947; Cabinet Document No. 491, 7 July 1947; Cabinet Conclusions, 14 May 1948; Cabinet Document No. 672, 7 May 1948. Keenleyside, *On the Bridge of Time*, 304-5.

41. Commission of Inquiry on War Criminals, *Report*, 12-13.

42. Philip Friedman, himself a survivor of the Holocaust in Poland, wrote: "The European countries reacted differently toward the Nazi Judenpolitik. The peoples of Western, Northern, and much of Southern Europe were almost totally against it, and many individuals aided the Jews in their struggle for survival. In Eastern and some parts of Central Europe, reactions varied. Nazi collaborators and sympathizers were in the majority; they were particularly numerous among Eastern European peoples— Ukrainians, Poles, Lithuanians, Latvians, Roumanians and Slovaks.... Active helpers, or 'righteous Gentiles', though a small minority in Eastern and Central Europe, were far more numerous in Western and Southern Europe, where a vast majority of the people were in sympathy with the Jews. Even among the collaborators and traitors in those countries the anti-Semitic program was not as popular as other parts of the Nazi plan": *Roads to Extinction*, 410. On the postwar pogroms in Eastern Europe (which may have killed 1,500 Jews in Poland alone by 1947), see Marrus, *The Unwanted*, 335-6. In general, see Howard Aster and Peter Potichnyi, *Jewish Ukrainian Relations: Two Solitudes* (Oakville 1985).

43. Ron Vastokas and Lubomyr Luciuk, "Soviet villains omitted: a flaw in Canada's search to uncover war criminals", *The Globe and Mail*, 4 Mar. 1986.

44. Paul Zumbakis, "Co-operation between the US Office of Special Investigations and the Soviet secret police", Boshyk, *Ukraine During World War II*, 131-5.

Chapter Seven

1. "Patricia Daniloff", *The Nation*, 1 Nov. 1986; Haynes Johnson, "A law fit for a police state", *Manchester Guardian Weekly*, 2 Nov. 1986; David Shipler, "Visas denied to bar critics, civil libertarians in U.S. fear", *The Globe and Mail*, 15 Nov. 1986.

2. Mowat, *My Discovery of America* (Toronto 1985); John Cruickshank, "Professor can enter U.S. only on 'Communist' visa", *The Globe and Mail*, 12 Feb. 1987. The well-known Canadian writer George Woodcock has also been barred for his "anarchist" past; Woodcock, "The political blacklisting of a Canadian writer", *Saturday Night*, August 1984, and "On being 'inadmissible' ", *The New York Review of Books* (September 1984).

3. Gary Evans, *John Grierson and the National Film Board: The Politics of Wartime Propaganda* (Toronto 1984), 224-68.

4. Washington, US National Archives, State Department records (USDS), 842.00B/4-1248, H. Earl Russell to Secretary of State, 12 Apr. 1948. DEA, v.2122 f.AR1171/1.

5. USDS, 842.00B/10-2748, Russell to Secretary of State, 27 Oct. 1948, and Charles F. Johnson to Russell, 27 Oct. 1948. The RCMP was occasionally embarrassed by the use of its subversive files, or those of municipal police forces, by the American immigration authorities, but there was little it could do but quietly grouch about it (see chapter 2).

6. USDS, 842.9111/12-1845, Lewis Clark to Secretary of State, 18 Dec. 1945; 842.91211/8-3049, Ambassador to Secretary of State, 30 Aug. 1949. "US closes doors to Margaret Gould", *The Toronto Telegram*, 15 Mar. 1949. *The Financial Post*, 26 Mar. 1949. *The Ottawa Citizen*, "US bans entry of Canadian reporter", 27 Aug. 1949. Her "undue influence" over the editorials of the *Star* may have had a more prosaic

basis than ideology. According to a former *Star* editor, she indeed had a "considerable influence" over Joseph Atkinson, the *Star* publisher, attributed "mainly to the fact that she was the only person Mr. Atkinson could hear without a hearing aid, for she had a clear, piercing voice...": Ross Harkness, *J. E. Atkinson of the Star* (Toronto 1963), 315.

7. "Professor's wife is held during Waldorf dinner", *The New York Times*, 26 Mar. 1949; "Columbia group protests barring of two Canadians", *The Globe and Mail*, 2 Apr. 1949; "John Goss and unstated charges", *BC Financial Times*, 7 May 1949; "Bar singer John Goss from Institute", *The Globe and Mail*, 12 Apr. 1949.

8. Woodcock, "Political blacklisting", 33. Frederick Gibson, *To Serve and Yet Be Free: Queen's University*, v.2: *1917–1961* (Montreal 1983), 273-96.

9. H. Kalman, G. Potvin, K. Winters, eds., *Encyclopedia of Music in Canada* (Toronto 1981), 925, 892.

10. C&I, v.172 f.3-10-111(1). At one point early in 1948 the minister wrote to R. A. Bryce, of Macassa gold mines (and the father of senior civil servant Robert Bryce), asking for more definite "proof" of Robinson's Communist activities so that the government could proceed quickly to bar Robinson before he entered Canada.

11. WLMK/M&N, v.419, Cabinet Conclusions, 6 and 10 Feb. 1948.

12. C&I, v.169 f.3-32-1(1), A. D. P. Heeney to J. A. Glen, 14 Feb. 1948 (with attached secret reports); Justice Department, "The Immigration Act and the admission of Communists", n.d.

13. WLMK/M&N, v.419, Cabinet Conclusions, 19 Feb. 1948.

14. C&I, v.169 f.3-32-1(1), Cabinet Committee on Immigration Policy, Minutes, 25 Feb. 1948; memorandum for the Minister, 23 Feb. 1948; S. T. Wood to Deputy Minister of Labour, 23 Feb. 1948. WLMK/M&N, v.421, Cabinet Document No. 619, "Entry of Communists into Canada", 26 Feb. 1948.

15. WLMK/M&N, v.419, Cabinet Conclusions, 27 Feb. 1948.

16. Ibid., A. D. P. Heeney to W. L. M. King, 27 Feb. 1948.

17. WLMK/M&N, v.419, Cabinet Conclusions, 1 Mar. 1948.

18. Ibid., 2 Mar. 1948.

19. C&I, v.169 f.3-32-1(1), E. W. T. Gill to C. W. Jackson, 23 Mar. 1948; "Memorandum regarding procedure for refusal of admission to Canada", 12 Mar. 1948.

20. The best contemporary analysis of the implications of the Pollitt case was in the Communist *Tribune*: Frank Williams (pseudonym for Frank Park), 20 Mar. 1948.

21. Examples of business pressures can be found in Department of Labour, v.4544 f.3-26-59; C&I, v.172 f.3-10-111(1); LSTL, v.38; John Bracken Papers, v.8 f.C-2000. Ontario Legislature, *Debates*, 5 and 11 Mar. 1948; House of Commons, *Debates*, 17 Mar. 1948. "Drew calls on Ottawa to expel alien reds", *The Globe and Mail*, 6 Mar. 1948, and "Guarding the border", editorial in same issue. "Find 79% of Canadians want Communists barred", *The Toronto Daily Star*, 24 Apr. 1948.

22. Reginald Whitaker, *The Government Party* (Toronto 1977), 317-22; Laurel Sefton MacDowell, *"Remember Kirkland Lake" : The Gold Miners' Strike of 1941–42* (Toronto 1983). Irving Abella, "Oshawa 1937", in Irving Abella, *On Strike: Six Key Labour Struggles in Canada, 1919–1949* (Toronto 1974), 93-128.

23. "Says US Communists trying to regain ground in Canada", *The Ottawa Citizen*, 10 Mar. 1948.

24. Irving Abella, *Nationalism, Communism, and Canadian Labour* (Toronto 1973), 98-9.

25. Ibid., 101; J. T. Morley, *Secular Socialists: The CCF/NDP in Ontario* (Kingston and Montreal 1984), 204-6.

26. WLMK/M&N, v.419, Cabinet Conclusions, 8 Apr. 1948. C&I, v.169 f.3-32-1(1), A. L. Jolliffe to Deputy Minister, 3 Mar. 1948; v.172 f.3-10-111(1), R. Forsythe to Minister of Mines and Resources, 11 Nov. 1948, and Director of Immigration to Minister, 2 Dec. 1948.

27. William Edward Kaplan, *Everything That Floats: Pat Sullivan, Hal Banks, and the Seamen's Unions of Canada* (Toronto 1987), 63.

28. *Toronto Daily Star*, 7 May 1948. C&I, v.169 f.3-32-1(1).

29. Ibid., H. Keenleyside to E. W. T. Gill, 29 May 1948.

30. C&I, v.169 f.3-32-1(1), E. W. T. Gill to H. Keenleyside, 30 June and 9 Nov. 1948. WLMK/M&N, v.419, Cabinet Conclusions, 1 July 1948. LSTL, v.40 f.C-20 (1948), Gill to A. D. P. Heeney, 6 Nov. 1948. One of the unionists who was on the Canadian banned list was a British subject who had worked for over two decades in the United States; when he visited Canada early in 1948 (before the Cabinet order was in effect) he was refused re-entry to the US. He re-entered anyway and was arrested and interned at Ellis Island on and off for some five years until he was finally deported to Britain: David Caute, *The Great Fear: The Anti-Communist Purge Under Truman and Eisenhower* (New York 1978), 235.

31. IB, v.856 f.555-10, Immigration Branch, Directive No. 10, 8 Dec. 1950; 83-84/347 box 5 f.SF-118(1), "Security screening procedure", 7.41(a) and (c).

32. USDS, 842.00B/6-1747, Howard K. Travers to Andrew B. Foster, 17 June 1947. IB, v.894 f.569-1(2) circular to posts abroad, 1 Nov. 1949 (earlier version dated 23 Sept. 1948).

33. USDS, 842.00B, American Consul to Secretary of State, 18 June 1948.

34. House of Commons, Standing Committee on External Affairs, *Minutes of Evidence*, 18 Nov. 1949, 11.

35. Ross MacDonald, "Too many Canadians barred from US for security—Pearson", *The Toronto Daily Star*, 30 Aug. 1956.

36. PCO 16, v.30, Cabinet Conclusions, 6 May 1952. Caute, *The Great Fear*, 176-7.

37. "Let him sing it", *Canadian Forum*, June 1947. PCO 16, v.14, Cabinet Conclusions, 1 Dec. 1948, with PCO memorandum to Special Cabinet Committee, 29 Nov. 1948.

38. Caute, *The Great Fear*, 164-5, 247-8.

39. PCO, Cabinet Conclusions, 28 July 1955 and 29 Mar. 1956. "Ottawa bars Robeson", *The Globe and Mail*, 11 Mar. 1956.

40. On the Red Dean, see David Caute, *The Fellow-Travellers: A Postscript to the Enlightenment* (New York 1973), 246-9.

41. DEA, v. 2486 f.102-CSA-40, J. George to Undersecretary of State, 25 Aug. 1948; L. Chance to L. B. Pearson, 26 Aug. 1948. LSTL, v.56 f.I-20-I-D, Adams to Spragge, 27 Oct. 1948.

42. Thirty years later, an obviously unrepentant Reuben is still at it: see Reuben, "The Gouzenko case: the documents that weren't there", *The Nation*, 20/27 July 1985, 44-7.

43. IB, v.750 f.514-15(3), D. N. McDonell to Pacific district, 7 July 1955.

44. PCO, Cabinet Minutes, 21 Dec. 1955; 29 Mar. and 12 Apr. 1956. Information provided to the author by Prof. John Jennings of Trent University.

45. PCO 2, v.83-84/213 f.S-100-5-0.

46. IB, 83-84/347 box 5 f.SF-S-118, Officer-in-Charge, Cologne, to Chief, Operations Division, 11 Dec. 1958; "Security screening procedure", 7.39—including the

warning to officers that "it is important that [Communist] diplomats and government officials do not receive the impression that they are being questioned more than is normally necessary".

47. PCO, Cabinet Minutes, 15, 19, and 29 Mar. 1956.

48. PCO, Cabinet Minutes, 31 July 1957, 24 Oct. 1959, 1 Mar. 1960. Two Chinese Communists were allowed to visit at the invitation of the Communist-led United Electrical Workers Union in 1959. This was described as an "exception": 12 and 24 Mar. 1959 and Cabinet Document No. 334/59, 23 Oct. 1959.

49. On Endicott and the Peace Congress, see Stephen Endicott, *James G. Endicott: Rebel Out of China* (Toronto 1980).

50. Harold Greer, "Monica Felton barred for Red activity", *The Toronto Daily Star*, 9 May 1953; *The Citizen*, 1 May 1953; *The Ottawa Journal*, 30 Apr. 1953; "City unions protest barring of writer", *The Vancouver Sun*, 29 Apr. 1953. The Cabinet decision to bar Felton simply cited her planned "participation in meetings being arranged by Communist front organizations": PCO 16, v.17, Cabinet Conclusions, 22 Apr. 1953. C&I, v.172 f.3-10-111(1), L. Fortier to W. E. Harris, 20 Apr. 1953, alerted the minister that Felton was sponsored by "the peace movement". IB, v.800 f.547-1(1), "Meeting on immigration matters", 22 Jan. 1954.

51. IB, v.856 f.555-10, covering letter by R. A. Mackay, Assistant Undersecretary of State for External Affairs, 3 June 1954.

52. IB, v.83-84/347 box 4 f.SF-SF-23(2), Security Panel Minutes, 17 July 1956; Security Panel Document No. 183, "List of Communist-controlled organizations in Canada", 10 Jan. 1957; Security Panel Minutes, 12 Mar. 1957. C&I, v.169 f.3-32-1(1).

Chapter Eight

1. Stanley Kutler, *The American Inquisition: Justice and Injustice in the Cold War* (New York 1982), 89-117; David Caute, *The Great Fear: The Anti-Communist Purge under Truman and Eisenhower* (New York 1978), 245.

2. Leopold Infeld, *Atomic Energy and World Government* (Toronto 1946); *Why I Left Canada: Reflections on Science and Politics* (Montreal 1978); RCMP Special Branch *Monthly Bulletin* (February 1951), 45-6.

3. PCO 16, v.21, Cabinet Conclusions, 22 Oct. 1950; v.22, Cabinet Conclusions, 22 Nov. 1950.

4. Cabinet Conclusions, 25 Oct. 1950.

5. PCO 18, v.139 f.C-22-1 (1951), W. K. Wardroper to L. Chance, 8 Jan. 1951.

6. C&I, v.169 f.3-32-1(1), R. Gordon Robertson to Norman Robertson, 2 Nov. 1950.

7. PCO 18, v.139 f.C-22-I(1951), Cabinet Document No. 24-51, "Possible measures directed at Communists", 23 Jan. 1951; R. G. Robertson to L. Chance, 26 Jan. 1951. PCO 16, v.23, Cabinet Conclusions, 24 Jan. 1951.

8. PCO 18, v.139 f.C-22-I(1951), A. D. P. Heeney for the Minister, 15 Feb. 1951; Heeney for the Minister, 7 Mar. 1951.

9. On the Second World War, see Reg Whitaker, "Official repression of Communism during World War II", *Labour/le Travail: Journal of Canadian Labour Studies* 16 (Spring 1987); on the postwar plans, see Lawrence R. Aronsen, "'Peace, order and good government' during the Cold War: Canada's internal security program", paper presented to the Canadian Historical Association Annual Meeting, Ottawa, 1982:

Aronsen's information on internment plans was based on files in the Department of National Defence Records, some of which are no longer open following the proclamation in 1983 of the Access to Information Act with its many exclusions.

10. A. D. P. Heeney, 7 Mar. 1951; PCO 16, v.23, Cabinet Conclusions, 8 Mar. 1951; v.25, Cabinet Conclusions, 24 May 1951. IB, v.895 f.569-1(4), Department of External Affairs, Circular Document No. 27/51A, 18 July 1951.

11. Stephen Endicott, *James G. Endicott: Rebel Out of China* (Toronto 1980), 289-302.

12. "Investigate Dr. Endicott", *The Vancouver Sun*, 17 Apr. 1952. House of Commons, Standing Committee on External Affairs, *Minutes of Proceedings and Evidence*, 24 Apr. 1952; PCO 16, Cabinet Conclusions, 15 May 1952; DEA, v.2412 f.102-AZW-40, Canadian Ambassador to the United States to Secretary of State for External Affairs, 3 June 1952.

13. C&I, v.739 f.570898, W. J. Bambruk to P. T. Baldwin, 7 Mar. 1950. DEA, v.2412 f.102-AZW-40(1), E. Reid to L. B. Pearson, 9 May 1952.

14. PCO Acc. No. 1983, box 3 f.C-20-5, Cabinet Document No. 267-52, L. B. Pearson to Cabinet, "Passports for travel to Iron Curtain countries", 20 Aug. 1952.

15. PCO 16, v.31, Cabinet Conclusions, 9 Oct. 1952.

16. PCO, Cabinet Minutes, 13 Sept. 1956; the mention of the Supreme Court was presumably a mistaken reference to the 1955 decisions of *Schachtman v. Dulles*, *Boudin v. Dulles*, and *Dulles v. Nathan*, all of which were actually decided in the District of Columbia Court of Appeal: Kutler, *The American Inquisition*, 97-101; Caute, *The Great Fear*, 248-51.

17. PAC, J. L. Cohen Papers, v.33 f.2977. C&I, v.172 f.3-20-111(1), J. E. Duggan, memorandum for the Deputy Minister, 14 Apr. 1954. IB, v.738 f.513109, especially "ALJ", memorandum for file, 3 Feb. 1949. When Carr's naturalization was revoked in the 1930s, an attempt was made to deport him to Russia, but the matter was dropped when the government could not prove *Soviet* citizenship (Carr had emigrated before the Russian revolution).

18. See chapter 4.

19. Infeld, *Why I Left Canada*, 60-61; C&I, v.169 f.3-32-1(1), L. B. Pearson to W. E. Harris, Dec. 1950.

20. PCO 16, v.27, Cabinet Conclusions, 31 Oct. 1951; PCO 18, v.138 f.C-20-5(1951), Cabinet Document No. 283-51, "Revocation of citizenship", 5 Oct. 1951.

21. C&I, v.169 f.3-32-1(1), R. G. Robertson to N. A. Robertson, 2 Nov. 1950.

22. PCO 16, v.23, Cabinet Conclusions, 24 Jan. 1951. PCO 18, v.139 f.C-22-I(1951), Cabinet Document No. 24-51, "Possible measures directed at communists", 23 Jan. 1951.

23. RCMP Special Branch *Monthly Bulletin*, 10 Sept. 1953, 14; PCO, Cabinet Minutes, 6 Sept. 1956 and 11 Apr. 1957; PC 1957-537, 11 Apr. 1957; Merrily Weisbord, *The Strangest Dream* (Toronto 1983), 168-9, 228.

24. "Government revokes citizenship of Rose, moves against Shugar", *The Globe and Mail*, 28 June 1957.

25. House of Commons, *Debates*, 30 Jan. 1958, 4054.

26. PCO, Cabinet Minutes, 27 May and 2 Sept. 1958; Cabinet Document No.128/58, 10 May 1958.

27. The Law Union of Ontario, *The Immigrant's Handbook: A Critical Guide* (Montreal 1981), 223-33; Commission of Inquiry Concerning Certain Activities of the RCMP, *Second Report*, v.2 (Ottawa 1981), 829.

28. RCMP Special Branch *Monthly Bulletin*, Nov.-Dec. 1948, 426-8.

29. PCO 18, v.188 f.S-100-D, Security Panel Document No. SP-79, "Issuance of certificates of citizenship", 20 Oct. 1950.

30. DEA, f.50207-A-40, Security Panel Minutes, 27 Oct. 1950.

31. PCO 16, v.23, Cabinet Conclusions, 27 Jan. and 5 Feb. 1951.

32. C&I, v.153 f.I-18-7(1), W. M. Haugan, "Cases submitted to the Interdepartmental Committee", 2 May 1957.

33. Caute, *The Great Fear*, 224-44.

34. C&I, v.169 f.3-32-1(1), R. G. Robertson to N. A. Robertson, 2 Nov. 1950.

35. PCO 18, v.139 f.C-22-I(1951), "J. L.", "Immigration entry", 24 Mar. 1951; "R. G. R." to N. A. Robertson, 4 May 1951.

36. Figures based on annual reports of the Department of Citizenship and Immigration.

37. PCO, Cabinet Document No. 110/60, "Deportation to Iron Curtain Countries", 30 Mar. 1960; IB, v.750 f.514-15(3), J. W. Dobson to Chief, Admissions Division, 24 Apr. 1958.

38. See chapter 3.

39. RCMP Special Section *Monthly Bulletin*, 1 Jan. 1946, 86-90; 1 Mar. 1946, 164-8.

40. PCO Acc. No. 83-84/213, box 16 f.S-100-5-D, P. M. Dwyer to N. A. Robertson, 26 Apr. 1952; Dwyer to R. G. Robertson, 5 June 1952.

41. Ibid., R. G. Robertson to J. W. Pickersgill, 7 June 1952; PCO 16, v.29, Cabinet Conclusions, 17 Mar. 1952; "Early arrests may bare new Canada spy ring", *The Toronto Telegram*, 27 June 1952, and "Passport lies charged", 28 June 1952; RCMP Special Branch *Monthly Bulletin*, 10 May 1954, 4.

42. William Edward Kaplan, *Everything That Floats: Pat Sullivan, Hal Banks, and the Seamen's Unions of Canada* (Toronto 1987) 82-3; PCO, Cabinet Conclusions, 30 June 1954. Thirty years later Pickersgill was just as expansively genial about the by now departed Banks when he was interviewed in the Donald Brittain NFB-CBC film *Canada's Sweetheart*.

43. PCO, Cabinet Minutes, 29 Aug. 1957.

44. Ibid., 21 Oct. 1959; 9 Feb. 1960.

45. Ibid., 25 June 1959; 30 June and 31 Aug. 1960.

46. Ibid., 5, 6, and 7 Apr., 10 and 19 May, 1960.

47. *Rebrin v. Bird and Minister of Citizenship and Immigration* (1961) SCR, 376.

Chapter Nine

1. See James Littleton, *Target Nation: Canada and the Western Intelligence Network* (Toronto 1986), for a thorough and searching analysis of the lasting impact of the Cold War on the Canadian national security state.

2. *Attorney General v. Brent* (1956), CSC 318. J. W. Pickersgill, *My Years with Louis St. Laurent: A Political Memoir* (Toronto 1975), 240. PCO, Cabinet Minutes, 17 May 1956.

3. PCO, Cabinet Minutes, 22 Mar., 17 and 24 May 1956; Cabinet Documents Nos. 110/56, 15 May; 113/56, 16 May; 117/56, 22 May 1956.

4. House of Commons, *Debates*, 18 Mar. 1957, 2411. Pickersgill, *My Years with Louis St. Laurent*, 241.

5. See chapter 4.

6. C&I, v.167 f.3-25-11-40, L. Fortier to D. Fulton, 10 July 1957. Fortier reiterated the same concerns to the RCMP commissioner, noting that public complaints normally were directed towards Immigration, rather than the RCMP (who actually made the decisions in specific cases), even though the immigration officers were almost as confused as the public itself by the "cumbersome" procedures: IB 83-84-1347 f.SF-C-35, Fortier to L. H. Nicholson, 24 July 1957.

7. IB, v.164 f.3-18-17(1), "Review of immigration security screening", 28 June 1957. The same document can also be found in EPP.

8. They also agreed with the waiver for wives destined to husbands in Canada on the rather patronizing ground that "most women, because of their role in life, are less inclined and have less opportunity to become interested in politics": "the majority of women are housewives and are not seriously interested in politics." The RCMP was also of the opinion that a woman usefully "occupied as a housewife" did not have time to engage in subversive activities and was thus a "reasonable risk": IB, v.164 f.3-18-17(1), Memorandum of meeting, 5 Sept. 1957.

9. A sixteen-page paper was prepared that detailed the comparative strength of Communism in elections and in trade unions in the various European countries, but it was not acted upon.

10. IB, v.164 f.3-18-17(1), Memorandum of meeting, 5 Sept. 1957.

11. House of Commons, *Debates* (1955), 1165; PCO, Cabinet Minutes, 4 July 1957.

12. PCO, Cabinet Document 142/58, "Immigration Policy and Procedures", 10 May 1958.

13. Quoted in Peter Stursberg, *Diefenbaker: Leadership Gained, 1956–62* (Toronto 1975), 71.

14. Freda Hawkins, *Canada and Immigration: Public Policy and Public Concern* (Montreal 1972), 121.

15. Ibid., 121-38; one exception to the security rule was the admission of Romanian Jews in 1960 (discussed in chapter 3), but this was merely a temporary response to a crisis. On RCMP–civilian tensions see EPP, Methods and Procedures Section to Acting Chief, Operations Division, 24 Sept. 1957.

16. PCO, Cabinet Minutes, 20 Jan. 1960.

17. Nancy Tienhaara, *Canadian Views on Immigration and Population: An Analysis of Post-War Gallup Polls* (Ottawa 1974), 60-73.

18. Ibid., 72.

19. Throughout the 1940s and 1950s, Canada had suffered a decisive net outflow of population over the US border. The political crises of the late 1960s, combined with a declining wage gap between the two countries, led to a sharp reversal of this pattern. In the years 1958–62, for example, 218,000 had emigrated from Canada to the US, while only 56,000 had gone in the reverse direction. Yet for the years 1968–73, the number of Canadian émigrés declined to 154,000 and the number of Americans emigrating to Canada rose dramatically to 140,000: Manpower and Immigration, *Immigration and Population Statistics* (Ottawa 1974), from tables at 34-5 and 88-9.

20. Gerald Dirks, *Canada's Refugee Policy: Indifference or Opportunism?* (Montreal 1977), 238.

21. Ibid., 233-5; Canada, Department of Manpower and Immigration, *The Immigration Program* (Ottawa 1974), 108-9.

22. The by now redoubtable Sedgwick had in 1931 prepared the case for the Ontario Attorney General's Department against Tim Buck and the other Communist leaders under the notorious section 98 (later repealed) of the Criminal Code (the famous *R. v. Buck et al.*, which led to the imprisonment of the eight Communist leaders). See

Lita Rose Betcherman, *The Little Band* (Toronto, n.d.), 171-97. He was also counsel to a special commission in 1945 that whitewashed Ontario premier George Drew's role in the infamous "Gestapo" affair, involving a special branch of the provincial police that sought to smear the CCF with the Communist brush (see David Lewis, *The Good Fight: Political Memoirs, 1909–1958* [Toronto 1981], 261-87). He also successfully defended in court one of those named as a Soviet espionage agent by the royal commission in the Gouzenko case: thus his long experience in such matters was not all one-sided.

23. Joseph Sedgwick, QC, *Report on Immigration*, Part II (Ottawa 1965), 16-7.

24. See Hawkins, *Canada and Immigration*, 150-61, for a general discussion of the reorganization and the White Paper.

25. Canada, Department of Manpower and Immigration, *Canadian Immigration Policy* (Ottawa 1966), 24-5.

26. Ibid., 36-7.

27. House of Commons, *Debates*, 20-23 Feb., 27 Feb., 1 Mar. 1967. The debate, and the changes in the act, are succinctly summarized in Hawkins, *Canada and Immigration*, 163-7.

28. Department of Manpower and Immigration, *Report on Applicants in Canada* (prepared by J. Sedgwick), November 1970.

29. J. L. Granatstein, *Canada 1957–1967* (Toronto 1986), 268-91.

30. IB, v.960 f.SF-S-129(1), T. Kent to M. Mackenzie, 16 Feb. 1967.

31. John Sawatsky, *Men in the Shadows: The RCMP Security Service* (Toronto 1980), 194.

32. Royal Commission on Security, *Report* (Ottawa 1969), 50.

33. Ibid., 51-2.

34. Ibid., 52.

35. Ibid., 52-3.

36. Ibid., 57.

37. On this battle, which included attempts by the RCMP to prevent publication of the commission's recommendations for civilianizing the Security Service, see Sawatsky, *Men in the Shadows*, 194-203; Littleton, *Target Nation*, 137-8; primary documents can be found in IB, v.960 f.SF-S-129.

38. IB, v.690 f.SF-S-129-(1), Security Panel Minutes, 9 June 1969.

39. The RCMP confirmed this when the commissioner informed the chairman of the Security Panel that "even detailed discussion at the interdepartmental level without the prior consent of the originating agency is in contravention of RCMP agreements with these foreign agencies": H. L. Higgitt to Gordon Robertson, 24 Apr. 1970.

40. IB, v.960 f.SF-S-129(1), draft letter to the Deputy Solicitor General for the signature of L. E. Couillard, n.d., and Couillard to R. B. Curry, 18 Apr. 1969.

41. "Aide mémoire: Security Review Board", n.d., n.a.

42. H. L. Higgitt to L. E. Couillard, 8 Dec. 1969; Couillard to A. J. MacEachen, 27 Feb. 1970; Robert M. Adams to Couillard, 25 Feb. 1970; Couillard to R. G. Robertson, 7 Apr. 1970; Assistant Deputy Minister (Immigration) to Director, Home Services Branch, 7 May 1970.

43. IB, v.960 f.SF-S-129(2), Wall, memorandum for the Security Panel, "Security Review Board", 6 July 1970.

44. W. K. Bell to Deputy Minister, 10 July 1970.

Chapter Ten

1. Canada, Manpower and Immigration, *A Report of the Canadian Immigration and Population Study*, v.2: *The Immigration Program* (Ottawa 1974), 143 (hereafter cited as "Green").

2. Green, 157.

3. Ibid., 176-7.

4. Ibid., 149.

5. Ibid., 151.

6. Ibid., 181-4.

7. Freda Hawkins, "Dilemmas in immigration policy-making", in Bernard Bonin, ed., *Immigration: Policy-Making Process and Results* (Institute of Public Administration of Canada 1976), 46.

8. Ellen W. Schreker, *No Ivory Tower: McCarthyism and the Universities* (New York 1986), 291-303.

9. IB, v.960 f.SF-S-129(1), draft letter for the Deputy Minister, n.d.

10. IB, v.960 f.SF-S-129(1), Security Panel Minutes, 13 June 1969. It is not clear which province was referred to; it would most likely have been Quebec.

11. IB, v.960 f.SF-S-129(2), Director, Home Services Branch, to Assistant Deputy Minister for Immigration, 13 Nov. 1970, with enclosure.

12. Diana Dilschneider, "List of academics barred by Canada's security is steadily growing", *The Toronto Star*, 14 Dec. 1972.

13. Paul Axelrod, "Businessmen and the building of Canadian universities: a case study", *Canadian Historical Review* 63:2 (1982), 202-22.

14. Interview with John Saywell, 6 Oct. 1986.

15. Dilschneider, "List of academics".

16. As indicated in earlier chapters, there is a shadowy history of using medical checks as cover for security probes. In an unguarded moment in the 1950s an immigration official told a journalist that the contemporary practice of not screening British immigrants presented no real security problem. "Didn't you know", he asked, "that all British Communists have tuberculosis?" (TB was grounds for barring immigrants): D. C. Corbett, *Canada's Immigration Policy* (Toronto 1957), 86.

17. York University Mészáros file, Dr. David Slater to Bryce Mackasey, 26 Sept. 1972. I am grateful to William D. Farr, vice-president of York University, for allowing me access to this file. Further references to correspondence are to this source. I would also like to thank my colleagues Neal and Ellen Wood of the political science department for providing me with their own clipping file on the Mészáros affair.

18. York University files, Slater to Mészáros, 6 Oct. 1972.

19. "The István Mészáros case and York University", undated document in the York University files.

20. Bruce Kirkland, "Immigration refusal 'slanderous', Marxist scholar says", *The Toronto Star*, 24 Oct. 1972.

21. "Ottawa begins action to deport scholar hired by York U", *The Globe and Mail*, 20 Oct. 1972.

22. York University files.

23. *Excalibur*, 26 Oct. 1972.

24. Melvyn Hill to Slater, 16 Nov. 1972.

25. Years later, with perhaps some poetic justice, Mackasey found himself declared *persona non grata* in another country. Appointed ambassador to Portugal in an

eleventh-hour flurry of much-criticized patronage appointments before the 1984 election, Mackasey was rejected by the Portuguese government.

26. House of Commons, Standing Committee on Labour, Manpower, and Immigration, *Minutes of Proceedings and Evidence*, 17 May 1973, 17-18.

27. Gerald Dirks, *Canada's Refugee Policy: Indifference or Opportunism?* (Montreal 1977), 243.

28. Quoted in Dirks, *Canada's Refugee Policy* (the best published source on the Chilean case), 246.

29. Ibid., 247.

30. Ibid., 248.

31. This continues to be the case in Pinochet's Chile in the late 1980s. Chilean support organizations do not recommend that those wishing to leave apply to the Canadian visa authorities, given what they perceive as an excessively low rate of acceptance. And any who do wish to try must first brave a swarm of General Pinochet's secret police in the lobby of the building, allegedly guarding the diplomatic property.

32. Quoted in Dirks, *Canada's Refugee Policy*, 249.

33. Green, 111.

34. Dirks, *Canada's Refugee Policy*, 258.

35. The statistical story of the movements is shown graphically in Michael Kidron and Ronald Segal, *The New State of the World Atlas* (London 1981), 26, based on UN and US figures.

36. Canada Employment and Immigration Commission, *Indochinese Refugees: The Canadian Response, 1979 and 1980* (Ottawa 1982).

37. "Civil liberties and immigration policy, brief submitted by the BC Civil Liberties Association", Dec. 1973, Green, 34-8.

38. Ibid., 26-8.

39. Warren Black, "Novel features of the Immigration Act, 1976", *Canadian Bar Review* (1978), 56.

40. Early in 1987 the government ordered the deportation of a Salvadorean on the grounds that he had been working against the government of El Salvador. Although they indicated he would not be deported to his country of origin because his life would thereby be endangered, the irony that he should be removed for political opposition to a state that threatens the lives of its own citizens seemed lost on the successive Canadian governments, both Liberal and Conservative, that initiated and carried out the deportation proceedings.

41. *Re Jolly and the Minister of Manpower and Immigration* [1975] 54 *Dominion Law Reports* [3d] 277; *Re Walter Irving Cronin* [1972] 3, Immigration Appeal Board Cases, 42; both cases are cited in the excellent Law Union of Ontario, *The Immigrant's Handbook: A Critical Guide* (Montreal 1981), 190-1. Interestingly, the Cronin case involved a physicist who had once been a member of the US Communist party, but who had sufficiently sanitized himself that he had actually done consulting work for the US government subsequent to his departure from the party. What was good enough for the FBI was not, in this case at least, good enough for the RCMP.

42. Commission of Inquiry Concerning Certain Activities of the RCMP, *Second Report: Freedom and Security under the Law* (Ottawa 1981), 818-9.

43. An internal immigration department document of 1975 indicated that there were 284 persons (114 cases) refused admission abroad on security grounds within the past year, 20 cases of sponsored or nominated applications, and only a single deportation order on security grounds alone out of 12,693 deportations ordered under all sections of the act (some of the latter may have involved security as well

as other causes), although there were security certificates presented in four cases before the Immigration Appeal Board: IB, v.960 f.SF-S-129(3), "Immigration Security Statistics", July 1975. These figures show that the main security rejection site was now abroad, and so the jurisdiction of the Special Advisory Board, from which were excluded cases abroad and sponsored cases, was certain to be of little significance in practical terms, a point of which the government was obviously quite aware.

44. IB, v.961 f.SF-S-129(2), J. L. Manion to T. D. Finn, 7 July 1978.

Chapter Eleven

1. Commission of Inquiry Concerning Certain Activities of the RCMP, *Second Report: Freedom and Security Under the Law*, v.2 (Ottawa 1981), 819-20.

2. Ibid., 824.

3. Ibid., 831-8.

4. James Littleton, *Target Nation: Canada and the Western Intelligence Network* (Toronto 1986), 135-6.

5. In the public service, an old Cabinet directive of 1963 indicating criteria for security-clearance rejections for public servants has been superseded by a new set of guidelines brought into line with the CSIS Act criteria: Treasury Board Circular 1986-26, "Government Security Policy", 18 June 1986.

6. SIRC is made up of five privy councillors not sitting in Parliament, appointed for five-year terms after consultation with the leaders of the opposition parties. It is currently chaired by Ron Atkey, a Conservative minister of employment and immigration in the Clark government.

7. Security Intelligence Review Committee, *Annual Report 1984–85*, 8.

8. Reg Whitaker, "Witchhunt in the Civil Service", *This Magazine* (October-November 1986), 24-9.

9. Letter to the author from Shirley Heafey, executive assistant, SIRC, 14 Oct. 1986; Peter Moon, "Panel says Irishman should be deported", *The Globe and Mail*, 20 Nov. 1986; Oakland Ross, "Journalist who applied for citizenship in 1977 now investigated as spy", *The Globe and Mail*, 23 May 1986.

10. SIRC, *Annual Report 1985–86*, 5-10, 22-3; Victor Malarek, "Mounties are trying to thwart agency, some in CSIS feel", *The Globe and Mail*, 28 June 1986; "Spy agency's troubles could impair security", 3 July 1986; "The security agency", 4 July 1986.

11. SIRC, *Annual Report 1985–86*, 20-1; see also Littleton, *Target Nation*, 180-2.

12. SIRC, *Annual Report 1985–86*, 21.

13. It should not be forgotten that Canada still maintains its own look-out list, albeit at a relatively lower profile than in the past. A recent example was the case of the West German scholar André Gunder Frank—barred in the past on a number of occasions—stopped at the border in 1985 attempting to visit Canada at the invitation of Queen's University. In this case, the minister of immigration, Flora MacDonald, happened to be the member of Parliament from Kingston, where Queen's is located. Representations from Queen's were successful and Frank was allowed to visit, at an unspecified cost to Canadian national security.

14. House of Commons, Standing Committee on Labour, Employment and Immigration, *Ninth Report*, 11 June 1986, 26.

15. Ibid., 25.

16. With the typical ambivalence of all inquiries into the immigration security process, the committee also expressed some concern that the low numbers of rejections

might reflect inadequate screening. They consequently recommended that SIRC be asked to analyse security information on individual immigrants that was not deemed sufficient to legally justify refusal, to determine if "Canada's Immigration Act is adequately protecting Canada": *Report*, 26.

17. Employment and Immigration Canada, *Annual Report 1984-85*; *Report to Parliament on the Review of Future Directions for Immigration Levels* (June 1985); *Annual Report to Parliament on Future Immigration Levels* (1986).

18. Irving Abella and Harold Troper, *None Is Too Many: Canada and the Jews of Europe, 1933–1949* (Toronto 1983).

19. Hugh Winsor, "Lifeboat people spark hardening attitude toward refugees", *The Globe and Mail*, 18 Aug. 1986. The flavour of some of the hostile public reaction can be garnered from the letters-to-the-editor column of the newspapers. One woman from Welland, Ontario, for instance, wrote to *The Toronto Star*: "Foreign governments take note. The easiest way to get your espionage agents into Canada is to load them in a lifeboat close by a fishing vessel and have them pretend to be refugees dumped at sea for several days. They will be welcomed by the minister of employment and immigration..." (23 Aug. 1986). Not all the public reaction is negative, however.

20. Andrew McIntosh, "Canadian people to be awarded Nansen medal for aid to refugees", *The Globe and Mail*, 6 Oct. 1986; *Annual Report on Future Immigration Levels* (1986), 8.

21. Michael R. Marrus, *The Unwanted: European Refugees in the Twentieth Century* (New York 1985), 81-121.

22. Dorothy Thompson, *Refugees: Anarcy or Organization?* (New York 1938), quoted in Marrus, *The Unwanted*, 3.

23. G. J. Beijer, "The political refugee: 35 years later", *International Migration Review* 15 (1981), 18.

24. Based on statistics compiled by C. Michael Lanphier, Refugee Documentation Project, York University (November 1986).

25. Aristide Zolberg, "International factors in the formation of refugee movements", *International Migration Review* 20:2 (1986), 153.

26. Gil Loescher and John Scanlan, *Calculated Kindness: Refugees and America's Half Open Door, 1945 to the Present* (New York 1986).

27. On the national security reasons for this reluctance, see above, 57-8.

28. Gerald Dirks, "A policy within a policy: the identification and admission of refugees to Canada", *Canadian Journal of Political Science* 17:2 (June 1984), 288.

29. W. Gunther Plaut, *Refugee Determination in Canada* (A Report to the Honourable Flora MacDonald) (Ottawa 1985), 16-7.

30. Section 55 of the Immigration Act provides that refugees may be returned if "(b) they have engaged in acts of espionage or subversion, or there are reasonable grounds for believing they will do so, unless the Minister is satisfied the national interest will not be hurt by their admission; (c) there are reasonable grounds to believe they will engage in the subversion or instigation of subversion by force of any government while in Canada; (d) there are reasonable grounds to believe they will engage in violenct activities which would threaten the lives or safety of persons in Canada."

31. Article 32 reads: "1. The Contracting States shall not expel a refugee lawfully in their territory save on grounds of national security or public order.

"2. The expulsion of such a refugee shall be only in pursuance of a decision reached in accordance with due process of law. Except where compelling reasons of national security otherwise require, the refugee shall be allowed to submit evidence to clear himself, and to appeal to and be represented for the purpose before competent authority or a person or persons specially designated by the competent authority."

Article 33 reads: "1. No contracting state shall expel or return a refugee in any manner whatsoever to the frontiers of territories where his life or freedom would be threatened on account of his race, religion, nationality, membership of a particular social group, or political opinion.

"2. The benefit of the present provision may not, however, be claimed by a refugee whom there are reasonable grounds for regarding as a danger to the security of the country in which he is, or who, having been convicted by a final judgment of a particularly serious crime, constitutes a danger to the community of that country."

32. (1985) 1 SCR.

33. Section 7 reads: "Everyone has the right to life, liberty and security of the person and the right not to be deprived thereof except in accordance with the principles of fundamental justice."

34. The remainder was accounted for by refugees from Iran, Iraq, Lebanon, and Sri Lanka, who are not readily categorizable in political terms.

35. Employment and Immigration Canada, *Annual Report 1984–85*.

36. Employment and Immigration Canada, *Report to Parliament on Future Immigration Levels* (1985).

37. Reg Whitaker, "Murder by Decree: the New Tory Refugee Policy", *This Magazine* 21:2 (May–June 1987).

38. 35–36 Eliz. II, 1986–87, Bill C-55, An Act to Amend the Immigration Act, 1976.

39. *Report to Parliament*, 7.

40. Dirks, "A policy within a policy", 297.

41. Senate, *Debates*, 30 Jan. 1986, 1937; *The Report of the Senate Special Committee on Terrorism and the Public Safety* (Ottawa 1987).

42. "Rise of terrorism in Canada is likely, security experts say", *The Globe and Mail*, 28 Apr. 1986. In fact all the legal machinery is in place to bar someone like Nidal, even in the rather unlikely event that an internationally wanted terrorist would reveal himself by publicly claiming refugee status.

43. An academic conference on the Middle East at the University of Calgary invited Soviet and Iraqi scholars; they were denied entry to Canada on national security grounds even though the Helsinki accords, to which Canada is a signatory, call for the free passage of scholars and researchers across borders: *CAUT Bulletin* (Oct. 1986), 18.

Afterword

1. R. Kenneth Carty and W. Peter Ward, "The making of a Canadian political citizenship", in Carty and Ward, eds., *National Politics and Community in Canada* (Vancouver 1986), 67-8.

2. Thomas Powers, *The Man Who Kept the Secrets: Richard Helms and the CIA* (London 1980), 297.

3. John Sawatsky, *Men in the Shadows: The RCMP Security Service* (Toronto 1980), *x*.

4. Treasury Board Circular No. 1986-26, "Government Security Policy", 18 June 1986, section 6.7.

Index